D0916980

SECULAR CHORAL MUSIC IN PRINT

Second Edition

ARRANGER INDEX

Music-In-Print Series, Vol. 2c

MUSICDATA, INC.

Philadelphia, 1987

The Music-In-Print Series to date:

Vols. 1a,b. Sacred Choral Music In Print, Second Edition (1985)

Vol. 1c. Sacred Choral Music In Print, Second Edition: Arranger Index (1987)

Vols. 2a,b. Secular Choral Music In Print, Second Edition (1987)

Vol. 2c. Secular Choral Music In Print, Second Edition: Arranger Index (1987)

Vol. 3. Organ Music In Print, Second Edition (1984)

Vol. 4. Classical Vocal Music In Print (1976) (out of print)

Vol. 4s. Classical Vocal Music In Print: 1985 Supplement

Vol. 5. Orchestral Music In Print (1979) (out of print)

Orchestral Music In Print: 1983 Supplement

Educational Section of Orchestral Music In Print (1978)

Vol. 6. String Music In Print, Second Edition (1973) (out of print)

String Music In Print: 1984 Supplement

Music-In-Print Annual Supplement 1986

Music-In-Print Series: ISSN 0146-7883

Printed by Port City Press, Baltimore, Maryland

Musicdata, Inc.
P.O. Box 48010
Philadelphia, Pennsylvania 19144-8010

Library of Congress Cataloging-in-Publication Data

Secular choral music in print, second edition.
    Arranger index.

    (Music-in-print series, ISSN 0146-7883 ; vol. 2c)
    1. Daugherty, F. Mark, 1951-   Secular choral
music in print—Indexes.   2. Choral music—Bibliography—
Indexes.   I. Series: Music-in-print series ; v. 2c.
ML128.V7S37   1987   016.7841   87-24033
ISBN 0-88478-021-X

Guide to Use

The Arranger Index is designed to be used in conjunction with Secular Choral Music In Print, 2nd Edition. Secular Choral Music In Print provides access to the music by composer or title; the Arranger Index provides an additional means of access: by the name of the arranger or editor.

The Arranger Index lists in alphabetical order all arrangers and editors cited in Secular Choral Music In Print. The arranger's or editor's name is listed in all capital letters. Each name is followed by a listing of all the secular choral works arranged or edited by that person.

The listing under each arranger name gives the composer and title of each arranged work, in alphabetical order. If a work has no composer, it is listed by title.

This arrangement allows the user to look up any desired arranger or editor, and then scan for the composers and titles of desired works. Once the composer and title have been determined, the work may then be looked up in Secular Choral Music In Print to obtain complete bibliographic and ordering information.

Another way of using the Arranger Index is to look up the same person in the role of composer in Secular Choral Music In Print, and in the role of arranger in the Arranger Index. Since the distinction between composer and arranger is frequently problematic, this technique of looking in both places can often afford a more complete view of the person's complete output.

The Arranger Index has been derived from the data of Secular Choral Music In Print by a computer process. As a result, all names and titles are listed exactly as they appear in Secular Choral Music In Print. In the case of multiple arrangers, the arranger names appear together, separated by semi-colons. In the case of uniform and translated titles, the uniform titles are the ones appearing in the index.

Musicdata welcomes reaction from users concerning the format and utility of this index, as well as any suggestions as to other possible indexes or formats.

609
Bright, Houston
Reflection

AAFLOY, HELGE
Grieg, Edvard Hagerup
Bruremarsj Fra Telemark

AAGARD, POVL
Aagaard, Thorvald
Varen

AAMODT, VALTER
Fiskaren Pa Sejegrunnen

AARON; HAYWARD
Bauch
Two Songs For Hanukkah

AAS, ELSE BERNTSEN
Julesanger Fra Mange Land

Trubadurvise

Turesson, Gunnar
Balladen Om Birkebeinarne Og Kong
Sverre
Balladen Om Norsk Gamalost Og 6
Andre Songar

Vise Fra Tommerskogen

ABBOTT
Marais, Josef
Marching To Pretoria

ABBOTT, R.
Twelve Days Of Christmas, The

ABBOTT, RUTH
Rich Old Miser Courted Me, The

Sun Had Sunk Behind The Hill, The

ABEL; ROTHENBERG; SCHREIBER
Sing Dein Lied

ABEL-STRUTH, SIGRID; BIALAS, GUNTER
Hirtenweihnacht

ABOTT, R.
Wassail Bough, The

ABOTT, RUTH
Christmas Day Is Coming

ABRAHAMSEN, NILS
Auld Lang Syne

ABRIL, MARIO
African Trilogy

ABT
Ach Wie Ist Moglich Dann

ABT; AMMANN
Z'Basel An Mim Rhi

ABT, FRANZ
Thuringian Volkslied

Umrauschen Auch Freuden

ADAMIS, MICHAEL
Karavaki

ADAMS
Gibbons, Orlando
Silver Swan, The

Gounod, Charles Francois
Ring On, Sweet Angelus

Morgan
Clorinda

ADAMS, COURTNEY S.
French Chansons For Three Voices,
Part 1

French Chansons For Three Voices,
Part 2

ADE
Meinberg, Karl
Es Scheinen Die Sternlein

ADES
Anderson
Sleigh Ride

Andersson
Knowing Me, Knowing You
Name Of The Game
Thank You For The Music

Bacharach, Burt F.
As Long As There's An Apple Tree
Do You Know The Way To San Jose
Magic Moments

Berlin, Irving
Great Songs By Irving Berlin
There's No Business Like Show
Business

ADES (cont'd.)
Brahms, Johannes
Four Songs For Treble Voices

Brown
Sentimental Journey

Burt, Alfred
Alfred Burt Carols For Children
Alfred Burt Carols, Set 1
Alfred Burt Carols, Set 2
Alfred Burt Carols, Set 3

Burt, Francis
All On A Christmas Morning
Come, Dear Children
We'll Dress The House

Cates
With Everything Changing

Coburn
Blossoms Are Beautiful
I'm A Dreamer
Love Is...

Davis
Have A Good Day

Di Novi
Brand New Morning

Dickinson, Clarence
Brand New Morning

Drake, Ervin
I Believe

Eddleman, David
Hanukkah Time

Eisenberg, Sylvia White
Min Skol, Din Skol

Evans
Feelin'
Think Summer

Fields
Let All The People In

Folk Singers, The

Four To Sing

Fox, Charles
Ready To Take A Chance Again

Fred Waring Christmas Song Book

Fred Waring Olden Goldies Songbook

Fred Waring Song Book

Friedman, Ignaz
Let Me Call You Sweetheart

Fulton
Make America Proud Of You

Gallina
Just Give Me Music

Goodman
Christmas Was Meant For Children

Green
Sentimental Journey

Grieg, Edvard Hagerup
Three Songs By Edvard Grieg

Hague
Did I Ever Really Live?

Hilliard
Dear Hearts And Gentle People

Jackson
Let There Be Peace On Earth

Jones
Many Rains Ago

Kane
Carlos Dominguez

Kaplan
Harmony

Kern, Jerome
Show Boat, A Choral Montage

Kingsley, Gershon Gary
Popcorn Legend

Lantz, Dave
Sunshine

Laurence
Hurry Home For Christmas

Lawrence
Hurry Home For Christmas
Meaning Of Christmas, The

ADES (cont'd.)
Lee
It's A Good Day

Leigh
Search Your Heart

Leisy, James Franklin
Greatest Show On Earth
Isn't This A Lovely Christmas

Levene
Ring Those Christmas Bells

Loesser
Once In Love With Amy
Wonderful Copenhagen

McHugh, Jimmy
On The Sunny Side Of The Street

MacKenzie
Banamba, The

Mancini, Henry
Sometimes

Manning
Happiness Comes, Happiness Goes

Marenzio, Luca
Three Sixteenth Century Madrigals

Marks
A-Caroling We Go
Rudolph The Red-Nosed Reindeer

Martine
Everybody Needs A Rainbow

Meece
Almost Christmas Time

Mercer
Dream

Miller
I Believe In Sunshine
It's Up To You And Me
Let There Be Peace On Earth

Moller
Happy Wanderer, The

Moller, Friedrich W.
Happy Wanderer, The

Music, Men!

Mysels
Buy Me Chocolate

Noble
Christmas Comes But Once A Year

Noble, Jacquelyn
Come Join The Caroling

One For The Melody

Owens, Dewley
Hi, Neighbor

Parnes, Paul
Look On The Bright Side

Petkere, Bernice
Lullaby Of The Leaves

Pola
It's The Most Wonderful Time Of The
Year

Praetorius, Michael
Three Chorale Settings

Randl
Singing A Happy Song

Roberts
If Christmas Isn't Love

Rose
Me And My Shadow

Rowell, Glenn
Where In The World But In America

Sedaka, Neil
You Gotta Make Your Own Sunshine

Semola, Alfonse J.
Christmas Is The Warmest Time Of
Year

Shearing
Lullaby Of Birdland

Simon
Harmony

Simpson
Sing For America
Under The Umbrella Of The Red,
White And Blue

ADES (cont'd.)

Stainbrook
  Best Friend

Steele
  America Our Heritage
  America, Our Heritage

Stelle
  America, Our Heritage

Stevens, Halsey
  Peace Train

Stevens, Ray
  Everything Is Beautiful

Styne, Jule (Jules Stein)
  Let It Snow
  Let It Snow, Let It Snow
  Let It Snow, Let It Snow, Let It
    Snow
  Make Someone Happy

Sugar And Spice

Sugar And Spice For Christmas

Three To Make Music

Tilzer
  I Want A Girl

Two For The Holiday Song

Van Duzen
  New Day, A
  Sing, Sing America

Vance
  Catch A Falling Star

Vandross, Luther R.
  Everybody Rejoice

Waring, Peter
  Mistletoe
  Way Back Home

Weiss
  Ring Bell

Whorff
  Man With A Hundred Names

Wilkes
  What Color Is God's Skin

Williams, Paul
  Never Before, Never Again
  Rainbow Connection, The

Young
  Christmas Roundelay
  In A Shanty In Old Shantytown

ADES, HAWLEY
  Balay, Joan Rose
    Lemon Song, The

  Crupi, Joseph C.
    Turn Around

  Mitchell, Bob
    Good Time Music

  Noble, Jacquelyn
    Come Join The Caroling

  Parnes, Paul
    Makin' Music's Fun

  Pearls For Pretty Girls

  Zuker, Rickie
    Sing A Song, Song, Song!

ADLER
  Chic-A-Boom

  Cripple Creek

  Gypsy Laddie, The

  Hick's Farewell

  Young Hunting

ADLER, GUIDO; BAGGE, SELMAR; DAVID,
  FERDINAND; ESPAGNE, FRANZ;
  MANDYCEWSKI, EUSEBIUS; NOTTEBOHM,
  GUSTAV; REINECKE, CARL; RICHTER,
  E.F.; RIETZ, JULIUS

  Beethoven, Ludwig van
    Complete Works

ADLER, KURT
  Famous Operatic Choruses

ADLER, SAMUEL
  Blow The Wind Southerly

ADLER, SAMUEL DR.
  Agincourt Song

ADOLF, GUSTAV
  Burschen Aus Mystrina

ADRIO, A.
  Schein, Johann Hermann
    Diletti Pastorale. Hirtenlust 1624

AESCHBACHER, C.
  Gagliarda

AESCHBACHER, CARL
  Anneli, Wo Bist Gester Gsi

AESCHBACHER, W.
  S'Bluemli

  Volkslieder

AGAY
  Kaufman, Harry H.
    Caribbean Christmas

AGAY, DENES
  Pachelbel, Johann
    Kanon In D

AGER
  Barbara Allen

  Wade, Joseph Augustine
    Love Was Once A Little Boy

AGER, L.
  Barbara Allen

AGNESTIG, C-B.
  Churchill, Frank E.
    Snovit Och De Sju Dvargarna

AGNETA, SKOLD
  Theodorakis, Mikis
    Nar Dom Knyter Sin Nave

AGNOLUCCI
  Some Day

AGOCSY, L.
  Szallj Szep Enekszo

AGOSTINI, F.
  A Graciosa

  A La Sposa

  Ajaccio-La-Blanche

  Campane Di Natale

  Fior Di Rosa

  Mamma

  Minnana

  Myrtes Ajacciens

  Nanna Corsa

  Pasqua Di Zitelli

  U Sunador Di Viulinu

AGOSTINI, F.; ANJOU, P. D'
  Bocage Vendeen, Le

  Bresse, La

AGOSTINI, F.; TESSARECH, F;
  LAMBROSCHINI, A.

  A Pipa

  A Rustaghia

  Air Des Muletiers De Bogagnano

  Ajaccienne, L'

  Berceuse

  Hymne De Sampiero Corsu

  Lamentu

  Lamentu Di U Castagnu A U Corsu

  Voceru

AHLE
  Lissmann, Kurt
    Was Mag Doch Diese Welt

AHLEN, DAVID
  Krieger, Johann Philipp
    Rattfardige Blir Hadanryckt, Den

  Lubeck, Vincent(ius)
    Valkommen Var, O Herre Kar

AHLEN, WALDEMAR
  Helander, Maj
    Biet
    Blaklockan
    Fiskarens Visa
    Gunga, Gunga Pa Mitt Kna
    Hasselbusken
    Liten Visa Om Varen, En
    Lucia
    Nisse Och Nasse
    Nu Susa Grona Lindarna
    Tomtevisa
    Tripp Trapp Trull
    Ugglans Visa
    Visan Om Lillemor

  Leimontinus
    Frojder Eder Alla

  Olsson, K.E. Filip
    Blomstermanad

  Runback, Albert
    Burfageln
    Finken
    Goken
    Krakan I November
    Krakdialekter
    Talgoxen

  Sandberg, Folke
    Lys I Ett Manniskohjarta

  Schyter, Bengt
    Nu Har Vi Gymnastik

  Soderholm, Valdemar
    Dig Skall Min Sjal Stt Offer Bara
    Hur Ljuvt Det Ar Att Komma
    Staffan Stalledrang

  Wohlfart, Karl
    Blaklockorna

AHLM, HILMER
  Reesen, Emil
    To, Som Elsker Hinanden

AHROLD
  A-Roving

  Ah, The Syghes That Come Fro' My
    Heart

  Courting Of The Deaf Woman, The

  Early One Morning

  Es Steht Ein Lind

  Humphreys
    Maid Of Spain

  Humphreys, Don
    Fiesta
    Vocalitis

  I Wonder When I Shall Be Married?

  If I Should Die (Johnny's Gone To
    Hilo)

  One Hundred Years

AHROLD, F.
  Holly And The Ivy, The

  Lolly Too Dum

  Turtle Dove, The

  Wondrous Love

AIKEN
  Watson, Michael
    Anchored

AKERBERG
  Bedinger, Hugo
    Vuggesang

AKERBERG, ERIK
  Brolen, Carl Axel
    Vackra Sky

  Du Har Sorjit, Lilla Van

  Du Har Sorjit Lilla Van

  Myrberg, August M.
    Midsommardans

  Tanker Du Att Jag Forlorader Ar

  Tjanare, Mollberg, Hur Ar Det Fatt?

  Vackra Sky

  Vuggesang

AKERS
  America The Beautiful

AMABLE, J. (cont'd.)
Mendelssohn-Bartholdy, Felix
Bal Des Fleurs, Le

AMBUHL
S'Toggeburger Vreneli

AMELLER, A.
Rameau, Jean-Philippe
Clair Flambeau

Sakura

AMELN
Handel, George Frideric
Alexander-Fest, Das: Ode Zu Ehren
Der Heiligen Cacilia

AMELN, K.; HARMSEN, H.; THOMAS, W.;
VOTTERLE, K.

Quempas-Buch, Das

Quempas-Buch, Das

Quempas-Buch, Das

AMELN, KONRAD
Handel, George Frideric
Alexanderfest Oder Die Macht Der
Musik , Das

Innsbrucklied, Das

Lechner, Leonhard
Italienische Madrigale

Quempas-Heft, Das

Quempas-Heft, Das

Rhaw, Georg
Deutsche Zweigesange

AMIOT, J.C.
Bizet, Georges
Carmen: Avec La Garde Montante

AMMAN, BENNO
Tanzlied Aus Dem Elsass

AMMANN, B.
Jardiniere Du Roy, La

AMMANN, BENNO
Madchen Von Misox, Das

Montagnards, Les

S' Ramseyers Wei Go Grase

Schone Aus Dem Maggia-Tal, Die

Schone Von Onsernone, Die

Zanzi, G.
Lied Vom Becherlein, Das

ANAOUENNOU
Chants Bretons,recueil A Deux, Trois
Et Quatre Voix

ANDERLUH, A.
Auglan Voll Wassa, Die

Bei Da Lind'n Bin Is G'stand'n

Da Draussen In Wald Is A Wassale Kalt

Diandle, Was Fahlt Dir Denn?

Diandle, Wia Gfallt Da Der Neue Bua?

Do Liab, Do Recht Stark Is

Du Redst Allweil Von Scheid'n

Glei Ause Ban Ossiacher-See

Han Schon Viel Diandlan Gliabt

Hast Ma Ja Gsagg: Kimm Af D'nacht

Is Nix Mehr Wia Imma

Ja Gruass Enk Got'!

Kalt, Kalt Und Kalt, Kalt Waht Da
Lurnfelda Wind

Mei Dandle Is Sauba

Mei Diandle Hat Zwa Auglan, So
Schwarz Wia Die Kohln

O Dirndle Tief Drunt Im Tal

O Du Herzigscheans Diandle

O Rosntal

Setz Auf Mei Gruans Huatle

Steh Nar Auf, Du Junga Schweizerbua

ANDERLUH, A. (cont'd.)
Uber Die Alma, Ubers Halma

Und Im Feld Singt Die Lerch'n

Wann Du Mit Dein Herzlan So Haggli
Willst Sein

Wann I Hamgeh Von Diandlan

Was Fliagst Denn, Liabs Taubale

Was Kummert Mi Die Sternlan

Wia Mei Diandle, Mei Klans

Wia Schon Is, Wann I Sig Die Sunn
Aufgehn

Wohl In Der Wiederschwing

ANDERLUH, ANTON
Karntnerlieder Fur Gemischten
Viergesang

ANDERSEN, NORMA
Young
Lullaby Of The Leaves

ANDERSEN, OLAF
Uthmann, G. Ad.
Tord Foleson

ANDERSON
Lewis
Open Your Arms, My Alabamy

Ob I Lach Oder Sing

Parish
Syncopated Clock, The

Purcell, Henry
Fairest Isle

Soderberg
Bird's Song, The

ANDERSON, A.H.
By A Clear Fountain

ANDERSON; EDWARDS
Parish
Sleigh Ride

ANDERSON, LINDA ALLEN
Brahms, Johannes
Schwestern, Die

Hassler, Hans Leo
Ich Brinn Und Bin Entzundt Gen Dir

ANDERSON, NORMA
Ash, Frances
I'm Gonna Love That Guy

Whitney
No Man Is An Island

ANDERSON, RUTH
Rounds From Many Countries

ANDERSON, W.H.
All Through The Night

Gaelic Croon, A

Gay Is The Rose

Send Her On Along!

Smithery Box

Two French Folk Songs

Two French Folk Songs

Two Icelandic Folksongs

Two Ukrainian Folk Songs

Two Ukranian Folk Songs

ANDERSSON, KARL-ERIK; BERG, GOTTFRID;
ROSENQUIST, CARL E.; WIKANDER,
DAVID

Sju Lucia-Visor

ANDERSSON, OTTO
Runeberg, J.L.
Overgivna, Den

ANDRE
Meinberg, Karl
Bekranzt Mit Laub

ANDREAE, V.
Burschen Heraus

Pinzgauer Wallfahrt, Die

ANDREASSEN, O.
Larsen, N.
Hymne

ANDREWS
Dedrich
Kites Are Fun

Rock Around The Fifties

Seybold
Christmas Polka, The

ANDREWS, GEORGE
Let's Rock N' Roll

ANGELL
Graff
Children Of America

ANGELL; O'HARA
Sibelius, Jean
There Comes Another Morrow

ANREP-NORDIN, BIRGER
Bach, Johann Sebastian
Nyarsdagen

APEL, WILLI; ROSENBERG, SAMUEL N.
French Secular Compositions Of The
Fourteenth Century Vols. I-III

APPLE, ALAN
Three French Carols

APPLE, ALLAN
Simon, Paul
Mother And Child Reunion

APPLEBAUM
Mister Sandman

Mister Santa

APPLEBAUM, LOU
Of Love And High Times

APPLEBY; FOWLER
Firsts And Seconds

Sing In Harmony

Songs For Choirs

Sullivan, [Sir] Arthur Seymour
Six Four-Part Songs

APRILY, LAJOS
Sugar, Rezso
Tavaszodnik

ARANY, JANOS
Szonyi, Erzsebet (Elizabeth)
Elotted A Kuzdes

ARBERG, B.
Belles A-Singing

ARCH
Aignish On The Machair

Eriksay Love Lilt

Eriskay Love Lilt

Hebridean Waulking Song

Island Sheiling Song

Kennedy-Fraser, Marjory
Aignish On The Machair
Eriskay Love Lilt, An
Island Sheiling Song, An

Road To The Isles

Sleeps The Noon In The Deep Blue Sky

Wind On The Moor

ARCH, GWYN
Shortnin' Bread

Spinning Wheel, The

ARCHER, VIOLET
Three French-Canadian Folksongs

ARCHIBEQUE, CHARLENE
One May Morning

Prune Song, The

Scarborough Fair

ARCOLA; CASSEY
Whittaker, Roger
Last Farewell, The

AREND, A. DEN
Strauss, Johann, [Jr.]
An Der Schonen Blauen Donau

AVERRE (cont'd.)

Mann, Barry
Let The Song Last Forever

Milliman
Kissin' Mistletoe

AVERRE, DICK
Farrar, John
Hopelessly Devoted To You
You're The One That I Want

Hal Leonard Song Kit No.16 (Video Hits)

Hal Leonard Song Kit No.17 (Christmas Favorites)

Herman, Jerry
Mame

Lennon, John
All You Need Is Love
Blackbird
Norwegian Wood

Schwartz, Arthur
That's Entertainment

AVERRE, RICHARD
All My Trials

Carpenter, Richard Lynn
Goodbye To Love
Yesterday Once More

Farjeon, Eleanor
Morning Has Broken

Hayes, Isaac
John Shaft

Simon, Paul
American Tune
Me And Julio Down By The Schoolyard

AZELTON, PHIL
Heyman
When I Fall In Love

AZELTOR, PHIL
Christmas Song, The

BAAS, J.
Beveel Gerust Uw Bewegen

BACAK, JOYCE EILERS
Beavers
Like Flowers Are We

Berlin, Irving
White Christmas

Carol Of The Drum

Crocker, Emily
Drunken Sailor, The
Sunshine, Happiness

Do You Hear What I Hear

Dreamer

Fifty Nifty U.S.

Go Ye Now In Peace

God Bless America

Happiest Time Of The Year, The

Hendershott, Stacy
Look Out Your Window

Hughes
To The Future

Johnson, Neil
Maybe, But I Doubt It
Old Joe Clark
This Little Light Of Mine

Kerry Dance, The

Marks, Johnny D.
Rudolph The Red-Nosed Reindeer

Perry, Dave
Forest Shadows
Rosalee

Snyder
Guitar Man, The
I Believe In You
Proud Of Who We Are

Spevacek, Linda
Pass It Along!

Stocker
Hanukkah Dance

Strid, George L.O.
It's Christmas Time Again

BACAK, JOYCE EILERS (cont'd.)

Time, Love And Money

Ward, Samuel Augustus
America The Beautiful

Whole New World

Winter Wonderland

BACH, J.S.
Isaac, Heinrich
Nun Ruhen Alle Walder

BACH, L.E.
Drummer, G.
Kein Halmlein Wachst Auf Erden

BACH, STEVE
Adams, Skip
In The Arms Of Freedom

BACH; SWINGLE
Vivaldi, Antonio
Fugue

BACHL, H.
A Herz Wia A Vogerl

Alpara

Mir San Von Da Drinnat

Z'nachst Han I Ma D'Schneid

BACHL, HANS
Auf, Auf, Ihr Hirten

Auf, Hirten, Auf, Erwacht

Burkhart, Franz
Nachtigall, Ich Hor Dich Singen
Vogerl Schlafen Schon Im Wald, Die

Dreikonig

Frohlocket, Ihr Menschen

Geht's, Buama

Grunet, Felder, Grunet, Wiesen

Guten Abend, Liebe Hirten

O Bruader

O Wunna Uber Wunna

BACHLI
Tausendfussler

BACHMANN
Auf, Auf Zum Kampf

BACKER, H.
Blumlein Blaue, Das

Zwei Fruhlingslieder

Zwei Scherzliedchen

BACKER, HANS
Beste Zeit, Die

Kein Schoner Land

Keinen Schonern Tanz

BACON, BOYD
Tarrega, Francisco
Three Choral Pieces Of Tarrega

BADEN
Lissmann, Kurt
Beim Kronenwirt, Da Ist Heut Jubel Und Tanz

BADEN, CONRAD
Fehr, J.v.d.
Norge I Sol

BADEN, TORKIL
Teigen, Jahn
Do Re Mi

BAER, HOWARD
Canada's Favourite Folksongs For Kids

BAGGE, G.
Fille Allait Aux Champs, La

O Vermeland

Sous Le Dome Du Ciel

BAGLEY
Live-A-Humble

BAIKADAMOV, BAKHITZHAN
Sixteen Girls

BAILEY, LEON
Shanty Sequence, A

BAILEY, TERRENCE
Young Man Who Wouldn't Hoe Corn

BAINES; BARDWELL; SZABO
Humperdinck, Engelbert
Hungarian Nursery Rhymes

BAIRD
Coots, John Frederick
I Wouldn't Trade The Silver In My Mother's Hair

Rose
That Old Gang Of Mine

BAIRD, F.F.
Cantiones, Piae

BAIRD, J. JULIUS
Cantiones, Piae

BAIRD, JACK
Coots, John Frederick
I Wouldn't Trade The Silver In My Mother's Hair

Henderson, Raymond
That Old Gang Of Mine

BAIRD, MARGERY ANTHEA
Manchicourt, Pierre de
Twenty-Nine Chansons

BAIRD; SZABO
Dreyer
Wabash Moon

BAK, KARL
Ring, Oluf
Munken Og Fuglen

BAKKE, ARNT
Herr Ole

BALBO
Bach, Johann Sebastian
Light

BALDWIN
De Koven, (Henry Louis) Reginald
Oh Promise Me

Friml, Rudolf
Sympathy

Kountz, Richard
A La Russe

Manning, Kathleen Lockhart
In The Luxembourg Gardens

Speaks, Oley
Morning

Sullivan, [Sir] Arthur Seymour
Lost Chord, The
Night Is Calm And Cloudless, The

Tchaikovsky, Piotr Ilyich
Legend, A

BALL, ADRIAN
McCormick, Clifford
Christmas Is Coming
Yuletime

BALLA, GYORGY
Marton, Lajos
Kontrasztos Tajkep
Otthon

BALLARD, LOUIS W.
American Indian Sings, The

BALLING, MICHAEL
Wagner, Richard
Works Of Richard Wagner, Vol. 6:
Lieder Und Gesange And Chorgesange

BALOGH
Demeny, Dezso
Rococo Serenade

Sjoberg
Tonerna

BAMPTON
Come All Ye Friends Of Lyon

BAMPTON, R.
Christmas Nightingale, The

BAMPTON, RUTH
O Shenandoah

Shenandoah

BANG-MOLLER, F.
Sullivan, [Sir] Arthur Seymour
Leaves In Autumn Fade And Fall

BANNER, MARTIN
  Schumann, Robert (Alexander)
    I'm Being Drawn Into The Village
    Peaceful Night

BANTOCK, GRANVILLE
  Go Down Moses

  O Can Ye Sew Cushions?

  Sea Sorrow

  Swing Low Sweet Chariot

BANTOK
  O Dear, What Can The Matter Be?

BANTOK, G.
  German, [Sir] Edward (Edward German
    Jones)
    Big Steamers

BARAT-PEPPER
  Choeurs De L'Afrique Equatoriale

BARBERTONES
  Hamm
    Bye Bye Blues

BARDEZ, JEAN-MICHEL
  Memoires

BARDOS, L.
  Hetven Kanon

  Tabortuznel

BARDOS, LAJOS
  Bartok, Bela
    Fa Follott
    Icike-Picike

  Paix, Jacob
    Tambur

  Sag Du Noko To Kjerringa Mi

BARFOED, H.U.
  Bach, Johann Sebastian
    Es Nehme Zehntausend Dukaten
    Mer Hahn En Neue Oberkeet (Opening
      Chorus)
    Wir Gehn Nun

BARFOED, HANS-ULRIK
  Mads Doss

BARKER
  Christmas Gala, A

BARLOW
  Barnett
    Hola! Vamos A Cantor

  Jaffa
    Salut! Nous Allons Chanter

BARNARD, P.
  Widmann, Erasmus
    Geese, The

BARNBY, JOSEPH
  Sweet And Low

BARNES
  Beethoven, Ludwig van
    Heavens Are Declaring, The

  Big Rock Candy Mountain

  Coleman
    Rhythm Of Life

  Peacock
    Old Kris Kringle
    Three Wishing Candles
    Wreath Of Holly, A

BARNES, R.
  Isaac, Heinrich
    Innsbruck, Ich Muss Dich Lassen

BARNES, RICHARD
  Stoltzer, Thomas
    Entlaubet Ist Der Walde

BARNETT
  Deck The Halls And All That Jazz

BARNEY; WILSON
  Symonds, Norman
    These Things Shall Be

BARRETT; CRAIG
  Hildach
    Spring

BARRIE
  Byrd, William
    Nightingale, The

  Morley, Thomas
    Springtime Mantleth Ev'ry Bough

  Stodola Pumpa

BARRIE (cont'd.)

  Weelkes
    Take Here My Heart

BARRIE, WALTER
  Lassus, Roland de (Orlandus)
    Ah, Could My Eyes Behold Thee

BARRIS; LEYDEN
  Kohler
    Wrap Your Troubles In Dreams

BARROW, R.
  Chanson De Mai

BARROW, R.G.
  Agincourt Song, The

BARTELS, LEO
  Boccherini, Luigi
    Dancing Children

BARTH
  Beethoven, Ludwig van
    Flamme Lodert, Die
    Opferlied

BARTHEL, U.
  Als Ich Einmal Reiste

  Blaue Luft, Fruhlingsduft

  Horch, Was Kommt Von Draussen Rein

  Im Fruhtau Zu Berge

  Im Walde, Da Wachsen Die Beer'n

  Und Jetzt Gang I Ans Peter Brunnele

  Wenn Die Nachtigallen Schlagen

  Wohlauf In Gottes Schone Welt

BARTHEL, URSULA
  Csardas

  Cucaracha, La

  Festliches Lied

  Ich Bin Das Ganze Jahr Vergnugt

  Rhythmus Im Lied – Aus Nord Und Sud!

  Vive La Peperbusse

BARTHELMES, HEINRICH
  Brahms, Johannes
    Guten Abend, Gut' Nacht

  Du Sollst Mein Eigen Sein

BARTHELSON
  My Pretty Little Pink

  Somebody's Knockin' At Your Door

  Spin, Spin

  When I Was Single

BARTHELSON, J.
  Black Is The Color Of My True Love's
    Hair

  Johnny Has Gone For A Soldier

BARTHELSON, JOYCE
  Old Smokey

BARTHOLOMEW
  As Off To The South'ard We Go

  Away To Rio

  Emmett, Daniel Decatur
    Dixie

  Erie Canal

  Gaudeamus

  Gaudeamus Igitur

  Grandma Grunts

  Grieg, Edvard Hagerup
    Barn Song, A

  Haapalainen, Vaino
    Pan

  Hoodah Day

  I Wonder When I Shall Be Married

  Johansen
    Old Neighbors

  Nagler, Franciscus
    Serenade In The Snow

  Old Tom Wilson

BARTHOLOMEW (cont'd.)

  Riddle Song

  Scott, [Lady] John (Alicia Ann)
    Think On Me

  Shenandoah

  Songs Of Yale

  What Shall We Do With A Drunken
    Sailor?

BARTHOLOMEW, LELAND
  Banchieri, Adriano
    Canzoni Alla Frances (Of 1596)

BARTHOLOMEW, M.
  Arne, Thomas Augustine
    Punch

  Hame, Dearie, Hame

  We Be Soldiers Three

BARTLES
  Evans
    Lady Of Spain

BARTLETT
  Friml, Rudolf
    Allah's Holidays
    Love Is Like A Firefly
    When A Maid Comes Knocking At Your
      Heart

  Star-Spangled Banner, The

  Wilson, Henry Lane
    Carmena. Waltz-Song

BARTLETT, IAN
  Prokofiev, Serge
    Camp-Fire Chorus

BARTLITZ, E.; KUMMERLING, H.
  Weber, Carl Maria von
    Canons

BARTOK, B.
  Geh Nicht

  Magdlein, Sie Sind Teuer

  Rund Um Die Stadt Stehn Mauern

  Sag Mir Doch Den Weg

  Sonntag Ein Schluckchen Schnaps

  Unten, Neben Meinem Garten

BARTOK; SUCHOFF
  Three Hungarian Folk Songs

BASELT, FR.
  Giordani, Tommaso
    Caro Mio Ben

  Mozart, Wolfgang Amadeus
    Wiegenlied

BASTIAN, A.
  Singende Klingende Heimat

BATCHELOR, P.
  Greensleeves

BATES, K.
  Cain, Noble
    America, The Beautiful

BATESON
  Strauss, Johann, [Jr.]
    Fledermaus Selection

BATHHURST, EDITH
  Seventeen Well-Known Airs From
    Beggar's Opera

BATSANYI, JANOS
  Sugar, Rezso
    Biztatas

BATTANI
  Sundberg, John
    Can't Wait To Get Back

BATTKE, M.
  Lang, Hans
    Nun Will Der Lenz Uns Grussen

BATTNER, CARL
  Helan Gar

BAUERNFEIND, H.
  All Mein Gedanken

  Ca, Ca Geschmauset

  Drei Studentenlieder

  Ergo Bibamus

  Studio Auf Einer Reis

BAUERNFEIND, HANS
Klingende Tag, Der

BAUM, RICHARD
Bruder Singer

Geselliges Chorbuch, 1.

Geselliges Chorbuch, 2.

BAUM, RICHARD; EHMANN, WILHELM
Carmina Nova

BAUMANN
Langhans, Herbert
Es Geht Eine Helle Flote
Lasst Mich Nur Auf Meinem Sattel
Gelten

Peaceful

BAUMANN, LORRAINE
Backy, Don
In Time

Bell, Thomas
People Make The World Go Round

Davis, Mack
Baby Don't Get Hooked On Me

Fargo, Donna
Funny Face
Happiest Girl In The Whole U.S.A.

Gates, David A.
Guitar Man, The

Lane, Red
World Needs A Melody, The

MacDonald, Ralph
Where Is The Love

Mann, Barry
Make Your Own Kind Of Music

Singelton, Charles
Spanish Eyes

Wayne, Sid
See You In September

BAUR, P.
Bartholemey
Urbs Aquensis

BAYFORD
Foster, Stephen Collins
Beautiful Dreamer

Nairne
Wi' A Hundred Pipers

Stroud
Hail, Caledonia!

BAZIN
Moniuszko, Stanislaw
Cracoviak

BAZIN, F.
Colasse
Echos, Les

Helts
Vieille Ballade, Une

Rameau, Jean-Philippe
Fetes D'Hebe, Les

Weber, Carl Maria von
Chor Der Jager

BEADELL
Knight
Oh To Have Been

Porter, Cole
Let's Do It

Wilson
How Small We Are, How Little We
Know

BEAHM
Haydn, [Franz] Joseph
Haydn Seek

BEAHM, J.
1685

BEAHM, JACQUELYN
Goodbye, Liza Jane

Katy Cruel

Ringing, Singing

BEALL
Paterson, Suzanne Hunt
Little Song For Sharing, A

BEARD
Smalls, Charles
Ease On Down The Road

BEAT, J.
Carissimi, Giacomo
Nisi Dominus

BEATTIE; ET AL
Gray Book Of Favorite Songs, The

BECK, R.
Stenka Rasin

BECK, THOMAS
Bansull

Bull, Ole Bornemann
Seterjentens Sondag

Grieg, Edvard Hagerup
Varen

Hallingvisa

Jeg Lagde Mig Sa Sildig

Jeppe Og Trine

Julesanger-Enkeltvis

Limu, Limu, Lima

Markje Gronast

Proysen, Alf
Gaukelat
Husmannspolka
Skyldige, Den

Schubertiana

Schulz, Johann Abraham Peter
Allnaturen

Skifaerden Av Arnljot Gelline

To Norske Folkeviser

Visa Um Liti Kjersti

BECKER
Cacavas, John
My Jimmie O'

BECKER, GUNTHER
Drei Griechische Volkslieder

BECKER, H.-G.
Dalmatinisches Liebeslied

BECKER, HANS-GUNTHER
Dalmatinisches Scherzlied

Kaljinka

Magaschan

Mein Madel Hat Einen Rosenmund

Slowenisches Liebeslied

Sommergluck

Sur Le Pont D'Avignon

BECKER, P.
Blumlein Fein, Ein

Gott G'segn Dich Laub

Maienzeit Bannet Leid

Nach Gruner Farb Mein Herz Verlangt

Wach Auf, Meins Herzens Schone

Wann Ich Gedenk Der Stund

BECKERATH, A. VON
Fischer Und Das Madchen, Der

Schone Vom Lande, Die

Tic E Tic E Toc, Mein Schwarzer Knabe

BECKERS, ANTON
Reger, Max
Maria Wiegenlied: Maria Sitzt Am
Rosenhag

BECKMANN
Gluck, Christoph Willibald, Ritter
von
Fullt Mit Schalle

BECKWITH
Holovski
On The Mountain, On The Hill

Kol'Tsov
Bird Of Youth

BECKWITH, JOHN
Papineau

BEEGLE, RAYMOND
Spirit Of The Gilded Age

BEEKUM, J. VAN
Old Timers Medley, The

BEETHOVEN; BOYD
Charlie Is My Darling

Robin Adair

Save Me From The Grave And Wise

BEETHOVEN; FORBES
Three Irish Folk-Songs

BEETHOVEN; HEINREID
O Charlie Is My Darling

BEHAR, GY.
Bunkocska

Eisler, Hanns
Voros Csepel

Kel Es Lemegy A Nap

BEHENNA, DONALD
Deep River

Widdicombe Fair

BEHR, HERMANN
Drunten Im Unterland. Variations

BEHREND, JEANNE
Early American "Fuguing" Tunes

BEHREND, S.
Monteverdi, Claudio
Concerto De Madrigali

BEIN
Leverkuhn
Jugendzeit

BEIN, W.
Abt, Franz
Sehnsucht Nach Den Bergen

Apel, L.
Grusset Den Tag

Becher
Mein Schlesierland

Brahms, Johannes
Wiegenlied

Fesca, E.
An Die Glocke

Grote, H.
Heimat Am Meer

Kamm, Ferd.
Heimkehr

Mehul, Etienne-Nicolas
Lasst Uns Wie Bruder

Molck, H.
Nun Bricht Aus Allen Zweigen

Rahlfs
Auf Der Luneburger Heide

Rahusen
Chorlieder-Suite

Schulz, Johann Abraham Peter
Mond Ist Aufgegangen, Der

Silcher, Friedrich
Abschied, Der
Annchen Von Tharau
Frisch Gesungen
Lebewohl

Stuntz, Josef Hartmann
Ins Freie – Festmarsch

BELL
Choral Hits Of The Month No. 2

Choral Hits Of The Month No. 3

Didn't Ma Lawd Deliver Daniel

Grant
They All Call It Canada

Six Christmas Carols From Europe

BELLA, R.
Schweizer Volkslieder

BELLINGHAM, BRUCE; EVANS, EDWARD G. JR.
Sixteenth-Century Bicinia: A Complete
Edition Of Munich, Bayerische
Staatsbibliothek, Mus. Ms. 260

BELLMANN, R.
Entlebucher Kuhreihen

BEMENT
Early One Morning

Griffes, Charles Tomlinson
Auf Geheimen Waldespfade

Haydn, [Franz] Joseph
Come Gentle Spring

BEMENT; CLOUGH-LEIGHTER
Sibelius, Jean
For Thee, Suomi

BEMENT, G.S.
Early One Morning

Golden Day Is Dying, The

Let All Things Now Living

Swansea Town

Tiritomba

W Srod Nocnej Ciszy

Wiegenlied Der Hirten

BEMENT, G.S.; CLOUGH-LEIGHTER, H.
Sibelius, Jean
For Thee, Suomi

BEMENT, GWYNN S.
Golden Day Is Dying, The

Palestrina, Giovanni Pierluigi da
Vedrassi Prima

Poslechnete Mne Malo

W Srod Nocnej Ciszy

BEMENT, GWYNN S.; CLOUGH-LEIGHTER,
HENRY

Sibelius, Jean
For Thee, Suomi

BEMENT, R.G.
On Christmas Night All Christians
Sing

BEN-HAIM
Israelische Nationalhymne

BEN-HAIM, PAUL
Hatikva

BEN-PORAT, ZVI
Folk Songs No. 1

BENDER, AUGUSTA; POMMER, JOSEF
Oberschefflenzer Volkslieder

BENEDETTI-MICHELANGELI
Nove Canti Popolari

BENESTAD, FINN; HEGSTAD, ARNULF
Steenberg, Per
Koraler

BENNETT
Carey
America

Gershwin, George
Gershwin

Northern Lights

Revolutionary Etude

Southern Comfort

Steffe, William
Battle Hymn Of The Republic

Ward, Samuel Augustus
America, The Beautiful

BENNETT, LAWRENCE
Two Patriotic Odes For Men's Voices

BENNETT, R.R.
America

America The Beautiful

Battle Hymn Of The Republic, The

Columbia, The Gem Of The Ocean

BENSON
Jenkins
Ship Comes In, A

BENSON, LIONEL
Bateson, Thomas
Sister, Awake

Benet, John
All Creatures Now Are Merry Minded
Thyrsis, Sleepest Thou

BENSON, LIONEL (cont'd.)

Byrd, William
This Sweet And Merry Month Of May

Gibbons, Ellis
Round About Her Chariot

Gibbons, Orlando
O That The Learned Poets

Lassus, Roland de (Orlandus)
Hark, Hark, The Echo Falling
Ola! O Che Bon Eccho!

Marenzio, Luca
Cedan L'antiche
Yield Up Your Ancient Fame

Morley, Thomas
Arise, Awake, You Silly Shepherds
Damon And Phillis

Palestrina, Giovanni Pierluigi da
Vaghi Fiori, I

Weelkes, Thomas
As Vesta Was
On The Plains

Wilbye, John
Adieu, Sweet Amarillis
Why Dost Thou Shoot

BENTE
Rische, Quirin
In Einen Felsen Aus Granit

BENZING-VOGT
En Igeli Schloht d'Trummle

BEON, A.
A La Venue De Ce Doulx Temps

A l'Horta Del Meu Pare

Amour De Moy, L'

Av'Ous Point Veu La Perronnelle

Chanson D'Aventuriers

Chappeau De Saulge

Collection De Musique Ancienne,
premier Recueil

Collection De Musique Ancienne,
deuxieme Recueil

Della La Riviere

Dinderindine, La

En Venant De Lyon

Fleur De Gaiete

Gente Pastourelle

Gentilz Gallans De France

Hellas! Olivier Bachelin!

Ilz Sont Bien Pelez

Je Vous Escry De Ma Pencee

Mon Mari M'A Diffamee

Nuit, Le Jour, La

Qui Belles Amours A

Vecy La Doulce Nuyt De May

Vray Dieu D'Amours Confortez Moy

BERALDO, P.
Quarantadue Canoni

BERENS, H.
Vaggvisa

BERG, G.
Monteverdi, Claudio
O Mirtillo

BERG, GOTTFRID
Brudieu, Juan
Rena Jungfru, Vi Dig Vorda

Byrd, William
Ar Karleken Blott En Lustig Fyr

Cadeac, Pierre
Ack, Jag Ar Overgiven

Eccard, Johannes
Nu Vintern Star Sa Kall Och Svar

Fifty Madrigals And Partsongs

Franck, Melchior
O Underbara Skatt
Ung Brunett Ar Min Idol, En

BERG, GOTTFRID (cont'd.)

Gesualdo, [Don] Carlo (da Venosa)
Min Dyrkade Herdinna

Gibbons, Orlando
Silversvan, En

Goudimel, Claude
Vem Ar Den Som Ger Min Syn

Greytter, Mathias
Jagare I Skogen, En

Hassler, Hans Leo
Ack Jungfru Kar
All Lust Och Frojd
Satt Nu I Gang

Isaac, Heinrich
Nar Jag Star Upp I Morgonstunden

Janequin, Clement
Kom, Giv Mig Hjalp Och Stod
Pa Den Vackra Majfestdag

Kormusik For Sopran— Och Altroster

Lassus, Roland de (Orlandus)
Bonde, Vad Finns I Sacken?
Fly Som Elden Amors Makt
Snart Maj Ar Har

Lupi, Johannes (de)
Min Bors Har Rakat Illa Ut

Marenzio, Luca
Din Ogons Makt Jag Kanner
Glada Sefyrer
Hulda, Skymtande Herdinna
Nar Du Bortdrog
O Skank Mig Eder Karlek

Monteverdi, Claudio
Ack, Vor' Jag Bland De Dode
O, Myrtillus

Morley, Thomas
Med Frojd Och Gamman
Skona Nymf, Sa Natt Och Prydlig

Othmayr, Kaspar
Flicka Fin Med Brunt I Blick, En
Forsta Snon Har Fallit, Den

Praetorius, Michael
Du Grona Lind Dar Standar
Till Ljus Och Gronska Hjartat Trar

Purcell, Henry
I Denna Tacka, Ljuva Lund

Senfl, Ludwig
Elsalill
Hans Beutler
Jag Red Mig Ut En Morgon

Wilbye, John
Adieu, Sweet Amarillis

Willaert, Adrian
Lansmannens Frieri

BERGER, HUGO
Chorlieder Der Romantik

BERGER, JEAN
Senfl, Ludwig
Ich Stund An Einem Morgen

BERGMAN
Good King Wenceslaus

BERGMAN, E.
Tyttoset

BERGMAN, ERIK
Two Karelian Folksongs

BERGMAN, NANCY; OAKLEY, AUDREY
Coots, John Frederick
Strangers

BERGMANN
Blow, John
Shepherds, Deck Your Crooks

Clarke, Jeremiah
Music On Henry Purcell's Death

John Brown's Body

Marching Through Georgia

BERGSAGEL, JOHN
Anthem From The 16th Century

BERGSTROM, HARRY
Viihdekuoro 4

BERKE, DIETRICH
Schubert, Franz (Peter)
Lied Im Freien
Widerhall

BERKOWITZ
Sim Sholom

BERLIOZ, HECTOR
Weber, Carl Maria von
Recitatives

BERNER, OTTO A.
Gansedieb, Der

Ratsel

BERNTSEN, A.
Hoffding, Finn
Blaesten Og Sangen

BERNTSEN, ELSE
Hor Klokkene Ringer Til Ave

BERT, P.
Delalande, Michel-Richard
Ballet De La Jeunesse

BERTHE, JACQUES
McKuen, Rod Marvin
Allez, Allez Mon Troupeau

V'la l'Bon Vent

BERTHELOT, R.
Chabrier, [Alexis-] Emmanuel
Ile Heureuse, L'
Pastorale Des Cochons Roses
Villanelle Des Petits Canards

Levade, Charles (Gaston)
Vieilles De Chez Nous, Les

Rameau, Jean-Philippe
Hymne A La Nuit

BERTHIER, J.E.
Singing I'm

BERTHOLON, L.
Chants Populaires Harmonises

BERTIN, PAMELA
Wondrous Love

BESIG
Bryant
Bye, Bye, Love

DeSylva, George Gard (Buddy)
Button Up Your Overcoat

Feliciano, Jose
Feliz Navidad

Peoples
Christmas In A Small Town

BESIG, D.
Gibb, Barry
How Deep Is Your Love

BESIG, DON
Babe

Bryant, Boudleaux
All I Have To Do Is Dream

Cohan, George Michael
Cohan Salute!, A [1]
Cohan Salute!, A [2]

Kerr
I'll Never Love This Way Again

Ortolani, Riz
Till Love Touches Your Life

Preston, Billy
You Are So Beautiful

Voice Of Freedom, The

What Matters Most

BESSELER
Lassus, Roland de (Orlandus)
Madrigale Und Chansons

BESSIERES
Rimbaud, A.
Dormeur Du Val, Le

BEST
Three Highland Airs

BEVERIDGE, LOWELL P.
Touro-Louro-Louro!

BIALAS, G.
Dort Nied'n In Jenem Holze

Ecce, Dominus Veniet

Ees, Zwee, Drei, Vier

Rosel Wenn Du Meine Warst

'S Ging Einer Vorbei

Wenn Die Bettelleute Tanzen

BIALAS, GUNTHER
Czech Folksongs

Polish Folksongs

BIALOSKY, MARSHALL H.
E-Ri-E, The

Erie Canal, The

Three American Folk Songs

Wanderin'

BIANCHI
Fazioli
Who'll Take My Place

Von Tilzer, Albert
Why Doesn't Santa Claus Go Next
Door?

BIANCHI, BARBARA
Colby, Elmer
Church Bells Are Ringing For Mary,
The

BIANCHI, LINO
De Ponte, Giaches
Qual In Somm'e Questa, La

Palestrina, Giovanni Pierluigi da
Complete Works Of Giovanni
Pierluigi Da Palestrina, Vol. 31:
Libro II Dei "Madrigali Profani"

BIANCONI, LORENZO
Marsolo, Pietro Maria
Madrigali

BIBERAUER, J.
Wiegenlied Aus Mahren

BIEBL
Gregor

Himmel
Es Kann Ja Nicht Immer So Bleiben

Sacha

BIEBL, F.
Auf Wiedersehen In Froher Runde

Brotchenverkaufer, Der

Carmela

Dixie Land

Dort Bin Ich Daheim

Dort Drunten An Jenem Felsen

Es Ist Schon Zeit Zum Schlafengehen

Herr Rousselle, Der

Hirten Von Canigo, Die

Ich Wollt, Wenns Rosen Schneit

Ja, Charlie Ist Mein Liebling

Jingle Bells

Klopf Nicht An

Loch Lomond

Madele Mein

O Du Getreuer Gott

Oh! Susanna

Old Black Joe

Polly-Wolly-Doodle

Reiter, Der

Sarie Marais

Schatz, Steh Auf

Schwarze Kirschen

Tauber Und Die Taubin, Der

Unser Katz

Vier Edle Rosse

Vive L'amour

Wanderlied

Wenn Ich Morgens Fruh Aufsteh

Winter Hat Verloren, Der

Zum Tanze, Da Geht Ein Madel

BIEBL, FR.
Aber Heidschi Bumbeidschi

Alle Wiesen Sind Grun

Bitt Dich Gar Schon, Jungfer Lisichen

Der Kuckuck Fliegt Uber Mein Schatzle
Sein Haus

Gruss Dich Gott, Das Hor Ich Gern

Holdes Mariechen

Ich Wollt Ein Baumlein Steigen

Ihren Liebsten Zu Erwarten

Jetzt Wars Zum Heimgehn Zeit

Jetzt War's Zum Heimgehn Zeit

Rusla, Wenn Du Meine Warst

Und In Dem Schneegebirge

Wo Hast Du Hin Das Ringele

BIEBL, FRANZ
Abendlied

Adieu, Mein Kleines Madchen

An Dem Hutchen

Appenzeller Kuherlied

Arirang

Auf Dem Meer

Auf Der Brucke Von Avignon

Auf Matzlbach

Austrian Folksongs

Bald Gras Ich Am Neckar

Blumen Im Gras Ach, Knabe Willst Du

Brucke Von Avignon, Die

Deep River

Es Ist Mir Alles Eins

Ewige Trinker, Der

Foster, Stephen Collins
Old Folks At Home
Ring The Banjo

Frohliche Weihnacht Uberall

Frohlichen Zecher, Die

Funf Seemanslieder

Git On Board, Little Children

Glaubet Nicht, Was Man Spricht

Great Day

Hauslein, Das

Heissa, Kathreinerle

Heut Scheint Der Mond

Hopp, Madchen, Schwing Dein Rocklein

I Got A Robe

I Want To Be Ready

I'm A-Rolling

Im Tal Des Roten Flusses

In Old Joe's Schenke

Jagers Morgenlied

Joshua Fit The Battle Of Jericho

Kaminkehrer, Der

Kauft's Ein Lavendel

Kein Schoner Land

Kosakenlied

Leb Wohl, Mein Freund

Lebte Einst Ein Mann

Leis' Das Glockchen Ertont

Let Us Break Bread Together

Lieb, O Lieb

Liebchens Klage

BLANCHARD, R. (cont'd.)
  Rose Au Boue, La

  Roy A Fait Battre Tambour, Le

  Saint-Gilles

  Tic-Tac Du Moulin, Le

  Trois Belles Princesses

  Ville De Sarlat

  Voici La Pentecote

BLANCHARD, ROGER
  Chiffonnier, Le

  Dans Le Bois De FouilloUse

  Petit Mercelet, Le

  Tourne Mon Joli Moulin

  Walzer-Jodler

BLANCHE, F.
  Knipper, Lev Konstantinovich
    Plaine, Ma Plaine

BLAND
  Carry Me Back To Old Virginny

BLAND; HUNTLEY
  Oh Dem Golden Slippers

BLANKENBURG, WALTHER
  Frohliche Singradel

BLAREAU, L.
  Chabrier, [Alexis-] Emmanuel
    A La Musique

BLAREAU, LUDOVIC
  Ganne
    Marche Lorraine

BLECH; LENDVAI; WEBER
  Folk Song Settings

BLECH, LEO
  Kaferhochzeit

  Mein Madel Hat Einen Rosenmund

  Zwischen Berg Und Tiefen, Tiefen Tal

BLISS
  Dvorak, Antonin
    Violet, The

  Elgar, [Sir] Edward (William)
    Down In The Woodland

  Offenbach, Jacques
    Night In June

  Reichardt, Luise
    When The Roses Bloom

  Schubert, Franz (Peter)
    Hark! Hark! The Lark

BLOCH, WALDEMAR
  Heissa, Kathreinerle

BLOWER
  Handel, George Frideric
    Music From "Semele"

  Purcell, Henry
    Come Ye Sons Of Art

BLOWER, MAURICE
  Purcell, Henry
    Come Ye Sons Of Art
    Come Ye Sons Of Art. (Ode For The
      Birthday Of Queen Mary 1694)

BLUM, ROBERT
  Nageli, Johann (Hans) Georg
    Elf Ausgewahlte Gesange

  Vogel Juhei

  Vogel Juhei Blatt 1

  Vogel Juhei Blatt 2

  Vogel Juhei Blatt 3

  Vogel Juhei Blatt 4

  Vogel Juhei Blatt 5

  Vogel Juhei Blatt 6

  Vogel Juhei Blatt 7

  Vogel Juhei Blatt 8

  Vogel Juhei Blatt 9

  Vogel Juhei Blatt 10

BLUM, ROBERT (cont'd.)
  Zahler, R.
    Trutzliedchen

BLUME
  Weltliche Lieder

BLUMEL, FRANZ
  Zwoa Kohlschwarze Tauberl

BLYTON, CAREY
  Six Regional Canadian Folksongs

BOALCH
  Morley, Thomas
    Two-Part Canzonets For Voices And
      Recorders

BOCK
  Bach, Johann Sebastian
    Bouree

  Bricusse
    Time Is My Friend

  Glow-Worm

  Hamilton
    I'm So Glad We Had This Time
      Together

  Joplin, Scott
    Entertainer, The

  Leveen, Raymond
    Christmas Candles

  Regney, Noel
    I Sing Noel

  Scarborough Fair

BOEPPLE, P.
  Compere, Loyset (Louis)
    Le Renvoy

  Des Prez, Josquin
    Bergerotte Savoysienne
    Cueurs Desolez

  Handel, George Frideric
    Beato In Ver Chi Puo

  La Rue, Pierre de
    Pourquoi Non

  Lassus, Roland de (Orlandus)
    Twelve Motets

BOEPPLE, PAUL
  Brahms, Johannes
    Madchen, Das

  Schubert, Franz (Peter)
    Tanz, Der

BOERLIN, RICHARD
  Berlin, Irving
    Doin' What Comes Natur'lly

BOETTICHER, WOLFGANG
  Lassus, Roland de (Orlandus)
    Come La Notte
    Lucescit Jam O Socii
    Vier Madrigale

BOGENHARDT, HELMUT
  All Mein Gedanken

  Es Wollt Ein Schneider Wandern

  Gestern Beim Mondenschein

  Immer Rundherum

  Schafer Sag, Wo Tust Du Weiden

  Und Wieder Bluhet Die Linde

  Vermeland

BOGHEN, F.
  Frescobaldi, Girolamo
    Six Madrigals: Book 1

BOHLIN, FOLKE
  Ecce Quam Sit

BOHM, F.
  Haydn, [Franz] Joseph
    Beredsamkeit, Die "Freunde, Wasser
      Machet Stumm"

BOHN, WILLIAM
  O Tannenbaum

BOLAND; LEYDEN
  Jaffe
    Gypsy In My Soul

BOND, ANDERS
  Bortsalda, Den

  Dar Vaxte Upp En Lilja

BOND, ANDERS (cont'd.)
  Du Har Latit Din Karlek Fa Forsvinna

  Gangar Tva Jungfrur At Rosendelund,
    Det

  Jag Var Ej Mer An Sexton Ar

  Liten En Lilja, En

  Med Angslan Och Besvar

  Och Jungfrun Hon Gangar Pa Hogan Berg

  Vinteren Tar Anda

BONDS, M.
  Ezek'el Saw The Wheel

BONITZ, E.
  Drei Gesellige Chore

  Hassler, Hans Leo
    All Lust Und Freud
    Ihr Musici Frisch Auf

  Standchen, Das

BONITZ, EBERHARD
  Allerlei Kurzweil

  Jeep, Johann
    Zwei Liebeslieder

  Schein, Johann Hermann
    Zwei Trinklieder

  Steffens, Johann
    Kuckuck Auf Dem Zaune Sass, Der

BONNAL, E.
  Adios Ene Maitea

BONNAL, ERMEND
  Adios Ene Maitea

  Maritchu

BONNEAU, P.
  Jardins De France

BONSET, J.
  Schubart, (Christian Friedrich)
    Daniel
    Wiegelied Der Herders

BONSET, J.VAN
  Brandts-Buys, L.F.
    Mijn Moedertaal

BOODY, CHARLES
  Freedom Trail

BOORMAN, STANLEY H.
  Machaut, Guillaume de
    Complete Works Of Guillaume De
      Machaut, Vol. V

BORCH
  Cook, Will Marion
    Swing Along!

  Romberg, Sigmund
    Auf Wiedersehn!

BORDES
  Lassus, Roland de (Orlandus)
    Fuyons Tous D'Amour Le Jeu

BORGULYA, A.
  Harom Bolcsodal

BORNEFELD, HELMUT
  Handel, George Frideric
    Frohsinn Und Schwermut

BORNSCHEIN
  Robinson
    Water Boy

BORRIS, SIEGFRIED
  Wir Sind Die Kleinen Musici

BOSCH, ADR. SR.
  Glory, Glory Halleluja

BOTHIG
  Schubert, Franz (Peter)
    Nachtgesang Im Walde

BOTHIG, MAX
  Schubert, Franz (Peter)
    Dorfchen, Das
    Gondelfahrer, Der

BOTKA, V.; CSANYI, L.
  Fecske

  Feher Galamb

  Gyermekkarok I

  Gyermekkarok II

  Gyermekkarok III

BOTKA, V.; CSANYI, L. (cont'd.)

Gyermekkarok IV

Gyermekkarok V

BOTSFORD
Verdi, Giuseppe
Rigoletto Quartette

BOTTCHER
Frisch Auf, Gut G'sell

Madchenklage

BOUCHER, EDGAR
Quick We Have But A Second

Young May Moon, The

BOUGHTON, RUTLAND
Piper's Song

BOULTON, HAROLD; SOMERVELL
Our National Songsvol. I

Our National Songsvol. II

Our National Songsvol. III

Our National Songsvol. IV

BOURDILLON
Rieti, Vittorio
Night Has A Thousand Eyes, The

BOURGAULT-DUCOUDRAY, L.-A.
An Ader

An Anjelus

An Eol A Zao

Ar Boutaoner

Ar C'Hemener

Ar Paradoz

Ar Vaouez Tapet Mat

Ar Vrozig Ruz

Disul Vintin

Duhamel, M.
Adieu A La Jeunesse
Combien Ton Ble, Beau Matelot?
Dimanche A L'Aube
Douze Melodies Populaires De Basse-
Bretagne
Ma Douce Annette
Mona
Non, Le Tailleur N'est Pas Un Homme
Quand Une Fille Se Marie
Sabotier, Le
Semeur, Le
Soleil Monte, Le
Soupe Au Lait, La
Un Jour Sur Le Pont De Treguier

Eur Waladen En Ifern

Eur Zon Kerne

Gant Ar Vrombard Hag Ar Biniou

Gour'c Hemmennou Doue

Guerz Ar Vechantez

Kanouen Evit Dansal

Kaow D'Ar Youankis

Kenavo D'Ar Yaouankis

Kimiad An Ene

Kloareq Tremolo

Lavoromp Ar Chapeled

Me Voa Deut Beteg Aman

Mona

Pebeuz Kelou

Peden Au Arvoriz

Silvestrik

Skaperez

Souben Al Lez

Trente Melodies Populaires De Basse-
Bretagne

Va Dous Annaig

Var Bount An Naonet

Yannig Ar "Bon Garcon"

BOUSTEAD
Donizetti, Gaetano
Mary Stuart's Prayer

BOUTELLE
Berlin, Irving
Easter Parade

Bernard, Felix
Winter Wonderland

Brodszky, Ferenc
Because You're Mine

Edwards
Once In A While

Tiomkin
Friendly Persuasion

Winter Wonderland

BOUTELLE, CHARLES
Barber Shop Jubilee

BOUVARD, J.
Berceuse Polonaise

Chanson Espagnole

BOWDEN
Bell
Popcorn Popping On The Apricot Tree

BOWER
Geld
Purlie
Walk Him Up The Stairs

BOYCE; WILHOUSKY
I Love America

BOYD
Byrd, William
If Women Could Be Fair
Though Amaryllis Dance

Capehart
Turn Around, Look At Me

Cornelius, Peter
Monotone, The

Galway Piper, The

Grieg, Edvard Hagerup
Last Spring

Hahn
Gardez Le Trait De La Fenetre
Jour, La
Nuit, La

Have You Seen But A Whyte Lillie Grow

Lightfoot, Gordon
If You Could Read My Mind

Muss I Denn

Poor Wayfaring Stranger

Schumann, Robert (Alexander)
Requiem Aeternam

Sedaka, Neil
If I Could Write A Song

Tomkins, Thomas
Adieu, Ye City-Prisoning Towers

Tompkins
Too Much I Once Lamented

Weatherly, Fred E.
Need To Be, The

Webb
All I Know

Weelkes, Thomas
Give Me My Heart

Weil
If Love, Like Spring, Can Come And
Go
No Tears Have We To Shed
On Meadow And Hillside
Tears Are Idle And Said The Swallow

Wylie, Ruth Shaw
Madman's Song

Yarrow, Peter
Don't Ever Take Away My Freedom

BOYD, J.
Crystal Fountain, The

BOYD, JACK
Abt, Franz
Furchte Dich Nicht

Bizet, Georges
Carnaval
Entr'acte

BOYD, JACK (cont'd.)

Blue Bells Of Scotland, The

Donizetti, Gaetano
Ah, Che Il Destino

Rheinberger, Josef
Enticement

BOYD, WILLIAM
Berlioz, Hector (Louis)
Royal Hunt And Storm

BOYDE
Weil
Ye Winds Of Winter

BOYER
La Forge, Frank
Ballad Of Ira Hayes

BRADLEY
The Choral Repertory — Blue Book

The Choral Repertory — Red Book

BRADLEY, KARL
Twentieth Century Choral Music

BRADLEY, KURT
Schirmer's SSA Program Collection

BRADSHAW
Gimby
Canada Song

BRAEIN, EDVARD
Dansevise

Springar

BRAHMS
Dornroschen

Schubert, Franz (Peter)
Ellen's Second Song

Schwesterlein

Volkslieder

BRAHMS; DAVISON
Summer Day Had Passed Away, The

BRAHMS; FLETCHER
Cradle Song

BRAHMS, J.
Da Untem Im Tale

Fahr Wohl

Ich Fahr Dahin

In Stiller Nacht

O Lovely May

Wollust In Den Maien, Die

BRAHMS, J.; FIELD, R.
Nacht Wache

BRAHMS, JOH.
Charm Me Asleep

Dornroschen

Morgengesang

Reiter, Der

BRAHMS, JOH.; DAVIS, K.K.
Charm Me Asleep

BRAHMS, JOH.; WOODWORTH, G.W.
Summer Day Had Pass'd Away, The

BRAHMS, JOHANNES
Handel, George Frideric
O Happy Indeed

Satt En Fugl Pa Tornkvist, Det

Volksliedbearbeitungen Fur Frauenchor

BRAHMS, JOHANNES; BRUELL, IGNAZ; DOOR,
ANTON; EPSTEIN, JULIUS; FUCHS,
J.N.; GAENSBACHER, J.;
HELLMESBERGER, J.; MANDYCZEWSKI,
EUSEBIUS

Schubert, Franz (Peter)
Complete Works

BRAHMS; TRUSLER
Brahms, Johannes
Down Low In The Valley

BRAND, FRANZ
Smetana, Bedrich
Lied Der Landleute

BRANDENBURG, ARTHUR H.; DAVIS, HENRY
W.; SKORNICKA, JOSEPH E.; WELKE,
WALTER C. WERSEN, LOUIS G.;
WHISTLER, HARVEY S.; PREUSS,
THEO.

    Americana Collection

BRANDON
    Battle Of Stonington, The

    Revolutionary Tea Party

    Shenandoah

BRANDON, GEORGE
    Grandma's Advice

    Pioneers

    Root, George F.
      Contest, The

    Sad Song Of The Sea

    Seward, T.F.
      Skating Song

BRANLE DE L'OFFICIAL; WOOD
    Ding-Dong! Merrily On High

BRANSCOMBE
    Afar On The Purple Moor

BRASH, J.
    A Hunting We Will Go

BRATTON
    Wilson
      Call It America

BRAUN
    Brahms, Johannes
      In Waldeseinsamkeit

    Godowsky, Leopold
      Alt Wien

BRAUN, HORST-HEINRICH
    Madele Ruck, Ruck, Ruck

    Muss I Denn

BRAUTIGAM, H.
    Kume Geselle Min

BRAUTIGAM, HELMUT
    Im Schnutzelputzhausel

    Kuckuck Und Der Esel, Der

    Lustige Tierlieder

    Zwei Hasen, Die

BRAY
    Annie Laurie

    Gimby
      New Generation, The

    God Save The Queen

BREDNICH, ROLF WILHELM; SUPPAN,
WOLFGANG

    Gottscheer Volkslieder – Band III:
      Weltliche Lieder Und Volkstanze

BRENDEL, ENGELBERT
    Aus Meinem Brunnlein

    Gruss Gott, Du Schoner Maien

    Lustig Ist's Matrosenleben

BRESGEN
    Mozart, Wolfgang Amadeus
      Heil Dem Tag

BRESGEN, C.
    Abschied

    Als Ich Ein Junggeselle War

    An Der Grenze

    Auf, Auf Zum Frohlichen Jagen

    Es Blies Ein Jager Wohl In Sein Horn

    Five English Folksongs

    Hoi, Lustig, Mir Knechtlar!

    Liebste Buhle, Der

    Neun Tschechoslowakische Volkslieder

    Six English Folksongs

    Six English Folksongs

    Six German Folksongs I

    Six German Folksongs I

BRESGEN, C. (cont'd.)
    Six German Folksongs II

    Six German Folksongs II

BRESGEN, CESAR
    Funf Ungarische Volkslieder

    Improvisierte Chorlied, Das

BRETT
    Tallis, Thomas
      Spem In Alium Numquam Habui

BRETTNER, PETER
    Es Strahlt Die Welt

    Freu Dich, Erd Und Sternenzelt

    Weites Land

BRETTON
    Caear
      Crazy Rhythm

    Caesar
      Choral Selections From "No, No,
        Nanette"
      I Want To Be Happy
      Tea For Two

    Creamer, Henry
      If I Could Be With You

    Dubin
      Gold Diggers Forever! (Choral
        Selections)
      Lullaby Of Broadway

    James
      Freight Train

    Lennon, John
      Michelle
      Yesterday

    Porter, Cole
      Begin The Beguine

    Yellen, Jack
      Ain't She Sweet

BRETTON, ELISE
    Deutschendorf, Henry John (John
      Denver)
      Eagle And The Hawk, The

    Paull, Barberi Platt
      Sweet Benjamin, The Easter Pig

BRETTON, ELLIS
    Danoff, William Thomas
      Friends With You

    Deutschendorf, Henry John (John
      Denver)
      Victory Is Peace

BRETTON; FOX
    Deutschendorf, Henry John (John
      Denver)
      Eagle And The Hawk, The

BREVIG, AGNES
    Annie Laurie

    Ching A Ling

    Junita

    Lie, Harald
      Skinnvengbrev

    Old Black Joe

    Steal Away

BREWER
    Battle Hymn Of The Republic

    Mana-Zucca, Mme. (Augusta Zuckermann)
      Big Brown Bear, The

    March Of The Men Of Harlech

    Sullivan, [Sir] Arthur Seymour
      Lost Chord, The

BREWER, A. HERBERT
    Alexander

BRIDGE, FREDERICK
    Goslings, The

BRIDGE, J. F.
    Gibbons, Orlando
      Cryes Of London, The

    Morley, Thomas
      It Was A Lover And His Lass

BRIGHT
    Streets Of Laredo

BRIMHALL
    Alley Cat

    Chim Chim Cher-Ee

    Dominique

    Five Hundred Miles

    Green Green Grass Of Home

    I Left My Heart In San Francisco

    Lemon Tree

    Let There Be Peace On Earth

    Little Gray Donkey

    Spoonful Of Sugar, A

    Supercalifragilisticexpialidocious

    Taste Of Honey, A

    Tie Me Kangaroo Down, Sport

    Time For Us, A

    What Is A Youth

BRINCH, K.
    Bayly, T.H.
      Tell Me The Tales

BRISMAN, HESKEL
    Brahms, Johannes
      Songs Of Ophelia

BRITTEN
    Oliver Cromwell

    Sally Gardens

BRITTEN, BENJAMIN
    National Anthem, The

    Oliver Cromwell

BROADHEAD, G.
    To Daisies Not To Shut So Soon

BROADWOOD, LUCY E.
    Derby Ram, The

    Landmanns Lob

    Turmut-Hoeing

    Twankydillo

BROCHART, L.
    Gluck, Christoph Willibald, Ritter
      von
      Acte 1, Scene 1
      Agreable Sejour, L'
      Orphee, Acte 1, Scene 1
      Que D'attraits

    Gretry, Andre Ernest Modeste
      Choeur De L'Aurore

BROCKLEHURST, BRIAN
    Hindemith, Paul
      Pentatonic Song Book

BRODDE, OTTO
    Nun Lasst Uns Den Leib Begraben

    Nun Lasst Uns Den Leib Begraben

    Vom Aufgang Der Sonne Bis Zu Ihrem
      Niedergang

BRODDE, OTTO; KOCH, HANS OSKAR
    Thuringer Motetten-Band 1

    Thuringer Motetten-Band 2

BRODIN, YVES
    Brahms, Johannes
      Cygne Au Fil De L'eau

BRONSON
    Brahms, Johannes
      Sleep Under Bethlehem's Star

BROOKS
    Overstreet
      They'll Be Some Changes Made

BROUSSIER, JACQUES
    Michel, Paul-Baudouin
      Petit Zodiaque Sentimental, Part I
      Petit Zodiaque Sentimental, Part II
      Petit Zodiaque Sentimental, Part
       III

BROWER
    Martin, (Frederick John) Easthope
      Come To The Fair

BROWN
  Allison
    One And Only Me

  Londonderry Air

  Tchaikovsky, Piotr Ilyich
    Ye Who The Longing Know

BROWN, CHRISTOPHER
  A-Courting We Will Go

BROWN, F.E.
  If I Had Wings To Fly

  Massenet, Jules
    Elegy

  Schubert, Franz (Peter)
    Wand'ring Miller

  Tchaikovsky, Piotr Ilyich
    Legend, A

BROWN, GARY
  Codfish Shanty, The

BROWN; HOMER; ADES
  Green
    Sentimental Journey

BROWNING, PAUL
  Schumann, Robert (Alexander)
    Hymn Of The Evil Agencies

BRUCHHOLD
  Schulz, Johann Abraham Peter
    Lied An Die Freude

BRUCK; DEIS
  Gounod, Charles Francois
    Soldiers' Chorus

BRUCKER, HERMANN
  Ehemann's Leiden

BRUHN, OTTO
  Drink To Me Only

  Fjarran Han Drojer

  Jag Vet En Dejlig Rosa

  Mandom, Mod Och Morske Man

  Med Frojd Och Gamman

  Som Stjarnan Uppa Himmelen

  Tanker Du, Att Jag Forlorader Ar

  Vallvisa Fran Alvdalen

BRUMBY, COLIN
  Andy's Gone With Cattle

BRUNE, W.
  Wer Geht Mit, Juchhe, Uber See?

BRUNGS, PETER
  Tiroler Wollte Jagen, Ein

BRUNIER, FRANCOISE
  Quand Les Lilas Refleuriront

BRUNNER, H.; VONESCH, R.
  Ihr Berge, Lebt Wohl!

BRUNNER, M.
  Erinnerung

BRYDEN
  Autumn Leaves

BRYDSON, JOHN
  Green Broom

BRYMER, MARK
  Africa

  Alabama ... On Stage

  Automatic

  Celebrate America!

  Connor, Tommie
    I Saw Mommy Kissing Santa Claus

  Don't Cry

  Don't Touch That Dial!

  Dreamgirls

  Dreamgirls: Medley

  Eye Of The Tiger

  Good Ol' Country Music

  Human Nature

  I Am Woman Medley

  I Dig Rock And Roll Music

BRYMER, MARK (cont'd.)
  I Shall Sing

  I Won't Hold You Back

  Jackson, Michael
    Beat It

  Little Christmas, A

  McDonald, Michael
    Takin' It To The Streets

  Mann, Barry
    Make Your Own Kind Of Music

  Michael Jackson "Thriller" Medley,
    The

  Missing You

  Mountain Music

  My Inspiration

  Neutron Dance

  New World Coming

  No More Lonely Nights

  Shine Down

  So Far Away

  SRO — A Choral Revue Of Entertainment

  Stevens, Ray
    Can't Stop Dancin'

  Streets A-Fire!

  Surfin' With Jan And Dean

  This Is It

  Where The Boys Are

  Why Do Fools Fall In Love?

BUCHHOLZ
  Rostill
    Let Me Be There

  Wilson
    Most Beautiful Girl, The

  Zawinul
    Mercy, Mercy, Mercy

BUCHHOLZ, BUCK
  American Pop

  Jordan, Archie Paul
    It Was Almost Like A Song

  Last Blues Song, The

  Mann, Barry
    You've Lost That Lovin' Feeling

  Old Friends

  Read 'Em And Weep

  Richie, Lionel
    Stuck On You

  Rock And Roll Music

  Scott, [Robert W.] Bobby
    He Ain't Heavy.. He's My Brother

  Way We Were, The

  We've Got Tonight

  Whenever I Call You Friend

BUCHHOLZ, ROBERT
  Country Medley

BUCHTGER
  Strauss, Johann, [Jr.]
    Horet Zu, Gebet Acht

BUCHTIGER, F.
  Z' Lauterbach

BUCK
  Abt, Franz
    O Jugend, Wie Bist Du So Schon

  Annie Laurie

  Baumgartner
    Tage Der Rosen, Die

  Becker
    Wanderlied

  Beethoven, Ludwig van
    Heavens Are Declaring, The
    Opferlied

BUCK (cont'd.)
  Boseke
    Weinkanon

  Chopin, Frederic
    Ringelein, Das

  Es Steht Eine Lind'

  Mendelssohn-Bartholdy, Felix
    Abschied Vom Walde

  Peters
    Stromt Herbei, Ihr Volkerscharen

BUCK; DEIS
  Beethoven, Ludwig van
    Ehre Gottes Aus Der Natur, Die

BUCK, DUDLEY
  In Vocal Combat

BUHLER, PHILIPPE
  Foster, Stephen Collins
    Camptown Races

BULLARD, F.F.
  Johns, Clayton
    Dinah

BULLOCK, ERNEST
  Wauking O' The Fauld

BUNE
  Deutschendorf, Henry John (John
    Denver)
    Farewell Andromeda
    I'd Rather Be A Cowboy (Lady's
      Chains)
    Sunshine On My Shoulders

  Dylan, Robert (Bob)
    Blowin' In The Wind

  Lightfoot, Gordon
    Christian Island (Georgian Bay)
    Go My Way

  Paxton
    Going To The Zoo

  Tell Me What Month

  Tyson
    January Morning
    Someday Soon

  Wailie, Wailie

BUNE, ROBERT
  Deutschendorf, Henry John (John
    Denver)
    Farewell Andromeda (Welcome To My
      Morning)
    I'd Rather Be A Cowboy

  Paxton, Tom
    Going To The Zoo

BUNNELL
  Sanford
    Horse With No Name, A

BURDEN, JAMES
  Dodds
    N.R.G. Song
    Something For Tomorrow

  Hudson
    Understanding

  Raulston
    Spirit And Celebration
    Time Is My Friend

BURGHARDT
  Werner, Heinrich
    Sah Ein Knab Ein Roslein Stehn

BURKHARDT, H.; LIPPHARDT, W.
  Bach, Johann Sebastian
    Ausgewahlte Choralsatze

  Deutsche Kantionalsatze Des 17.
    Jahrhunderts

  Singer, Der. Ein Liederbuch Fur
    Schule Und Leben

  Singer, Der, Teil I: 1.-4. Schuljahr
    (Unterstufe)

  Singer, Der, Teil II: 5.-8. Schuljahr
    (Tageslauf; Jahreskreis)

  Singer, Der, Teil III: 5.-8.
    Schuljahr (Menschenleben)

BURKHARDT, HANS; LIPPHARDT, WALTHER
  Chorgesange Des 19. Jahrhunderts

  Weltliche Chorlieder Des 16.
    Jahrhunderts

BURKHART
  Mozart, Wolfgang Amadeus
    Wiegenlied

  Rosestock, Holderbluh

BURKHART, C.
  Deaf Woman's Courtship, The

  False Young Man, The

BURKHART, F.
  Abendchoral

  Ach Schonster Schatz, Mein Augentrost

  Ade Zur Guten Nacht

  Als Ich Auf Bergen Stand

  Als Ich Ein Jung Geselle War

  Andulka

  Baumlein Stand Im Tiefen Tal, Ein

  Bis Gott Willkomm, Frau Nachtigall

  Blumlein Auserlesen, Ein

  Brahms, Johannes
    Es Ist Ein Schnitter

  Cacilienlied

  Drei Rosen

  Drei Volkslieder Aus Niederosterreich

  Eccard, Johannes
    Nun Schurz Dich, Gretlein

  Es, Es, Es Und Es

  Es Ist Ein Lind

  Es Ist Ein Schnee Gefallen

  Es Sass Ein Schneeweiss Vogelein

  Handel, George Frideric
    Durch Harmonie
    Horch, Wie Das Tamburin Erklingt
    Kommt, Und Schwebend Schlingt Den
      Kranz
    Nymphen, Faune, Holde Flora
    Schallt Laut, Ihr Chore!
    So Wie Durch Heil'ger Lieder Macht

  Hans Spielmann

  Hassler, Hans Leo
    Feinslieb, Du Hast Mich G'fangen
    Jungfrau, Dein Schon Gestalt

  Hort, Ihr Herren

  Ich Spring An Diesem Ringe

  Isaac, Heinrich
    Innsbruck, Ich Muss Dich Lassen

  Jager In Dem Grunen Wald, Der

  Kein Feuer, Keine Kohle

  Kein Schoner Land

  Klopfet Mir Keiner An

  Kranichruf

  Lassus, Roland de (Orlandus)
    Annelein
    Audite Nova
    Ola! O Che Bon Eccho!

  Lechner, Leonhard
    Gott B'hute Dich

  Mei Mutter Mag Mi Net

  Mondhochzeit

  Mozart, Wolfgang Amadeus
    Giovinette Che Fate All'amore
    Singt Dem Grossen Bassa Lieder
    Strahlen Der Sonne Vertreiben Die
      Nacht, Die

  Nachtigall, Ich Hor Dich Singen

  Old Black Joe

  Peuerl, Paul
    Trau Gott Allein

  Praetorius, Michael
    Sie Ist Mir Lieb

  Rheinisch

  Schafer Tragt Sorgen, Ein

BURKHART, F. (cont'd.)
  Schein, Johann Hermann
    Holla, Gut Gsell

  Senfl, Ludwig
    Gelaut Zu Speyer, Das
    Im Meyen

  Sie Gleicht Wohl Einem Rosenstock

  S'ist Nichts Mit Den Alten Weibern

  So Geht Es In Schnutzelputz' Hausel

  Spee, F. von
    Bei Stiller Nacht

  Tagelied

  Tanz Mir Nicht Mit Meiner Jungfer
    Kathen

  Trutz Du Nur!

  Und In Dem Schneegebirge

  Verdi, Giuseppe
    Teure Heimat

  Verstohlen Geht Der Mond Auf

  Wach Auf, Mein's Herzens Schone

  Wagner, Richard
    Treulich Gefuhrt Ziehet Dahin

  Weiss Mir Ein Schones Roselein

  Wie Schon Bluht Uns Der Maien

  Wo Find Ich Denn Dein's Vaters Haus

  Wo Soll Ich Mich Hinkehren

  Wo Zwei Herzlieb Beinander Sein

  Zogen Einst Funf Wilde Schwane

  Zwischen Theiss Und Donaustrom

BURKHART, F.; VOGG, H.
  Handel, George Frideric
    Ritorni Omai Nel Nostro Core

BURKHART, FRANZ
  Bruckner, Anton
    Samtliche Werke, Band XXII-7:
      Germanenzug

BURNETT, MICHAEL
  Tenk You For De Chrismus

BURNETT, R.
  Deidre's Farewell

BURROUGHS
  Dylan, Robert (Bob)
    Don't Think Twice, It's All Right

  Lightfoot
    Early Mornin' Rain

  Mitchell, Joni
    Both Sides Now

  Stookey, Noel Paul
    I Dig Rock And Roll Music

BURROUGHS, BOB
  God Rest You Merry, Gentlemen

BURROUGHS; SEWELL
  Betts, Lorne M.
    Ramblin' Man

  Mitchell, John
    Joni Mitchell Medley

  Paxton
    If You're Happy Notify Your Face

  Webb
    MacArthur Park

BURROWS, DAVID L.
  Cesti, Marc' Antonio
    Four Chamber Duets

BURTHEL, JACOB
  Abends, Wenn Der Hirte Heimwarts
    Zieht

  An Einem Maientage

  Burschlein Sag Mir

  Csardas

  Cuckoo, The

  Es Fiel Ein Reif

  Froh Zu Sein Bedarf Es Wenig

  Ich Klage Dir, Lieber Mandelbaum

BURTHEL, JACOB (cont'd.)
  In Meiner Liebe Garten

  Robin Adair

  Sah Den Teufel Heute Nacht

  Sonne Kann Nicht Alle Tage Scheinen

  Still Und Trage Fliesst Die Wolga

  Vino Und Amore

  Zwei Englische Volkslieder

  Zwei Volkslieder

BURTHEL, JAKOB
  Au Clair De La Lune

  Doch Der Vater Sagte "Nein"

  Einst Hatt' Ich Mich Sehr Verliebt

  Hor, Liebchen

  Kleines Blumchen, Du Musst Welken

  Letzte Geld Vertrinken Wir, Das

  Londonderry Air

  Mochte Einmal Noch Ein Kind Sein

  Sonne Kann Nicht Alle Tage Scheinen

  Wollt Zur Frau Dich Nehmen

BUSCH, LOU
  All The Things You Are

BUSH, G.; HURD, M.
  Invitation To The Partsong, Book 1

BUSSER, H.
  Charpentier, Marc-Antoine
    Couronne De Fleus, La

BUSZIN, WALTER
  Sixty Canons On Secular Texts, Vol. 1

  Sixty Canons On Secular Texts, Vol. 2

BUTCHART, DAVID S.
  Gagliano, Marco da
    Three Madrigals

  Striggio, Alessandro
    Primo Libro De Madrigali A Sei
      Voci, Il

BUTLER
  Messenger Of The Heart

  Scott
    This Is My Own, My Native Land

  Verdi, Giuseppe
    Squilla, Echeggi La Tromba
      Guerriera

BUTLER, EUGENE
  Starshine

BUTTON, H. ELLIOT
  Drink To Me Only With Thine Eyes

  Morley, Thomas
    Sing We And Chant It

  Wallace, William Vincent
    Angels That Around Us Hover

BUTZ
  Alabiev, Alexander Nicholaevich
    Nachtigall, Die

  Brahms, Johannes
    Barkarole
    Minnelied

  Radecke, Robert
    Aus Der Jugendzeit

  Schulz, Johann Abraham Peter
    Drescherlied
    Liebeszauber
    Saemann Saet Den Samen, Der
    Sagt, Wo Sind Die Veilchen Hin
    Seht Den Himmel, Wie Heiter
    Sorgenfreie, Der

BUTZ, J. CHR.
  Wagner, Richard
    Wach Auf

BYRD
  Haralambi

BYRT
  Among The Leaves So Green-O

CABLE
Delanoe
Let It Be Me

Feltmate
Look Around

Gimbel
Bluesette

Hatch, Tony (Anthony Peter)
Downtown

Heyman
When I Fall In Love

Highlights From "Promises, Promises"

Holt
One Of Those Songs

Lees
Quiet Nights Of Quiet Stars

Livingston
Tammy

Loesser, Frank
Anywhere I Wander
Inch Worm, The
Ugly Duckling, The
Wonderful Copenhagen

Rodgers, Richard
It's The Little Things In Texas
Look No Further
Maine
Our State Fair
So Long, Farewell
Something Wonderful
Sweetest Sounds, The

Singleton
Strangers In The Night

Williams
How Do You Open A Show Without A
Curtain?

Willson, Meredith
Ask Not

Wright
Night Of My Nights

CABLE, HOWARD
O'Reilly, Dermott
Children's Winter

CACAVAS
Becker
Home, My Home

Ben Franklin In Paris

Danzig, Evelyn
Scarlet Ribbons

Dee
Bring Me Sunshine

Jingle Bells

Kramer
No Man Is An Island

Lustberg
Rachel My Own
You Can't Tell A Person

Magidson, Herbert Adolph
Gone With The Wind

Martyn
Shiver Ma' Timbers Jones
Shiver Ma'timbers Jones

Mitchell
Sand In My Shoes

Parsons, Robert
Eternally

Rodgers, Richard
Edelweiss
So Long, Farewell

Willson
America Calling

CACAVAS, JOHN
Cohan, George Michael
Yankee Doodle Boy
You're A Grand Old Flag

CACKLE
Starling
Chicken Song, The

CADOW, P
Flieg, Kleine Schwalbe

Komm Du, Mein Madel

Von All Den Madchen

CADOW, P (cont'd.)
Zwei Tschechische Volkslieder

CADOW, PAUL
Abendstern, Der

Abendstern Will Untergehn

Breitkopf, Bernhard Theodor
Amors Grab
Wunsch Eines Jungen Madchens
Zwei Lieder

Drei Schiffe, Die

Eberwein, Traugott Maximilian
Geniesset Den Mai

Gefangene, Der

Hammerschmidt, Andreas
Kunst Des Kussens, Die

Japanisches Wiegenlied

Krieger, Johann Philipp
Im Dunkeln Ist Gut Munkeln
Wurst Wider Wurst

Londonderry Air

Reichardt, Johann Friedrich
Veilchen, Das
Wahre Liebe, Die

Salieri, Antonio
Steter Tropfen
Waage Des Glucks, Die
Zwei Kanons

Serenade

Silcher, Friedrich
Es War Einmal

Wagner, Richard
Sangergruss

Zum Rio Grande

Zwei Frauenportraits

Zwei Gespielen

Zwei Heitere Barocklieder

Zwei Heitere Volkslieder Aus Ungarn

Zwei Slowakische Volkslieder

Zwei Volkslieder Aus Der
Tschechoslowakei

CADOW, PAUL; VETTER, KARL
Wagner, Richard
Sangergruss

CAILLARD, PH.
J'Entends L'Alouette

Route D'Amitie

V'la L'Bon Vent

CAILLAT, S.
Au Chateau De Mon Pere

Celui Que Mon Coeur Aime

Liseta

CAILLAT, STEPHANE
C'Etait P'tit Jean

CAILLET
Rubenstein
Voice Of Freedom

CAILLIET
Purcell, Henry
Passacaglia

Rubinstein, Anton
Voice Of Freedom

CAIN
Haydn, [Franz] Joseph
So Dim With Tears

Home In The Valley

Housman
White In The Moon

In That Great Gettin' Up Morning

Kalinnikoff, Paul
Let All Creatures Of God

Keep A-Inchin' Along

Kjerulf, Halfdan
Last Night The Nightingale

CAIN (cont'd.)
Martin, (Frederick John) Easthope
Come To The Fair

Mendelssohn-Bartholdy, Felix
Auf Flugeln Des Gesanges

Old Mac Donald's Farm

Ronald, [Sir] Landon
O Lovely Night
Prelude

Schubert, Franz (Peter)
Du Bist Die Ruh'
Du Bist Die Ruh
Flower Of June

Schumann, Robert (Alexander)
How Like Unto A Flower

Songs For Boys

Tennyson
Ring Out, Wild Bells
Sunset And Twilight

Tom Big-Bee River

CAIN, N.
Clough-Leighter, Henry
Let The Merry Bells Ring Out

Deep River

Early One Morning

Strickland, Lily Teresa
My Lover Is A Fisherman

CAIN, NOBLE
Mendelssohn-Bartholdy, Felix
Auf Flugeln Des Gesanges

Swing Low, Sweet Chariot

Vautor, Thomas
Mother, I Will Have A Husband

CAJANDER
Sibelius, Jean
An Das Vaterland

CALAHORRA, PEDRO
Ruimonte, Pedro
Parnaso Espanol; Madrigales Y
Villancicos A Quatro, Cinco Y
Seys

CALDER
Rodgers, Richard
Farmer And The Cowman, The

CALDICOTT, A.L.
Little Jack Horner

CALDWELL
Brahms, Johannes
Abendlied

CALDWELL, MARY E.
Brahms, Johannes
Abendlied

CALKINS-HOEKJE, BETH
Wreck Of The John B., The

CALMEL, R.
Mon Petit Poney

CALMEL, ROGER
Mon Petit Poney

CALVIN, DOT
Chaplin
Smile

CAMMAROTA, LIONELLO; DEL GIOVANE DA
NOLA, GIAN DOMENICO
Polifonia Napoletana Del Rinascimento

CAMMIN, HEINZ
Geese, Heinz
Seefahrt Nach Rio, Die

CAMPBELL
Slumber Song

Vecchi, Orazio (Horatio)
Let All Our Lives Be Joyous

CAMPBELL, A.
Songs

CAMPBELL, D.
Search-Songs Of The Sun

CANDLYN
What Shall We Do With A Drunken
Sailor

CANTELOUBE, J.
A La Claire Fontaine

Ah! Si Mon Moine Voulait Danser

Ah! Toi, Belle Hirondelle

Alouette

C'est La Belle Francoise

En Roulant Ma Boule

Fringue, Fringue

Isabeau S'y Promene

Mon Per' N'avait Fille Que Moi

Mon Pere A Fait Batir Maison

Par Derrier' Chez Mon Pere

[Six] Noels D'Europe

V'l'a L'bon Vent

CANTELOUBE, JOSEPH
Autre Jour, En Voulant Danser, L'

CAPPS, AL
Bacharach, Burt F.
Knowing When To Leave

CARAPEZZA, PAOLO EMILIO
Pari, Claudio
Lamento d'Arianna, Il

CARBUCCIA, MARIE-FRANCE
Le Forestier, Catherine
Petite Fugue, La

CARDAMONE, DONNA G.
Willaert, Adrian
Canzone Villanesche Alla Napolitana
And Villotte

CAREME, MAURICE
Bernier, Rene
Sabots De La Vierge

Middeleer, Jean De
Blauwe Schuur, De
Grange Bleue, La

CAREY, HENRY
Flocks Are Sporting

CARL, ROBERT
Mendelssohn-Bartholdy, Felix
Abendlied
Herbstlied
Ich Wollt' Meine Lieb'

Mozart, Wolfgang Amadeus
Due Pupille Amabile
Ecco, Quel Fiero Istante
Piu Non Si Trovano
Se Lontan, Ben Mio, Tu Sei

Schumann, Robert (Alexander)
So Wahr Die Sonne Scheinet

CARLETON, B.
Hahn, Carl
Green Cathedral, The

CARLETON, BRUCE
Sousa, John Philip
Liberty Bell, The

CARLSEN, CARSTEN
Annie Laurie

Auld Lang Syne

Forsyth, Cecil
Beautiful Dreamer

Krane, Kjell
Var Engang En Konge, Det

Loch Lomond

Londonderry Air

CARLSTEDT, JAN
Lille Per Stabbe

Schottisch Fran Dalarna

Tva Skanklatar Fran Mora

CARLTON
Boosey And Hawkes Choral Series

CARLYLE
Allen
Home For The Holidays

Bart, Lionel
Consider Yourself
Where Is Love?
Where Is Love

CARLYLE (cont'd.)
Drake, Ervin
I Believe

Fields
Chantez, Chantez

Guthrie, Woody (Woodrow Wilson)
This Land Is Your Land

Kent, Walter
I'll Be Home For Christmas

Large
Holiday Polka, The

Newley, Anthony
Gonna Build A Mountain
Nothing Can Stop Me Now
Nothing Can Stop Ne Now
Wonderful Day Like Today, A

Seeger, Pete
If I Had A Hammer
Turn! Turn! Turn!

Simon
Harmony

Styne, Jule (Jules Stein)
Let It Snow! Let It Snow! Let It
Snow!

CARMINES
America The Beautiful

CARPENTER
Crecquillon, Thomas
What Greater Love Can Come

CARROLL
Rock-A My Soul

CARRUTHERS-CLEMENT, ANN
Aleotti, Vittoria
Baciai Per Haver Vita
Hor Che La Vaga Aurora

CARTER
Beall, John Oliver
Wheels

Hark! What Mean Those Holy Voices

CARTER, ANDREW
Ding Dong! Merrily On High

Make We Merry On This Fest

Three English Folk-Songs

Twelve Days Of Christmas, The

Two For The Price Of One

CARTER, JOHN
Deutschendorf, Henry John (John
Denver)
Follow Me

CARTRIGHT
Hawkins
Tuxedo Junction

CASADESUS, F.
Charbonnel, R.
Berceuse De "Moissoneur"
Lisetta, La
Rossignolet

CASAGRANDE, EFREM
Quattordici Canti Internazionali

CASEY
Brel
Ne Me Quitte Pas

CASEY, CHUCK
Holler, Dick
Abraham, Martin And John

Tennessee Wig-Walk

CASHMORE
Drunken Sailor, The

CASHMORE, DONALD
Drink To Me Only With Thine Eyes

Gentle Maiden

Pretty Polly Oliver

Rio Grande

CASIMIRI, RAFFAELE; BIANCHI, LINO
Palestrina, Giovanni Pierluigi da
Complete Works Of Giovanni
Pierluigi Da Palestrina, Vol. 2:
Libro I Dei "Madrigali Profani"

CASSEY
Applause

Beatles, Chipmunks And Red-Nosed
Reindeer

Beckley
I Need You

Benton, Otis
Endlessly

Blue Velvet

Carmichael, Hoagy
Star Dust

Choral Hits Of The Month No. 1

Christmas Day

Coleman
Tennessee Wig Walk

Come Saturday Morning

Curtain Time

Danoff
Take Me Home, Country Roads

Danzig, Evelyn
Scarlet Ribbons

Dear World

Dear World Medley

Ellington, Edward Kennedy (Duke)
Caravan

Evans
Tongue Twister

Everything Is Beautiful

Geld, Gary
Hurting Each Other

Golden Boy

Gundry
Tomorrow Belongs To The Children

Half The Battle

He Ain't Heavy

Hudson
Moonglow

I Couldn't Sleep A Wink Last Night

Jericho

John
Tiny Dancer

Jolson, Al
Back In Your Own Back Yard

Kiss Her Now

Koehler
Let's Fall In Love

Lennon, John
Across The Universe
And I Love Her
Birthday
Carry That Weight
Give Peace A Chance
Goodbye
Here, There And Everywhere
If I Fell
Imagine
In My Life
Maxwell's Silver Hammer
Ob-La-Di, Ob-La-Da
Penny Lane
Strawberry Fields Forever
Uncle Albert-Admiral Halsey
When I'm Sixty-Four
Yellow Submarine

Loggins, David A.
Sounds Of Loggins And Messina

Love Story

Lovely Way To Spend An Evening, A

McCartney, [John] Paul
That Would Be Something

MacGimsey, Robert
Shadrack

Make Me Smile

Medley

Music From The Broadway Shows

My Great, Grandfather

CASSEY (cont'd.)

No More

Nyro
  Save The Country

Ode To Joy

O'Kun, Lan
  Ring Little Triangle

One Less Bell To Answer

One Person

Ortolani
  More

Pass Me By

Pops Of The 70's—Group 6

Promises, Promises

Raindrops Keep Fallin' On My Head

Russell, Bobby
  Little Green Apples

Sedaka, Neil
  Laughter In The Rain

Snowbird

Stills, Stephen
  Isn't It About Time

Sunrise Serenade

Think How It's Gonna Be

Till Love Touches Your Life

Vaya Con Dios

Waller, Thomas (Fats)
  Ain't Misbehavin'

Wedding Song

We've Only Just Begun

Withers
  Ain't No Sunshine

CASSEY, CHUCK
  Arkin, David F.
    Black And White

  Axton, Hoyt
    Joy To The World

  Bacharach, Burt F.
    Living Together, Growing Together
    Look Of Love, The
    Lost Horizon
    Reflections
    World Is A Circle, The

  Bennett, Richard Rodney
    Too Beautiful To Last

  Bergman, Alan
    Hands Of Time, The (Brian's Song)

  Black, Don
    Born Free
    To Sir, With Love

  Bricusse, Leslie
    Candy Man, The

  Buie, Buddy
    Traces

  Cochran, Hank
    Make The World Go Away

  Danoff, William Thomas
    Take Me Home Country Roads

  Davis, Mack
    I Believe In Music

  De Vorzon, Barry
    Bless The Beasts And Children

  Gates, David A.
    If

  Gershwin, George
    Foggy Day, A
    Love Is Here To Stay
    Nice Work If You Can Get It
    They Can't Take That Away From Me

  Goffin, Gerry
    Hi-De-Ho (That Old Sweet Roll)

  Hamilton, Nancy
    How High The Moon

  If You Were Me And I Were You

CASSEY, CHUCK (cont'd.)

  King, Carole
    Back To California
    Carole King Choral Collection
    Home Again
    I Feel The Earth Move
    It's Going To Take Some Time
    Music
    Song Of Long Ago
    Sweet Seasons
    Tapestry
    You've Got A Friend

  Like It Is Today Choral Book

  MacColl, Ewan
    First Time Ever I Saw Your Face,
      The

  Mann, Barry
    New World Coming
    Rock And Roll Lullaby

  Marks, Johnny D.
    Choral Christmas Medley

  Music

  Porter, Cole
    Ev'ry Time We Say Goodbye
    I Love Paris
    You'd Be So Nice To Come Home To

  Putman, Curly
    Green Green Grass Of Home

  Rodgers, Richard
    It Never Entered My Mind

  Schwartz, Arthur
    I See Your Face Before Me

  Schwartz, Stephen Lawrence
    Beautiful City
    Pippin

  South, Joe
    Don't It Make You Wanta Go Home
    I Never Promised You A Rose Garden
    Walk A Mile In My Shoes

  Styne, Jule (Jules Stein)
    People

  Sweet Inspiration — Where You Lead

  Turk, Roy
    Walkin' My Baby Back Home

  Weidler, Warner Alfred
    Love Means (You Never Have To Say
      You're Sorry)

  Wood, Haydn
    Roses Of Picardy

CASSIMIR, HEINRICH
  Stehn Vor Den Leuten Wir

CASTELLAZZI
  Arcadelt, Jacob
    Bianco E Dolce Cigno, Il

  Azzaiolo, Filippo, [Publisher]
    Due Villotte Del Fiore

  Banchieri, Adriano
    Contrappunto Bestiale Alla Mente
    Intermedio Di Solfanari
    Mascherata Di Villanelle

  Dieciocho Obras Corales De Autores
    Antiguos

  Lassus, Roland de (Orlandus)
    Ola! O Che Bon Eccho

  Monteverdi, Claudio
    Ecco Mormorar L'onde
    Lasciatemi Morire
    Su, Su, Su, Ch'el Giorno E Fore

  Palestrina, Giovanni Pierluigi da
    Ahi Che Quest' Occhi Miei
    Alla Riva Del Tebro
    Da Cosi Dotta Man
    I Vaghi Fiori E L'amorose Fronde

  Scandello, Antonio (Scandellus,
    Scandelli)
    Bonzorno Madonna

  Vecchi, Orazio (Horatio)
    Gioite Tutti
    Imitazione Del Veneziano
    Margarita Dai Corai

CASTELLAZZI, LUIGI
  Cori Popolari Italiani

CASTELZZI
  Anonymous
    Pastorella, La

CATON
  Tchaikovsky, Piotr Ilyich
    March

CATSIFF
  Newman, Herbert
    Wayward Wind

CAUCHIE
  Janequin, Clement
    Caquet De Femmes, Le
    Jalouzie, La
    Plus Belle De La Ville, La
    Thirty Songs

CAUCHIE, MAURICE
  Quinze Chansons Francaises Du XVI
    Siecle

CAUSEY, C. HARRY
  Lonesome Valley

CAVALIERI, ANGELO
  Cavalieri, Lucille
    Where You Are

CAWTHORNE
  Raff, Joseph Joachim
    Day Dawns Anew

CAZEAUX, I.
  Senfl, Ludwig
    Ceulx De Picardie

  Sermisy, Claude de (Claudin)
    Ceulx De Picardie
    Elle A Bien Ce Ris Gracieux
    J'ay Fait Pour Vous Cent Mille Pas
    Je Suis Tant Bien

CHAFFIN
  Poldini
    Dancing Doll, The

  Speaks, Oley
    Morning
    On The Road To Mandalay

CHAGNON, R.
  Becaud, Gilbert
    Bateau Blanc, Le

  Misraki, P.
    Chiens Perdus Sans Collier

  Salvador
    Apres Nous
    Dis Monsieur Gordon Cooper
    Maman
    Mousquetaires, Les
    Tu Reviens

  Salvador, Henri
    Apres Nous
    Dis, Monsieur Gordon Cooper
    Maman
    Mousquetaires, Les
    Tu Reviens

  Schaffenberger, W.
    Marin

  Van Parys, Georges
    Si Tous Les Gars Du Monde

CHAILLEY
  Dufay, Guillaume
    Belle Se Seid, La
    Belle Se Sied, La

  Poulenc, Francis
    Marianita
    Troyak

  Reveillez-Vous, Picards

CHAILLEY, J.
  Adam de la Hale
    Rondeaux

  Lully, Jean-Baptiste (Lulli)
    Venerabilis Barba Capucinorum

CHAILLEY, JACQUES
  Marianita

  Passant Par Paris

  Simon, Louis-Victor
    Il Pleut, Bergere

  Touati, Raymond
    Au Gre Du Vent
    Elle A Passe

  Troyak

CHAITMAN, A.
  Weisgal, A.
    Hashkivenu

CHAIX
  Cinq Chansons Populaires De Savoie

CHALLINOR
  Balfe
    Vocal Fantasia On Bohemian Girl

  Gounod, Charles Francois
    Choral Fantasia On Faust

  Wagner, Richard
    Choral Fantasia On Tannhauser

  Wallace, William Vincent
    Choral Fantasia On Maritana

CHALLINOR, F.A.
  Arne, Michael
    Lass With The Delicate Air, The

  Balfe, Michael William
    Bohemian Girl, The: Choral Fantasia

  Barnby, [Sir] Joseph
    Sweet And Low

  Gentle Night

  Gounod, Charles Francois
    Faust, Choral Fantasia

  Lass With The Delicate Air, The

  Last Rose Of Summer, The

  Schubert, Franz (Peter)
    Fischer, Der

  Wagner, Richard
    Tannhauser, Choral Fantasia

  Wallace, William Vincent
    Maritana, Choral Fantasia

CHAMBERLAIN
  Three German Folksongs

CHAMBERS
  Arne, Michael
    Lass With The Delicate Air, The

  Atkey, Olive
    Watermelon Man

  Byrd, William
    When As I View Your Comely Grace

  Handel, George Frideric
    Where'er You Walk

  Hares Of The Mountain

  Haydn, [Franz] Joseph
    Now Mine Eyes Are Grown Dim

  Is There Anybody Here?

  Schubert, Franz (Peter)
    Shepherdess
    To Spring

  Sullivan, [Sir] Arthur Seymour
    Lost Chord, The

  World Itself Is Bright And Gay

CHAMBERS, H. A.
  All Through The Night

  Bonnie Banks O' Loch Lomond, The

  Bonnie Banks Of Loch Lomond, The

  Coleridge-Taylor, Samuel
    Hiawatha's Wedding-Feast

  Country Gardens

  Elgar, [Sir] Edward (William)
    Banner Of Saint George, The

  Ford, Thomas
    Since First I Saw Your Face

  German, [Sir] Edward (Edward German
      Jones)
    Shepherds' Dance

  Golden Slumbers

  Handel, George Frideric
    Dove Sei
    Now On Land And Sea

  Lincolnshire Poacher, The

  Lully, Jean-Baptiste (Lulli)
    Bois Epais

  March Of The Men Of Harlech

  March Of The Men Of Harlech

  Miller Of The Dee, The

  Monro, George
    My Goodness, Celia

  O No, John

CHAMBERS, H. A. (cont'd.)
  Stanford, Charles Villiers
    Revenge, The

  Wagner, Richard
    Spinnerlied

  Weel May The Keel Row

  Young, Anthony
    Phillis Has Such Charming Graces

CHAPMAN, HENRY G.
  Borodin, Alexander Porfirievich
    Polovetzian Dance And Chorus

CHAPPELL
  Christmas Jazz, The

  Daniel Jazz, The

  Goliath Jazz, The

  Jericho Jazz, The

  Noah Jazz, The

  Prodigal Son, The

  Red Sea Jazz, The

CHAPPELL, HERBERT
  English Country Garden

CHAPUIS, A.
  Handel, George Frideric
    Air De Xerxes

  Rouget de l'Isle, Claude Joseph
    Marseillaise, La

CHARLES, RAY
  Arkansas Traveler

  Comin' Round The Mountain

  Ezekial Saw The Wheel

  Foster, Stephen Collins
    Old Black Joe

  Get A Musical Log

  Hi Ho, Nobody Home

  Hi Ho Nobody Home

  Jingle Bells

  Kohan, Angelos
    Nut Song, The
    One More Time

  Latham
    Hiawatha's Mittens

  Nobody Knows De Trouble I've Seen

  Polly Wolly Doodle

  Sweet Little Mountain Bird

  There's No Place Like Rome

  Twinkle Twinkle Little Star

  Wilson
    It's Time To Sing

  Yo Te Amo

CHENEY, SIMON PEASE
  American Singing Book

CHENNEVIERE, G.; DOYEN, A
  Chant Des Haleurs De La Volga

  Chant Des Haleurs De La Volga

CHINN, TEENA
  Berlin, Irving
    Let Yourself Go

  Blues In The Night

  Body And Soul

  Celebration

  Davis, Mac
    Stop And Smell The Roses

  Embraceable You

  Gershwin, George
    Man I Love, The
    Someone To Watch Over Me

  Hearts To Heart

  Markham, Sheely
    Step Out In Front

  New-Fashioned Christmas, A

CHINN, TEENA (cont'd.)
  See You In September

  Soul And Inspiration

  Try A Little Kindness

  What's New?

  Wilson, Bob
    Shout

CHIRINOS
  Picaflor

CHOMINSKI, JOZEF
  Szymanowski, Karol
    Szesc Piesni Kurpiowskich

CHORBAJIAN
  Dvorak, Antonin
    Song To The Moon

CHOUDENS
  Debussy, Claude
    We Sing To Spring

CHRIST
  Adam
    Abendlied

  Adam de la Hale
    Minnelied

  Ade Zur Guten Nacht

  Blumelein, Sie Schlafen, Die

  Brahms, Johannes
    Abschiedslied
    Barcarole
    In Stiller Nacht

  Braune Maidelein, Das

  Dieffenbacher
    Harmonie Fuhrt Uns Zusammen

  Dowland, John
    Come Again! Sweet Love Doth Now
      Invite

  Eccard, Johannes
    Hans Und Grete

  En Ding

  Es Waren Zwei Konigskinder

  Grell, Eduard August
    Gnadig Und Barmherzig
    Herr, Deine Gute Reicht So Weit

  Haydn, [Franz] Joseph
    Du Bist's, Dem Ruhm Und Ehre
      Gebuhret

  Heimliche Liebe

  Herbststimmung

  Isaac, Heinrich
    Innsbruck, Ich Muss Dich Lassen

  Latann
    Frei Weg

  Letzte Tanz, Der

  Litterscheid
    Sonniger Lenz Am Rhein

  Mond Ist Aufgegangen, Der

  Mozart, Wolfgang Amadeus
    Wiegenlied

  Ratsel

  Rosabella-Fidolin

  Schubert, Franz (Peter)
    Im Abendrot
    Liebe
    Lobt Den Gewaltigen
    Ruhe (Leise, Leise Lasst Uns
      Singen)
    Weihegesang
    Zwei Tugendwege, Die

  Schwabisches Tanzlied

  Schweinauer Tanz, Der

  Silcher, Friedrich
    Nur Du Allein

  Verstohlen Geht Der Mond Auf

  Wandrers Nachtlied

  Winter Ist Vergangen, Der

CHRIST (cont'd.)

Zuccalmaglio, Anton Wilhelm Florentin
von
Verstohlen Geht Der Mond Auf

CHRIST, JACOB
Rosabella-Fidolin

Schwabisches Tanzlied

Schweinauer Tanz, Der

Wandrers Nachtlied

CHRIST, JAKOB
Siebzehn Volkslieder

CHRISTENSEN
Ride The Chariot

CHRISTIANSEN
Marlowe
Come Live With Me And Be My Love

CHRISTIANSEN, LARRY A.
Pensive Dove

Sometimes I Feel

CHRISTIANSEN, P.
Grieg, Edvard Hagerup
Spring

CHRISTIANSEN, PAUL
Ahnfelt
Day By Day

CHRISTIANSEN, SIGURD
Charlottown Is Burning Down

CHRISTIE, K.
Blue-Tail Fly, The

CHRISTIE, N.
Fletcher, Percy Eastman
Galway Piper

CHRISTOFER, JOHN
Biggest Little Song Book, The

CHRISTOPHER, CYRIL S.
Girl I Left Behind Me

CHRISTY
Fontaine, Paul
Some Like Dogs

CHURCHILL
Black Is The Color Of My True Love's
Hair

Landlord, Fill The Flowing Bowl

Morey
Heigh-Ho

Morley, Thomas
April Is In My Mistress' Face

Willson
Here Comes The Springtime
I See The Moon
It's Beginning To Look Like
Christmas
It's Easter Time
Laura Lee
Mother Darlin'

Yellow Rose Of Texas, The

CHURCHILL; CRAIG
Wolf
Old Painting, An

CHURCHILL; JAMES
Morey
Someday My Prince Will Come
Whistle While You Work

CHURCHILL, JOHN
I'se The B'y

Trois Canes, Les

CHURCHILL, KENNETH
Morley, Thomas
April Is In My Mistress Face

CHURCHILL; RHEA
Morey
Someday My Prince Will Come

CIERI
Croce, Giovanni
Ove Tra L'Herbe E I Fiori

Vecchi, Orazio (Horatio)
Al Bel De' Tuoi Capelli
Hor Ch'Ogni Vento Tace

CISILINO, SIRO
Greghesche, Libro I (1564)

CISNEROS
Gaudeamus Igitur

CLARK
Mango Walk

Shield
Wolf, The

Tinga Layo

CLARKE
Let Us Cheer The Weary Traveller

Lightfoot
Canadian Railroad Trilogy
Cotton Jenny
Love And Maple Syrup
Your Love's Return

CLARY
Blind Man Stood On The Road And
Cried, The

Le's Have A Union

CLAUDIUS; GERSTER
Schulz, Johann Abraham Peter
Mond Ist Aufgegangen, Der

CLAUDIUS, H.
Werner, Fritz
Apfelkantate

CLAUSEN, C.
Mendelssohn-Bartholdy, Felix
Nine Songs

CLAUSEN, KARL
Al Pris Og Lov Og Aere Bor

Arnholtz, Arthur
Nederlaget

Brahms, Johannes
Abschiedslied
Ach Lieber Herre Jesu Christ
Bei Nachtlicher Weil
Deutsche Volkslieder I
In Stiller Nacht
Mit Lust Tat Ich Ausreiten
Schnitter Tod
Von Edler Art
Wollust In Den Maien, Die

English And French Folk Songs

Far Dog Fort

Hjertesorg

Hor Dog, O Hor Dog

Hvorledes Gar Det Her

Jeg Gik Mig Ud En Sommerdag

Kavalerdansen

Mendelssohn-Bartholdy, Felix
Abschied Vom Walde
Im Walde
Mailied
Morgengebet
Nachtigall, Die
Ni Sange
Tre Folkeviser
Waldvogelein, Die

Op! Hen Op Til Fryd Og Glaede

Saerhefte II

Saerhefte III

Urtegarden

CLAYTON, J.
Strauss, Johann, [Jr.]
Morning Leaves

CLEMENS, A.
Es Taget Vor Dem Walde

Jetzt Kommt Die Zeit, Dass Ich
Wandern Muss

Roslein Auf Der Heiden

Schwarzbraunes Madchen, Ein

Und Wenn Das Glocklein Funfmal
Schlagt

Weiss Mir Ein Blumlein Blaue

Wohlan, Die Zeit Ist Kommen

CLEMENS, ADOLF
Fruhjahrsanfang

Reichardt, Johann Friedrich
Wach Auf, Meins Herzens Schone

Schreinergesell, Der

CLEMENT, N.
Steuerlein, Johann
J'Entends Une Chanson

CLEMENTS
Blow The Wind Southerly

Donkey Riding

Logan
Pale Moon

Openshaw
Love Sends A Little Gift Of Roses

Parr Davies
Sing As We Go

Ray
Sunshine Of Your Smile

Romberg, Sigmund
When I Grow Too Old To Dream

Schubert, Franz (Peter)
Hark! Hark! The Lark
Question, The

Stuart
Soldiers Of The Queen

Tennyson
There Is Sweet Music Here

CLEMENTS, J.
Clarke, Emile
Sincerity

Sharpe, Evelyn
When The Great Red Dawn Is Shining

CLEMENTS, JOHN
Drink To Me Only With Thine Eyes

Hill, [Lady] Arthur
In The Gloaming

CLEMS, ADOLF
Sag, Ich Lass Grussen

CLEVELAND
Hart
Sesame Street

Moss
Circles
I've Got Two

Raposo, Joseph G.
Canta Una Cancion
Picture A World
Sing

CLOUGH-LEIGHTER
Heseltine, Philip ("Peter Warlock")
Rest, Sweet Nymphs

CLOUGH-LEIGHTER, H.
Berlioz, Hector (Louis)
Choruses From "The Damnation Of
Faust"

Handel, George Frideric
Where E'er You Walk

Morley, Thomas
Now Is The Month Of Maying

Purcell, Henry
Come Unto These Yellow Sands

CLOUGH-LEIGHTER, H.; WOODWORTH, G.W.
Sullivan, [Sir] Arthur Seymour
Finale From "The Gondoliers"

CLOUGH-LEIGHTER, HENRY
A Cappella Singer, The

Brahms, Johannes
Four Love Songs
Six Love Songs

Bridge, Frank
Pan's Holiday

Bullock, Ernest
Tragic Story, A

Sibelius, Jean
For Thee, Suomi

Sullivan, [Sir] Arthur Seymour
Entrance Of The Peers
Finale From "The Gondoliers"

CLOUGH-LEIGHTER, HENRY; DAVISON,
ARCHIBALD T.

Galway Piper, The

CLOUGH-LEITER, HENRY
Schubert, Franz (Peter)
Miriams Siegesgesang

CLUWEN, P.
  Deep River

CLYNSEN
  Mignan, Edouard-Charles-Octave
    Hymne National A Jeanne D'Arc

COATE
  Bacharach, Burt F.
    You'll Never Get To Heaven

COATES
  Addrisi
    Time For Livin'

  America

  Bacharach, Burt F.
    Message To Michael, A

  Brubeck
    Summer Song

  Buie, Buddy
    Stormy
    Traces

  Chapin
    I Hear Bells

  Chaplin, N.W.
    I Hear Bells

  Dedrich
    Like To Love-Like To Sing About
      Sunshine
    One By One People Come, Sing
      Together

  Dedrick
    Like To Love, Like To Sing About
      Sunshine

  Eiler
    Fly Away

  Friedman
    Windy

  Goldenberg, William Leon (Billy)
    Suddenly There's You

  Hamilton
    Sing A Rainbow

  Hamilton, Arthur
    Sing A Rainbow

  Harris
    You Bring Me Love

  Hatch, Tony (Anthony Peter)
    Who Am I

  Kern, Jerome
    Look For The Silver Lining

  Le Coat
    World Is My Home, The

  Liliedahl
    Mother Country

  McGlohon, Loonis
    On This Day

  Mancini, Henry
    Moon River

  Mitchell
    Both Sides Now
    Circle Game, The

  Ornadel
    If I Ruled The World

  Paxton
    You Can Build A Bridge

  Priesing, Dorothy M.
    Now Is The Carolling Season

  Robinson
    Black And White

  Scott
    He Ain't Heavy

  Simple Gifts

  Sweney
    Sunshine In My Soul

  Sweney, John R.
    Sunshine In My Soul

  Whittaker
    I Am But A Small Voice

  Woods
    Side By Side

COATES, H.
  Palestrina, Giovanni Pierluigi da
    Che Splendor De'luminosi Rai
    Gioja M'abond Al Cor

COBB; GORDY; COATES
  Buie, Buddy
    Traces

COBINE, AL
  British Grenadiers, The

  Christmas Rose, A

  Kirkman, Terry
    Enter The Young

  MacLellan, Gene
    Put Your Hand In The Hand

  Meadowlands

  Miller, Ned
    Invisible Tears

  Owens, Buck
    Together Again

COCKBURN
  Des Prez, Josquin
    Grillo, El

  Passereau
    Il Est Bel Et Bon

COCKSHOTT, GERALD
  Au Port Du Havre

  Bird's Song, The

  Bon Roi Dagobert, Le

  Borobondo, Lo

  Chanson De L'aveine

  Compagnon Cordonnier, Le

  Cornemuseux, Le

  Cueillette Des Pommes, La

  Cure Et La Servante, Le

  Depart Pour L'island

  Fils Du Cordonnier, Le

  Greenland Fishery

  Il Etait Une Bergere

  Je N'ai Pas De Barbe Au Menton

  Komt, Vrienden, In Het Ronden

  Little Sailor, The

  May Carol

  Mon Merle

  Mon Pere Avait Cinq Cents Moutons

  My Boy Billy

  Our Donkey

  Paper Of Pins

  Paul And The Hens

  Petit Jean Revenant De Lille

  Quete Pour La Mariee

  Savez-Vous Planter Les Choux?

  Shanty And Two Folk Songs From
    France, A

  Sur Les Bords De La Loire

  Three French Songs

  Three Songs For Boys

  Troix Marins La Loire, Les

  Two Eighteenth Century Songs

  Wiltshire Wedding, The

COGGIN
  When I Can Read My Title Clear

COHN
  Lamport
    Bronx River Puzzle
    Dress Parade
    Equable Explanation
    Gamut, The
    Technical Advice To Persons
      Planning To Erect Memorial
      Statues To Themselves
    Who He?

COLBRIE
  Siegl, Otto
    Durch Den Park

COLE
  Astol
    Borinquena, La

  Chappell
    Song Of The Dove

  Herzog
    God Bless The Child

  Johnson
    Lift Ev'ry Voice And Sing

  Mandel
    Lucky, Lucky

  Philipps, P.
    Nightingale, The

  Prokop, Walther
    One Fine Morning

  Wayne
    Port Au Prince

COLE, B.
  Harmony Gems

COLEBY, GEOFFREY
  Through The Sound Barrier

COLEMAN
  Bare Necessities, The

  Ev'rybody Wants To Be A Cat

  Gentle On My Mind

  Handel, George Frideric
    Pack Clouds Away

  Honey

  Ode To Joy

  Schubert, Franz (Peter)
    An Die Musik

COLEMAN, H.
  Bizet, Georges
    Smugglers' Chorus

COLEMAN, HENRY
  All Through The Night

  Gathering Daffodils

  Gentle Maiden, The

  Keys Of Heaven

  Snowy Breasted Pearl, The

  Somervell, Arthur
    Go From My Window, Go

  Sullivan, [Sir] Arthur Seymour
    Never Mind The Why And Wherefore

  Wild Hills Of Clare

COLLINS
  Christmas Medley

  Weelkes, Thomas
    O Jonathan
    When David Heard

COLLINS, WALTER
  Lassus, Roland de (Orlandus)
    Echo Song

COLVIN
  Billings, William
    Now Shall My Inward Joys Arise
    Time, What An Empty Vapor 'Tis

COMMER; ESPAGNE; HABERL; RAUCH; DE WITT
  Palestrina, Giovanni Pierluigi da
    Collected Works, Vol. 28: Madrigals
    Collected Works, Vol. 29: Madrigals

COMPANEETZ, GREG.
  Engel, U.
    Adoizdechic

CONDIE
  Huss, Henry Holden
    Crossing The Bar

CONLEY
  Bill Grogan's Goat

CONLEY, LLOYD
  Bernard, Felix
    Winter Wonderland

  There's No Place Like Home For The
    Holidays

  We Wish You A Merry Christmas

CRAIG; MASON (cont'd.)

Mascagni, Pietro
Gli Aranci Olezzano Sui Verdi
Margini

Monteverdi, Claudio
Orfeo: Two Choruses

Purcell, Henry
Dido And Aeneas, Three Choruses

Rossini, Gioacchino
Duetto Buffo Di Due Gatti

CRAMER
Daughter Will You Marry

Daughter, Will You Marry?

Handel, George Frideric
Draw The Tear From Hopeless Love
Music, Spread Thy Voice Around

CRANMER
Hughes, H.
My Lagan Love

CRESSA, HELMY
Blackburn, Bryan
Love Is Blue

CRESTANI, MARCO
Pasci Angionedda

CRESTON
Tagore
None Lives Forever

CROCKER, EMILY
Blow Ye Winds

Children Go Where I Send Thee

Hanukkah Again Is Here

John Henry

Just Put Some Love In Your Heart

Mayfield, Percy
Hit The Road, Jack

Newman, Herbert
Wayward Wind, The

Song Is A Gift, A

CROMIE, M.
Gaelic Song

CROSS
Ward, Samuel Augustus
America The Beautiful

CROSS, RONALD
Pipelare, Mathaes
Opera Omnia Vol. I: Chansons And
Motets

CROUCH, DONALD
Me Gustan Todas

CROWLEY
Cowan, Marie
Christmas In Foreign Lands And Home

CSUKAS, ISTVAN
Balazs, Arpad
Csufolo

CUMMING
Martinu
Plaisir D'Amour

Purcell, Henry
Man Is For The Woman Made

CUMMINGS, D.
See The Radiant Sky Above

CUNDICK
American Tribute, An

CUNNINGHAM; WORK
Newton
Casey Jones

CURRIE, E.
Morley, Thomas
Beside A Fountain

Wilbye, John
Lady, When I Behold

CURRY; RAYMOND
Handel, George Frideric
Verdi Prati

CURTIS
Squire
When You Come Home

Willard
My Heart Sings

CURTRIGHT, CAROLEE
Danoff, William Thomas
Take Me Home, Country Roads

Deutschendorf, Henry John (John
Denver)
Aspenglow
Druthers
Farewell Andromeda (Welcome To My
Morning)
Fly Away
Follow Me
How Can I Leave You Again

Henson, James Maury (Jim)
Muppet Show Theme, The

Lennon, John
Yesterday

Sommers, John Martin
Love Is Everywhere

Two In The Middle

CURWIN, CLIFFORD
Celtic Lullaby

CZAJKOWSKI, MICHAEL
Three Shaker Songs

White Lent

CZERNIK, W.
Hymnen Der Nationen

D513
Schubert, Franz (Peter)
Pastorella Al Prato, La

D'ACCONE, FRANK
Layolle, Francesco
Music Of The Florentine Renaisance
Vol.III & VOL. IV

DAGNINO, EDOARDO
Nenna, Pomponio
Madrigals

DAGSVIK, ARNE
Noringen

Sulle, Rulle, Gullodokka Mi

Three Songs About Longing

Two Songs

Wedding March

DAHL
Krasinsky, Fritz
Das War In Meinen Kindertagen

DAHLEN
Brel
Ne Me Quitte Pas

Gorney, Jay (Daniel Jason)
Bill Of Rights, The

Mandel
Homework
Human Brain, The

Satie
River, The

DAHLSTROM, GRETA
Nu Maste Jag Resa

DAHMEN
Asriel
Viel Blut Ward Hingegeben

Els Segadors

Fromm, Herbert
Huttens Kampflied

Gunther, A.
Vergass Dei Haamit Net

DALAMORINIERE, G.
Au Petit Vent De Galerne

Ce Joli Mois Nouveau

Chanson De Quete Du Velay

Danse, La

Dialogue Des Metamorphoses

Fileuses, Les

Guignolot D'Saint-Lazot

J'Ai Cueilli La Belle Rose

Noel

Noel Des Garrigues

Patre Des Montagnes, Noel De Saboly

DALAMORINIERE, G. (cont'd.)

Prisonnier De Nantes, Le

Queteurs De L'An Neuf, Les

Saint Joseph A Fait Un Nid

V'la L'Bon Vent

D'ALBERT; BUSONI; RAABE, PETER;
STRADEL, AUGUST; V. DA MOTTA, J.;
KELLERMANN, B.; BARTOK, BELA;
TAUBMANN, OTTO; WOLFRUM, PHILIPP;
STAVENHAGEN, B.

Liszt, Franz
Collected Works

DALE
Foster, Stephen Collins
Oh Susanna!

Music In The Round

Strauss, Johann, [Jr.]
Thousand And One Nights, A

DALE, P.
Strauss, Johann, [Jr.]
An Artist's Life
Morning Leaves

DALLINGER, FRIDOLIN
Schone Minka

DALOS, LASZLO
Farkas, Ferenc
Vallon Szerenad

DAMROSCH
All Through The Night

Janequin, Clement
Au Joly Jeu Du Pousse Avant Fait
Bon Jouer

DAMROSCH, FRANK
Debussy, Claude
Blessed Damozel, The

DANHAUSER, A.
Mendelssohn-Bartholdy, Felix
Hiver Et L'Ete, L'

Silcher
Nymphe Des Eaux, La

DANIEL, D'ETIENNE
Dix Chants De Bretagne

DANIEL, E.
Amants, Les

Doulces Douleurs, Les

Ma Liberte

Sur La Route De Chatillon

Voici Venir Le Bel Ete

Voyage

DANIEL, ETIENNE
Berceuse Cosaque

C'etait Dedans Un Petit Bois

Fille Au Coupeur De Paille, La

Moustaki, Georges
Hiroshima

Remplis Ton Verre Vide

Robin, Marie-Therese
Aujourd'hui Je Chanterai
Compter Les Nuages
J'ai Jete Mon Ame Au Vent
Java Du Temps Perdu, La
Mon Ami Inconnu
Printemps Est Court, Le
Prisonnier Oublie, Un
Quand S'en Va La Derniere Voile

Sylvestre, Anne
Dans Le Brouillard D'Automne

DANIEL, OLIVER
Billings, William
Chester
Fare You Well, My Friends
I Am The Rose Of Sharon
Lamentation Over Boston
Modern Music

DANIELS, E.
Morley, Thomas
April Is In My Mistress' Face

DANIELSEN, RAGNAR
Du Gronne Glitrende

DANT
  Purcell, Henry
    My Dearest, My Fairest

DARASZ; JOY
  Sight And Sound

DARBY
  Blue Tail Fly, The

  Kaihan, M.
    Now Is The Hour

DARCIEUX
  Mehul, Etienne-Nicolas
    Chant Du Depart, Le

  Pierne, Gabriel
    Bergerie

  Strauss, Johann, [Jr.]
    An Der Schonen Blauen Donau

DARCIEUX, F.
  Handel, George Frideric
    Hymne A Bacchus
    Ombra Mai Fu
    Tombez Mes Larmes

  Indy, Vincent d'
    Six Chants Populaires Francais
    Six Chants Populaires Francais
    Trois Chansons Populaires
      Francaises

  Lully, Jean-Baptiste (Lulli)
    Isis

  Martini, Jean Paul Egide
    (Schwarzendorf)
    Plaisir D'Amour

  Mehul, Etienne-Nicolas
    Cantilene D'Ariodant

  Monsigny, Pierre-Alexandre
    O Ma Tendre Musette

  Rameau, Jean-Philippe
    Chantons Sur La Musette, Chantons!
    Fetes D'Hebe, Les
    Hymne Au Soleil

  Schumann, Robert (Alexander)
    Deux Grenadiers, Les
    Gai Printemps

  Severac, Deodat de
    Ma Poupee Cherie

  Vingt Chansons Populaires Du Massif
    Central

  Weber
    Robin Des Boix

DART
  Invitation To Madrigals, Book One

  Invitation To Madrigals, Book Two

  Invitation To Madrigals, Book Three

  Invitation To Madrigals, Book Four

  Invitation To Madrigals, Book Five

DART, T.
  Invitation To Madrigals-Book 1

  Invitation To Madrigals-Book 2

  Invitation To Madrigals-Book 3

  Invitation To Madrigals-Book 4

  Invitation To Madrigals-Book 5

  Invitation To Madrigals-Book 6

  Invitation To Medieval Music-Book 1

  Invitation To Medieval Music-Book 2

DASHNAW, A.
  Ives, Charles
    Circus Band

DASHNAW, ALEXANDER
  Ives, Charles
    Son Of A Gambolier, A
    They Are There!

DAUGHERTY; REYNOLDS; JAMES
  Neiberg
    I'm Confessin'

DAULY, G.
  Chanson Bretonne

  Voulez-Vous Savoir

DAUMER, M.
  Va Dous Annaig

DAUNTON, FRANK
  Faithful Johnny

DAUPHIN, L.
  Soixante Petits Airs Francais Du Dix-
    Septieme Siecle, premier Recueil

  Soixante Petits Airs Francais Du Dix-
    Septieme Siecle, deuxieme Recueil

DAUTREMER, A.-M.; DAUTREMER, M.
  Trente Noels Anciens, Deuxieme Livre

DAUTREMER, M.
  Monsigny, Pierre-Alexandre
    O Ma Tendre Musette

  Pergolesi, Giovanni Battista
    Que Ne Suis-Je La Fougere

  Tambourin

DAVID, H.
  Billings, William
    Consonance
    Modern Music

  French Chansons

  Palestrina, Giovanni Pierluigi da
    Two Madrigals

DAVID, JOHN NEPOMUK
  Bretonisches Abendlied

  Du Mein Einzig Licht

  Es Taget Vor Dem Walde

  Gar Lieblich Hat Sich Gesellet

  Grimmig Tod Mit Seinem Pfeil, Der

  Herzlich Tut Mich Erfreuen

  Ich Schell Mein Horn Im Jammerton

  Ich Wolltgern Singen

  Mayen, Der Mayen, Der

  Was Wolln Wir Auf Den Abend Tun?

  Zehn Neue Volksliedsatze

DAVIDSON, CHARLES
  Saenu

DAVIE, CEDRIC THORPE
  Four Scottish Folk Songs

DAVIE; MCVICAR
  Oxford Scottish Song Book

DAVIES
  Bach, Johann Sebastian
    I Know A Flow'r It Springeth

  Mentra Gwen

  Praetorius, Michael
    I Know A Flow'r It Springeth

  Three Spanish Carols

DAVIES, BRYAN
  Hava Nagila

DAVIES, H.
  Linger, Carl
    Song Of Australia

DAVIES, IVOR R.
  Begone! Dull Care

  I Saw Three Ships

  Lincolnshire Poacher, The

DAVIES, L.H.
  Widmann, Benedikt
    Kling Glockchen Kling!

DAVIES, LAURENCE H.
  Cornelius, Peter
    Kings, The

  Dvorak, Antonin
    Moon Rainbow

  Sullivan, [Sir] Arthur Seymour
    Brightly Dawns Our Wedding Day

DAVIES, WALFORD
  Davy, John
    Bay Of Biscay, The

  Paxton, William
    Breathe Soft, Ye Winds

  Stevens, Richard John Samuel
    Cloud-Capt Towers, The

DAVIS
  Abt, Franz
    Laughing

  Adrian
    X And Why

  Ding Dong, Merrily

  Dunhill, Thomas Frederick
    Cloths Of Heaven

  Foster, Stephen Collins
    Oh Susanna!

  Holmes
    Rock The Boat

  I Never Want To Go

  Loring, Richard Edwin
    They Have No Song

  Schubert, Franz (Peter)
    Gretchen At The Spinning Wheel
    Lindenbaum, Der

DAVIS, ALFRED
  Beethoven, Ludwig van
    An Malzel

  Rossini, Gioacchino
    Duetto Buffo Di Due Gatti

DAVIS, BERTRAN E.
  Vincenet, Johannes
    Collected Works, The

DAVIS, K. K.
  Babe, So Tender, A

  Basque Lullaby

  Cobbler's Jig, The

  Cock-a-doo-dle-doo

  Come, Lasses And Lads

  Cui, Cesar Antonovich
    Radiant Stars, Above The Mountains
      Glowing

  Day Of The Fair, The

  Dowland, John
    Come Again! Sweet Love Now Doth
      Invite

  Early One Morning

  Gay Young Jack

  German, [Sir] Edward (Edward German
    Jones)
    Orpheus And His Lute

  Gossip Joan

  Handel, George Frideric
    Where E'er You Walk

  Has Sorrow Thy Young Days Shaded?

  Jon, Come Kisse Me Now

  Let All Things Now Living

  Mein Madel Hat Einen Rosenmund

  Monro, George
    My Lovely Celia

  Morley, Thomas
    My Bonny Lass She Smileth
    Sing We And Chant It

  Morning Comes Early

  My Inmost Thoughts Are All Of Thee

  Nightingale, The

  O Little Star

  Oaken Leaves

  Old Woman And The Pedlar, The

  Schubert, Franz (Peter)
    Where Are Those Who Long Have
      Striven?

  Sicilian Mariner's Hymn

  Tessier, Charles
    Au Joli Bois

  Tu Mi Vuoi Tanto Bene

  Turn Ye To Me

  Wassail Song

DAVIS, K. K. (cont'd.)

Wilbye, John
Adieu, Sweet Amarillis

Zwischen Berg Und Tiefem, Tiefem Tal

DAVIS, K.K.; DARCIEUX, FRANCISQUE
Noel Of The Bressan Waits

DAVIS, MICHAEL
Gabriel, Charles H., Sr.
Little Teetotalers

DAVISON
Touro-Louro-Louro!

DAVISON, A.T.
Annie, The Miller's Daughter

Arensky, Anton Stepanovich
Crystal Brook
Mystic Stars

Bonnie Dundee

Brahms, Johannes
Es Tont Ein Voller Harfenklang
Gesang Aus Fingal

Brennan On The Moor

Campbells' Are Comin', The

Canto Di Caccia

Crudele Irene

Cui, Cesar Antonovich
Radiant Stars

Dowland, John
Come Again, Sweet Love

Evensong In French

Foggy Dew, The

Franck, Cesar
Choeurs Des Chameliers
Far O'er The Bay

Galway Piper, The

Gluck, Christoph Willibald, Ritter
von
From The Realm Of Souls Departed
If Here, Where All Is Dark And
Silent

Gounod, Charles Francois
Chorus Of Bacchantes

Gray, DeLacy
Valley, The

Gretchaninov, Alexander Tikhonovich
Autumn
Sun And Moon

Has Sorrow Thy Young Days Shaded?

Kullo

Lassus, Roland de (Orlandus)
Bon Jour, Mon Coeur
Ola! O Che Bon Eccho!

Marenzio, Luca
Spring Returns

Monks' March, The

Monteverdi, Claudio
Ohime! Ohime

Morales, Cristobal de
Me Ye Have Bereaved

Morley, Thomas
April Is In My Mistress' Face
Dainty, Fine, Sweet Nymph
Fire, Fire, My Heart
My Bonny Lass
Now Is The Month Of Maying
Shoot, False Love, I Care Not

Pedlar, The

Purcell, Henry
With Drooping Wings, Ye Cupids Come

Rantin', Rovin' Robin

Rimsky-Korsakov, Nikolai
Choruses From "Sadko"

Spanish Ladies

Sullivan, [Sir] Arthur Seymour
Choruses From "H.M.S. Pinafore"
Choruses From "Princess Ida"
Choruses From "Ruddigore"
Choruses From "The Mikado"
Choruses From "The Yeomen Of The
Guard"

DAVISON, A.T. (cont'd.)

How Sweet The Answer Echo Makes

Turn Ye To Me

Wagner, Richard
Chorus And Finale

Weelkes, Thomas
Nightingale, The

DAVISON, A.T.; DAVIS, K.K.
I Would We Lived As Angels Do

DAVISON, ARCHBALD T.
Caisson Song, The

DAVISON, ARCHIBALD T.
Dol-li-a

Dowland, John
Now, O Now, I Needs Must Part

Ford, Thomas
Since First I Saw Your Face

Lover's Curse, The

Rantin', Rovin' Robin

Rozhinkes Mit Mandeln

Sacramento

Shenandoah

Sullivan, [Sir] Arthur Seymour
Magnet And The Churn, The

Touro-Louro-Louro!

DAVISON; SURETTE
Concord Book For Women's Voices, The

Home And Community Song Book

One Hundred Forty Folk Songs

DAVISON; SURETTE; ZANZIG
Book Of Songs, A

Concord Junior Song And Chorus Book

DAVISON; WOODWORTH
At Father's Door

Fireflies

Song Of The Life-Boat Men

Sullivan, [Sir] Arthur Seymour
Finale From "The Gondoliers"

DAWE, MARGERY
New Road To Hymn Tunes

DAWN, MURIEL; DAWN, DOUGLAS
My Aunt Jane

DAWSON, WILLIAM L.
King Jesus Is A-Listening

My Lord, What A Mourning

Talk About A Child That Do Love Jesus

DE BRANT
All Through The Night

DE CESARE, RUTH
They Came Singing

DE CORMIER
A La Claire Fontaine

African Drinking Song

Ahrirang

Alouette

Bella Bimba

Coulters, Candy
Scotch Lullaby

Coulters Candy

Dance Ti' Thy Daddy

Deep Blue Sea

Eres Alta

Free, My Lord, Free At Las'

Hunter's Song

If I Had A Ribbon Bow

Ilkey Moor Baht At

In The Good Old Colony Days

Jenny Jenkins

DE CORMIER (cont'd.)

Johnny Has Gone For A Soldier

Kissin's No Sin

Loch Lomond

Lolotte

May There Always Be Sunshine

Pick A Bale Of Cotton

Play Party

Rainbow 'Round My Shoulder

Raise A Ruckus

Revolutionary Portrait

Rounds Of Israel

Rozhinkes Mit Mandeln

Singing School, The

Soldier, Soldier, Won't You Marry Me?

Stars Shinin' By N' By

Suliram

Tail Toddle

Tumbalalaika

Wailie, Wailie

Welcome Here

Whistling Gypsy, The

Who Killed Cock Robin

Who Killed Cock Robin?

DE CORMIER; OKUN
One And Seven Pennies

DE FRUMERIE, GUNNAR
Wibergh, Olof
Ryttare Tre, De

DE LA CROIX, J.
Chants De La Route Et De La Mer

DE LOURDES-MARTINS, MARIA
Portuguese Folksongs

DE NITO
Perez Freire
Ay, Ay, Ay!

Quaratino, Pascual
El Flechazo

Tchaikovsky, Piotr Ilyich
Danza Arabe

DE PAUR
Ay, Ay, Ay

In Bright Mansions Above

Jerry (Lord, Dis Timber Gotta Roll)

Marry A Woman Uglier Than You

Pauline, Pauline

Ye Ke Omo Mi

DE PAUR, LEONARD
Brahms, Johannes
Five Songs For Male Chorus

Roberts, Ruth
Legend Of The Twelve Moons, The

DE PEARSALL, R.
When Allen-A-Dale Went A-Hunting

DE PUE
Jump Down, Turn Around

Mr. Rabbit

Tomorrow Shall Be My Dancing Day

DE REVERE, JON
Anonymous
Cyfri'r Geifr

Earnest, John David
Shine On Me

Gomes, Antonio Carlos
Coro Di Cacciatoria

Klein, Nancy Kirkland
Shady Grove

DE ROSE; STATON
    Brown
        Have You Ever Been Lonely?

DE SOUSA, FILIPE
    Portuguese Folksongs

DE SURCY, BERNARD BAILLY
    Monteverdi, Claudio
        A Che Tormi Il Ben Mio
        All'hora I Pastori Tutti
        Almo Divino Raggio
        Amor Per Tua Merce
        Amor S'il Tuo Ferire
        Ardi O Gela
        Ardo Si Ma Non T'amo
        Arsi E Alsi
        Baci Soavi E Cari
        Ch'io Ami La Vita Mia
        Donna S'io Miro Voi
        Filli Cara E Amata
        First Book Of Madrigals, The
        Fumia La Pastorella
        La Vaga Pastorella
        Poi Che Del Mio Dolore
        Questa Ordi Il Laccio
        Se Nel Partir Da Voi
        Se Per Havervi, Oime
        Se Por Non Mi Consenti
        Tra Mille Fiamme
        Vsciam Ninfe Homai

DE TRILLA
    Massotti Littel, M.
        Black Suns

DE VAAL, O.
    Ketelbey, Albert William
        In Een Kloostertuin

DE WITT
    Haydn, [Franz] Joseph
        Beredsamkeit, Die

DE WITT, THEODOR; RAUCH, J.N.; ESPAGNE,
    FRANZ; COMMER, FR.; HABERL, FR.
    X.

    Palestrina, Giovanni Pierluigi da
        First Critical Edition

DE WOLFF
    Elgar, [Sir] Edward (William)
        Nederland En Oranje

    Sullivan, [Sir] Arthur Seymour
        Lost Chord, The

    Wat De Toekomst Brenge Moge

DEACON
    Norden
        Ocean Lore

DEACON; DEIS
    Norden
        Call Of The Sea

DEALE, EDGAR
    Down By The Salley Gardens

    Drinking Song

    Fairest Rose In All The Garden

    Follow Me Up To Carlow

    I Will Walk With My Love

    Lark In The Clear Air

    My Lady Celia

    Oft In The Stilly Night

DEALE, EDGAR M.
    Castle Of Dromore

    Lark In The Clean Air, The

    Yellow Boreen

DEANT, PIERRE
    Barron, Bob
        Cindy

    Beart, Guy
        Souliers, Les

    Popp, Andre
        Kalinka

    Raiter, Leon
        Roses Blanches, Les

DECESARE
    My Horses Ain't Hungry

DECESARE, RUTH
    Candu

    Dinah Oh!

    Song Of The River

DECHANT, A.
    Wiesner, R.
        Fruhlingswonne

DECKER
    Joplin, Scott
        Solace

DECKER, H.
    Pearsall, Robert Lucas de
        Shoot, False Love

    Pilkington, Francis
        Rest, Sweet Nymphs

DECKER, HAROLD
    Canons On Music

    Monteverdi, Claudio
        Lasciatemi Morire

DECORMIER
    Canzone, La De Vino

DEDEKIND, A.
    Ebel, Eduard
        Leise Rieselt Der Schnee

DEDRICK, A.
    Nichols
        Christmas Waltz, A

    Wilder
        Child Is Born, A

DEFORD, RUTH I.
    Ferretti, Giovanni
        Secondo Libro Delle Canzoni A Sei
        Voci (1579), Il

DEFOSSEZ, R.
    Damme, P. van
        Deux Chansons Populaires

    Mozart, Wolfgang Amadeus
        Berceuse

DEHNE
    Brahms, Johannes
        Da Unten Im Tale

    Kremberg, Jacob (James)
        Hoffnung

    Meinberg, Karl
        Was Hab Ich Denn Meinem
            Feinsliebchen Getan

    Mendelssohn-Bartholdy, Felix
        Comitat

    Mozart, Wolfgang Amadeus
        Bruder, Reicht Die Hand Zum Bunde
        Sehnsucht

    Silcher, Friedrich
        Hoffe Das Beste
        In Der Ferne

DEHNE, P.
    Bettelmanns Tanz

    Es Geht Nichts Ubers Singen

    Mozart, Wolfgang Amadeus
        Sehnsucht

    Praetorius, Michael
        Winterlied

DEIBLER, SEAN
    Who Killed Cock Robin?

DEIS
    All Through The Night

    Bizet, Georges
        Ouvre Ton Coeur

    Bridge
        Love Went A-Riding

    Charles, Ernest
        Clouds

    Curran, Pearl Gildersleeve
        Dawn
        Nursery Rhymes
        Rain

    Dichmont, William
        Ma Little Banjo

    Edwards, Clara
        By The Bend Of The River

    Enders, Harvey
        Russian Picnic

    Gibbons, Orlando
        Silver Swan, The

    Grieg, Edvard Hagerup
        Ich Liebe Dich

DEIS (cont'd.)

    Guion, David Wendall Fentress
        Mam'selle Marie
        Ol' Paint
        Yellow Rose Of Texas, The

    Lemlin, Lorenz
        Gutzgauch, Der

    Leoncavallo, Ruggiero
        Mattinata

    Mana-Zucca, Mme. (Augusta Zuckermann)
        Big Brown Bear, The

    Mozart, Wolfgang Amadeus
        Alphabet, The

    Purcell, Edward C.
        Passing By

    Rasbuch, Oscar
        Mountains
        Trees

    Romberg, Sigmund
        Auf Wiedersehn!

    Schubert, Franz (Peter)
        Allmacht, Die

    Speaks, Oley
        Morning
        Sylvia

    Strauss, Johann, [Jr.]
        Your Eyes Shine In My Own

    Strickland, Lily Teresa
        Mah Lindy Lou

    Tchaikovsky, Piotr Ilyich
        Legend, A

    Wagner, Richard
        Pilgerchor

DEKKER, WIL
    Tomkins, Thomas
        Two Madrigals

DELAMORINIERE, G.
    A La Claire Fontaine

    Allons, Brebis

    Autre Jour, Pastourelle, L'

    Brouillards De Noel, Les

    Ce Sont Les Dames De Paris

    C'Est Un Petit Pauvre

    Cette Nuit

    Chanson De La Mariee

    Chanson Du Lait, La

    Chant Du Patre, Le

    Chevre, La

    Choral Des Adieux

    Coucou, Le

    Depechons-Nous

    Eveillez-Vous

    Fanfare

    Fille Du Laboureux, La

    Fille Du Roi Loys, La

    Fille Du Vigneron, La

    Fille Qui S'Engage, La

    Garcons De Chez Nous, Les

    Gare Au Loup

    Gentil Coqu'licot

    Hiver, L'

    Jardin, Le

    Je Fis Un Reve

    Je Suis De La Requisition

    Jour De La Noel, Le

    La-Bas, Ces Montagnes

    Lou Roussignou Que Volo

    Magali

    Mal Mariee, La

DELAMORINIERE, G. (cont'd.)

Margoton Va A L'Eau

Marions Les Roses

Minuit Sonne

Mon Agneau

Mon Petit Oiseau

Mort Du Roi Renaud, La

Nez De Martin, Le

Noel De Provence

Pauvre Laboureur, Le

Pendant Que Le Four Chauffe

Pluie Et Le Vent, La

Printemps Dans La Foret, Le

Reveillez-Vous

Riviere, La

Ronde

Rossignolet Du Bois

Rossignolet Sauvage

Semeur, Le

Si Je Savais Voler

Sont Trois Jeun's Capitaines

Suite De Bourrees

Sur Les Bords De La Loire

Trois Marins De Groix, Les

Ville De Sarlat, La

Violette Dans Les Gants, La

V'La L'bon Vent

Vogue, Vogue, Petit Bateau

Voici La Noel

Voici La Saint-Jean

Voici Le Mois De Mai

DELAMORINIERE, GUY
 Aloette Sur La Branche, L'

Chanson Bretonne

Dors, Mon Jacquinou

D'ou Viens-Tu, Bergere

Entre Le Boeuf Et L'ane Gris

Faucheurs, Les

La-Haut, Dessur Ces Roches

La-Haut, Sur La Montagne

Noel Auxois

Noel Nouvelet

Petrouchka

Peureux, Le

Trimousett'

Trois Princesses, Les

DELANEY
 Old Zip Coon

DELANEY, R.M.
 Gadie, The

Hunt The Wren

Irish Gentleman, An

Morley, Thomas
 Festival

Oh, Congo River

Old Satan

Sally Brown

Tarantella

DELANEY, ROBERT M.
 Arkansaw Traveler, The

Changement, Le

Down Among The Dead Men

Hunt The Wren

Mozart, Wolfgang Amadeus
 Song Of The Courtiers
 With Voices Rejoicing

On The Mountain

River, The

Three Ravens, The

DELINEAU, J.
 C'Est Derriere Chez Nous

DELLER
 Gibbons, Orlando
  Silver Swan, The

 Pygott
  Quid Petis O Fili

 Weelkes
  On The Plains, Fairy Trains

DELLO JOIO
 Chopin, Frederic
  Lovers, The
  Ring, The
  Wish, The

DELMORE; WILSON
 Smith
  Beautiful Brown Eyes

DEMENY, OTTO
 Vary, Ferenc
  Korus-Szvit

DEMERATH, F.
 Winter Ist Vergangen, Der

DEMERATH, FRITZ
 Zuccalmaglio, Anton Wilhelm Florentin
 von
  Verstohlen Geht Der Mond Auf

DENESSEN
 Mahlberg, Eugen
  Drei Wunsche
  Sei Stark Mein Herz

DENGSO, EJVIND
 Can't Help Falling In Love

Could You Be Loved

Exactly Like You

Long And Winding Road, The

No Woman No Cry

People Get Ready

Rivers Of Babylon

Smoke Gets In Your Eyes

Stir It Up

DENHAM
 Goober Peas

 Ward
  Beautiful America!

DENHOFF, J.
 Ach, Blumlein Blau

Bluh Nur, Bluh, Mein Sommerkorn

Ihr Kleinen Vogelein

Morgenstern Der Finstern Nacht

DENNIS, H.
 Walmisley, Thomas Forbes
  Music, All Powerful

DENNISON, MICHAEL
 Mozart, Wolfgang Amadeus
  Peter, Peter

DENT
 Purcell, Henry
  My Beloved Spake

DERIVIS, L.
 Mendelssohn-Bartholdy, Felix
  Barcarolle Venitienne
  Belle Jeunesse
  Chanson De Printemps
  Chanson Du Rouet
  Hymne A L'Aurore
  O Nuit Tranquille
  Ronde De Lutins
  Sur Les Ailes Des Songes
  Tarentelle

DERIVIS, L. (cont'd.)

  Voici L'Automne

DERWINGSON, RICHARD; EMERSON, ROGER
 Competition

DESCH, R.
 Es Ging Ein Knab Ins Niederland

 Hohne, H.
  Hoch Auf Dem Gelben Wagen

Ich Sag Ade

Karolinchen

Limpiate Con Mi Panuelo

Maccheroni

Schmiede, Die

War' Ich Ein Vogelein

Wie Lieblich Schallt Durch Busch Und
 Wald

DESCH, RUDOLF
 All Mein Gedanken

Auf, Auf Zum Frohlichen Jagen

Demantius, Christoph
 Frisch Auf, Singet All

Es Sass Ein Klein Wild Vogelein

Frisch Auf, Zum Jagen

Gluck Auf, Ihr Bergleut

Ich Schreit' Auf Grunen Wegen

In Die Stille Fallt Ein Leiser Regen

Komm, Lieber Mai Und Mache

Lassus, Roland de (Orlandus)
 Cara Madonna Mia

Nun Ist Die Schone Fruhlingzeit

Peuerl, Paul
 O Musica, Du Edle Kunst

Ride The Chariot

Schlaf, Mein Kindchen

Sherman
 Chim-Chim-Cheri

Sommerreigen

Tanzchen

Tiritomba

Was Soll Ich In Der Fremde Tun

Wir Gniessen Die Himmlischen Freuden

Zieht Langsamer

Zu Frankfurt An Der Oder

DETEL, ADOLF
 Ci Jsou To Konicky

Coz Ten Slavicek Vo Pul Noci Zpjiva

Drunten In Der Grunen Au

Inverno E Passato, L'

Jager Wollte Schiessen Gehn, Der

Jestli Mne, Sedlacku, Dceru Nedas

Kaksipa Poikaa Kurikasta

Kjinise I Jerakjina

Minun Kultani Kaunis On

O Korano

Oj Devojce

Po Vijn'krushqit Maleve

Siva Holubic-Vku

Skoda T'a

Sont Les Filles De La Rochelles

Stole Mi Se Ozeni

Sunce Zarko

Tancuj, Vy Krucaj

Yelenka

DEUTSCH, WALTER
Am Montag, Da Fang Ma Vorn Wieder An

An Auflauf Gibt's Bei Uns

Ord'ntlichen Leut, Die

Pfeifenkramer-Lied, Das

Unfehlbar

Wann I Von Wean Weggageh

Was Uns Noch Fehlt

Wer A Geld Hat

DEUTSCHMANN, G.
Naschhafte Katzchen, Das

Reizende Drohung

Vergangliches Gluck

DEUTSCHMANN, GERHARD
Ade Zur Guten Nacht

Da Drunten Im Tale

Im Walde, Da Wachsen Die Beer'n

Melodiosen Volkslieder, Die

Schubert, Franz (Peter)
Im Abendrot

Schumann, Robert (Alexander)
So Wahr Die Sonne Scheinet

Zwei Abendlieder

DEVATY, A.
Jindrich, Jindrich
Ceske Pisni

DEVITO
Down By The Riverside

Li'l Liza Jane

DEWS
Friml, Rudolf
Sympathy

Goulding, Edmund
Lovely Song My Heart Is Singing,
The

Romberg, Sigmund
Will You Remember (Sweetheart)

Winner, Septimus ("Alice Hawthorne")
Whispering Hope

DEXTER
Alfie

Alley Cat

Bastow
Galloping Major, The

By The Time I Get To Phoenix

Christmas On The Moon

De Meglio
Santa Lucia

Gounod, Charles Francois
Light As Air

Greensleeves

Haydn, [Franz] Joseph
Farewell

I'd Like To Teach The World To Sing

In The Year 2525

Jean

Little Silver Bell, The

Mermaid, The

Montagu
Advance Australia

My Way

Noble
Love Is The Sweetest Thing

Olivieri
Au Revoir

Pops Of The 70's-Group 3

Silcher
Song Of Farewell, A

Smith
Little Peach In An Orchard Grew, A

DEXTER (cont'd.)
Snowy-Breasted Pearl

Steffani
God Bless Elizabeth

Stuart
Lily Of Laguna
Tell Me, Pretty Maiden

Sullivan, [Sir] Arthur Seymour
Sigh No More, Ladies

Winner, Septimus ("Alice Hawthorne")
Whispering Hope

Wynn
Be A Friend

You're So Vain

DEXTER, H.
Carey, Henry
Spring

Debussy, Claude
En Bateau

Maypole, The

Robin Hood And Little John

Schumann, Robert (Alexander)
Wild Horseman, The

Yradier, Sebastian
Paloma, La

DEXTER, HARRY
Arnheim, Gus
Sweet And Lovely

Boll Weevil, The

Brown, Nacio Herb
Paradise

Clutsam, George H.
Love Comes At Blossom Time

Constant Lover, The

Crawdad Song, The

Davson, Gordon
Druid's Prayer

Dupont, Paul
Rosita

Fibich, Zdenek (Zdenko)
My Moonlight Madonna

Foggy, Foggy Dew

Geiger, Oskar
Just For A While

Gourley, Ronald
Dicky Bird Hop

Haines
Sally

Hill, Mildred J.
Happy Birthday To You

Hughes, J.
Bless 'Em All

I Want To Go Home

Jonasson, J.E.
Cuckoo Waltz

Ketelbey, Albert William
Bells Across The Meadows

King, Charles E.
Song Of The Islands

Lennon, John
Michelle

Mary Anne

May, Hans von
Starlight Serenade

Mill-Wheel, The

Nelson, Ed G.
In A Shady Nook

Norton, Frederic
Any Time's Kissing Time

Once I Had A Sweetheart

Peanut Song, The

Posford, George
At The Balalaika
Goodnight Vienna

DEXTER, HARRY (cont'd.)
Rapee, Erno
Charmaine
Diane

Songs The Whole World Knows

Stasny, A.J.
Rose Dreams

Steffe, William
Battle Hymn Of The Republic

Swain, Frank
Just A Rose In Old Killarney

Young
Beautiful Love

Zamecnik, J.S.
Nights Of Splendour

DEXTER, HARRY; MELFI
Chopin, Frederic
So Deep Is The Night

DEXTER, HARRY; VIENNA, FRANZ
Sleep, My Baby, Sleep

DEXTER; OLIVER
It's Over

DIACK
Handel, George Frideric
Pastoral Cantata

Purcell, Henry
I'll Sail Upon The Dog Star

Scott, [Lady] John (Alicia Ann)
Think On Me

DIACK; BAKER
Bach, Johann Sebastian
Choruses
Mer Hahn En Neue Oberkeet

DIACK, J.M.
Two Czech Folksongs

DIACK, J. MICHAEL
All Nature Smiles

All Through The Night

Anonymous
Have You But Seen A White Lily
Grow?
My Little Pretty One

Bach
Come, Let Us To The Bagpipe's Sound

Begone, Dull Care

Blow, My Bully Boys

Blue Bells Of Scotland, The

Bonnie Banks O' Loch Lomond

Brahms, Johannes
Schmied, Der
Wiegenlied

British Grenadiers, The

Carey, Henry
Pastoral

Charlie Is My Darling

Dowland, John
Fine Knacks For Ladies

Drink To Me Only

Early One Morning

Golden Slumbers

Haul Away, Joe

I Left My Dearie

It Was A Lover And His Lass

John Peel

Mozart, Wolfgang Amadeus
Cradle Song
If I Had A Donkey

Reuben Ranzo

Rosebud By My Early Walk, A

Schubert, Franz (Peter)
Call Of The Wood, The
Hark! Hark! The Lark
Wandernimg
Wild Rose, The

DIACK, J. MICHAEL (cont'd.)

Schumann, Robert (Alexander)
  Ladybird

This Old Man

White Sand And Gray Sand

Ye Banks And Braes

DICKINSON, PETER
Anonymous
  When I Was A Sailor

DICKS
Tchaikovsky, Piotr Ilyich
  One Summer Morn

DICKS, E.A.
Adam, Adolphe-Charles
  Comrades' Song Of Hope, The

Foster, Stephen Collins
  Come, Where My Love Lies Dreaming
  Come Where My Love Lies Dreaming
  Old Folks At Home

Goss, John
  O Thou Whose Beams

Gounod, Charles Francois
  Choeur Des Soldats

Hatton, John Liptrot
  Softly Fall The Shades Of Ev'ning

Macey, J.C.
  Simple Simon

Oakeley, Herbert Stanley
  Evening And Morning

Pinsuti, Ciro
  Crusaders, The
  Good Night, Good Night, Beloved!
  In This Hour Of Soften'd Splendour
  Sea Hath Its Pearls, The

Rossini, Gioacchino
  Carita, La

Sullivan, [Sir] Arthur Seymour
  Beleaguered, The
  If Doughty Deeds My Lady Please

Verdi, Giuseppe
  Squilla, Echeggi La Tromba
    Guerriera

Walmisley, Thomas Forbes
  Music All Powerful

DICKS, ERNEST A.
Golden Slumbers Kiss Your Eyes

On The Banks Of Allan Water

DICKSON
O'Hara
  This Train

DIDAM
Englert
  Wir Sind Jung

Englert, Eugene E.
  Wann Wir Schreiten Seit' An Seit'

Lustigen Bettelleute, Die

DIDAM, O.
Abendglocken

Beethoven, Ludwig van
  Flamme Lodert, Die

Lyra, Justus Wilhelm
  Mai Ist Gekommen, Der

Wer Geht Mit Uber See?

Werner, Heinrich
  Sah Ein Knab Ein Roslein Stehn

Zelter, Carl Friedrich
  Es War Ein Konig In Thule

DIEKEMA
Willson, Meredith
  Till There Was You

DIEKEMA; BARBER
Hey, Look Me Over

DIEKERHOF
Barnby, [Sir] Joseph
  Sweet And Low

DIEMER, EMMA LOU
Men Are Fools That Wish To Die

So I Have Seen A Silver Swan

DIENER, T.
Drei Alte Studentenweisen

DIENY, A.
Capello, Il

DIEPENBEEK, F.
Gounod, Charles Francois
  Gloire Immortelle

DIES, WERNER
Translateur, S.
  Auf Dem Rummel

DIETERICH
When Will I See My Home?

DIETRICH, FRITZ
Hirtenbuchel Auf Die Weihnacht

DIETSCH, F.
Freier, Der

Liebeslied

DIJK, JAN VAN
Binge, Ronald
  Elizabethan Serenade

DILLER
Roberts
  North Doth Blow, The

Star-Spangled Banner, The

DILSNER, L.
Schubert, Franz (Peter)
  Sound Of The Cymbal

D'INDY
Janequin, Clement
  Guerre De Renty, La

DINGEMANN, G.
Hab Meine Liebe Wohl Verborgen

In Meines Vaters Garten

DINHAM, K.J.
I'll Bid My Heart Be Still

She's Like The Swallow

DINN
Grainger, Percy Aldridge
  Sir Eglamore

DIPIAZZA, O.
Anonymous
  Dodici Canti Popolari Friulani
  Quattordici Canti Popolari Friulani

DISTLER, HUGO
Lassus, Roland de (Orlandus)
  Grosse Nasenlied, Das

DITE, L.
Lanner, Josef
  Romantiker, Die

DITE, LOUIS
Bruckner, Anton
  Edle Herz, Das
  Standchen
  Sternschnuppen

Des Abends Kann Ich Nicht Schlafen
  Gehn

Du Mein Einzig Licht

Erlaube Mir, Fein's Liebchen

Es Steht Ein' Lind

Fiedler, Der

Reissiger, F.A.
  Schlesische Zecher Und Der Teufel,
    Der

Wach Auf Mein' Herzensschone

DITON, CARL
Thirty-Six South Carolina Spriituals

DOBBS
Blow The Wind Southerly

Bobbie Shaftoe

King Arthur's Servants

DOBBS, J.P.B.
Foster, Stephen Collins
  Oh Susanna!

Li'l Liza Jane

DOBOS, A.
Anonymous
  Vidam Vadaszat

DOBRZANSKI
Wodzicka, Woda

DODD, M.
Old Bang'am

Per Spelmann

Preston, Walter H.
  Shuckin' Of The Corn

Wee Cooper Of Fife, The

DODS, MARCUS
Jolly Miller, The

DOEBLER, LARRY
Clemens, Jacobus (Clemens non Papa)
  Friendships

DOERLEMANN, E.
Ein Schwarzbraunes Madel

Es Blies Ein Jager Wohl In Sein Horn

Wer Will Mit Uns Nach Island Ziehn

DOLANSKA
Volkslieder Aus Der Tschechoslowakei

DONAHUE
Bronte
  Tell Me, Tell Me

DONATH
Fassbinderlied

Handel, George Frideric
  Ja, Noch Susser Ist Die Liebe
  Lob Der Musik
  Totenfeier
  Vorwarts, Weichen Muss Die Not

DONATH, P.
Glaslein Muss Ja Wandern, Das

Volkslieder Aus Dem Lande
  Sachsenanhalt, Heft 1: Dreissig
  Volkslieder

Volkslieder Aus Dem Lande
  Sachsenanhalt, Heft 3: Funfzehn
  Volkslieder

DOPPELBAUER, J. F.
Bluh Nur, Bluh Mein Sommerkorn

Gesegn Dich Laub

Ich Bin Dein

Ich Weiss Mir Ein Maidlein

Krakauer, Der

Zwischen Dem Esel Und Dem Rind

DOPPELBAUER, JOSEF FRIEDRICH
Flogen Einst Drei Wilde Tauben

Roter Wein

Rusla, Wenn Du Meine Warst

Wie Schon Ist's Draussen

DORITY; PFAUTSCH
Ol' Joe Clark

DORNBUSCH, GERHARD
Brandvakstrop

Pierina

Ramsa Fran Varmland

Sjung Med!

Tukku, Tukku, Ulliga Faren

DOTTIN
Zwolf Chansons Vom Hofe Franz' I

DOTTING, G.
Cahiers Du Plein Jeu, Les

DOUGHERTY
Across The Western Ocean

Blow Ye Winds

Mary Ann

Mobile Bay

Shenandoah

DOUGHTY
Don Gato

DOUGLAS
Brooks
  Little Bird Told Me, A

DOUGLAS (cont'd.)

Kahn
Charlie My Boy

Quadling, Lew
Careless

When The Saints Go Marching In

Wright
It's A Blue World

DOUTY, N.
Peri, Jacopo
Invocation Of Orpheus

Ravel, Maurice
Slumber, Beloved One

DOVO, BERT
Greatest Love Of All, The

DOWNEY
Gaudeamus Igitur

DOWNING
Beethoven, Ludwig van
Heavens Are Declaring, The

De Koven, (Henry Louis) Reginald
Winter Lullaby, A

Edwards, Clara
Into The Night

Firestone, Idabelle
If I Could Tell You

Malotte, Albert Hay
For My Mother
Little Song Of Life, A

Rasbuch, Oscar
Mountains

DOYEN, A
Borodin, Alexander Porfirievich
Chanson De La Foret Sombre
Chanson De La Foret Sombre

Brahms, Johannes
Chant Magyar

Gossec, Francois Joseph
Hymne A La Nature

Mehul, Etienne-Nicolas
Hymne A La Raison

Melodies Populaires, Deuxieme
Fascicule: Deux Chants Russe

Melodies Populaires, Premier
Fascicule: Trois Chants Russes

Wagner, Richard
Choral De Sachs

DOYEN, ALBERT
Chabrier, [Alexis-] Emmanuel
Roi Malgre Lui, Le: Fete Polonaise

DRAKE, JIM
Jones
Hideaway Place
New Tomorrows

DRECHSLER
Marenzio, Luca
Zwei Madrigale

DREO, HARALD
Zechmeister, Rudolf
Burgenlandhymne

DRESSLER, L.
Sullivan, [Sir] Arthur Seymour
Long Day Closes, The

DREWES
Stewart
I Am The Nation

DREXLER
Beethoven, Ludwig van
Bitten Lied

DREXLER, J.
Lang, Hans
Oho, Schon Wieder

Palm, Emil
Regentropfen

Ziehrer, Carl Michael
Sei Gepriesen, Du Lauschige Nacht

DREXLER, JOS.
Fullekruss, E.
Treue Mutterherz, Das

DREXLER, JOSEF
Abt, Franz
Waldandacht

Benatzky, Ralph
Ich Muss Wieder Einmal In Grinzing
Sein

Dostal, Hermann
Kerzengrad Steig Ich Zum Himmel

Filip, Frank
Servus Grinzing, Servus Wein

Lang, Hans
Jetzt Ist Es Still
Marianne Hopsassa
Unterm Fensterl

Lehar, Franz
Ach, Die Weiber!
Es Lebt' Eine Vilja, Ein
Waldmagdelein

Loube, Charles
I Red Im Schlaf

Nicolai, Otto
Chor Der Elfen

Schubert, Franz (Peter)
Forelle, Die

Straus, Oscar
Walzertraume

DREYER; JAMES
Ruby
Cecilia

DRIESSEN, R.
Rossini, Gioacchino
Danza, La

DRISCOLL
Norton
My Melancholy Baby

DRISCOLL, DENNIS
Jolson, Al
Me And My Shadow

DROUIN
Beethoven, Ludwig van
Hymne Au Soleil
Mon Joli Moulin

Chopin, Frederic
Mazurka

Gounod, Charles Francois
Bonjour, Bonsoir

Mendelssohn-Bartholdy, Felix
Au Bord Du Lac
Voici L'Automne

Missa, Edmond Jean Louis
Petits Loups, Les

Mozart, Wolfgang Amadeus
Hymne Triomphal
Rossignolet, Le
Tendresse Filiale

Rameau, Jean-Philippe
Fetes D'Hebe, Les
Hymne A La Nuit

Rouget de l'Isle, Claude Joseph
Marseillaise, La

Schubert, Franz (Peter)
Adieu
Chant Du Meunier
Standchen
Valse Printaniere

Schumann, Robert (Alexander)
Petit Choral

Weber, Carl Maria von
Jagerchor

DU VINAGE
Buchtger, Fritz
Hohe Stunde

Cadow, Paul
Drei Frauen Hat Der Hein Gehabt
Frauen, Hort Doch Auf Zu Jammern

Clemens, Adolf
Wir Stehen Auf Den Klippen

Erdlen, Hermann
Nun Jubiliert Der Morgen

Lissmann, Kurt
Heimat, Du Mutterlich Herz
Musik, Du Bist Die Welt
Zwei Schreiber Ruderten

Sendt, Willy
Nicht Nach Dem Blinden Wunsch

DU VINAGE (cont'd.)

Unger, Hermann
Dach Und Wiesen Sind Vom Frost
Silbern Uberzogen
Wo Ich Ferne

Weber, Ben Brian
Hochste Buch, Das

DUBUQUE; FLEIG
Rasposchol

DUCREST
Curran, Pearl Gildersleeve
Nocturne

Edwards, Clara
Into The Night

Friml, Rudolf
Donkey Serenade, The

Guion, David Wendall Fentress
Carry Me Home To The Lone Prairie

Hageman, Richard
Do Not Go My Love

DUEY
Ain't Got Time To Die

Bach, Johann Sebastian
Good Fellows Be Merry

Jones
Women, What Are They

Minstrel Boy, The

My Good Ol' Man

DUHAMEL, M.
A La Claire Fontaine

A Lorient Vient D'Arriver

Au Beau Clair De La Lune

C'Est Trois Garcons

Chansons Populaires De Haute-Bretagne

Couturier De Ruffigne, Le

Dans La Cour Du Palais

Dans La Ville De Rennes

Dessus Les Sables De La Mer

Dieu! Que Les Femmes Sont Betes!

Filles De Saint-Briac, Les

Galant Mal Recu, Le

Gars De Locmine, Les

Gas De Locmine, Les

J'Ons Un Voyage A Faire

Laboureur Et Les Hommes D'Armes, Le

Passant Par Paris

Pelo De Betton

Perrine Etait Servante

Tablier Vole, Le

Veille De La Saint-Louis, La

Vivent Les Matelots!

DUIS, ERNST
Europa Singt

DUNCAN
Steffe, William
Battle Hymn Of The Republic

DUNCAN, CATHY
Isaacson, Michael Neil
Music Is Heart To Heart

Mulcey, David
Very Small

DUNCAN, CHESTER
Then And Now

DUNHAM
Bayly
Long, Long Ago
Sweet And Low

DUNHILL
Mozart, Wolfgang Amadeus
Oh Come, Sweet Spring

EHRET (cont'd.)

Wiseman
Tenderly He Watches

Woods
Side By Side

Yarrow, Peter
Day Is Done

Yellow Rose Of Texas, The

Youthful Chorister

EHRET; JENKINS
Gannon, James Kimball (Kim)
Under Paris Skies

EHRET, W.
Hammerschmidt, Andreas
Note Well, My Heart

I Know My Love

In That Great Gettin' Up Mornin

It's Song Time

Time Draws Nigh, The

Wilbye, John
Come, Shepherd Swains

EHRET, WALTER
Beers, Bob
Peace Carol, The

Choral Time

Cindy

Cohan, George Michael
You're A Grand Old Flag

Fare You Well, My Love

Gershwin, George
Summertime

Gibbons, Orlando
Silver Swan, The

Hassler, Hans Leo
Come Now, Let's All Drink Cool Wine
I Wish To Spend My Time Rejoicing

Hava Nagila

I Know An Old Lady

I Pack She Back To She Ma

I Saw Three Ships

I'm Goin' To Ride Up In The Chariot

Jamaica, Farewell

Loewe, Frederick
They Call The Wind Maria

Louchheim, Stuart F.
Spirit Of Christmas, The

Mem'ries Vanish Never

Mozart, Wolfgang Amadeus
Alphabet, The
Sing A Song Of Merry Christmas

My Masters, Be Merry

Myers, Ronald Charles
I Want To Be Everything
Of All The Good Things
Wakin' Up
We're For America
Where Is Happiness?

Nine Hundred Miles

O It's Good-Bye Liza Jane

Old Ark's A Moverin, The

Paxton, Tom
Marvelous Toy, The

Porter, Cole
Another Op'nin, Another Show

Purcell, Henry
Man Is For The Woman Made
Sound The Trumpet

Regney, Noel
Sweet, Sweet, Sweet Little Jesus

Roberts, Ruth
Brave And The Bold, The
Our Country 'Tis Of Thee
Tall Tom Jefferson

EHRET, WALTER (cont'd.)

Robinson, Earl Hawley
House I Live In, The

Rodgers, Richard
Climb Ev'ry Mountain
Do-Re-Mi
Getting To Know You
It's A Grand Night For Singing
Oh, What A Beautiful Mornin'
Oklahoma!
Oklahoma!: Choral Selections
Sound Of Music, The

Rome, Harold Jacob
Be Kind To Your Parents

Seeger, Pete
Where Have All The Flowers Gone?

Simon, Paul
April Come She Will
Mrs. Robinson
Scarborough Fair-Canticle

Sow Took The Measles, The

Styne, Jule (Jules Stein)
Everything's Coming Up Roses
People

Swann
Hippopotamus Song, The

There's A Little Wheel A-Turnin'

Vreneli Auf Dem Gugisberg, 'S

Wailie, Wailie

Wayfaring Stranger

We Are Crossing Jordan River

Wilbye, John
I Love, Alas, Yet Am Not Loved

Winter's Night

EHRET; WALTON
Kjerulf, Halfdan
Last Night The Nightingale

EHRET; WARNICK; MILLER
Rodgers, Richard
Sound Of Music, The: Selections

EHRISMANN
Reichardt, F.
Festlied

EHRISMANN, HANNS
Strauss, Johann, [Jr.]
Rosen Aus Dem Suden

EHRISMANN, HANS
Lehar, Franz
Gold Und Silber

S' Heimelig

EIELSEN, STEINAR
Fem Folkeviser Og Negro Spirituals

Sanghefte 1

Springar 1 Fra Bergen

Tre Folkeviser

EIKEN, PETER
Dahl, Kare
Voggesong Til Siri

EILERS, JOYCE
Millet, Kadish (Kay)
What's More American?

Reynolds, Malvina
If You Love Me

EINSTEIN, ALFRED
Golden Age Of The Madrigal, The

EISENBART, KARL M.
I Hab A Schons Haus

EITNER, ROBERT
Publikationen Aelterer Praktischer
Und Theoretischer Musikwerke

EKLOF, EJNAR; GUSTAFSON, JOHN;
WIKANDER, DAVID; AHLEN, WALDEMAR;
OVERSTROM UNO

Skolkoren Uppl. A

Skolkoren Uppl. B

EKLUND, STIG
Taube, Evert
Har Ar Den Skona Sommer

EKWUEME
Hombe

ELAINE, SR. M
Grieg, Edvard Hagerup
I Love You

ELBIRK, HENNING
Buket Danske Folkemelodier, En

Ehrling, Thore
Ole Bole Bum

Mortensen, Ole
Fire Sange

ELBIRK, V.H.
Bonfils, Kjeld
Abadilje-En Skaeg Familie

ELGAR
Arne, Michael
God Save The Queen

As Torrents In Summer

How Calmly The Evening

My Love Dwelt In A Northern Land

Snow, The

Weary Wind Of The West

ELGAR, EDWARD
Snow, The

ELIOT
Foster, Stephen Collins
Gentle Annie

ELKAN
Bizet, Georges
Flowers Of Flame

Lecuona, Ernesto
Andalucia

Ravel, Maurice
Bolero

ELKAN, HENRI
Debussy, Claude
Clair De Lune

Granados, Enrique
My Blossom

Jones
Rittenhouse Square

Offenbach, Jacques
Song Of The River, The

Tchaikovsky, Piotr Ilyich
Oh Lovely Spring

ELKUS, J.
Ives, Charles
Thanksgiving And Forefathers' Day

ELKUS, JONATHON
Ives, Charles
Circus Band

ELLIOTT
Handful Of Keys

ELRICH
Lai, Francis
Love Story

Prager
Christmas Means Love

ELSAESSER
Lissmann, Kurt
Mit Hellem Sang Und Frohem Tanz

ELSMITH, BERTA
Sullivan, [Sir] Arthur Seymour
Iolanthe

ELSNER
Sturmer, Bruno
Es Singt Das Herz

EMBORG, H.B.
Schubert, Franz (Peter)
Standchen

EMBORG, J.L.
Agnete Og Havmanden

Emborg, Jens Laurson
Den Vilde Rosenbusk
Jomfruen Og Gogen

Hamburger, Povl
Hvor Klart Dog Stjernen Ses I Nat
Mester Ole Vind
Og Kom Den Ode Vinter

Jeg Taenkte Pa Verden

ERBELDING, DIETRICH (cont'd.)

  Wo Die Wolga Fliesst

ERDELYI, JOZSEF
  Farkas, Ferenc
    Szivarvany

ERDLEN
  Beim Kronenwirt

  Blume, Karl
    Grun Ist Die Heide

  Brahms, Johannes
    Guten Abend, Gut' Nacht

  Ebel, Eduard
    Leise Rieselt Der Schnee

  Schulz, Johann Abraham Peter
    Mond Ist Aufgegangen, Der

ERDLEN, H.
  Alleweil Ein Wenig Lustig

  Auf, Auf Zum Frohlichen Jagen

  Auf Dem Berg, So Hoch Da Droben

  Auf Dem Berg So Hoch Da Droben

  Das Lieben Bringt Gross Freud

  Den Schonsten Fruhling Seh'n Wir
    Wieder

  Des Besenbinders Tochter

  Die Gedanken Sind Frei

  Feinsein, Beinander Bleibn

  Frau Schwalbe Ist 'Ne Schwatzerin

  Frohliches Frankenland

  Gedanken Sind Frei, Die

  Horch, Was Kommt Von Draussen Rein?

  Jan Hinnerk

  Lasst Uns Jauchzen, Lasst Uns Singen

  Lieben Bringt Gross Freud, Das

  Mein Lieb Ist Wie Der Morgenstern

  Schon Ist Die Welt

  Singt Mit Uns

  Und In Dem Schneegebirge

  Und Jetzt Gang I Ans Peters Brunnele

  Wahre Freundschaft

  Winter Ist Vergangen, Der

  Wohlauf, Die Luft Frisch Und Rein

ERDLEN, HERMANN
  Bohmische Wind, Der

  Ebel, Eduard
    Leise Rieselt Der Schnee

  Goldene Ringelein, Das

  Neckische Geisslein, Das

  Silcher, Friedrich
    Wie Lieblich Schallt

  Wenn Hier Een Pott Mit Bohnen Steiht

ERDMANN, VEIT
  Stehn Zwei Stern Am Hohen Himmel

ERDTMAN, SIGURD
  Harteveld, Wilhelm Napoleonovich
    Svenskmannaed. Karl XII Marsch

ERHARD, KARL
  Monteverdi, Claudio
    Orfeo: Zwei Festliche Chore

ERICSON, CHRISTOPHER
  Sally Gardens

ERIKSEN, REIDAR
  Moller, Friedrich W.
    Glade Vandrer, Den

ERIKSSON, JOSEF
  Fjarran Han Drojer

  Jag Lagde Mig Sa Sildig

  Jeg Lagde Mig Sa Sildig

  Limu, Limu, Lima

  Nar Majdagen Lockar

ERIKSSON, JOSEF (cont'd.)
  Ola Glomstulen

  Segerstam, Selim
    Bon

  Weber, Carl Maria von
    Bon

ERKKO
  Sibelius, Jean
    Im Morgennebel

ERNRT, N.
  Auf Unserer Brucke Zwei Madchen

  Gut G'sell Und Du Musst Wandern

  Hinterm See Dort

  Ihr Madchen, Sammelt Wasser Ein

  Jesu, Zu Dir Schreien Wir

  Klinge Lieblich Und Sacht

  Mein Schatzlein Kommt Von Ferne

  Viele Tranen Ich Vergoss

  Wenn Sonne Kommt Am Morgen

ERVIN, MAX T.
  Tunes And Countertunes

ESDORF, PETER
  Raymond, Fred
    Komm, Trink Und Lach Am Rhein! "Ich
     Liebte Vor Jahren Ein Madchen"

ESNAOLA
  Parera
    Himno Nacional Argentino

ESPOSITIO, JIM
  Tierney, Thomas
    Christmas Round, A

ESPOSITO
  Christmas Wish, The

  I'm The Man Who Built The Bridges

ESPOSITO, JIM
  Christmas Is Coming

  Deutschendorf, Henry John (John
    Denver)
    I'm Sorry

  Gibb, Steve
    She Believes In Me

  Hall, Daryl
    It's A Laugh

  Lennon, John
    All My Loving
    Imagine
    Maxwell's Silver Hammer
    When I'm Sixty Four
    Yellow Submarine

  Paxton, Tom
    I'm The Man That Built The Bridges
    What Did You Learn In School Today?

  Tierney, Thomas
    Tune Of Our Own, A

  Twelve Days Of Christmas, The

ETTI, K.
  Haydn, [Franz] Joseph
    Acht Lieder
    An Die Freundschaft
    An Iris
    Gebet Zu Gott
    Landlust, Die
    Lob Der Faulheit
    Mit Wurd' Und Hoheit Angetan
    Sympathie
    Wunsche Der Liebe
    Zufriedenheit

  Liszt, Franz
    Es Muss Ein Wunderbares Sein

  Mozart, Wolfgang Amadeus
    Erbarmt! Ha, Welcher Sturm!
    O Wie Schon, Soldat Zu Sein
    Secondate, Aurette Amichi

  Schubert, Franz (Peter)
    Der Rache Opfer Fallen
    Ich Mochte So Gerne Sie Kosen
    Schone Stunde, Die Uns Blendet!
    Wenn Mut Und Schonheit Sich Vereint
    Wie Lebt Sich's So Frohlich Im
     Grunen

ETTI, KARL
  Abt, Franz
    Vaterland, Ruh' In Gottes Hand

  All Mein Gedanken

  Handel, George Frideric
    Grablied

  Haymerle, F.
    Lied Von Osterreich, Das

  Kreutzer, Konradin
    Schutz Bin Ich, Ein

EURINGER
  Sendt, Willy
    Und Ob Lieb Sorge Schier Verzagt

EVAN, HARRY
  David Of The White Rock

EVANS
  Colahan, Arthur
    Galway Bay

EVANS, EDWARD G. JR.
  Martini, Johannes
    Secular Pieces, The

EVANS, H.
  Cottrau, Teodoro
    Santa Lucia

  James, James
    Hen Wlad Fy Nhadan

EVANS, HAL
  John Peel

  Joshua Fit' De Battle Ob Jericho

  Lassen, Eduard
    When Thy Blue Eyes

EVANS; NAYLOR
  Livingston
    Silver Bells

EVANS; SECHLER
  Shields
    In The Good Old Summertime

EXPERT
  Arbeau, Thoinot (Jehan Tabourot)
    Pavane

  Bertrand
    Adieu, Adieu, Ma Nymphette Amiable
    Ce Ris Plus Dous Que Le L'Oeuvre
     D'Un Abeille
    Hola, Caron, Nautonnier Infernal
    Je Meurs, Helas! Je Meurs, Mon
     Angelette
    O Doux Plaisir, O Mon Plaisant
     Dommage

  Bonnet, Pierre
    Alors Que Mon Coeur S'Engage
    C'Est Trop Peu Pour Moy De Pleurer
    Voulez Vous Donc Tousjours, Madame

  Costeley, Guillaume
    Allon Gay, Gay Bergeres
    Las! Je N'Eusse Jamais Pense
    O Que Suis Trouble

  Des Prez, Josquin
    Mille Regretz
    Mille Regretz De Vous Abandonner

  Goudimel, Claude
    Qui Au Conseil Des Malins N'A Este

  Janequin, Clement
    Au Joly Jeu
    Ce Moys De May
    Chant De L'Alouette, Le
    Chant Des Oyseaux, Le
    Cris De Paris, Les
    Guerre, La
    Laissez Cela
    Ouvrez Moy L'Huis
    Petite Nymphe Folastre
    Qui Vouldra Voir Comme Un Dieu Me
     Surmonte
    Si J'Ay Este Vostre Amy
    Sy Celle La Qui Oncques Ne Fut
     Myenne

  Lassus, Roland de (Orlandus)
    Bon Jour, Mon Coeur
    De Fond De Ma Pensee

  Le Jeune, Claude
    Autant En Emporte Le Vent
    Belle Aronde, La
    Ce N'Est Que Fiel, Ce N'Est
     Qu'Amerq
    Je Pleure
    Je Suis Desheritee
    Qu'Est Devenu Ce Bel Seil
    Revecy Venir Du Printans
    S'Ebahit-On Si Je Vous Aime
    Voicy Du Gay Printans

FARGO, MILFORD (cont'd.)
  There Is No Christmas Like A Home
    Christmas

FARQUHAR
  Engel
    Return Of Maytime

FARRELL, DENNIS
  Do You See That There Bird

FAUQUET, JOEL-MARIE
  Janequin, Clement
    En Amour Y A Du Plaisir

FAVRE, G.
  Berger Qui Me Fait La Cour, Le

  Chant Du Meunier

  Choeurs A Deux Voix, Premier Recueil

  Choeurs A Deux Voix, Deuxieme Recueil

  Deux Chants Populaires De Provence

  Deux Chants Populaires Du Maine

  Dix Chants Populaires

  En Passant Par Un Echalier

  En R'venant D'Saint-Savinien

  Guenillon

  Il Etait Un Bonhomme

  Je M'en Fus Cueillir La Rose

  Ma Mere M'a Berce

  Nez De Martin , Le

  Trois Chants D'Afrique

  Trois Chants De Rouergue

  Trois Noels Francais

FAY, VERNON
  Down Saint Petersburg Road

FAYAU, O.
  Agnel, L'

  Au Bois Rossingnolet

  Berceuse D'Auvergne

  Bourree

  Deux Brunettes Du Dix-Huitieme Siecle

FEARIS
  Barnard, Charlotte Alington
    ("Claribel")
    Come Back To Erin

  Comin' Thro' The Rye

  Fearis Two-Part Song Album

  Flow Gently, Sweet Afton

  Gray, Hamilton
    Two Cities, The

  Grieg, Edvard Hagerup
    Apple Blossoms

  Jensen, Adolf
    Mill, The

  Marks, Godfrey
    Sailing

  Molloy, James Lyman
    Kerry Dance, The
    Love's Old Sweet Song

  Offenbach, Jacques
    Lightly Floats Our Bonny Boat

  Schuler, George S.
    Cowboy, The

  Strauss, Johann, [Jr.]
    An Der Schonen Blauen Donau

FEARIS, J.S.
  Beethoven, Ludwig van
    When Grandmother Dreams

  Flow Gently, Sweet Afton

  High School Glee Club, The

  Ideal Collection Of Three Part Songs,
    The

  S.A.B. Collection, The

FEARIS, J.S. (cont'd.)
  Strauss, Johann, [Jr.]
    Rosen Aus Dem Suden

FEARIS, JOHN S.
  Fearis Quartet And Chorus Book

  Girls' Glee Club, The

  Junior High School Glee Club, The

  Practical Twp-Part Songs

  S.A.B. Chorus Collection

  Select Trios, Chorus Collection For
    Male Voices

FEDERLEIN
  Tchaikovsky, Piotr Ilyich
    Light Of Dawning, The

FEDERLEIN, G.
  Schubert, Franz (Peter)
    Rosamunde

FEGERS, K.
  Auf, Ihr Freunde

  Es Fliegt Gar Manches Vogelein

  Es Kam Ein Schuster Ohne Frau

  Und Jetzund Kommt Die Nacht Herein

FEIBEL, NORBERT
  Lied, Kling In Die Welt

  Lied, Klingt In Die Welt

FELDSHER, HOWARD M.
  Lochlainn, Colm O.
    Mrs. McGrath

FELDSTEIN
  Strommen
    Hope For The Future
    Wind Of Life, The

FELINE, A.
  Rossini, Gioacchino
    Duetto Buffo Di Due Gatti

FELLERER
  Gosswin
    Newe Teutsche Lieder-1581

FELLOWES, E.H.
  Elizabethan Two-Part Songs

  Elizabethan Two-Part Songs

FELLOWES, EDMUND; MORONEY, DAVITT
  Bennet, John
    Madrigals To Four Voices

FELT, GERHARD
  An Des Haffes Anderm Strande

  De Oadeboar

  Et War Emoal Twee Schwestre Jung

  Memel, Ach Memel

  O Kam Das Morgenrot Herauf

  Welch Ein Wunder

FELTON
  Speaks, Oley
    On The Road To Mandalay

FENBY
  Delius, Frederick
    Wedding Music

FENGER, B.R.
  Down Among The Dead Men

FENGER, R.
  Jag Unnar Dig Anda Allt Gott

  Wennerberg, Gunnar
    Har Ar Gudagott Att Vara

FENLON, IAIN
  Music And Patronage In Sixteenth-
    Century Mantua, Vol. 2

FENNER; KARLIN
  Chadieu
    Rock Me In The Cradle

FENNER, THOMAS P.
  Cabin And Plantation Songs As Sung By
    The Hampton Students

FENWICK
  Booth
    Cheer For Canada, A

  Schumann
    Spring Lullaby

FERGUSON
  Coffee Grows On White Oak Trees

  Two Shaker Songs

FERGUSON, GREGORY F.
  Irish Girl, The

FERNAND
  Gounod, Charles Francois
    Marche Pontificale

FERNSTROM, JOHN; HAGLUND, ALLAN;
    RANTZEN, TORSTEN; RALF, EINAR

  Ficksangbok

FERRARI
  Rimsky-Korsakov, Nikolai
    Chanson Indoue

  Tchaikovsky, Piotr Ilyich
    Legende

FERRELL, JOHN
  Twelve Days Of Christmas, The

FERRIS; FRANK
  Skelton
    Red's White And Blue March

FETTKE
  Leech
    Children Are The World's Tomorrow

  MacFarren
    Fy Upon You, Fy!

FIALA, JAROMIR
  Smetana, Bedrich
    Mitgift, Die

FIELD
  Weelkes, Thomas
    Four Arms, Two Necks, One Wreathing
    Hence, Care, Thou Art Too Cruel

  Wilbye, John
    Weep, O Mine Eyes

FIELD, R.
  Brahms, Johannes
    Es Geht Ein Wehen Durch Den Wald
    Verlorene Jugend

  Monteverdi, Claudio
    If I Should Part From You

  Vecchi, O.
    My Sweetest Love, I'm Grieving

FIELD, ROBERT
  Buffalo Gals

  Gabrieli, Giovanni
    Music Be Praised

  Hassler, Hans Leo
    Ich Scheid Von Dir Mit Leide
    Oh, The Good Life Gives Me Pleasure

  Lassus, Roland de (Orlandus)
    Qui Dort Ici?

  Morley, Thomas
    Leave, Alas, This Tormenting

  Peuerl, Paul
    Frischauf Und Lasst Uns Singen

  Stodola Pumpa

FIELDS
  Lippe
    How Do I Love Thee

FINCH, ALFRED
  Janequin, Clement
    Ce Moys De May

FINCK
  Ach Herzigs Herz

FINE
  Brahms, Johannes
    Mainacht, Die

  Copland, Aaron
    Boatmen's Dance
    Ching-A-Ring Chaw
    Dodger
    I Bought Me A Cat

  Debussy, Claude
    Beau Soir

FINLAY, K.
  Flowers Of Edinburgh, The

FINLAY, KENNETH
  When She Answered Me

FORSBLAD
Just For Young Men

Morley, Thomas
O Sleep, Fond Fancy
Though Philomela Lost Her Love

Rounds For Beginning Chorus

Young Men Singing

FORSTER
Rosenstock, Holderbluh

FORSTER, CUTHBERT
Elfin Eightsome Reel

FORSTER, P.
Schoch, J.
Mailied

FORSTER, PETER
Es Wollte Sich Einschleichen

O Du Schoner Rosengarten

Rosenstock, Holderbluh

FORTUNE
Dylan, Robert (Bob)
Blowin' In The Wind
Times They Are A-Changin', The

Fast
These Things I've Known

Lightfoot
Pony Man, The
Pussywillows, Cat-Tails

Stookey, Noel Paul
A'Soalin'

Tyson
Four Strong Winds

Yarrow, Peter
Day Is Done
There Is A Ship

FOSS
Manning, Kathleen Lockhart
Shoes

Nin, Joaquin
Captive Heart, The
Ill-Requited Love
Linnet With The Golden Beak, The
Minuet In Song

FOSTER, ARNOLD
Dabbling In The Dew

O Sally, My Dear

Sharp, Cecil James
Dabbling In The Dew
O Sally, My Dear

Simon The Cellarer

There Was A Pig Went Out To Dig

FOSTER, DONALD
Clerambault, Louis-Nicolas
L'Histoire De La Femme Adultere

FOTE
Backer
I'd Like To Teach The World To Sing

McGlohan
Christmas Eve
It's Christmas Time

Zynczak, S.
Love You

FOTE, RICHARD
McGlohon, Loonis
It's Christmas Time

FOUQUE, MARTIN
Bial, Rudolf
Wohin Ich Wand're Durch Die Welt

Einmal Kehr' Ich Wieder, Prachtiges
Berlin!

Kummer, W.
Waldschenke, Die

Link
Es War Einmal
Gluhwurmchen-Idyll

Meine Freud' Ist Die

Mittmann, Paul
Mein Schlesierland

Rickels, K.
Hinter Einer Gartenmauer

FOUQUE, MARTIN (cont'd.)
Schultze, Norbert
Drei Rote Rosen
Lili Marleen
Salut!
Weit Hinter Frisco

FOUST, ALAN
Harvey, Alex
Someone Who Cares

Kirkman, Terry
Cherish
Everything That Touches You
Requiem For The Masses

MacLellan, Gene
Put Your Hand In The Hand

FOWELLS, R.M.
Broadway Ballads

FOWKE, EDITH; JOHNSTON, RICHARD
Folk Songs Of Canada

Folk Songs Of Quebec (Chansons De
Quebec)

FOWKE; JOHNSTON
Folk Songs Of Canada II

FOX
Cherish

FOX, DAN
Deutschendorf, Henry John (John
Denver)
Back Home Again
Fly Away
Leaving On A Jet Plane
Rocky Mountain High

FRACKENPOHL
Bishop
Morning Star

Brahms, Johannes
Mainacht, Die

Irish Elegy, An

Joplin, Scott
Entertainers, The

Mozart, Wolfgang Amadeus
Tale Of A Pigtail

Oh, Breathe Not His Name

When Love Is Kind

FRACKENPOHL, ARTHUR
Annie Laurie

Londonderry Air

Orpheus And His Lute

FRANCISCI, O.
Rozhor Sa, Vatra

FRANCK, M.
Kommt, Ihr G'spielen

FRANCOEUR; BACAK
Jesse

FRANK
Ahlert
Two Thousand Years

Arlen, Harold
All Out For Freedom

Bach, Wilhelm Friedemann
No Blade Of Grass Can Flourish

Barouh
Man And A Woman, A

Bassett, Karolyn Wells
Take Joy Home

Beach
I Wish You Love

Beethoven, Ludwig van
Fruhlingsruf

Bruckner, Anton
Trosterin Musik

Cahn
Thoroughly Modern Millie

Carmichael
Dreams
Three Little Ships
Whale Song, The

Chaplin
This Is My Song

FRANK (cont'd.)
Dvorak, Antonin
Song To The Moon

Easterbrook
Chatterbox, The
Little Pigs, The
Lollipop Song

Glazer
Musicians, The

Gluck, Christoph Willibald, Ritter
von
Tout Dans La Nature

Green Fields

Hague
Did I Ever Really Live

Harrer
Mein Herz Ist Bereit

Hatch, Tony (Anthony Peter)
Call Me
Who Am I?

Haydn, [Franz] Joseph
Augenblick, Der
Very Ordinary Story, A

Heiberg
This Is The Day

Herbeck
Wohin Mit Der Freud

Homilius, Gottfried August
Frolocket Und Singet

Impossible Dream, The

Keith
Yellow Bird

Kessler
Travelin' Bank

King
Song Of The Islands

Kretzmer
In The Summer Of His Years

Kreutzer, Konradin
Abendlied

Lampell
Pass It On

Loesser
Music Of Home, The
Summertime Love

Loesser, Frank
Anywhere I Wander
Faraway Boy
Gideon Briggs, I Love You
Greenwillow Christmas
Inch Worm, The
King's New Clothes, The
New Ashmolean Society And Students
Conservatory Band, The
Once In Love With Amy

Mancini, Henry
Lonely Winter

Marnay
Once Upon A Summertime

Mendelssohn-Bartholdy, Felix
Andenken

Merry Madrigals, The

Moller
Happy Wanderer, The
Santa, The Happy Wanderer

Myddleton, William H.
Down South

One, Two, Three, Caroline

Raye
I'll Remember April
Ways Of Love, The

Rimsky-Korsakov, Nikolai
Nightingale And The Rose, The

Rome
Music Lessons

Sapienza
My Father

Schneider
Thank You

Schubert, Franz (Peter)
Des Tages Weihe
Lebenslust

FRY (cont'd.)

Deutschendorf, Henry John (John Denver)
Perhaps Love

Ham, Albert William (Al)
Without You

Just Once

Porter, Cole
C'Est Magnifique
Do I Love You?
From This Moment On

Yesterday Once More

FRY, GARY D.
Danoff, William Thomas
California Day
Friends With You
Liberated Woman
Light Of My Life, The
Take Me Home, Country Roads
Take Me Home Country Roads
Take Me Home, Country Roads

Deutschendorf, Henry John (John Denver)
Aspenglow
Druthers
Farewell Andromeda (Welcome To My Morning)
For Baby (For Bobbie)
How Can I Leave You Again
I Want To Live
It Amazes Me
Singing Skies And Dancing Waters

Jabara, Paul
Enough Is Enough (No More Tears)

Johnston, Bruce
I Write The Songs

Lennon, John
Every Little Thing
Good Day Sunshine
Hard Day's Night, A
Ob-La-Di, Ob-La-Da
Penny Lane
With A Little Help From My Friends

Marks, Johnny D.
Rudolph, The Red-Nosed Reindeer

Moroder, Giorgio
On The Radio

Sommers, John Martin
Love Is Everywhere
Thank God I'm A Country Boy

Williams, Paul
Can You Picture That?
I Hope That Somethin' Better Comes Along
I'm Going To Go Back There Someday
Magic Store, The
Movin' Right Along
Never Before, Never Again
Rainbow Connection, The

FUCHS, J.N.
All' Mein Gedanken

Hun I Nit A Schians Dianal?

Hut' Du Dich

FUHRER, RUDOLF H.
Bruckner, Anton
Samtliche Werke, Band XXII-8:
Helgoland

FULLER
Bemberg, Herman
'Tis Snowing

FULLEYLOVE
This Old Man

FUNCK
Deutsche Lieder Des 15. Jahrhunderts
Aus Fremden Quellen

FUNK, GARY
Moten Swing

GAARTZ
Lied Der Wolgaschlepper

Rote Fahnen

GABEAUD, A.
Indy, Vincent d'
Dans La Tour Du Palais
Marche Des Conscrits Dans La Montagne

GAD, HELGA
Syv Tosserier

GAGLIANO
Lecuona, Ernesto
Cordoba

GAGNEPAIN, BERNARD
Quinze Vaudevilles Ou Rondes De Table

GAGNON, A.
Ani Couni

GAILEY
Have Yourself A Merry Little Christmas

GAINES
Speaks, Oley
Sylvia

GAINES, S.
Yonder! Yonder!

GAITO
Dvorak, Antonin
Humoresca

Grieg, Edvard Hagerup
A La Primavera

Haydn, [Franz] Joseph
Serenade

Mozart, Wolfgang Amadeus
Canto De Cuna

Schubert, Franz (Peter)
Marcha Militar

Schumann, Robert (Alexander)
Traumerei

Wagner, Richard
Pilgerchor

GAL, HANS
Binzgauer Wallfahrt, Die

Es Wollte Sich Einschleichen

Hons Ging Zum Tor Hinaus

Leinweber, Die

GAL, HANS; MANDYCZEWSKI, EUSEBIUS
Brahms, Johannes
Complete Works

GALKO, LADISLAV
Slovak Songs, Vol. I

Slovak Songs, Vol. II

Slovak Songs, Vol. III

Slovak Songs, Vol. IV

GALLINA, JILL
Danoff, William Thomas
Take Me Home, Country Roads

Gotta Sing

Happy Holidays

In His Eyes

That's What Friends Are For

GAMBAU, V.
Noel De France

Reve De Celui Qui Boit, Le

Turelurelu

GAMBLE, EDWIN
Dowland, John
Two Elizabethan Encores

GARAY, JANOS
Bardos, Lajos
Uj Szovetneket

GARBERS
Gross
Freiheit, Die Ich Meine

GARBOLETTO, ANTONIO
Anthology

GARDEN
Brahms, Johannes
Rhapsodie

GARDINER, H. BALFOUR
And How Should I Your True Love Know?

Sir Eglamore

GARDINER; HOLST
I Love My Love

I Sowed The Seeds Of Love

Swansea Town

GARDNER
Banks Of Jordan

Big White Ship

Billings, William
Chester

Brahms, Johannes
Hymn Of Freedom

Chopin, Frederic
Prelude No. 7
Prelude No.7
Prelude No. 20

Deep Blue Sea

Down, Down, Down

Enesco, Georges (Enescu)
Roumanian Rhapsody

Foster, Stephen Collins
Beautiful Dreamer
Some Folks
Swanee River

Gastoldi, Giovanni Giacomo
Festival In Sienna

Goin' To Be A Mighty Day

Good News

Hear The Bells

Home In That Rock

I Done Done

I Want To Be Ready

In This Land

Kitty Of Colraine

Lassus, Roland de (Orlandus)
Serenade

Lead Me

Little Black Train

Michael, Row The Boat Ashore

Mozart, Wolfgang Amadeus
Calypso Canon
Two Canons

Old Joe Clark

Pick A Bale Of Cotton

Ride On Moses

Satan Is Mad

Send The Light

Sing Sorrow

Sourwood Mountain

Strauss, Johann, [Jr.]
Pizzicato Polka

Three Nineteenth Century Canons

Three Sixteenth Century Canons

Turn Around

Ward, Samuel Augustus
America The Beautiful

GARDNER, JOHN
Sing For Pleasure, Book 7: Three Popular Songs

GARDNER, M.
All Night, All Day

Frere Jacques

Kum Ba Yah

GARDNER, MAURICE
Bow Down

By'm By

Clap Your Hands

Down By The Bayou

Down By The Riverside

Early One Morning

Every Night When The Sun Goes In

Four Spirituals

Galilee

GEOFFRAY, CESAR (cont'd.)

Boheme, La

Brume

Charbonnier, Le

Connaissez-Vous La-Bas

Dans Les Bois

Distler, Hugo
    Wanderlied

J'Ai Mon Coeur A Mon Aise

Jean-Bart

O Ma Belle Aurore

O Sari Mares

Retour Du Marin, Le

Sont Les Filles De La Rochelle

Sur La Route De Dijon

Terre De Nos Peres, La

Vieille Ronde, La

Ya Se Van Los Pastores

GEOFFRAY, CESAR; CAILLAT, STEPHANE
    Falala

GEOFFROY-DECHAUME, ANTOINE
    Rameau, Jean-Philippe
        Incas, Les

GEORGE
    Smith
        Sing Out America

GERBER
    Madrigale Nordischer Gabrieli-Schuler

GERBER, REBECCA L.
    Cornago, Johannes
        Complete Works

GERG, GOTTFRID
    Willaert, Adrian
        Vad Tanker Du, Mitt Hjartas
        Harskarinna

GERHOLD, NORBERT
    Alt-Ausseer Postillion, Der

    Alte Hutte, Die

    Anuschka

    Auf Nach Mailand

    Bela Bimba

    Da Pfarrer Hat Gsagt

    Din, Don

    Es Blies Ein Jager

    Frisch Auf, Gut G'sell

    Frohliche Bruder

    Gut'n Abend

    Ja, Mir Scheint Es So

    Jager Aus Kurpfalz, Ein

    Jager Jagt Ein Wildes Schwein, Ein

    Jager Langs Dem Weiher Ging, Ein

    Jetzt Tanzt Hannemann

    Juchhe, Tirolerbua

    Kleine Maritschu, Die

    Komzak, Karl
        Marchen
        Volksliedchen

    Kurfurst Friedrich

    Lasst Die Peitschen Knallen

    Lerche, Die

    Madl Heirat Mi'

    O, Hast Du Noch Ein Mutterlein

    Rameau, Jean-Philippe
        O Nacht

    Tiritomba

    Un'grischen Husaren, Die

GERHOLD, NORBERT (cont'd.)

    Von Luzern Uf Waggis Zue

    Weg Zu Mein Diandl, Der

GERICKE, H.P.; MOSER, H.; QUELLMATZ,
    A.; VOTTERLE, K.

    Bruder Singer

    Kleine Bruder Singer, Der

GERMAN, EDWARD
    Beauteous Morn

    Camel's Hump, The

    My Bonnie Lass She Smileth

    O Peaceful Night

    Orpheus With His Lute

    Rolling Down To Rio

GEROLD
    Sturmer, Bruno
        Aber Die Nacht Muss Sich Wandeln
        Zum Morgen

GERSBACH
    Bein, Wilhelm
        Lied Der Treue

GERSDORF
    Sturm-Biel, Wilhelm
        Es Zog Der Maienwind Zu Tal

GERSTENBERG
    Eisler, Hanns
        Deutsche Heimat, Sei Gepriesen

    Frohe Jugend

    Wenn Hier Son Pott Mit Bohnen Steiht

    Willaert, Adrian
        Opera Omnia Vol. XIII: The
        Madrigals Of The Musica Nova

GERSTER
    Bruder, Zur Sonne, Zur Freiheit

    Nowikow
        Lied Der Weltjugend

    Unsterbliche Opfer

    Werner, Heinrich
        Sah Ein Knab Ein Roslein Stehn

GERSTER, OTTMAR
    Gluck, Christoph Willibald, Ritter
        von
        Festgesang "Freudenklange, Frohe
        Festgesange"

GEVAERT, F.
    Reveillez-Vous Picards

GEVAERT, F.-A.
    Abandonnee, L'

    Boite A Pandore, La

    Bouquet A Madeleine Au Jour De Sa
        Fete

    Brunette

    Chanson De Mai

    Chanson Flamande

    Chanson Satyrique

    Chanson Soldatesque Du Temps De
        Charles VIII

    Collection De Choeurs,deuxieme
        Fascicule

    Collection De Choeurs,quatrieme
        Fascicule

    Collection De Choeurs,sixieme
        Fascicule

    Deguisement Inutile, Le

    En Venant De Lyon

    Felicite Passee

    Gentils Galants De France

    Gluck, Christoph Willibald, Ritter
        von
        Choeur D'Introduction Du Prologue

    Il Fait Beau Voir Ces Hommes D'Armes

    Laissez Jouer, Jeunes Gens

    Mai, Le

GEVAERT, F.-A. (cont'd.)

    O Nuit, Heureuse Nuit

    Paysans De Chatou A Leur Seigneur,
        Les

    Ronde Villageoise

    Temps Passe, Le

    Vache Egaree, La

GEVAERT, F.-A.; BEON, A.
    Amaryllis

    Au Clair De Lune

    Beaux Yeux

    Chanson De La Mariee

    Collection De Choeurs,huitieme
        Fascicule

    Ma Femme Est Morte

    Petit Bossu

    Va Dous Annaig

    Vous Me Tuez Si Doucement

GEVAERT, F.-A.; DU BOIS, L.
    Collection De Choeurs,neuvieme
        Fascicule

    De La Riviere

    Fortune A Tort

    Jamais Je N'Aurai Envie

    Jamais Printemps

    Ne Revenez Plus, Lisette

    Patapatapan Allons

    Petite Fleur

    Que Je Vous Aime!

    Vous Avez Beau Vous Defendre

GHISI, FEDERICO SARTORI
    Canti Artigiani Carnascialeschi

GIASSON
    Chopin, Frederic
        How Sweet The Wine

    Dvorak, Antonin
        Gypsy Heart

    Marchetti, F.D.
        Music Of Love, The

GIBB
    Beethoven, Ludwig van
        Flame Color
        Freemen Are We All

    Brahms, Johannes
        Quiet Wood, The
        Within My Heart Breathes Music

    Elgar, [Sir] Edward (William)
        As Torrents In Summer

    Nobody Knows The Trouble I See

    Ravel, Maurice
        Blossom Falls, A

    Steal Away To Jesus

GIBBONS
    Locke
        Cupid And Death

GIBBS
    Heseltine, Philip ("Peter Warlock")
        Yarmouth Fair

GIEFER, W.
    Drei Laub Auf Einer Linden

    Guten Abend, Gut' Nacht

    Ich Geh Durch Einen Grasgrunen Wald

    Lass Nur Der Jugend Ihren Lauf

GIEHNE
    Beethoven, Ludwig van
        Ehre Gottes Aus Der Natur, Die

GIELAS
    Pachelbel, Johann
        Kanon In D

GIELGE, HANS
Klingende Berge

GIESBERT, F.J.
Erde Braucht Regen, Die

O Du Schoner Rosengarten

Rosen Und Die Nelken, Die

Wer Ein Lammlein Weiden Will

GIESEN, WILLY
Ciku, Ciku, Grabu

Denza, Luigi
Funiculi-Funicula

Drei Junge Madchen

Es Geht Nichts Uber Die Gemutlichkeit

Gestern Abend, Da Ging Ich Wohl

Morgen Will Mein Schatz Verreisen

O Tannenbaum

Schiffer Auf Dem Blanken Rhein, Der

GIETZ, BERND HANS
Alle Vogel Sind Schon Da

Hab Mein Wage Vollgelade

Jager Langs Dem Weiher Ging, Der

Loch Lomond

Romberg, Sigmund
Trink! Trinkt!

Swing Durch Die Welt

Yellow Rose Of Texas, The

GILBERT
Strawberry Fair

GILBERT; BOTKIN
Coffee Grows On White Oak Trees

GILBERT, N.
Dance To Your Daddy

GILBERT, NORMAN
Haul Away, Joe

GILBERT, REANEY
Early Fifteenth-Century Music Vol. II

Early Fifteenth-Century Music Vol.
IV: Anonymous Chansons From The
Ms Oxford, Bodleian Library

GILDAY, E.F.
Brahms, Johannes
Gang Zum Liebchen, Der

GILES
Poor Lonesome Cowboy

GILLAM
Snow Lay On The Ground, The

GILLES, O.
Beim Kronenwirt

GILLIAM
Soon One Mornin'

GILLIES, DOUGLAS
Sambalele

GINGRICH
Mendelssohn-Bartholdy, Felix
Gondolier's Evening Song
Jagdlied, Op.120 No. 1

GIRARD, H.A.
Inverno E Passato, L'

GIRAUD, Y.
Friderici, Daniel
Amis Sur Cette Terre

Suite "Au Joli Bois"

GIRAUD, YVES
Fleur Des Chansons Rustiques De La
Renaissance Francaise, La

Le Jeune, Claude
Voici Le Vert Et Beau Mai

GIVERT, YVON
Leduc, Jacques
Soleil d'Orties, Six Impressions
Fugaces

GLADSTONE, JERRY; BOCK, FRED
Joplin, Scott
Entertainer, The

GLARUM
Papa Didn't Know

GLASER
Canzone D'i Zampognari

Cuckoo Carol, The

GLASER, V.
Brahms, Johannes
Gang Zum Liebchen, Der

Cup Of Old Stingo, A

Isaac, Heinrich
Mein Freud Allein

O Magali, My Most Beloved

Pilkington, Francis
Rest, Sweet Nymphs

Rameau, Jean-Philippe
Votre Amour, Berger

Twelve Days Of Christmas, The

GLASER, VICTORIA
Ah! Gabriel

Cambric Shirt, The

Canzone Di Zampognari

Fireflies

Lassus, Roland de (Orlandus)
Mon Coeur Se Recommande A Vous

Morley, Thomas
Fire, Fire My Heart

Peerson, Martin
Upon My Lap My Sov'reign Sits

Rich Old Miser Courted Me, The

Touro-Louro-Louro!

GLAZER; FORTUNE
Hassler, Hans Leo
Because All Men Are Brothers

GLAZER; FRANK
Hassler, Hans Leo
Because All Men Are Brothers

GLEDHILL, C.
I Will Give My Love An Apple

Mary The Virgin Sings A Song

GLEDHILL, CHRISTOPHER
I Will Give My Love An Apple

Mary The Virgin Sings A Song

GLINSKI, M.; BOK, J.
Pacelli, Asprilio
Four Madrigals

GLINSKY, M.
Pacelli, Asprilio
Madrigali, Libro I

GLUCK, F.
Klage

GLUCK, FR.
In Einem Kuhlen Grunde

Vier Grablieder

GNAU, A.
Gently, Johnny My Jingalo

GOEBEL, G.
Es Fiel Ein Reif In Der
Fruhlingsnacht

GOEHR
Little Folk Songs

GOETSCH, C.
De Hirtechnab

GOETZ
Krietsch, Georg
Vor Den Augen Der Gotter

GOETZL
Friml, Rudolf
Sympathy

GOITRE, R.
Balazs, Arpad
Due Composizioni A Tre Parti

Bardos, Lajos
Cinque Composizioni A Due E Tre
Parti
Quattro Continenti
Tredici Composizioni A Due Parti

GOITRE, R. (cont'd.)

Jardanyi, Pal
Sette Composizioni Facili A Tre
Parti

Kocsar, Miklos
Invocazione Della Primavera

Olsvai, Imre
Girandola Di Colori

GOLD
Kellem, Milton
Gonna Get Along Without You Now

Kern, Jerome
All The Things You Are

GOLDFARB; SUCHOFF
I Have A Little Dreydl

GOLDMAN
Bach, Johann Sebastian
Siciliano

Brahms, Johannes
Sandmannchen

Chopin, Frederic
Choral Etude, A

Faure, Gabriel-Urbain
Sicilienne

Hava Nageella

Hava Nevtzey B'Machol

How Good It Is

Kaleenka

Lameedbar

Merry Christmas Song, A

Rossini, Gioacchino
Danza, La

Schubert, Franz (Peter)
Night And Dreams

Simple Gifts

Verdi, Giuseppe
Song Of The Little Fairies

Ya Ba Bom

GOLDMAN, MAURICE
Hatikvah

GOLDMAN, RICHARD FRANKO
Landmarks Of Early American Music,
1760-1800

GOLDSBROUGH
Purcell, Henry
Trumpet Song

GOLDSBROUGH; FORTUNE
Purcell, Henry
In Guilty Night

GOLGEVIT, J.
Ballade En Novembre

Nomades, Les

GOLMAN, STEPHANE; MARBOT, ROLF
On Top Of Old Smoky

GONZALES
La Hora Del Canto

GOODALE
Encina, Juan del
Gasajemonos De Husia

Goncales, Bernal
Navego En Hondo Mar

Guerrero, Francisco
Huyd, Huyd, O Ciegos Amadores
Ojos Claros Y Serenos

Ju Me Leve Un Belle Maitin

Morata, Gines de
Ninpha Gentil

Ponce, Juan
Ave Color Vini Clari

Vasquez, Juan
De Los Alamos

GOODCHILD, ARTHUR
Cuckoo, The

GOODHART
Agincourt Song

Sweet Lavender

GOODHART; CALLAHAN
Sing, Men

GOODMAN
Hava Nageela

GOODWIN
Schubert, Franz (Peter)
Du Bist Die Ruh'

GORDON
Bach, Johann Sebastian
To Spring

Green Grow The Rushes O

Jock O'Hazeldean

Schubert, Franz (Peter)
Evening Song

Shenandoah

Steiner
Theme From A Summer Place

Yuletide Festival, A

GORDON, PHILIP
Christmas Cheer

Palestrina, Giovanni Pierluigi da
Arbor Decora

GORE
Lassus, Roland de (Orlandus)
Ola! O Che Bon Eccho!

GOTTWALD, CLYTUS
Berg, Alban
Nachtigall, Die

Mahler, Gustav
Ich Bin Der Welt Abhanden Gekommen

GOTZ, ROBERT
Zoll, Paul
Jenseits Des Tales Standen Ihre
Zelte

GOTZE-KOHLER
Schubert, Franz (Peter)
Nachtigall, Die

GOUDIMEL, C.; COUPER, A.
As A Hart Longs For The Brooklet

GOULD, GRETCHEN
Deutschendorf, Henry John (John
Denver)
Baby Just Like You, A

GOULDING; JAMES
Janis
Love, Your Magic Spell Is
Everywhere

GOUNOD
Lully, Jean-Baptiste (Lulli)
Hiver, L'

Rameau, Jean-Philippe
En Ce Doux Asile

GOUNOD; DROUIN
Rameau, Jean-Philippe
Castor Et Pollux

GRABNER, H.
Abschied

Dirnle, Dirnle, Jetzt Geh'n Wir In'
Garten Raus

Es Bluhen Die Maien

Es Flog Ein Kleins Waldvogelein

Es Steht Ein Lind In Jenem Tal

Es Wollt Ein Magdlein Fruh Aufstehn

Hirtenlied

Ich Hort Ein Sichelein Rauschen

Ich Weiss Mir Ein Maidelein

Isaac, Heinrich
Innsbruck, Ich Muss Dich Lassen

Kleine Mann, Der

Sie Gleicht Wohl Einem Rosenstock

So Liegst Denn Auf Erden

Taublein Weiss

Zogen Einst Funf Wilde Schwane

Zuccalmaglio, Anton Wilhelm Florentin
von
Es Fiel Ein Reif In Der
Fruhlingsnacht

GRABNER, HERMANN
Ach Schonste, Allerschonste

Draussen Auf Der Grunen Au

Gefangene Zeisele, Das

Heiland Ist Geboren, Der

Hirtenlied

Isaac, Heinrich
Innsbruck, Ich Muss Dich Lassen

Klopfet Mir Keiner An

Schulz, Johann Abraham Peter
Mond Ist Aufgegangen, Der

Schwalangschor-Lied

So Liegst Denn Auf Erden

Vulpius, Melchior
Helle Sonn, Die

GRAETZER
Antologia Coral, Fasciculo I

Antologia Coral, Fasciculo II

Antologia Coral, Fasciculo III

Antologia Coral, Fasciculo IV

Antologia Coral, Fasciculo V

Finck
Ach, Herzigs Herz

Garcimunoz
Una Montana Pasando

Gesualdo, [Don] Carlo (da Venosa)
Non T'amo O Voce Ingrata

Hassler, Hans Leo
Wenn Mein Stundlein Vorhanden Ist

GRAF, HARRY
Haydn, [Johann] Michael
Lob Des Sanges
Sehnsucht Nach Dem Landleben

GRAFF, OLA
Tre Viser Fra Nord

GRAHAM, HERMANN
Lied Vom Bauerndorf, Das

GRAHAM, R.
Rocking Carol

GRAHAM; SHIRL; STILLMAN; ADES
Drake, Ervin
I Believe

GRAINGER
I'm Seventeen Come Sunday

GRAINGER; HUGHES
Dunstable, John
O Rosa Bella

GRAM, J.
Brahms, Johannes
In Stiller Nacht
Wiegenlied

Dansevise

Kaereste Ven

Molholm, Louis
Om Jeg Ta'r Mig En Livsens Ven

Muss I Denn

Schwartz, J.
Nej, Smuk Er Min Skat Ej

GRAMSS, K.
Pfiffige Pal, Der

Schlafende Schaferin, Die

GRAMSS, KNUT
Franck, Melchior
Lustig, Ihr Herren, Allzumal

GRANVILLE
Buxtehude, Dietrich
Alles, Was Ihr Tut

Franck
In Dem Armen Dein
Wer Ueberwindet

Hammerschmidt, Andreas
Das Ist Je Gewisslich Wahr

Schuetz
So Far Ich Hin
Wer Will Uns Scheiden?

GRASBECK, GOTTFRID
Halvan

Helan

Kesapaiva Kangasalla

Konneveden Kotiseutulaulu

Ringlek

Sakkijarven Polkka

Taivas On Sininen

Tersen

Vinechko

GRASCHER, F.
An Bock Hab I G'schoss'n

Bin A Lustig'r Fuhrmann

Da Drauss'n Im Wald

Dirndle Hast G'hort

Dirndle Magst Du An Rot'n Apfel?

Funfundzwanzig Dirnd'lan

Ja Wann I's Stundle Nur Wusst

GRAULICH, GUNTER
Schutz, Heinrich
Alma Afflitta, Che Fai?
Cosi Morir Debb'io
Di Marmo Siete Voi
D'orrida Selce Alpina
Dunque Addio, Care Selve
Feritevi, Ferite
Fiamma Ch'allaccia
Fuggi, Fuggi, O Mio Core!
Giunto E Pur, Lidia
Io Moro, Ecco Ch'io Moro
Mi Saluta Costei
O Dolcezze Amarissime
O Primavera
Quella Damma Son Io
Ride La Primavera
Selve Beate
Sospir, Che Del Bel Petto
Tornate, O Cari Baci
Vasto Mar

GRAVELLE
Glazer, Carl
Christmas Present To Santa Claus, A

GRAVES
Adam
Sergeant's Song

Arnold
In Search Of A Wife

Blow The Wind Southerly

Caleno Custure Me

Dibdin, Charles
Tol De Liddle Li

Foom, Foom, Foom!

Four Eighteenth Century Chorus Songs

Linley, Thomas
Departure Of Robinson Crusoe, The

Old John Braddle-Um

Pepusch, John Christopher
Charming Sounds That Sweetly
Languish

Shield, William
Song For The Winter, A

Snow It Melts The Soonest

Storace, Stephen
Peaceful Slumb'ring On The Ocean
Quarreling Duet

GRAVES, RICHARD
I Am A Brisk And Sprightly Lad

GRAY
Von Tilzer, Albert
Wait Till You Get Them Up In The
Air, Boys

GRAY, DON
I Never See Maggie Alone

Morey, Larry
Heigh-Ho

GRAY, W.J.
Cindy

Great Day

GRAYSON
Noel, Noel

Praetorius, Michael
Sie Ist Mir Lieb

Purcell, Henry
In These Delightful Pleasant Groves

GRAZIANI-WALTER, C.
Rossini, Gioacchino
Preghiera Del Mose

Verdi, Giuseppe
O Signore Dal Tetto Natio
Va Pensiero Sull'ali Dorate

GREEN
Little Bull

GREENBERG
Choral Songbook

E la don, don, Sweet Virgin Mary

Isaac, Heinrich
Quis Dabit Capiti Meo Aquam?

Riu, Riu, Chiu

Sons Of Eve, Reward My Tidings

Wilbye, John
Come Shepherd Swains
Weep O Mine Eyes

GREGOR; KLAUSMEIER; KRAUS
Europaische Lieder In Den Ursprachen-
Band 1

Europaische Lieder In Den Ursprachen-
Band 2

GREIG, HILDA
Poston, Elizabeth
Ladybird, The

GRELL
Buhkoken Von Halberstadt

GREPPI
Gounod, Charles Francois
Coro De Los Soldados

GRESSER, H.
Stehst So Still, Mein Pferdchen

GREVE, C.J.
Bayless, J.
Candida

GREYSON
Arbeau, Thoinot (Jehan Tabourot)
Belle Qui Tiens Ma Vie

Arne, Thomas Augustine
Which Is The Properest Day?

Banchieri, Adriano
Contrappunto Bestiale Alle Mente

Bennet, John
Weep, O Mine Eyes

Berger, Jean
Night, Lovely Night

Brahms, Johannes
Evening, The
Gentle Heart, The
Im Herbst
Morning Song
O Susser Mai

Byrd, William
Lullaby
While The Bright Sun

Cara
Forsi Che Si, Forsi Che No

Certon, Pierre
Le Ne L'o Se Dire

Cui, Cesar Antonovich
Dawn, The

Des Prez, Josquin
Parsons Regretz

Donato
All Ye Who Music Love

Dowland, John
Come Again! Sweet Love Doth Now
Invite

Dvorak, Antonin
This Day
Up Sprang A Birch Tree

Encina, Juan del
Pues Que Jamas

GREYSON (cont'd.)
Festa, Costanzo
Se'l Pensier Che Mi Strugge

Gastoldi, Giovanni Giacomo
Amor In Nachen
Questa Dolce Sirena

Gesualdo, [Don] Carlo (da Venosa)
Ecco Moriro Dunque!

Gibbons, Orlando
Silver Swan, The

Gombert, Nicolas
Hors Envieux! Retirez Vous

Gretchaninov, Alexander Tikhonovich
Autumn

Hassler, Hans Leo
Ach, Schatz, Ich Singe Und Lache
Ah, Love, I Laugh While Singing
All Happiness Love Gives To Me
All Lust Und Freud
Herz Tut Mir Aufspringen, Das
Jungfrau, Dein Schon Gestalt
My Heart With Love Is Springing
Nun Fanget An Ein Gut's Liedien
Nun Fanget An Ein Gut's Liedlein
Tanzen Und Springen

Jeune
Revecy Venir Du Printemps

Lassus, Roland de (Orlandus)
Bon Jour Mon Coeur
Bon Jour, Mon Coeur
Matona, Mia Cara
Ola! O Che Bon Eccho!

Lemin
Gutzgauch, Der

Martini
Come Sing This Round With Me

Mendelssohn-Bartholdy, Felix
Farewell To The Wood
May Song

Morley, Thomas
Fire, Fire My Heart
I Go Before, My Charmer
My Bonny Lass She Smileth
Now Is The Month Of Maying

Palestrina, Giovanni Pierluigi da
Ve Drassi Prima Sensa Luce Il Sole

Passereau
Il Est Bel Et Bon
Il Est Bel, Et Bon

Peuerl, Paul
Frolich Zu Sein In Deiser Zeit

Pinsuti, Ciro
In This Hour Of Softened Splendor

Ponce
Como Esta Sola Mi Vida

Purcell, Henry
In These Delightful Pleasant Groves
With Drooping Wings

Scandello, Antonio (Scandellus,
Scandelli)
Little White Hen

Schubert, Franz (Peter)
Tanz, Der

Schuman
Trust

Sermisy, Claude de (Claudin)
Au Joli Bois
Qui Se Pourroit Plus Desoler

Stephani, Johann
Kuckuck Hat Zich Zu Tod Gefall'n,
Der

Vautor, Thomas
Mother, I Will Have A Husband

Vecchi, Orazio (Horatio)
Fa Una Canzone
So Ben Mi Ch'a Bon Tempo

Volkman
At Evening

Weelkes
Donna Il Vostro Bel Viso
I Bei Ligustrie E Rose

Weelkes, Thomas
Nightingale, The

Widmann, Erasmus
Wer Lust Und Lieb Zur Musichat

GREYSON (cont'd.)
Wilbye, John
Change Me, O Heavens

Willaert, Adrian
Sempre Mi Ride Sta

GREYSON, N.
Brahms, Johannes
Falke, Der

Martini, [Padre] Giovanni Battista
Come Sing This Round With Me

GREYSON, NORMAN
Arensky, Anton Stepanovich
O'er The Mountains And The Valleys

Bateson, Thomas
Your Shining Eyes And Golden Hair

Bennet, John
Weep, O Mine Eyes

Brahms, Johannes
Abschiedslied
Beherzigung
Madchen, Das
Nein, Es Ist Nicht Auszukommen Mit
Den Leuten
Rede Madchen

Demantius, Christoph
Lieblich Ich Horte Singen

Donati, Baldassare (Donato)
All Ye Who Music Love

Dowland, John
Come Again! Sweet Love Doth Now
Invite

Ford, Thomas
Since First I Saw Your Face

Hassler, Hans Leo
Nun Fanget An Ein Gut's Liedlein
Von Dir Kann Ich Nicht Scheiden

Leslie, Henry David
Charm Me Asleep

Martini, [Padre] Giovanni Battista
Come Sing This Round With Me

Mendelssohn-Bartholdy, Felix
Andenken
Gluckliche, Der
Lerchengesang

Morley, Thomas
Now Is The Month Of Maying

Purcell, Henry
In These Delightful Pleasant Groves

GRIES, JEROME
Be Merry And Wise

GRIFFIN
Wayne
Miss America

GRIFFITHS, VERNON
Work, Henry Clay
Grandfather's Clock

GRIMBERT, JACQUES
Amour De Moy, L'

Beau Matin A La Fraiche, Un

Belle Est Au Jardin d'Amour, La

Cockenpot, F.
Colchiques Dans Les Pres

De Toute La Semaine

En Passant Par La Lorraine

Ma Douce Annette

Ma Foret

Mois d'Avril S'en Est Alle, Le

Oi Kas Sodai

Ronde De Table

Ronde Des Baisers

Soleil Monte, Le

Sur Le Pont d'Avignon

Vendanges, Les

Yannos Et Parona

GRIMES, G.
Twelve Days Of Christmas

GRINDEL, J.
Au Chant De L'Alouette

Heureux

Histoire Ancienne

Ile Saint Louis, L'

Loin

Nomades, Les

Philippe-Gerard, M.
Chat De La Voisine, Le

Poetes, Les

Tendresse, La

Vieux Pelerin, Le

Vieux Soldat, Le

Voir

GRINDEL, JACQUES
Sylvestre, Anne
T'En Souviens Tu La Seine

GRISCHKAT, H.
Schein, Johann Hermann
Wenn Filli Ihre Liebesstrahl

GRISCHKAT, HANS
Lassus, Roland de (Orlandus)
Landsknechtsstandchen

GROHE
Zelter, Carl Friedrich
Durch Feld Und Buchenhallen

GROLL, OTTO
Amapolita

Amazing Grace

Amen

American Folksongs

Annie Laurie

Auf Grunen Wanderwegen

Balalaikaklange, Nach Russischen
Volksweisen

Bortniansky, Dimitri Stepanovich
Ich Bete An Die Macht Der Liebe

Bunte Welt

Durch Die Welt

Einsam Is Der Weg

Einsam Ist Der Weg

Es Fuhrt Nur Ein Weg

Es Ist Fur Uns Eine Zeit Angekommen

Es Klingt Ein Lied

Espagnola

Fiesta Brasiliana

Foster, Stephen Collins
Swanee River

Freude Am Leben

Glory-Land

Golondrina, La

Hava Nagila

Igelhoff, Peter
Wir Machen Musik

Israelisches Liebeslied

Jingle Bells

Kalinka

Katjuscha

Kosakenpatrouille

Kuhlo, Karl
Ich Bin Durch Die Welt Gegangen

Lied Der Verbannten

Lopez, Francis
Mexico

My Bonnie Is Over The Ocean

GROLL, OTTO (cont'd.)
My Lord, What A Morning

Nobody Knows

Poor, Lonesome Cowboy

Schnell Vergeht Ein Tag

Schone Nau Haka

Somebody's Knockin'

Tscherkessenlied

Warjag, Die

Wenn Der Abendwind

GRONQUIST, ROBERT
Hassler, Hans Leo
Jungfrau, Dein Schon Gestalt

GROOT, C.; ANDRIESSEN, J.; STRATEGIER,
H.; FLOTHUIS, M.; MENGELBERG, K.;
HORST, A.
Dresden, Sem
Thema En Variaties Op "Des Winters
Als Het Regent"

GROS
Kremberg, Jacob (James)
Grunet Die Hoffnung

GROSSE-SCHWARE
Zwei Abendlieder-Quodlibets

GROSSE-SCHWARE, H.
Abendlieder-Quodlibet

Drei Tag' Sind's, Dass Ich
Zuruckgekehrt

Drei Volkslieder-Quodlibets

Gluck Auf, Ihr Bergleut

Hore Mich, Mein Herr Und Gott

Lass Doch Der Jugend Ihren Lauf

Quodlibet

Sag, Warum Bliebst Du Aus

Zwei Abendlieder-Quodlibets

GROSSJUNG, HEINZ
Kosaken-Wiegenlied

GROSSMAN, F.
Auf Der Wildbahn

Maria Und Der Schiffer

GROSSMANN, F.
Ich Weiss Nicht: Bin Ich Arm Oder
Reich

Jetzt Wird Der Feste Schluss Gemacht

GROTE
Bruckner, Anton
Am Grabe

GROTENHUIS, JOHN
He Came Singing Love

GROVE
Vautor, Thomas
Sweet Suffolk Owl

GROVEN, EIVIND
Bukkevisa

Fanteguten

Kvam, Oddvar S.
Olav Liljukrans

Om Kvelden

Salme

GRUN, B.
Dvorak, Antonin
Deep Blue Ev'nin
Summer Song

GRUNDY
Willson, Meredith
Goodnight My Someone

GRUSNICK
Franck, Cesar
Musikalische Bergreihen

GRUSZCZYNSKA, MARIA
Polish Folksongs

GRYTTER, RUD.
Gluck, Christoph Willibald, Ritter
von
Elysium, I

Mozart, Wolfgang Amadeus
Duet
Forbundssang
Klokkespil-Kor
Terzet

Rung, Henrik
Hr. Peder Kasted Runer Over Spange
Hvor Nilen Vander Aegypterens Jords
Hytten Er Lukket, Natten Er Stille
Pa Tave Bondes Ager
Sommerdag Mig Gores Lang, Den
Syv Romancer
Under Det Gronne Trae
Vilde Ravn Er Flojet Bort, Den

Sange For Lige Stemmer

GRYTTER, RUDOLF
Schubert, Franz (Peter)
Af Musiken
Geisterchor
Hirtenchor
Jagerchor

GRYTTER, RUDOLF; HATTING, CARSTEN
Gebauer, Joh. Chr.
Foraret
Forarsbudskab
Fuglekvidder
Graeshoppen
I Skoven
Jaegersang
Kanon
Moderen Med Barnet
Nye Ar, Det
Ridder Kalv
Rimfrosten
Sange Til Skolebrug
Sommeraften
Storste Mand, Den
Tommeliden
Torbisten Og Fluen
Varsang
Vise Om Varen, En

Kuhlau, Daniel Frederik Rudolph
Kor Nr. En
Kor Nr. To
Kor Nr. Tre
Tre Alfescener

GUBITOSI, E.
Scarlatti, Alessandro
Colpa, Il Pentimento E La Grazia,
La

GUDEWILL
Zehn Weltliche Lieder Aus Forsters
"Frische Teutsche Liedlein"

GUENTHER
Evans
In The Good Old Summer Time

Johnson
Lift Ev'ry Voice And Sing

GUETTLER
Hassler, Hans Leo
Ach Schatz Ich Dir Klagen

GUILLORE, LUC
C'est Dans Dix Ans Il N'y A Plus De
Printemps

GUION; DOWNING
Sail Away For The Rio Grande

GULBRANDSEN
Purcell, Henry
Passing By

GURLITT
Binchois, Gilles (de Binche)
Sechzehn Weltliche Lieder

GUSTAFSON
Billings, William
Chester

GUSTAFSON, STIG
Sommarn A En Ljuveli Ti

GUTTMANN
Schonlank
Fahnenschwur

GUTTMANN, OSKAR
Samlaich, E.
Dzunay

GYARFAS
Balazs, Arpad
Ropteto

HAASE, BRUNO
Heulied, Das

HABASH
Emmett, Daniel Decatur
Dixie

I'll Never Fall In Love Again

It's A Big Wide World

My Great, Grandfather

Ward, Samuel Augustus
America The Beautiful

Yellow Rose Of Texas, The

HABASH, JOHN MITRI
Walt Disney Choral Showcase

HABERL, F.X.; SANDBERGER, ADOLF
Lassus, Roland de (Orlandus)
Collected Works

HABERLEN, JOHN
Byrd, William
Cast Off All Doubtful Care

Country Diversion

English Christmas, An

Schubert, Franz (Peter)
Liebe

Toss The Pot

HABERLEN, JOHN B.
Certon, Pierre
Je Ne Fus Jamais Si Aise

Herbert, J.B.
Temperance Drum, The

Schumann, Robert (Alexander)
Wenn Ich Ein Voglein War

Wilbye, John
As Fair As Morn

HABERLEN, JOHN; MCKELVY, JAMES
Flaming Pudding Carol, The

HABETIN
Sturmer, Bruno
Unter Dem Tieferen Himmel

HADAR, JOSEPH
Famous Songs Of Israel

HADDOCK
Schubert, Franz (Peter)
Erlkonig

Schumann
Springtime

HADOW, W.H.
Market Day

HAFNER
Motetten Alter Meister

HAGELIN, TORVAL
Dar Sitter En Duva Pa Liljona Kvist

HAGEMANN, P.
Schuman, W.
Spring Song

Tchaikovsky, Piotr Ilyich
Echoes Of Gladness

HAGEMANN, PHILIP
This Special Season

Wagner, Richard
Wach' Auf! Es Nahet Gen Den Tag

HAGEN
Lowe, Mundell
Ain't It The Gospel Truth
That Old Fashioned Gospel Band

HAGLER, P.
D'r Rosegarte Z'Mailand

HAGNI, R.
Schmid, Walter
Lob Des Gesanges

HAHN, G.
Taube, Evert
Anglamark
Har Gar Stigen
Minnet Och Tystnaden

HAHN, GUNNAR
Delsbovalsen

Djaknevisa

Fyra Folkvisor

Ganglat Fran Mockfjard

Gardebylaten

HAHN, GUNNAR (cont'd.)
God Morgon, Min Docka

Greensleeves

Huldas Karin

Iringorad

Jag Gar I Tusen Tankar

Jungfru Maria Till Betlehem Gick

Kavaljersvisa Fran Varmland

Kvallen Stundar

Minns Du Ej?

Minstrel Boy, The

Olsson, Hjort Anders
Gardebylaten

Schenell, Per
Delsbovalsen

Stopa Klockor

Taube, Evert
Huldas Karin
Rosa Pa Bal
Stockholmsmelodi

Voici Venir Le Joli Mai

HAHN, GUNNER
Greensleeves

HAIRSTON
Adams
Tataleo

Dosoo
No Ne Li Domi

Let The Church Roll On

Live A-Humble

Oh, Rocka My Soul

Sometimes I Feel Like A Motherless
Chile

Steal Away

Swing A Lady Gum-Pum

What Kind O' Shoes You Gonna Wear?

HAIRSTON, J.
Deep River

Dis Ol' Hammer

Dis Train

Don't Be Weary Traveler

Elijah Rock

Hand Me Down

Hold On

Home In Dat Rock

In That Great Gittin' Up Mornin'

It's All Over Me

Jones
Gossip, Gossip

Joshua Fit De Battle Of Jericho

HAIRSTON, J.; WILSON, H.R.
Free At Last

HAIRSTON, JESTER
Sakura, Sakura

HAIRSTON; WILSON
Jester Hairston's Negro Spirituals
And Folk Songs

HALASZ, KALMAN
Cutting Down The Pine

HALES
Keel, Frederick
Lullaby

HALL
Cindy

Dooley
Johnny Has Gone For A Soldier

High Barbary

Orff, Carl
Nursery Rhymes And Songs
Singing Games And Songs

HALL (cont'd.)
Scott
Annie Laurie

Sourwood Mountain

HALL, JOHN
Coasts Of High Barbary, The

HALL, RICHARD
Foster, Stephen Collins
Camptown Races

HALL, W.D.
Brahms, Johannes
Neckereien

HALL, WILLIAM
All The Pretty Little Horses

Black Is The Color

Brahms, Johannes
Weg Der Liebe

Go Tell Aunt Rodie

I Know Where I'm Goin'

Lord Randall

My Gentle Harp

Schumann, Robert (Alexander)
Liebesgram
Wenn Ich Ein Voglein War

So Far From My Own

Umrem

HALL, WM.D.
Arcadelt, Jacob
Alma Mia Donna E Bella, L'

Aura Lee

Banchieri, Adriano
Ad Un Dolce Usignolo
Zabaione Musicale, Il

Brahms, Johannes
Boten Der Liebe, Die
Fragen
Klosterfraulein
Wechsellied Zum Tanz
Weg Der Liebe

Deep River

Gently, Johnny, My Jingalo

I Know Where I'm Goin'

Kirbye, George
Sorrow Consumes Me
Sweet Love, O Cease Thy Flying

Lonesome Dove, The

Marenzio, Luca
Scaldava Il Sol

Schumann, Robert (Alexander)
Dunkler Lichtglanz
Herbstlied
Landliches Lied
Schon Blumelein

Weelkes, Thomas
All At Once Well Met Fair Ladies

When Love Is Kind

Willaert, Adrian
Madonn' Io Non Lo So Perche Lo Fai

Willie, Take Your Little Drum

HALLENBERG, H.
Kullan Ylistys

HALLORAN
Arlen, Harold
I Love A Parade

Brown
We Wish You The Merriest

Elliott
It's Christmas Time Again

Gershwin, George
Somebody Loves Me

Ray
You're A Lucky Fellow, Mr. Smith

Schwartz
You And The Night And The Music

Van Heusen
You Never Had It So Good

HALSEY, LOUIS
Three Shanties

HAMBURGER, POVL
Schulz, Johann Abraham Peter
Einladung
Heulied
Knabe An Ein Veilchen, Der
Kukuk Traurte, Der
Liebeszauber
Lied
Lieder Im Volkston
Lieder Im Volkston
Mailied
Mailied Eines Madchens
Minnelied
Mutter Bei Der Wiege, Die
Trost Fur Mancherlei Tranen
Wiegenlied

HAMILL
Hamilton, Arthur
Sing A Rainbow

HAND
Ten French Songs

HANDLE, J.
High Level Ranters Song And Tune Book

HANNENFORD, N.
Arditi, Luigi
Bacio, Il

Strauss, Johann, [Jr.]
An Der Schonen Blauen Donau

Sullivan, [Sir] Arthur Seymour
Orpheus With His Lute

HANSEN
Beers, Bob
Peace Carol, The

Christmas Is Coming

HANSEN, CURT
Cornelius, Peter
Christmas Tree, The

HANSEN, E.
Clewing, C.
Alle Tage Ist Kein Sonntag

Heiser, W.
Zieht Im Herbst Die Lerche Fort

HANSEN, WILHELM
Lewkovitch, Bernhard
Tre Madrigali Di Torquato Tasso

Rabe, Folke
Rondes

HANSON
Cohan, George Michael
Barbershop Medley

HANSON, ELIS
Jag Gar I Tusen Tankar

Sommarvisa Fran Dalarna

Varvindar Friska

HANSSEN, DANIEL
Schumann, Robert (Alexander)
Til Slutt

HANSSLER, F.
Ebel, Eduard
Leise Rieselt Der Schnee

HANUS, JAN
Autumn

Spring

Summer

Winter

HARDING
Sibelius, Jean
O Mighty Land

HARDWICKE
Ding, Dong, Merrily On High

Down In The Valley

Old Man Noah

Sweet Be Thy Slumber

Wilbye, John
Weep, O Mine Eyes

HARDWICKE, ARTHUR
When I Was Single

HARE, M.
Bamba, La

HARING
Adair
In The Blue Of Evening

Creamer, Henry
'Way Down Yonder In New Orleans

Englemann
Melody Of Love

HARK, FRIEDRICH
Ade Zur Guten Nacht

All Mein Gedanken

Es Blieds Ein Jager Wohl In Sein Horn

Es Geht Eine Dunkle Wolk Herein

Es Steht Ein Lind In Jenem Tal

Jetzt Kommen Die Lustigen Tage

Kuckuck Auf Dem Zaune Sass, Der

Lieben Bringt Gross Freud, Das

Wach Auf, Meins Herzens Schone

Wohlan, Die Zeit Ist Kommen

Zehn Alte Lieder

HARLAN, VERN
Deutschendorf, Henry John (John
Denver)
Autograph
Dancing With The Mountains
My Sweet Lady

Holdridge, Lee Elwood
Whalebones And Crosses

Kahn, Gus
Charley, My Boy

Rogers, Kenneth Ray (Kenny)
Sweet Music Man

HARLINE
Washington
Pinocchio Choral Showcase

HARLINE; BOUTELLE
Washington
When You Wish Upon A Star

HARLINE; RHEA
Washington
When You Wish Upon A Star

HARMAN, ALEC
Marenzio, Luca
Invitation To Madrigals No. 12
Invitation To Madrigals No. 13

Oxford Book Of Italian Madrigals, The

Popular Italian Madrigals Of The
Sixteenth Century

HARNED, ALFRED
Roes, Carol Lasater
E Kuu Lei
Hymn Of Supplication
Mahalo Nui
Merry, Merry Monarch, A
Song Stories Of Hawaii

HARPER, EDWARD
Gibb, Barry
Stayin' Alive

HARPER, F.
Sailor's Song, A

HARQUEL, F.
Villa-Lobos, Heitor
Balaio

HARRIMAN
Crumhorn Consort Music, Vol. I

Crumhorn Consort Music, Vol. II

Four Late 14th Century Pieces

Italian Caccias Of The 14th Century,
Vol. 1

Senfl, Ludwig
Three Secular German Lieder

HARRIMAN, RALPH
Dufay, Guillaume
Guillaume Dufay, Vol. I: Four 4-
Part Works

Eight Pieces With Original
Ornamentation

Landini, Francesco
Four Ars Nova Trios

HARRIS
Bolero

Brahms, Johannes
Abendstandchen
Wie Melodien Zieht Es Mir

Creston, Paul
Here Is Thy Footstool

Des Prez, Josquin
El Grillo

Dichmont, William
Ma Little Banjo

Dowland, John
Come Again, Sweet Love!

Eccard, Johannes
Now Come And Join The Song

Hassler, Hans Leo
Come, All Musicians, Come

Lassus, Roland de (Orlandus)
Mon Coeur Se Recommande A Vous
O Occhi, Manza Mia

Leoni, Franco
Tally-Ho!

Morley, Thomas
Beside A Fountain
Now Is The Month Of Maying
Since My Tears And Lamenting
Sing We And Chant It

Purcell, Henry
Mavis, The

Rachmaninoff, Sergey Vassilievich
Floods Of Spring

Rasbuch, Oscar
Trees

Scandello, Antonio (Scandellus,
Scandelli)
Little White Hen, The

Schein, Johann Hermann
Das Ist Mir Lieb

Strauss, Richard
Morgen

Strickland, Lily Teresa
Mah Lindy Lou

To Schumann With Love

Vecchi, Orazio (Horatio)
Fa Una Canzone

Weber
Abu Hassan

Weelkes
Welcome, Sweet Pleasure

When Johnny Comes Marching Home

HARRIS, ED
Brahms, Johannes
Schlaf, Kindlein, Schlaf!

I Saw Three Ships

Von Tilzer, Harry
Take Me Out To The Ball Game

HARRIS, JERRY WESELEY
Cindy

In That Great Gettin' Up Mornin'

MacFarren
You Stole My Love

Schubert, Franz (Peter)
An Die Musik
Nachthelle

HARRIS, JERRY WESLEY
Homilius, Gottfried August
Sing Joyfully

HARRIS, V.
Schubert, Franz (Peter)
Allmacht, Die

HARRISON
Brahms, Johannes
Come Soon

Eton Choirbook 1

Eton Choirbook 2

Eton Choirbook 3

Mendelssohn-Bartholdy, Felix
Night Ride Of Elves

HAYWARD (cont'd.)

Van Heusen, James
Darn That Dream
Here's That Rainy Day

Wayne
Blue Velvet

Webb
Up, Up And Away
Up, Up, And Away

Zynczak, S.
Love You

HAYWARD, LOU
Bixio, Cesare Andrea
Tell Me That You Love Me Tonight

Kern, Jerome
Way You Look Tonight, The

McHugh, Jimmy
Lovely Way To Spend An Evening

HEADING
Gluck
Mill Wheel, The

HEARTZ
Nevin
Rosary, The

HEATH
Death, Be Not Proud

General William Booth Enters Into
Heaven

He's Got The Whole World In His Hands

Sometimes I Feel Like A Motherless
Child

This Train

When Johnny Comes Marching Home

HEBBEL
Willner, Arthur
Erleuchtung

HEBBLE
Polistina, Anthony Thomas
There Is A Child

Prokofiev, Serge
Midnight Sleigh Bells

HECHT, G.
Lortzing, (Gustav) Albert
Gesangprobe, Die

HECHT, GUSTAV
Weber, Carl Maria von
Es Blinken So Lustig Die Sterne

HECKE
Mozart, Wolfgang Amadeus
Abendruhe

HECKE, H.
Schubert, Franz (Peter)
Morgenstandchen

HECKMANN, HAROLD
Mozart, Wolfgang Amadeus
Thamos, Konig In Agypten

HEDENBLAD
Kor-Album

HEDENBLAD, IVAR; DURING, EDV.;
HULTQUIST, GUST.; KALLSTENIUS,
GOTTFR.; STROMBERG, ALFR.

Sangarforbundet Del. I

HEDGES, ANTHONY
Ally Croaker

Leezie Lindsay

HEDGREN
Barnby, [Sir] Joseph
Sweet And Low

HEENAN, ASHLEY
Four American Folk Songs

HEERUP, GUNNAR
Albert, Heinrich
Der Nordvind Lasst Sich Horen

Dedekind, Henning
Wer Will Mir Helfen Klagen

Marenzio, Luca
Kommt, Ihr Lieblichen Stimmen Alle
Von Einem Fliessenden Brunnen

Regnart, Jacob
Ach Gott, Wie Soll Ich Singen

Sange Fra Ca.1600

HEERUP, GUNNAR (cont'd.)

Schaerer, Melchior
Wo Soll Ich Mich Hinkehren

Schein, Johann Hermann
Kuhle Maien, Der
Viel Schoner Blumelein

HEFTI, J.
Sould Auld Acquaintance

HEFTI, JACQUES
Sould Auld Acquaintance

HEGEL, WILHELM
Nobody Knows The Trouble I've Seen

HEIBERG
German Songs

Gretchaninov, Alexander Tikhonovich
In Crimson Clouds

Kabalevsky, Dmitri Borisovich
Merry King, The
One Fine Morning
Song Of The Birds
Song Of The Clever Crocodile
Toy Ship, The

Schumann
Epigram

Schumann, Robert (Alexander)
Elegy For A Songbird
Song Of Sorrow
Tambourine, The
Triolet

HEIBERG; MAIZEL
Marshak
Three Brave Hunters

HEIDUCZEK, ALOIS
Ruschla, Wenn Du Meine Warst

HEIM, IGNAZ
Weber, Carl Maria von
Wanderlied
Wanderlied "Die Sonn' Erwacht, Mit
Ihrer Pracht"

HEIM, J.
Sammlung Von Volksgesangen,
Liederbuch Fur Schule, Haus Und
Verein

Sammlung Von Volksgesangen,
Liederbuch Fur Schule, Haus Und
Verein Band I

Sammlung Von Volksgesangen,
Liederbuch Fur Schule, Haus Und
Verein Band II

Sammlung Von Volksgesangen,
Liederbuch Fur Schule, Haus Und
Verein Band II

HEIN, H.
Hort, Ihr Jungen Bursch'

HEINRICHS
Harder
Geh' Aus, Mein Herz

Kremberg, Jacob (James)
Hoffnung

Mendelssohn-Bartholdy, Felix
Wisst Ihr, Wo Ich Gerne Weil

Pfusch, W.
Auf Wiedersehen

Rahlfs
Eine Allein, Der

Werner
Heidenroslein

HEINRICHS, H.
Mozart, Wolfgang Amadeus
Standchen

Schumann, Robert (Alexander)
Sonntags Am Rhein

HEINRICHS, HANS
Auf, Auf Frohlichen Jagen

Lustig Klingt Matrosensang

Mein Madel Hat Einen Rosenmund

Und In Dem Schneegebirge

HEINRICHS, W.
Am Weiten Strand Am Meer

Barba Jere, Draussen Ist Ein Segel

Fanden Sie Doch Am Fruhen Morgen

Farewell Und Adieu, Ihr Spanischen

HEINRICHS, W. (cont'd.)

Madchen

Gar Nicht Weit Von Montpellier

In Die Fremde Zog Er Fort

Jascha Spielt Auf

Joshua Fit De Battle Ob Jericho

Kad Si Bila Mala, Mare

La Zandunga, So Geht Deine Melodie

Little David Play On Your Harp

Little David, Play On Your Harp

Seerauberlied

Tanzen Soll Die Danitza

U Ranu Zoru

Und Nun Soll Erklingen Ein Frohliches
Lied

When The Stars Begin To Fall

Wir Kamen Einst Von Piemont

HEINRICHS, WILHELM
Cielito Lindo

Deep River

Go Down, Moses

Nordwind

Wenn Es Tag Wird In Den Bergen

HELFMAN, M.
Gorochov, Y.
Saleynu

HELFMAN, MAX
Ani Maamin

Atzey Zeydim Omdim

Mi Yemalel

Shir Namal

HELLDEN, DANIEL
All American Promenade

Ant Han Dansa Med Mej

Bellman, Carl Michael
Bacci Bone-Och Sententie Bok
Blasen Nu Alla
Boljan Sig Mindre Ror
Bort Allt Vad Oro Gor
Bort Allt Vad Oro Gor
Fjariln Vingad Syns Pa Haga
Fjariln Vingad Syns Pa Haga
Glada Bygd
Liksom En Herdinna
Ulla! Min Ulla!

Blasen Nu Alla

Boljan Sig Mindre Ror

Bort Allt Vad Oro Gor

Dina Ogon

Duvans Sang Pa Liljekvist

Fjariln Vingad Syns Pa Haga

Greensleeves

Gut Shabes Aich I-II

Ilu Natan I-II

Ja Blaste I Min Pipa

Kordans 1, Se Rubr

Liksom En Herdinna

Red River Girl

Sangdans Vid Valborgsmass

Should Auld Acquaintance

Slutsang

Sorjande, Den

Staffansvisa

Tvastammigt

Ulla! Min Ulla!

Uti Var Hage

HELLDEN, DANIEL (cont'd.)
Vem Kan Segla Forutan Vind?

HELLER, RUTH
Our Singing Nation

HELLER, RUTH; GOODELL, WALTER
Singing Time

HELM
Heinrichs, Wilhelm
Bitte Dich, Mein Schones Kind
Einsam Ein Wilder Reiter

HELM-BASISTA, W.
Bach, Johann Sebastian
Bouree

HELM, E.
Arcadelt, Jacob
Deh Come Trista

HELMBORG, BJORN
Monteverdi, Claudio
Ecco Mormorar L'onde

HEMBERG, ESKIL
Jerusalems Skomakare

Pettersson, Allan
Svit Ur Barfotasanger

Tillfallighetskompositioner Och
Hyllningsvisor I Urval

HEMES
Steffen, Wolfgang
Ist Nicht Ein Jeder Tag Ein Neues
Leben

HEMMER
Tilleul, Le

HEMSTREET
Edwards, Clara
By The Bend Of The River

HENAULT
Costeley, Guillaume
Mignonne, Allons Voir Si La Rose

Janequin, Clement
Ce Moys De May

Lassus, Roland de (Orlandus)
Fuyons, Fuyons Tous Le Jeu
Quand Mon Mari

Passereau
Il Est Bel Et Bon

HENDERSON
Beethoven, Ludwig van
An Die Freude

Nemec
Huskin' Bee

HENDICKSON, PAUL
Samiotissa

HENDRICKSON, PAUL
Gypsy, The

Shepherd's Song

Under Heaven's Radiance

When You Go To The River

HENNAGIN
Cucaracha, La

Go 'Way From My Window

Waillie, Waillie

Walking On The Green Grass

HENNIG, W.
Barbel Und Uli

Lustiges Handwerklied

HENNIG, WALTER
Noble Duke Of York, The

HENSON, BEV
Brahms, Johannes
Abendstandchen

Duson, Dede
What Is Gold
With All My Spirit

HENTSCHEL, R.
Jetzt Kommen Die Lustigen Tage

HERDER
Ives, Charles
Charlie Rutlage
Evening
Walking

HERDER, RONALD
Des Prez, Josquin
Parfons Regretz

HERMANN, HUGO
Roslein, Das

HERMANN, W.
Schein, Johann Hermann
Zwolf Gesange

HERMANNS, WILLY
Ich Habe Den Fruhling Gesehen

HERNRIED
Beethoven, Ludwig van
O Charlie Is My Darling
Soldier's Song

HEROLD
Lass Fragen Sein Alteres

HERRAND, ALEC
Siniavine, Alec
Vent, Le

HERRAND, MARC
Grassi, Andre
Marie, La

Valery, Claude
Comme Un P'tit Coquelicot

Villard, Jean (Gilles)
Trois Cloches, Les

HERRAND, PIERRE
Romans, Alain
Jean Le Pecheur

HERRESTHAL, HARALD
Short Master Pieces From The 15th And
16th Centuries

HERRGOTT, FRITZ
Gruass Enk Alle Miteinand

Treffpunkt 1.

Treffpunkt 2.

HERRICK
Harris
Tie Me Kangaroo Down, Sport

Kent
Time

HERRMANN
Purcell, Henry
Come Ye Sons Of Art

HERRMANN, H.
Hinunter Ist Der Sonne Schein

Ich Wollt Ein Baumlein Steigen

Kein Schoner Land

Und Jetzo Kommt Die Nacht Herein

Zum Tanze, Da Geht Ein Madel

HERRMANN, HUGO
O Du Schoner Rosengarten

Roslein, Das

HERTZ
Wagner, Richard
Hail, Bright Abode

HERZMANN
Volkstumliche Italienische Lieder

HERZOGENBERG, HEINRICH
Deutsches Liederspiel

HESCH
Yo Dee Oh Dee Ay

HESS, ERNST
Chellelander Spinnerlied

Nancy-Lied

HESS, JOHN J.
Deck The Halls

HESS, REIMUND
Au Clair De La Lune

Cotton Fields

Golondrina, La

Guantanamera

Jurgens, Udo
Zeig Mir Den Platz An Der Sonne

HESS; RINES
Baer, Charles E.
Those Good Old Fluffy- Ruffle Days

HESSENBERG, K.
All Mein Gedanken, Die Ich Hab

Jager Aus Kurpfalz, Ein

Kein Feuer, Keine Kohle

HETSCH, JOSEPH
Noels

Saboly, Nicholas
Noels De Provence

HEUBERGER, R.
Mozart, Wolfgang Amadeus
O Klage Nicht

HEUKEN, HANSJAKOB
Hopsa, Mein Madele

HEWITT
Blaauw, P.
Clock Is Playing, The

HEWITT, T.J.
Andrew, Paul
Winding Road, The

Parr Davies
Fairy On The Christmas Tree, The

Scott, Clement
Now Is The Hour

Song Of The Volga Boatmen

HEWSON, G. H. P.
Where'er I See Those Smiling Eyes

HICKOCK, R.
Othmayr, Kaspar
Ich Schell Mein Horn

HICKS
Dreyer
Cecilia

Hamm
Bye Bye Blues

Kahn
Yes Sir, That's My Baby

Monaco
Row, Row, Row

O Mister Moon

HICKS, MARY
Come Lasses And Lads

Comin' Thro' The Rye

HIGGINS, G.
Li'l Liz, I Love You

HIGGINS, JOHN
Gershwin, George
Gershwin! A Concert Panorama

Let's Fall In Love

HIGGINS, JOHN: LAVENDER, PAUL
Williams, John
America, The Dream Goes On

HIGH
Freeman
Tom, Tom, The Piper's Son

Kalman
Love's Own Sweet Song

Myddleton, William H.
Down South

Ramos
Rancho Grande, El

Smith
In The Northland

HILBER, B.
Es Chond All' Obe-N-Es Musali

HILBER, J.B.
Alte Tellenlied, Das

Luegid Vo Barg Und Tal

Veilchen Blau

HILD, FRANZ
Jungbrunn, Der

Zum Reigen Herbei!

HILL, A.
Zerbrochene Ringlein, In Einem Kuhlen
Grunde, Das

HILL, HARRY
At Pierrot's Door

Second Book Of The Singing Period
Series

HUBER
  Strauss, Johann, [Jr.]
    Fledermaus-Walzer
    Schatz-Walzer

HUBER, F.
  Beethoven, Ludwig van
    Auf Dunklem Irrweg
    Du Hast In Deines Armels Falten
    Heil Unserm Konig! Heil!
    Ruhend Von Seinen Taten
    Tochter Des Machtigen Zeus!

  Cornelius, Peter
    Heil Diesem Hause

  Donizetti, Gaetano
    Sehet, Wie Diener Sich Muhen Und
      Plagen

  Flotow, Friedrich von
    Hort Die Glocken!

  Glinka, Mikhail Ivanovich
    Lustig Ergiessen Frei Von Dem Eise

  Handel, George Frideric
    Ombra Mai Fu

  Lehar, Franz
    Lippen Schweigen, Lockt Zum Reigen

  Lortzing, (Gustav) Albert
    Auf, Munter, Bruder
    Ein Schuster, Jung An Jahren
    Greifet An Und Ruhrt Die Hande
    Seht Dort Den Muntern Jager
    Spruhe, Flamme, Gluhe Eisen
    Zuchtig Brautlein

  Marschner, Heinrich (August)
    Juchheissa! Heut' Durft Ihr Die
      Kannen Nicht Schonen
    Segne, Allmachtiger, Segne Dies
      Paar

  Mozart, Wolfgang Amadeus
    Corriamo, Fuggiamo Quel Mostro
      Spietato!
    Godiam La Pace
    Nettuno Sonori!
    Placido E Il Mar, Andiamo
    Ricevete, O Podioncina
    Scenda, Amor, Scenda, Imeneo
    Schon Weichet Dir, Sonne
    Servate O Dei Custodi

  Nedbal, Oskar
    Nach Der Arbeit Schweren Tagen

  Offenbach, Jacques
    Drig, Maitre Luther!

  Rossini, Gioacchino
    Lasst Froh Die Horner Erschallen

  Sehnsucht Nach Der Heimat

  Smetana, Bedrich
    Kirchweihtag! Ein Fest Der Freude!

  Suppe, Franz von
    Was Wir Verdammen

  Thomas, Ambroise
    Auf, Ihr Lustigen Zecher

  Verdi, Giuseppe
    Auf, Gebet Raum
    Heil Dir, Agypten, Isis Heil
    O Signore!
    O Signore
    Sind Wir Denn An Die Feinde
      Verraten?
    Wir Leben Vom Raub
    Wir Sind Zigeunermadchen

  Wagner, Richard
    Gesegnet Soll Sie Schreiten
    Jubelt In Das Fest Hinein
    Zum Letzten Liebesmahle

  Ziehrer, Carl Michael
    Faschingskinder

HUBER, F.; NIGGLI, F.
  Ustig Wott Cho, Der

HUBER, F.; PFIRSTINGER, F.
  Luegit, Vo Bergen Und Tal

HUBER, FERDINAND
  Abendlied

  Heimweh

HUBER, PAUL
  Mendelssohn-Bartholdy, Felix
    Bacchus-Chor

HUBER, W.S.
  Es Chunnt E Luschtiga Beckerchnab

  Schein, Johann Hermann
    Musica Boscareccia

HUBER, WALTER SIMON
  Schein, Johann Hermann
    Frau Nachtigall Mit Sussem Schall
    Jucholla, Freut Euch Mit Mir!
    O Cordion, Heut Bluht Dein Gluck!
    O Fili, Schon Und Subtil
    O Luft, Du Edles Element
    Wohlauf, Du Edle Lyr

HUBSCH-PFLEGER, LENI
  Lechner, Leonhard
    Auf Sie Hab Ich Mein Herz Gestellt
    Ei, Ei, Wie So Ganz Freundlich
    Freundlicher Held
    Halt Hart Herz, Hochster Hort
    Neue Teutsche Lieder, Nurnberg 1577
    O Lieb, Wie Suss Und Bitter
    Ohn Ehr Und Gunst
    So Wunsch Ich Ihr Ein Gute Nacht
    Unfall Reit Mich Ganz Und Gar, Der
    Wohl Kommt Der Mai

HUBSCHMANN
  Englert, Eugene E.
    Wann Wir Schreiten Seit' An Seit'

  Grimmig Tod Mit Seinem Pfeil, Der

  Tod Von Basel, Der

  Verkehrte Welt

HUCH, RICARDA
  Bergh, Rudolph
    Requiem Fur Werther

HUDSON
  Three English Madrigals

HUDSON, BARTON
  Brumel, Antoine
    Opera Omnia Vol. VI: Magnificats,
      Secular Works

HUDSON, HAZEL
  Mary Ann-Jamaica Farewell

  Will You Be My Partner?

HUFF, MAC
  Ashford, Nickolas
    Ain't No Mountain High Enough

  Build A Better World

  Dancin' In The Streets

  DiMicro, Vincent
    Up The Ladder To The Roof

  Friends

  Hallelujah – Get Happy

  In A Simple Way I Love You

  Music In My Life

  Strouse, Charles Louis
    Let's Go To The Movies

  We've Got Stars

HUFF, RONN
  Patriotic Medley

HUGHES
  Second Youth Song Book

  Second Youth Song Book

  Westmore
    It's Who You're With That Counts

  Youth Song Book

HUGHES, BRIAN
  Two Old Testament Spirituals

HUGHES, D.
  Blow The Wind Southerly

HUGHES, ROBERT J.
  Dry Bones

HUGO
  Meyer
    Heimat

HUHN
  Rasbuch, Oscar
    Trees

HUHN, BRUNO
  Rasbuch, Oscar
    Trees

HULT, JOHN
  Du Har Sorjit Nu Igen

  Hej Dunkom

  Jag Vet En Dejlig Rosa

  Jungfrun Hon Gar I Ringen

HULT, JOHN (cont'd.)

  Nackens Polska

  Varvindar Friska

HUMAN, F.
  O Du Schone, Susse Nachtigall

HUMAN, L.
  Praetorius, Michael
    Sehnsucht Nach Dem Sommer

HUMMEL
  Bland
    Carry Me Back To Old Virginny

  Foster, Stephen Collins
    My Old Kentucky Home
    Old Folks At Home

HUMMEL, FERD.
  Schumann, Robert (Alexander)
    Zigeunerleben

HUMMEL, HERMAN A.
  Home On The Range

HUMPHREYS, ALWYN
  Nobody Knows De Trouble I've Seen

HUMPHREYS, HENRY
  Songs Of The Confederacy

  Songs Of The Union

  When The Saints Go Marching In

HUNT PATERSON, SUZANNE
  Poor Girl's Lament, The

HUNTER
  All The Things Are You

  Chanita

  Five Nursery Rhymes

  For Me And My Gal

  I Was Born Almost 10, 000 Years Ago

  Jack Was Every Inch A Sailor

  Kern, Jerome
    Smoke Gets In Your Eyes

  Rodgers, Richard
    You'll Never Walk Alone

  Softly Flows The Nieman

  Streets Of Laredo, The

  Sullivan, [Sir] Arthur Seymour
    Ah, Leave Me Not Alone
    Flowers That Bloom In The Spring,
      The
    H.M.S. Pinafore Medley
    Hail Poetry
    I Built Upon A Rock
    Willow, Tit-Willow

  Viva Tutti

  Where Did You Grow?

  Y'minah

HUNTER; PARKER; SHAW
  Poulton, George R.
    Aura Lee

  Webster, J.P.
    Lorena

HUNTER, ROBERT
  Mon Petit Coeur Soupire

HUNTER; SHAW
  Good Night, Ladies

HUNTER; WEALE
  Highland Laddie

HUNTLEY
  Glover, S.
    Song Bird Of The Night

  Rogers, J.H.
    Star, The

  Schubert, Franz (Peter)
    Hark! Hark! The Lark

HUNTLEY, FRED H.
  Go, Tell It On The Mountains

  It's Me

  Nobody Home

JAUFRE, C.
  Gobbo So Pare

JEFFERY, BRIAN
  English Songs

  French Songs

  Spanish Songs

JEHN, MARGARETE; JEHN, WOLFGANG
  Kinderlieder Aus Aller Welt, 48

  Kinderspiele Aus Aller Welt, 28

  Pam Pam Trumma Trumma: Kinderlieder
      Aus Aller Welt

  Weihnachtslieder Aus Aller Welt, 50

JEHN, WOLFGAnG
  Zena Zena

JEHN, WOLFGANG
  A Ram Sam Sam

  Ana Halach Dodech

  Auf Bahias Marks

  Auf Brautschau Ging Herr Frosch

  Bauer Und Die Krahe, Der

  Blaue Farbe, Die

  Cindy

  Flog Ein Vogel

  Gehn Nicht Zum Tanze

  Hej, Schnelles Wasser

  Ich Weiss Ein Schone Rose

  In Einem Schonen Garten

  Kleine Erbsen, Kleine

  Kleines Boot Mit Rotem Segel

  Land Of The Silver Birch

  Lieder Aus Aller Welt, 38

  Linstead Market

  Michael, Row The Boat Ashore

  Mockingbird, The

  Navidad

  Play And Sing

  Play Fo' Ma Dogoma

  Rock-A-My-Soul

  Sag, Wolln Wir Heut Zum Tanze Gehn

  Tanzlied

  Tingluti Tangluti

  Tumbalalaika

  Vedavid Yefei Einayim

  Warum Zieht Johnny In Den Krieg

  Who's Dat Yonder

  Zwolf Europaische Weihnachtslieder

JEHRLANDER, K.F.
  Lennon, John
    Blackbird
    Michelle
    Norwegian Wood

JEHRLANDER, KARL-FREDRIK
  Ack, Varmeland Du Skona

  Allt Under Himmelens Faste

  Bellman, Carl Michael
    Gubben Noach
    Joachim Uti Babylon
    Sa Lunka Vi Sa Smaningom

  Brudmarsch Fran Jamtland

  Emigrantvisa

  Fjarran Han Drojer

  Shield, William
    Bondpojken

  Sommarvisa Fran Dalarna

  Taube, Evert
    Nocturne

JELMOLI
  Quattro Cavai Che Trottano

JENKINS
  Brahms, Johannes
    Sapphische Ode

  DeMoraes
    Boy From Ipanema, The
    Girl From Ipanema, The

  Gannon, James Kimball (Kim)
    Under Paris Skies

  Goell, Kermit
    How Wonderful To Know

  Hoffman
    Hawaiian Wedding Song, The

  Icini
    Summertime In Venice

  Lowe
    I'll Never Smile Again

  Mendelssohn-Bartholdy, Felix
    Automne, L'
    May Song

  Minstrel Boy, The

  Parsoni
    If You Love Me, Really Love Me

  Prince
    Sing, It's Good For You

  Rome
    All Of A Sudden

  Schubert, Franz (Peter)
    An Die Musik
    Hark, Hark! The Lark
    Who Is Sylvia

  Seelen
    C'est Si Bon

  Simon, Paul
    Sound Of Silence, The

  Sullivan, [Sir] Arthur Seymour
    Long Day Closes, The

  Werner
    Two Roses, The

JENKINS, C.
  Arne, Thomas Augustine
    Lle Bo'r Mel

JENKINS, CYRIL
  Hot Cross Buns!

  Little Jack Horner

  Old King Cole

  Summer Is Icumen In

JENKINS, JR
  Hanley
    Zing! Went The Strings Of My Heart

  Roberts
    Smiles

  Whiting
    Breezing Along With The Breeze

JENKYNS, PETER
  Old King Cole

JENNINGS, C.
  Here We Come A-Caroling

JENNINGS, CAROLYN
  Dance And Turn

  I Saw Three Ships

JENNINGS, PAUL
  If

  Jackson, Michael
    Eat It!

  Kander, John
    How Lucky Can You Get

JENNINGS; SPIEGL
  Mozart, Wolfgang Amadeus
    Magic Carpet, The

JENSEN, SOREN
  On Ilkley Moor Baht'at

JENTSCH, M.
  Ach, Wie Ist's Moglich Dann

  Konig Der Himmel- Ein Kind, Der

JERGENSON
  Lover's Lament, The

JEROME
  Foster, Stephen Collins
    Old Black Joe

  Watson, Michael
    Babylon

JESSLER
  Greifenberg, Armin
    Tausend Wege

JESSLER, FRITZ
  Mein Schatzlein Kommt Von Ferne

JESSYE
  E-I-O

  Hand Car Blues

  Henry
    By Heck!

  Lecuona, Ernesto
    Breeze And I, The

  Smith
    Ballin' The Jack

JOANNIDIS, JANNIS
  Greek Folksongs

JOCHUM, O.
  Bucklige Mannlein, Das

  Ich Reit Auf Einem Rosslein

  O Tannenbaum!

  Schaferlied Aus Schwaben

  Wo A Kleins Huttle Steht

JOCHUM, OTTO
  Jungfer Mit Dem Roten Rock

JODE
  Alte Madrigale

  Bach, Johann Sebastian
    Bach Fur Alle

  Chorbuch Alter Meister-Band 1

  Chorbuch Alter Meister-Band 2

  Chorbuch Alter Meister-Band 3

  Mozart, Wolfgang Amadeus
    Dir, Seele Des Weltalls

  Musikant, Der: Heft 5 Und 6

JODE, FRITZ
  Hindemith, Paul
    Wer Sich Die Musik Erkiest

  Reichardt, Johann Friedrich
    Beherzigung
    Felsen Stehen Gegrundet
    Lied Der Parzen
    Wanderers Nachtlied
    Warnung, Wecke Den Amor Nicht Auf

  Singkreisel, Der

JODE, FRITZ; KRAUS, EGON
  Funfton, Der

JOHANSEN, JENS; KULLBERG, ERLING
  Lille Paris; 7 Viser Af Birger
      Sjoberg

JOHANSON
  Garcia
    Chiton!

  Holmdahl
    Herr Andersson... Eller Den Skulle
      Ni Ha Hort!

JOHANSON, SVEN-ERIC
  Och Flickan Hon Gar I Ringen

  Per Spelman

JOHNSON
  Dvorak, Antonin
    Songs My Mother Taught Me

  Oh, Freedom!

  Penny, The

  Scandalize My Name

JOHNSON, CLAIR W.
  Alma Mater

JOHNSON, DAVID
  Ten Georgian Glees For Four Voices

KALLIPKE, ERNST (cont'd.)

Translateur, S.
Sportpalast-Walzer
Wiener Praterleben

KALLSTENIUS, E.
Du Gamla, Du Fria

KALLSTENIUS, EDVIN
A Janta A Ja

Bellman, Carl Michael
Sa Slar Min Glock

Dahlgren, Fredrick A.
A Janta A Ja

Sitter En Duva, Det

Soldaten Han Kommer

KAMMEIER, H.
Blaue Beeren

Es Sass Ein Katerlein Auf Dem Dach

Es Taget Vor Dem Walde

Weib, Komm Nach Haus

KAMMERER, I.
Auf, Du Junger Wandersmann

KAMMERER, J.I.
Mullerin, Die

KAMP
Friderici, Daniel
Ade, Ich Muss Nun Scheiden

Gumpeltzhaimer, Adam
Nacht Ist Kommen, Die

Lechner, Leonhard
Gott B'hute Dich

Regnart, Jacob
Wann Ich Gedenk Der Stund

KAMP, R.
Ich Hab Die Nacht Getraumet

KAMP, RICHARD
Cornelius, Peter
Salam Aleikum

Es Wollt Ein Jagerlein Jagen

Monteverdi, Claudio
Senecas Abschied Und Tod

Schubert, Franz (Peter)
Wandrers Nachtlied I

KAMPP, E.
Charlie Is My Darling

KANAOUENNOU
Chants Bretons, recueil A Une Voix

Dix Chants Bretons

KANEDA, BILL
Roes, Carol Lasater
Aloha, America

KANETSCHEIDER
Genee, Richard
Italienischer Salat

KANETSCHEIDER, ARTUR
D'Zit Ischt Do

Sandwirt, Der

KANTELETAR
Sibelius, Jean
Was Die Amsel Rackert

KAPLAN
Hava Nagila

O, Beautiful Young Maiden

Schumann, Robert (Alexander)
Zigeunerleben

Wilbye
Ah, Thou Golden Month Of May

KAPLAN, A.
Brahms, Johannes
Four Folk Songs

Dvorak, Antonin
Golden Harvest
Oh, Here's A Day For Joyful Singing
Songs Filled My Heart
Up Sprang A Birch Tree Overnight
When Evening Comes, Chimes Fill The
Forest

Pergolesi, Giovanni Battista
Per Voi Mi Struggo In Pianto

KAPLAN, A. (cont'd.)

Telemann, Georg Philipp
Werfet Panier Auf Im Lande

KAPLAN, ABRAHAM
Mendelssohn-Bartholdy, Felix
Lerchengesang

KAPPHAHN, CHRIS
Ward, Samuel Augustus
America The Beautiful

KARKOFF
Boom-Da-Li-Da

KARKOFF, MAURICE
Ach Ya Chabibi

Boom-Da-Li-Da

Skona Afton

Vallkullans Locksang

Vallvisa Fran Vastdalarna

Var Markens Ros

KARLIN
Bliss, P. Paul
Pro Phundo Basso

Bristow
Call John!

Case
I Was Glad

Foster, Stephen Collins
Hard Times, Come Again No More

Jacobs
Peter, Peter, Pumpkin Eater

Palmer
Rap-ple-te Rouch

Three Nineteenth Century Christmas
Carols

KARLSEN, ROLF
Lars Lenkelifot

KARNGARD, BENGT
Pierina

KARNTEN
Erdlen, Hermann
Auf, Auf Zum Frohlichen Jagen

KARPOWITSCH
Abendglocken

Kalinka

Kosakisches Wiegenlied

Rote Sarafan, Der

Suliko

Zwolf Rauber, Die

KARPOWITSCH, A.
Kalinka

Katjuscha

Kosakenpatrouille

Kosakisches Wiegenlied

Schwarze Augen

Suliko

Tschubtschik

KASCHNER, ORTWIN
Glutvolle Liebe

Roter Apfel

KATT, LEOPOLD
Heilmann, Harald
Jugend Singt II: Von Liebe Und
Treue, Abschied Und Herzelied
Jugend Singt III: Zur
Weihnachtszeit

KAUDER, HUGO
Three English Folk Songs

KAUFFMANN, RONALD
All Through The Night

Allen, Peter
Don't Cry Out Loud

Gibb, Barry
Tragedy

Hamlisch, Marvin F.
Last Time I Felt Like This, The

KAUFMANN, E.J.
Cucu, Il

Vieni Sulla Barchetta

KAUFMANN, HENRY H.
Vincentino, Nicola
Collected Works

KAY
Dickinson
Emily Dickinson Set

KAYSER, LEIF
Adam de la Hale
Kume, Kum Geselle Min

Schierbeck, Poul
Tre Sange

KEAN
Foster, Stephen Collins
Beautiful Dreamer

KEATS
Kent
Bright Star

KECHLEY
Le Jeune, Claude
Tu Ne L'Enten Pas, La La La

KEENE, TOM
Williams, Byron Olsen
Fiesta, La

KEETMAN
Orff, Carl
Chansons Enfantines
Chansons Originales Francaises

KEETMAN, GUNILD
Orff, Carl
Lieder Fur Die Schule Heft I
Lieder Fur Die Schule Heft III
Lieder Fur Die Schule Heft V
Lieder Fur Die Schule Heft VII

KEETMAN, GUNILD; MURRAY, MARGARET
Orff, Carl
Orff Schul-Werk Vol. 2: Major
Orff Schul-Werk Vol. 3: Dominant
Major
Orff Schul-Werk Vol. 4: Minor
Orff Schul-Werk Vol. 5: Dominant
Minor

KEIGHLEY, THOMAS
Afton Water

Banks Of Allan Water, The

Benet, John
All Creatures Now Are Merry Minded

Callcott, John Wall
O Snatch Me Swift

Comin' Thro' The Rye

Handel, George Frideric
Where'ere You Walk

Hullah, John [Pyke]
Three Fishers Went Sailing

MacFarren, [Sir] George Alexander
Sands Of Dee, The

Meeting Of The Waters, The

Morley, Thomas
Fire, Fire, My Heart
It Was A Lover And His Lass
Now Is The Month Of Maying

Purcell, Henry
Nymphs And Shepherds

Webbe, Samuel, Sr.
When Winds Breathe Soft

Ye Banks And Braes

You Gentlemen Of England

KELDORFER, V.
Mozart, Wolfgang Amadeus
Wiegenlied

KELDORFER, VIKTOR
Ade!

Es War Einmal Ein Magdelein

Hinaus

Wagner, Joseph Frederick
Tiroler Holzhackerbuam-Marsch

KELIN, E.
Von Land Zu Land

KIMMELL
    Swets
        Magic In The Heart Of The Universe

KINDALL
    Millet
        Join Hands

KING
    Becaud, Gilbert
        What Now My Love

    Christmas Day

    Dear Hearts, Gentle People

    Dear World

    Doodlin' Song, A

    Dylan, Robert (Bob)
        Mr. Tambourine Man

    Flamingo

    Gershwin, George
        Clap Yo' Hands

    Haggart, Robert Sherwood
        What's New?

    Heather

    If You Don't Look Around

    I'll Never Fall In Love Again

    It Was A Very Good Year

    It's A Big Wide World

    Jones
        It Had To Be You

    Kiss Her Now

    One Person

    Porter, Cole
        I Get A Kick Out Of You
        Night And Day

    Previn
        You're Gonna Hear From Me

    Promises, Promises

    Riders In The Sky

    River Is Wide, The

    Rodgers, Richard
        Thou Swell

    Romberg, Sigmund
        Lover Come Back To Me
        One Kiss
        Wanting You

    Schwartz
        If There Is Someone Lovelier Than
            You

    Sing Out

    Something

    Spirit In The Sky

    There Will Never Be Another You

    This Is That Time Of Year

    Weill, Kurt
        Mack The Knife

    Youmans
        Hallelujah!
        Sometimes I'm Happy

KING, P.
    Morey, Larry
        Snow White Revisited

KING, PETER
    Clap Yo' Hands

    Hallelujah!

    Strike Up The Band

KINGSBURY
    Climb Up, Ye Children, Climb

KINGSBURY, JOHN
    Bateson, Thomas
        Nightingale In Silent Night, The

    Jones, Robert [1]
        Farewell, Dear Love

    Pilkington, Francis
        Look, Mistress Mine

KINGSLEY
    Croswell
        Journey Through Yourself
        Rebirth
        Save A Little Love For Yourself

    Jackson
        Rivers To The South

    Larimer
        My Rock

    Rosenbaum
        Art Of Living
        Lady Of Valor, A
        Rock, Rock, Rock

KINSMAN
    Down In The Valley

    Johnny Has Gone For A Soldier

KINYON
    Battle Hymn Of The Republic

    Ward, Samuel Augustus
        America, The Beautiful

KIRCHL, A.
    Schubert, Franz (Peter)
        Daphnis

    Ziehrer, Carl Michael
        Weaner Mad'ln

KIRCHL, ADOLF
    Storch, A.M.
        Nachtzauber

KIRK
    Des Prez, Josquin
        Cricket

    Hassler, Hans Leo
        Dear Love, Of Thee Alone

    Haydn, [Franz] Joseph
        Der Greis

    Little Wheel A-Turnin'

    Schumann
        Fairest Of Flowers
        Only One, The

KIRK, THERON
    Choral Art

    Four French Folk Songs

    Three Seventeenth Century Poems

KIRKPATRICK, JOHN
    Ives, Charles
        Crossing The Bar
        Johnny Poe

KIRMSSE
    Ging Auf Den Jahrmarkt

    Lefler
        Heimat

    Seid Nicht Bose, Vater, Mutter

    Tief In Dem Herzen Innen

KIRMSSE, H.
    Fur Die Sozialistische Feier, Heft 2:
        Totengedenken

    Fur Die Sozialistische Feier, Heft 3:
        Eheschliessung

KIRMSSE, H.; IRRGANG, H.
    Volker Singen, Die, Folge 1

    Volker Singen, Die, Folge 2

KIRNBAUER, FRANZ
    Deutsche Bergmanns-Volkslied, Das

KISS, D.
    Bartok, Bela
        Csillagok, Csillagok

KISS, L.
    Ketszolamu Korusgyujtemeny

KISTLER, CYRILL
    Wagner, Richard
        Apotheose Des Hans Sachs

KITE, HUGH W.
    Chantons Noel

KJELDAAS, GUNNAR
    Norske Folkeviser Med Klaver Innhold

KJELSON
    Come Live Your Life With Me

    Gute Nacht

KJELSON (cont'd.)

    Marks
        I Heard The Bells On Christmas Day
        Night Before Christmas Song
        Rudolph, The Red-Nosed Reindeer

    Pastures Green

    Praetorius, Michael
        Sie Ist Mir Lieb

    Shenandoah

    Vance
        Cindy

KJELSON; BRAZ
    Black And White

KJELSON; VANCE
    Mayday Carol

KLAUER
    Heinrichs, Hans
        Morgenwanderung

KLEFISCH
    Arcadelt, Jacob
        Im Wind Verwehen Alle Meine Klagen
        So Wie Die Tauben Zart

    Azzaiolo, Filippo, [Publisher]
        Bauernmadchen, Ein

    Corteccia, Francesco Bernardo
        Ich Hab Dich Geliebt

KLEFISCH, W.
    Arcadelt, Jacob
        Ihr Muden Augen

    Salzburger Glockenjodler

    Spanisches Wiegenlied

KLEFISCH, WALTER
    Dachkraxler, Der

    Schone Lola, Die

    Strauss, Johann, [Jr.]
        Leichtes Blut

KLEFISCH, WALTER; BENDEL, FRANZ
    Liszt, Franz
        Schaut Her, Wir Sind's

KLEIN
    Brahms, Johannes
        Abendlied
        Ach Arme Welt
        Bei Nachtlicher Weil
        Brausten Alle Berge
        Im Herbst
        In Stiller Nacht
        Letztes Gluck
        Nachtens
        Nachtwache
        O Schone Nacht
        Sehnsucht
        Spatherbst
        Wollust In Den Maien, Die
        Zigeunerlieder

    Donati, Baldassare (Donato)
        Chi La Gagliarda

    Gabrieli, Giovanni
        Lieto Godea Sedendo

    Gastoldi, Giovanni Giacomo
        Bell' Umore, Il

    Janequin, Clement
        Au Joly Jeu
        Petite Nymphe Folastre

    Lassus, Roland de (Orlandus)
        Fuyons Tous D'Amour Le Jeu
        Ich Waiss Mir Ein Miedlein
        Io Ti Voria
        O Bella Fusa
        Sauter, Danser, Faire Des Tours
        S'io Fusse Ciaul
        Tutto Lo Di Mi Dici "Canta"
        Un Jour Vis Un Foulon Qui Foulait

    Mozart, Wolfgang Amadeus
        Ecco Quel Fiero Istante
        Luci Care Belle
        Mi Lagnero Tacendo

    Schumann, Robert (Alexander)
        In Meinem Garten
        Von Dem Rosenbusch

    Senfl, Ludwig
        Song Of The Shepherd

    Sermisy, Claude de (Claudin)
        Languir Me Fais
        Puisqu'en Amour A Si Grand Passe-
            Temps

KNUTSEN, TORBJORN
Jeg Lagde Mig Sa Sildig

KOCH
All Mein Gedanken

Jetzt Gang I Ans Brunnele

Lieben Bringt Gross Freud, Das

Rumbala

Standchen

Tulikow
Friede Der Welt

KOCH, ERLAN VON
Didl Didl Didl

KOCH, ERLAND V.
Brollopslek Fran Sarna

KOCH, ERLAND VON
Didl Didl Didl

I-I-O-Hi-Ho

Orren Han Kuttrar

Rovorna

Sa Draga Vi Upp Till Dalom Igen

Tuss Lullerilull

Vaxte Upp En Lilja, Det

KOCH, H.
Volkslieder Der Volker Der
Sowjetunion, Heft 3

Volkslieder Der Volker Der
Sowjetunion, Heft 5

Volkslieder Der Volker Der
Sowjetunion, Vol. 1

Volkslieder Der Volker Der
Sowjetunion, Vol. 2

KOCH, JOHANNES H.E.
Irish Folksongs

KOCHAN
Wir Sind Die Rote Garde

KODALY
Horvath, Josef Maria
Horatii Carmen

KOECHLIN, C.
Bourgault-Ducoudray, Louis-Albert
Adieu A La Jeunesse
Angelus, L'
Disons Le Chapelet

KOEMMENICH
Wagner, Richard
Hail Bright Abode
Pilgerchor

KOEN, W.
Com Nu Met Sang Van Soete Tonen

Winter Is Voorbij, De

KOENIG
Brahms, Johannes
Ich Fahr Dahin

KOENIG, F.
Es Scheinen Die Sternlein

Gade, Niels Wilhelm
Morgengesang

Grell, Eduard August
Erhaben, O Herr

Isaac, Heinrich
Innsbruck, Ich Muss Dich Lassen

Lechner, Leonhard
Gott B'hute Dich

Mayer, Otto
Zum Volkstrauertag

Palestrina, Giovanni Pierluigi da
Jede Schonheit, Geliebte
Selig Ist Es Zu Sterben

KOENIG, FRANZ
Brahms, Johannes
In Stiller Nacht

Ebel, Eduard
Leise Rieselt Der Schnee

Im Schonsten Wiesengrunde

Wahre Freundschaft

KOEPKE, P.
Brahms, Johannes
Wie Melodien Zieht Es

KOESTER, WERNER
Kleine Mariana

KOHL, FR.
Auf Tirolerischen Almen

KOHLER-GOTZE
Schubert, Franz (Peter)
Gondelfahrer, Der

KOHLHASE
Tchaikovsky, Piotr Ilyich
Na Son Grjadusci
Nocevala Tucka Zolotaja
Vecer

KOKALY, STEFAN
Thiel, Hans R.
Rheinwein, Ja Das Ist Mein Wein

KOKELAAR, K.
Offenbach, Jacques
Chor Der Studenten

KOLCSEY, FERENC
Bardos, Lajos
Batorsag Ad Erot

KOLSCH
Knab, Armin
Lowenzahn, Zunde Deine Lichtlein An

KOMPANEETZ
Orloff
Bright Shawl, The

KONOWITZ, BERT
Deutschendorf, Henry John (John
Denver)
Calypso

Diamond, Neil
America
Hello Again
Love On The Rocks
On The Robert E. Lee
Songs Of Life

KONZ
Lira Popular

KOPOSSOW
Donau Tont Nach Alter Weise

KORDA
Offenbach, Jacques
Barcarolle

Strauss, Johann, [Jr.]
Sangerlust-Polka

Weber, Carl Maria von
Wiegenlied

KORDA, V.
Deine Wangelein Sind Roselein Rot

Es Burebuebli

Golondrina, La

Haydn, [Franz] Joseph
Geheimnis
Lachet Nicht Madchen
Mutters Lied
Sinn Des Lebens
Unzufriedenen
Verganglichkeit

Kaiser, Otto
Mein Sorg

Maria Und Der Schiffmann

Mendelssohn, B.
Morgenlied
Wanderlied

Mozart, Wolfgang Amadeus
Begluckte Herz, Das
Fruhlingsanfang
Guter Vorsatz
Kinderspiel
Lebensreise
Tag Der Freude
Zufriedene, Der

Rathgeber, Valentin
Von Der Weise Zu Leben

Santa Lucia

Schonigh, H.
Firsch Auf, Ihr Musikanten

Schubert, Franz (Peter)
Bald Tonet Der Reigen
Heiter Strahlt Der Neue Morgen
Spinnerinnenchor
Wir Bringen Dir Die Kette Hier

KORDA, V. (cont'd.)

Schumann, Robert (Alexander)
Gartnerin, Die

Strauss, Johann, [Jr.]
Du Und Ich
Du Und Ich Aus Jakuba
Ewiges Lied
Intermezzo
Jagerball Aus Karneval In Rom
Musik Von Johann Strauss
Biedermeier- Intermezzo
Musikalische Liebeslektion
Prinz Karneval
Schone Welt
Spinnliedchen
Verliebte Madchen, Das
Wiener Busserl Marsch

Szene, Szene, Szene

Telemann, Georg Philipp
Tra-Ri-Ra-Rum

Tiritomba

Tiz Par Csokot

Vieni Sul Mar

Von Luzern Auf Weggis Zue

Wahre Freundschaft

Weisst Du Keinen Schatz

KORDA, VIKTOR
Annamirl

Funfundzwanzig Volkslieder Aus
Osterreich

Hammerschmiedselln, Die

Handwerksburschen, Die

Holzknechtbaum, Die

Im Lesachtal

Kehr Ich Abends Heim

Lavntal

Strauss, Johann, [Jr.]
An Der Schonen Blauen Donau

Strauss, Josef
Wiener Kinder

KORINGER, FRANZ
Babusch

Dunja

Jovo

Regen

Ziganka

KORLING, FELIX
Dans I Sommarkvall

Hej, Bjorkelov

Kan Man Tro!

Kom, Kamrat! Sangmarsch

Stolz, Robert
Kom, Kamrat! Sangarmarsch

Storstugans Marsch

KORN
Driessler, Johannes
Lilie Gleich, Der
Willkomm Und Abschied
Zwischen Erstehen Und Tod

KORNYEI, ELEK
Bardos, Lajos
Szekesfehervar

KORT, J.
Diepenbrock, Alphons
Wandrers Nachtlied

KORTEKANGAS, OLLI
Sakkijarven Polkka

KOSAKOFF, REUVEN
Hatikvah

KOSCHINSKY
Haussmann, Valentin
Tanz Mir Nicht Mit Meiner Jungfer
Kathen

Mozart, Wolfgang Amadeus
Venerabilis Barba Capucinorum

KRISTOFFERSEN, D.
Heggen, Bodvar
Bon

Sonstevold, Maj
Blaklokkeleiken

KRISTOFFERSEN, DAG
Bixio, Cesare Andrea
Torna Piccini Mia

Bull, Ole Bornemann
Saeterjentens Sondag

Grieg, Edvard Hagerup
Varen

Gruber, Ludwig
Min Mor Var Fodt I Valsens

Horton, George Vaughn
Mockin' Bird Hill

Popularserie Nr. 1

Popularserie Nr. 2

Popularserie Nr. 3

Popularserie Nr. 4

Popularserie Nr. 5

Saus, Anders
Alle Vakre Jenters Hambo

Sorte Oyne

KRONE
Morley, Thomas
Sing We And Chant It

Ravenscroft, Thomas
In The Merry Spring

Ronald, [Sir] Landon
Down In The Forest

Songs From Many Lands

Songs From The Four Corners

Songs To Sing With Descants

Spanish And Latin American Songs

Wagner, Richard
Festival Prelude

KRONE, B.
Christmas Star

Noel

O Music, Sweet Music

On A Winter's Night

KRONES
Descants For Christmas

From Descants To Trios

Inter-Americana

Our First Songs To Sing With Descants

Our Third Book Of Descants

Songs And Stories Of The American
Indians

Songs For Fun

Songs Of Norway And Denmark

Songs Of Sweden And Finland

Who'll Buy My Lavender

KROSS, SIEGFRIED
Brahms, Johannes
Dreizehn Volkslieder Fur Frauenchor

KRUMNACH
Three Kings

World Is Ours Today, The

KRUMNACH, WILHELM
Three Kings

KRUNNFUSZ
Christmas Is Coming Again

Sigman, Carl
Marshmallow, A

Twelve Days Of Christmas, The

KUBAT, K.
Auf Der Hochstattner Alm

KUBIK
Aguirre, Julian
Triste No. 4
Triste No. 5

Anonymous
Cuando, El

Beethoven, Ludwig van
Ehre Gott Aus Der Natur, Die

Boccherini, Luigi
Minue Celebre En La

Brahms, Johannes
Danza Hungara No. 5
Vals

Caba
Kollavina

Centeno
Fragata Sarmiento

Chopin, Frederic
Anhelo
Polonesa
Primavera

Couperin
Segadores, Los

Denza, Luigi
Funiculi-Funicula

Dvorak, Antonin
Largo

Foster, Stephen Collins
Swanee River

Gauchito
Ofrenda Gaucha

Gluck, Christoph Willibald, Ritter
von
En La Ribera

Gomez Carrillo, Manuel
Vida Mia
Yerba Buena

Grieg, Edvard Hagerup
Cancion De Solveig

He's Goin' Away

Liadov, Anatol Konstantinovich
Cajita De Musica

Liszt, Franz
Nocturno No. 3

McCord, William Patrick
Pregon Serrano

Mussorgsky, Modest Petrovich
Gopak

Oh, Dear! What Can The Matter Be?

Paganini, Niccolo
Caza, La

Pergolesi, Giovanni Battista
Tre Giorni Son Che Nina

Polly-Wolly-Doodle

Rodriguez, Augusto
Cancion Del Agua (Canaveral)
Noches Coloniales

Ronda En El Cielo

Rossini, Gioacchino
Danza, La

Sammartino, Luis
Caballito Pampa

Schubert, Franz (Peter)
Heidenroslein

Soon One Mornin' Death Comes Creepin'

Strauss, Johann, [Jr.]
Sangre Vienesa

Tee Roo

Veinte Y Cinco De Mayo

Volver A Sonar

Waldteufel, Emil
Patinadores, Los

KUBIK, G.
Little Bird, Little Bird

KUBIK, GAIL
Annie Laurie

As I Went A-Walking One Fine Summer's
Evening

KUBIK, GAIL (cont'd.)

Black Jack Davy

Creep Along, Moses

Foster, Stephen Collins
Jeanie With The Light Brown Hair

Hop Up, My Ladies

I Ride An Old Paint

John Henry

Johnny Stiles

Listen To The Mocking Bird

Little Bird, Little Bird

March Of The Men Of Harlech

Oh, My Liver And My Lungs

KUBIZEK, A.
Mundus Cantat, Heft 2

KUBIZEK, AUGUSTIN
A Schisserl Und A Reindl

All Mein Gedanken

Balm In Gilead

Bei Meiner Liebsten

Bin I Nit A Purschle

Bin I Nit A Purschle?

Bose Rauber, Der

Brennende Liebe

By An' By

Das War Der Zwerg Perkeo

Deep River

Des Teufels Ritt

Dreh Dich Um, Mein Kindchen

Es Liegt Ein Schloss In Osterreich

Go Down, Moses

Ich Denke Dein

Ich Hort Ein Sichelein

Im Schwarzen Walfisch

In Jedem Vollen Glase Wein

Juchhe, Tirolerbua

Juhe, Tirolerbua

Krambambuli

Kubizek, Augustin
Makkaroni

Madchen Und Bursche

Maimorgen

Mein Schatzchen

Mundus Cantat, Heft 1

Nach Suden Nun Sich Lenken

Nekutej

Ohne Freude, Ohne Sonne

Oj Korana

Sang Ist Verschollen, Der

Schafermadchen, Das

Sitzt A Klans Vogerl

Sometimes I Feel

Stan' Still, Jordan

Swing Low, Sweet Chariot

Tausend Goldne Sterne

Traurige Weise

Und Die Ferne Ruft

Ungluckliche Liebe

Verlassenes Madchen

Wanns Heumahn

KUBIZEK, AUGUSTIN (cont'd.)

Was Machst Du

Winter Ist Vergangen, Der

Wutend Walzt Sich

Zehn Satze Von Studentenliedern

KUBY; MYROW
Choral Arrangements

KUCHLER
Krauss, R.
Musikantenlied

KUHLENTHAL, FRED
Siebzig Volksliedsatze

KUHN, RUDOLF
Nach Haus

KUKUCK
Fidelbogen, Der

KUKUCK, FELICITAS
Dutch Folksongs

KULENKAMPFF
Girnatis, Walter
Holla, Jungs, Und Jacken Aus

KULLNES, AKE
Och Jungfrun Hon Gangar Pa Hogan Berg

KUN
Jessel
Parade Of The Wooden Soldiers

Lincke
Glow-Worm
Glowworm

Wilson
In The Little Red School House

KUNAT, K.
Auf Da Steirischen Grenz

KUNZ
Housman
White In The Moon

KUNZ, ALFRED
Frauenstrophe

In Der Fremde

Lied

Spruch

We'll Rant And We'll Roar

KUNZ, E.
Hassler, Hans Leo
Jungfrau, Dein Schon Gestalt

Jeep, Johann
Musica, Die Ganz Lieblich Kunst

KUNZ, JACK
Child Is Born

KUNZEL
Berlioz, Hector (Louis)
Chant Des Bretons

Liszt, Franz
Gaudeamus Igitur – Humoreske

KUPFERSCHMID
Althouse, Jay
Sail Away On A Song

KURIG, H.
Es Blies Ein Jager Wohl In Sein Horn

Lieben Bringt Gross Freud, Das

KURIG, HANS-HERMANN
Da Drauss', Da Steht Ein Haselbusch

Ich Bin Kuckuck Und Bleib Kuckuck

Kuckuck Als Liebesbote, Der

Sonne Scheint Nicht Mehr, Die

KURING, H.
Ade Zur Guten Nacht

KURTEN
Lissmann, Kurt
Aus Dem Hohen Mullerhaus
Katz, Die Lasst Das Mausen Nicht,
Die
Von Lippe Uber Die Heide

Sturmer, Bruno
Komm, Mein Herz

KURZBACH
Aturow
Partisanen Vom Amur

Eisler, Hanns
Einheitsfront, Die

Rote Fahne, Die

KUTZER, ERNST
Hore Mein Meister

Welch Ein Wunder

KUUSISTO, TANELI
Merikanto, Oskar
Laatokka

KUXHAVEN, D.
Brollops Mars

Lassus, Roland de (Orlandus)
Super Flumina Babylonie

Neefe, Christian Gottlob
Wie Sie So Sanft Ruhn

Stjenka Rasin

KUXHAVEN, DOOR D.
Kom Nu Met Sang

KUXHAVEN, J.
Vers 1 En 2

KVAM, ODDVAR S.
Min Onkel Hadde En Bondegard

Three Folk Songs

KVANDAL, JOHAN
Kjerulf, Halfdan
Lokkende Toner

KYSAR
Barbey, Bob
I Like It—Bein' Me!

KYSAR, MICHAEL
Anderson, Paula
Wherever You're Going

Payne, Warren
Questions

Strand
Wintersong

LA FONTAINE
Shalom Chaverim

LACHEUR, REX
O Canada

LADMIRAULT, P.
Charbonnier, Le

Poule Blanche, La

LAGERKVIST, KJELL
Inte Skall Du Falla En Tar

Taube, Evert
Nocturne

LAGGER, OSCAR
Bateliere, La

LALLEMENT, B.
Aussitot Que La Lumiere

Buchtger, Fritz
Es Ist Nur Einer Ewig

Chansons A Danser Et A Repondre

Chevalier Du Guet, Le

Cloques, Sounnez!

Douze Chansons A Danser De Bretagne

Filles, Chantez Le Mois De Mai

Gesegn Dich Laub

Ils Etaient Trois P'tits Freres En
France

J'Ai Traverse Neuf Landes

Meiland, Jacob
Tant Que Boirai

N'Allez Pas Au Bois

Pendant La Messe

Petite Suite Franco-Allemande

Vespres Du Falgoux, Les

Ville De Sarlat, La

Vive Henri IV

LALLEMENT, BERNARD
Avril Pres De Finir

Combien J'Ai Douce Souvenance

Coupo Santo

De Bon Matin Me Suis Leve

Filles De Marmande, Les

Guilaneu, Le

La-Bas, Dans Mon Jardin

Lullaby Of Itsuki

Melodie Cevenole

Ou Allez-Vous Fillette?

Passant Par Paris, Mon Cousin

Pauvre Laboureur, Le

Pierre De Grenoble

Tiau Plaisir d'Etre A Table

Touati, Raymond
Pauvre Madeleine

Voici L'Hiver Passe

LAMB, GORDON H.
Gilmore, Patrick S.
When Johnny Comes Marching Home

LAMBERT
Leisy, James Franklin
Child Knows, The

LAMBERT, JACK
Leisy, James Franklin
Songs From Alice

LAMBOTTE, L.
Aupres De Ma Blonde

LAMERS, H.
Air De Table

Amusons Toujours Nos Desirs

Heureux Lindor, L'

Jeune Iris, Vous Allez Apprendre

Langage Des Soupirs, Le

Pastorale

Reciproque, Le

Rossignol, Le

Sure De Ta Foi

Tu Ne Dois Pas, Jeune Lisette

Venez, Amours

Vous Regnez Sur Mon Coeur

LAMMERS, H.
Anonymous
Pavane

Aux-Cousteaux, Artus (Arthur)
Estime Qui Voudra La Mort
Et Cette Ambition
Vie Est Une Table, La

Beaujoyeulx, Baltasar de
Ballet Comique De La Reine, Le

Collection De Musique Ancienne,
Premiere Recueil

Collection De Musique Ancienne,
Deuxieme Recueil

Collection De Musique Ancienne,
Troisieme Recueil

Des Prez, Josquin
Deploration De Jehan Ockeghem, La

Janequin, Clement
Cris De Paris, Les
Guerre Ou La Bataille De Marignan,
La
Las, Povre Coeur

Lassus, Roland de (Orlandus)
Beau Le Cristal
Fuyons Tous D'Amour Le Jeu
Puce J'Ay Dedans L'Oreille, Une

Monte, Philippe de
Comme La Tourterelle
Premiere Jour Du Mois De May, Le

LAMMLE
Krietsch, Georg
Von Dem Tau Des Himmels

LAMONT
Loewe, Frederick
Almost Like Being In Love

Morley, Thomas
Now Is The Month Of Maying

LAMPE, C.I.F.
Catch Club, Or Merry Companions

LANCIEN, NOEL
Lancien, Noel
Soum, Soum

LAND
Christmas Party

Sing Noel

LAND, E.
Horn, Charles Edward
Cherry Ripe

LANDECK
Git On Board

LANDON, H.C.R.
Haydn, [Franz] Joseph
Qual Dubbio Omai

LANE
Byram-Wigfield, Rebekah
Christmas Bell Song

LANE, PHILIP
Lady Mary

LANG
Carnival Suite

Schulz, Johann Abraham Peter
Abendlied

LANG, C. S.
De Battle Ob Jericho

LANG, H.
Abend Ist Da, Der

Abscheid

Ach Schatz, Jetz Muss Ich Wandern

Bauerlein, Das

Bin Ein Lust'ger Jagersknecht

Da Der Vogel Auf'm Baum Sass

Der Hat Vergeben

Dort Unten In Dem Tale

Es Kam Ein Jung Herr

Es Wohnte Eine Mullerin

Frohliche Quodlibets

In Der Morgenfruhe

In Meines Vaters Garten

Ist Etwas So Machtig

Jager, Der

Kuckuck Auf Dem Nussbaum Sass, Der

O Wie So Schon Und Gut

Regiment Sein Straussen Zieht

Seid Nun Lustig Und Frohlich

Tiroler Wollte Jagen, Ein

Und Wir Gingen Mit Lust Und Freude

Viel Freuden Mit Sich Bringet

Vivat Dem Brautigam

Was Fang Ich Denn An

Wer Jagen Will

LANG, HANS
Bindergesell, Der

Butzemann, Der

Drei Tanzlieder

Es Blies Ein Jager Wohl In Sein Horn

Frohlich Handwerk

Gebhard, Hans
Kirmes

Glucksring, Der

LANG, HANS (cont'd.)
Hab Mein Wage Vollgelade

Horch, Was Kommt Von Draussen Rein

Ich Ging Durch Einen Grasgrunen Wald

Ich Hab Die Nacht Getraumet

Inmitten Der Nacht

Je Hoher Der Kirchturm

Kleine Geige, Eine

Kommet, Ihr Hirten

Kuckuck Auf Dem Zaune Sass, Der

Lyra, Justus Wilhelm
Bange Nacht Ist Nun Herum, Die

Mannlein Steht Im Walde, Ein

Muss I Denn

Nachtigall, Ich Hor Dich Singen

Nachtigall, Ich Hor Dich Singen
[Chorus]

O Laufet, Ihr Hirten

Rathgeber, Valentin
Von Der Edlen Musik "Der Hat
Vergeben"

Reichardt, Johann Friedrich
Wach Auf, Meins Herzens Schone

Schneider-Ballade

Schneiders Hochzeit

Schott's Chorbuch Band II

Schott's Chorbuch Band III

Silcher, Friedrich
Nichts Kann Auf Erden

Sitzt A Schons Vogerl

Sonne Scheint Nicht Mehr, Die

Sterben Ist Ein Schwere Buss

Still, Weil's Kindlein Schlafen Will

Tod Und Die Konigstochter, Der

Vogelein Im Tannenwald

Vogelhochzeit

Vogelkonzert

Weizen Bluht, Der

Wer Geht Mit?

Widele, Wedele

Zollner, Karl Friedrich
Wandern Ist Des Mullers Lust, Das

Zschieche, Alf
Wenn Die Bunten Fahnen Wehen

Zuccalmaglio, Anton Wilhelm Florentin
von
Blumelein, Sie Schlafen, Die

Zwei Hasen

LANGER, HANS-KLAUS
Ist's Nicht Wirklich So?

Kristalle, Die Feinen

My Bonnie

Seid Nicht Bose

Suliko

LANGLEY, JAMES W.
Tailor And The Mouse, The

LANGOSCH, K.
Lissmann, Kurt
Drei Vagantenlieder

LANGREE, A.
Akepsimas, Jo
Vassilis, L'Enfant Grec

Brassens, Georges
Mauvaise Reputation, La
Sabots D'Helene, Les

Chez Madame Duvivier

Gars De Senneville, Les

LANGREE, A. (cont'd.)
Mon Cher Amant

Nuit Passee, La

Ou Est Mon Galant

Pauvre Martin

Quand Le Bon Homm'

LANGREE, ALAIN
Beart, Guy
Couleurs Du Temps, Les

Borel-Clerc, Charles
Ah! Le Petit Vin Blanc

Dans La Plaine

Fau, Raymond
Dans Mon Vieux Coucou

Hereu Riera, L'

Humenry, Jean
Ballade Des Rues Qui Ont Change De
Nom, La

J'entends, Ma Lisette

Renard, A.
Temps Des Cerises, Le

Tilloliers, Les

Vian, Boris
Prisonnier, Le

LANGSCHIED
Sturmer, Bruno
Beim Regen In Der Kleinen Stadt
Dass Zweie Eins Geworden
Glaube, O Herz

LANGSTROTH, I.
Melodies Of The Middle Ages

LANTZ
Dyer, D.
Santa's Sleigh

LAPIN
Candy Man, The

Never Been To Spain

LAPLANTE, PIERRE
Three Dishes And Six Questions

LAPORTE, BERNARD
Lincolnshire Poacher, The

LARGE
Elliot
Bill Bailey's Comin' Home

I've Been Working On The Railroad

My Darling Clementine

Sarlow
Holiday Polka, The

Woodbury
Sound On!

LARMANJAT, J.
Clerc, Le

Doute, Le

Fin De Journee

Pardon, Le

Promenade, La

Soldat, Le

LARSSON, RUNE
Visa Vill Jag Sjunga, En

LASALA
Obras Corales A Dos Voces Iguales

Obras Corales A Tres Voces Iguales

Obras Corales A Una Voz

LASSEN
Lowe, Mundell
It's Not Where You've Been

LAUB, THOMAS
Dronning Dagmar

Jomfru I Hindeham

Jomfru I Ormeham

Lave Og Jon

Liden Kirsten

LAUB, THOMAS (cont'd.)

  Marsk Stigs Dotre

  Salmer Og Folkeviser

  Valravnen. Stalt Vesselil

LAUDER; CLEMENTS
  Dillon, Fannie Charles
    End Of The Road, The

LAUGHTON, WALLACE
  Ride On Moses

LAUREL, J.
  Abeille, L'

  Adieu, Cher Petit Village

  Venez Petits Enfants

LAVAGNE, E.
  Beethoven, Ludwig van
    Ehre Gott Aus Der Natur, Die

LAVATER
  Gentle Maiden, The

  Mendelssohn-Bartholdy, Felix
    Fruhlingslied

  Strauss, Johann, [Jr.]
    Tales From The Vienna Woods

LAVATER, H.
  D'Meitschi Vum Emmetal

  Minnelied

  Morley, Thomas
    Tanzlied

LAVATER, LOUIS
  Brahms, Johannes
    Red Rose And Dead Rose

  Gentle Maiden

  Invitation To The Dance

  Lully, Jean-Baptiste (Lulli)
    Bois Epais

  Strauss, Johann, [Jr.]
    An Der Schonen Blauen Donau
    Tales From The Vienna Woods

LAVERE; ANSON
  Jason
    Chapel In The Valley

LAVI, HAVA
  Choral Works

LAVOGLER, V.
  Andreas Hofers Abschied Vom Leben

LAWSON, GORDON
  L'il Liza Jane

LAWSON, MALCOLM
  Flowers Of The Forest, The

LAWTON, F.V.
  Rosas, Juventino
    Over The Waves

LAZARENO, MANUEL
  Three Spanish Folk Tunes

LAZZAROTTI, J.
  Nelli Monti Di Cuscioni

LE FLEMING
  O Waly, Waly

LE FLEMING, CHRISTOPHER
  Spring Has Now Unwrapped The Flowers

LEAMAN
  All Kinds Of People

  By The Time I Get To Phoenix

  Caste Your Fate To The Wind

  Chim Chim Cher-Ee

  Cycles

  Didn't We

  Flamingo

  Gentle On My Mind

  He Ain't Heavy, He's My Brother

  Hello, Goodbye

  Hi-De-Ho

  Holly Holy

  I Never Promised You A Rose Garden

LEAMAN (cont'd.)

  Isn't It A Pity

  It Was A Very Good Year

  King Of The Road

  Little Green Apples

  Loesser
    My Darling, My Darling

  Love Story

  Make The World Go Away

  Mr. Touchdown U.S.A.

  Pops Of The 70's-Group 5

  Rubber Duckie

  Silver Bird

  Songs From "Mary Poppins"

  Spoonful Of Sugar, A

  Sweetheart Of Sigma Chi

  They Long To Be Close To You

  This Is My Country

  Tom Dooley

  Twelve Days Of Christmas

  Vaya Con Dios

  Whatever Will Be, Will Be

LEAMANN
  Taste Of Honey, A

LEBOWSKY
  Cannon
    Bill Bailey, Won't You Please Come
    Home?

  Cugat
    My Shawl
    Ruisenor, El

  Espinosa
    Altenitas, Las

  Grenet, Eliseo
    Mama Inez

  Herzog
    God Bless The Child

  Lecuona, Ernesto
    Andalucia
    Comparsa, La
    Dame De Tus Rosas

  Ortolani
    More

  Rodgers, Richard
    Sentimental Me

  Schultze
    Lilli Marlene

LECHTHALER, J.
  Ich Sinne Hin Und Her

  Sennin, Die

LEDGER, PHILIP
  Oxford Book Of English Madrigals, The

LEE
  Raposo, Joseph G.
    Sing

LEE, E. MARKHAM
  Gentle Maiden, The

  Handel, George Frideric
    Minuet

  Old King Cole

  Purcell, Henry
    Sound The Trumpet

  Spring And Summer

  Strauss, Johann, [Jr.]
    An Der Schonen Blauen Donau
    Fledermaus, Die: Waltz
    Spring's Refrain

LEE, F. MARKHAM
  Wagner, Richard
    O Star Of Eve

LEEDS; RUSSELL; ROUBANIS
  Wise
    Misirlou

LEEDS; RUSSELL; ROUBANIS; HABASH
  Wise
    Misirlou

LEES, HEATH
  Iona Boat Song

LEEUWEN, S.
  Zeller, Carl
    Vogelhandler, Die: Selections

LEFEBVRE
  Fourteen Folk Tunes For Young Men

  Kernochan
    As I Ride By

  Straus
    Here Comes The Band

LEFEBVRE, C.
  Fourteen Folk Tunes For Young Men

  Greensleeves

  Here We Come A-Wassailing

  Holly And The Ivy

LEGUY, JACQUES
  Binchois, Gilles (de Binche)
    Se Je Souspire, Plains Et Pleure

  Dufay, Guillaume
    Belle Se Siet, La
    Se La Face Est Pale

  Ockeghem, Johannes
    Ma Bouche Rit

LEGUY, SYLVETTE
  Machaut, Guillaume de
    Ballades
    Lais
    Motets
    Remede De Fortune, Le
    Rondeaux
    Virelais

LEHNER
  Schandl, Ernst
    Wachau

  Strauss, Johann, [Jr.]
    Bauern-Polka

  Strauss, Josef
    Spharenklange

LEHNER, J.
  Mozart, Wolfgang Amadeus
    Standchen

LEHNER, L.
  Beethoven, Ludwig van
    Opferlied

  Brahms, Johannes
    Wiegenlied

  Bruckner, Anton
    Wenn Ich Den Wanderer Frage

  Burger-Seeber, N.
    O Hoamatle

  Flies, J. Bernhard
    Wiegenlied

  Fruhlingsliebe

  Haydn, [Franz] Joseph
    Zur Feierstunde

  Jurgens, A.
    Drauss Ist Alles So Prachtig

  Kothe, Wilhelm
    Waldkonzert

  Kreipl, Joseph
    S'Mailufterl

  Kuhlau, Friedrich
    Wanderers Nachtlied

  Lehar, Franz
    Es Lebt' Eine Vilja, Ein
     Waldmagdelein
    Jeg Velger Wien

  Lyra, Justus Wilhelm
    Wanderschaft

  Mozart, Wolfgang Amadeus
    Standchen

  Neuendorff, A.
    Rattenfanger, Der

LEHNER, L. (cont'd.)

Rieder, C.
  Wann I Amol Stirb

Schnopfhagen, H.
  Hoamatland

Schubert, Franz (Peter)
  Allmacht
  Wiegenlied

Schumann, Robert (Alexander)
  Fruhlingsgruss

Seydler, L.K.
  Hoch Vom Dachstein An

Skopicek, M.
  Wie Konnt' Ich Dein Vergessen

Strauss, Johann, [Sr.]
  Kathinka Polka

Strauss, Johann, [Jr.]
  An Der Schonen Blauen Donau
  Auf Der Jagd
  Demolirer Pola Francaise
  Eljen A Magyar
  G'schichten Aus Dem Wienerwald
  Im Krapfenwaldl
  Im Krapfenwald'l
  Kunstlerleben
  Leichtes Blut
  Liebeslieder
  Morgenblatter
  Pester Csardas
  Seid Umschlungen Millionen
  Tritsch Tratsch
  Unter Donner Und Blitz
  Veilchen Polka
  Wiener Bonbons
  Wo Die Citronen Bluhn

Strauss, Josef
  Auf Ferienreisen
  Buchstaben
  Buchstaben Polka Francaise
  Dorfschwalben Aus Osterreich
  Feuerfest
  Mein Lebenslauf Ist Lieb Und Lust
  Moulinet
  Plappermaulchen
  Plappermaulchen Polka
  Wiener Kinder Singen Gern

Tief Im Bohmerwald

Untreue

Vancura, A.
  Blumenstrauss Aus Wien, Ein
  Frohliches Wandern

Weisst Du Wievielle Sterne Stehen

Woyna, F. von
  Und Der Hans Schleicht Umher

Ziehrer, Carl Michael
  Endlich Allein
  Faschingskinder
  Urwiener-Polka
  Weaner Mad'ln

LEHNER, LEO
  A Waldbua Bin I

A Weni Kurz, A Weni Lang

Abendglocke, Die

Ade Zur Guten Nacht

Alleweil Kann Mer Net Lustig Sein

Almfahren

Als Wir Jungst In Regensburg Waren

Andulka Me Dite

Auf Der Fladnitzer Alma

Auf Einem Buschele Haberstroh

Auf Und An

Aupres De Ma Blonde

Awa Z' Sittendorf

Bald Gras Ich Am Neckar

Bayrischen Maidle, Die

Braun Meidelein

Bruchner, F.
  Wenn Ich Der Wandrer Frage

Bursch Und Madel Hin Zum Tanze Gehn

Coeur De Ma'mie, Le

Crambambuli

LEHNER, LEO (cont'd.)

Csillag Elag

D' Tanzmusi

Da Lahnsadler Holzknecht

Deine Wangelein Sind Roselirot

Dirndle Geh Zum Zaun

Drauss Ist Allein So Prachtig

Drei Lilien

Drunt Im Lichtental

Drunten Im Unterland

Es Burebuebli

Es Fiel Ein Reif In Der
  Fruhlingsnacht

Es Hat Sich Halt Eroffnet Das
  Himmlische Tor

Es Liegt Ein Schloss In Osterreich

Es Sass Ein Klein Wild Vogelein

Es Waren Zwei Konigskinder

Es Wollt Ein Jager Wohl Jagen

Fein Sein, Bei 'Nander Bleib'n

Foster, Stephen Collins
  Old Folks At Home

Freier Mut

Gedanken Sind Frei, Die

Gestern Auf Die Nacht

Gluck, Fr.
  Dort Unten In Der Muhle
  In Einem Kuhlen Grunde

Greane Fensterl

Gruass Di God Is A Scheans Wort

Gute Nacht, Mein Allerliebster Schatz

Haydn, [Franz] Joseph
  Kommt Der Lenz Im Winter Schon

Heidschi Bumbeidschi

Heimliche Liebe

Heut Gien Mar Auf Die Alma

Hopsa! Schwabenlied

Horch, Was Kommt Von Draussen 'Rein?

Ihren Schafer Zu Erwarten

Im Fruhjahr Bei Der Niada

Im Fruhjahr, Wann's Grean Wird

Im Wald Und Auf Der Heide

In Den Fruhling, In Den Sommer

In Die Berg Bin I Gern

Ja Die Holzknechtbaum

Juhe, Tirolerbua

Knebelsberger, L.
  Andreas Hofer

Komzak, Karl
  Bad'ner Madln

Kothe, Wilhelm
  Waldkonzert

Kreipl, Joseph
  'S' Mailufterl

Laub Fallt Von Den Baumen, Das

Leben Auf Der Alm, Das

Leben Bringt Grosse Freud', Das

Leineweber

Lied Vom Spaten Abend, Das

Lippitzbach

Lore Am Tore

Madle Ruck Ruck

Mai Ist Gekommen, Der

LEHNER, LEO (cont'd.)

Mozart, Wolfgang Amadeus
  Sehnsucht Nach Die Fruhling

Muss I Denn Zum Stadtle 'Naus

O, Den I Hatt' So Gern

O Dirndle Tief Drunt Im Tal

O Du Schone, Susse Nachtigall

Pacius, Fredrik
  Soumis Sang

Pfiat Di Gott, Mein Liabs Tiabele

Rieder, C.
  Wann I Amal Stirb

Rote Rosen

'S Herzl

'S Peterbrundl

Schnadahupfeln Vom Grundlsee

Schon Ist Die Jugend

Schonste Auf Der Welt Ist Mein
  Tirolerland, Das

Schubert, Franz (Peter)
  Lindenbaum, Der
  Wiegenlied

Schumann, Robert (Alexander)
  Fruhlingsgruss

Schwefleholze

Seydler, L.K.
  Hoch Vom Dachstein An

Silcher
  Lebewohl

Silcher, Friedrich
  Annchen Von Tharau
  Loreley

Spinn! Spinn!

Strauss, Johann, [Sr.]
  Kathinka Polka
  Sperl Polka

Strauss, Johann, [Jr.]
  An Der Schonen Blauen Donau
  Annen Polka
  Auf Der Jagd
  Demolirer-Polka
  Eljen A Magyar
  Geschichten Aus Dem Wienerwald
  Im Krapfenwaldl
  Kunstlerleben
  Liebeslieder
  Morgenblatter
  Perpetuum Mobile
  Pester Csardas
  Pizzicato Polka
  Rosen Aus Dem Suden
  Sangerlust Polka
  Seid Umschlungen, Millionen
  Seufzer Polka
  Tritsch-Tratsch-Polka
  Unter Donner Und Blitz
  Veilchen Polka
  Vergnugungszug
  Wien-Strauss
  Wiener Bonbons
  Wo Die Citronen Bluhn

Strauss, Josef
  Auf Ferienreisen
  Buchstaben-Polka
  Dorfschwalben Aus Osterreich
  Feuerfest
  Mein Lebenslauf Ist Lieb Und Lust
  Moulinet
  Plappermaulchen

Ubers Bacherl Bin I G' Sprungen

Und I Hab Dir In D'Augerln G'schaut

Unter Der Linden

Var En Lordag Asten, Det

Vierzeiler Aus Dem Burgenland (Wia
  Hocha Da Turm)

Vogelein Im Tannenwald

Von Meinem Bergli Muss I Scheiden

Wachauer Schifferlied

Wachtelschlag, Der

Wahre Freundschaft

Waldvogelein

LEROLLE
  Janequin, Clement
    Ou Mettra L'On Ung Baizer Favorable

LESBINES
  Yerakina

LESLIE, C.E.
  Zollner, Karl Friedrich
    Bill Of Fare, The

LESLIE, H.
  Hook, James
    Lass Of Richmond Hill, The

  Weelkes, Thomas
    Nightingale, The

LESSKY, FR.
  Alter Wiener-Bitz, Ein

  Das Kriag'n Ma Nimmermehr

  Na, Da Hab'n Ma's G'fangt

  'S Waschermadl Von Lichtenthal

  Wann I Anmal Stirb

  Weaner Geht Net Unter, Der

LESTER
  Stravinsky, Igor
    Dance Of The Princesses

LESTER, WILLIAM
  Cossack Lullaby

  Last Rose Of Summer, The

  Londonderry Air

  Spinning Song

LESUR, DANIEL
  Ah! Dis-Moi Donc Bergere

  Chanson De Mariage

  Deux Chansons De Bord

LETBRIDGE, H.O.; BRUMBY
  Andy's Gone With Cattle

LETHBRIDGE
  Bach
    Open My Heart

  Delibes, Leo
    Barcarolle

  Mahler
    Cuckoo, The Nightingale, And The
      Donkey

LETHBRIDGE, H.O.; LOAM, ARTHUR S.
  Jabbin Jabbin

  Maranoa Lullaby

LETHBRIDGE; LOAM, ARTHUR S.
  Two Aboriginal Songs

LEU, FRANZ
  Bruch, Max
    Carmosenella

LEUPOLD, U.S.
  Mozart, Wolfgang Amadeus
    In The Starlight
    Sing Care Away

LEVANON, A.
  Zur Michelo Akhalnu

LEWENTHAL, RAYMOND
  Alkan, Charles-Henri Valentin
    Marcia Funebre Sulla Morte D'un
      Pappagallo

LEWIN, OLIVE
  Alle, Alle, Alle

LEWIS
  Anonymous
    Skinnamarink

  Beachem
    Sweet Mama Tree-Top Tall

  Brand
    Something To Sing About

  Charlottetown Is Burning Down

  Freedom Land

  Hanukkah Holiday Today!

  If You Will Marry Me

  Johnny-Go-Round

  McAlister
    Kids Are People Too!

LEWIS (cont'd.)
  Mama Don't 'Low No Music Played In
    Here

  Miz Santa Claus

  Nelson
    Believe
    Good Morning Life

  Olman
    Down By The O-HI-O

  Sing A Song Of Singing

  Smith, Chris
    Ballin' The Jack

  This Little Light Of Mine

  Tripp
    I've Got A Date With Santa

  Tripp, Paul
    Why Can't Every Day Be Christmas

  Tum Balalaika

  Upidee

  We Shall Not Be Moved

LEWIS, ADEN
  Bart, Lionel
    Food Glorious Food
    I'd Do Anything

  Bricusse, Leslie
    Beautiful Land, The

  Wilder, Alec
    Cast Your Bread Upon The Waters

LEWIS; BARTLES
  Bach, Johann Sebastian
    Ricercar A 6

  Purcell, Henry
    When I Am Laid In Earth

LEWIS; FORTUNE; GOLDBROUGH
  Purcell, Henry
    O, I'm Sick Of Life

LEWIS; FORTUNE; GOLDSBROUGH
  Purcell, Henry
    When On My Sick Bed I Languish

LEWIS, JOHN
  Bach, Johann Sebastian
    Canonic Fugue XII

  Purcell, Henry
    When I Am Laid In Earth

LEWIS, L.
  Bullard, Frederick Field
    Winter Song

LEWIS; PLATT
  Christmas Party

  Country Christmas Time

  Harrington, Karl Pomeroy
    There's A Song In The Air

  Hose
    Christmas Party
    Reuben And Rachael At Christmas
      Time

  Palmer
    Let's Dance

  This Land Is Your Land

LEWIS, W.
  Verdi, Giuseppe
    Hail To Our Native Land

LEYDEN
  Bock, Jerry
    Fiddler On The Roof: Choral
      Selections
    If I Were A Rich Man
    Matchmaker, Matchmaker
    Sabbath Prayer
    Sunrise, Sunset

  Porter, Cole
    Anything Goes
    Don't Fence Me In
    Friendship

  Schwartz, Stephen Lawrence
    Beautiful City
    Day By Day
    Godspell: Choral Selections
    Prepare Ye The Way Of The Lord

  Simon
    Harmony

  What A Wonderful World

LEYDEN (cont'd.)
  Willson
    Freedom Song, The

LEYDEN, NORMAN
  Alphabet Song, The

  Cabaret

  Cabaret Medley

  Company Medley

  Dearie

  Far Away Places

  Fiorello Melody

  Happy Time, The

  One Paddle, Two Paddle

  Thank You Song, The

  Til Tomorrow

  Wonderful World Of Children, The

L'HOSTE-PAIR, H.
  Temps Passe, Le

LIANI
  Kodaly, Zoltan
    Coccinella

LIANI, DAVIDE
  Kodaly, Zoltan
    Canti Per Bambini, 50

LICHT
  Deck The Hall

LIDBERG, JORGEN
  Rosenberg, Gunnar
    Fulabergsvisan

LIDDELL, CLAIRE
  Ae Fond Kiss

  Fine Flowers In The Valley

  I'll Ay Ca' In By Yon Toon

  Where Are The Joys?

  Ye Banks And Braes

LIDEN, KARL
  Duben, Anders von
    Karolinermarsch

  Karolinermarsch

LIEBARD, L.
  Eis Freit Ein Wilder Wasserman

  Moleirinha

  Monts Retentissent, Les

  Village Detruit, Le

LIEBE, K.M.
  Ach Elslein, Liebes Elselein

  Auf, Ihr Jagersleut Erwacht

  Es Blies Ein Jager Wohl In Sein Horn

  Lasst Uns All Nach Hause Gehen

  Mir Ist Ein Feins Brauns Maidelein

  O Mein Gott, Ich Armes Weiblein

LIEBE, KURT MARIA
  Kluge Mannlein, Das

LIEBE, L.
  Mendelssohn-Bartholdy, Felix
    On Music's Wing

LIEBERT, BILLY; SVARDA, BILL
  Pledge Of Allegiance, The

LIEBLEITNER
  A Waldbua Bin I

LIEBLEITNER, K.
  Altdeutsches Weinachtslied

  Auf D'r Karntnarischn Alm

  Auf Nimmer-Nimmer Wiedersehn

  Awer, Miazal, Ha Ha!

  Es Jagt Ka Hund

  Hast Mir Ja G'sagg

  Hat's Laterl Anglant

  Hinta Mein Vodan Sein' Stadl

LOFFLER, GERHARD (cont'd.)

War Immer So, 'S

LOJESKI, ED
At The Hop

Book Of Love, The

Careless Whisper

Carmichael, Hoagy
Skylark

Elvis: Pure Gold

Gershwin, George
Porgy And Bess (Medley)

Guthrie, Woody (Woodrow Wilson)
This Land Is Your Land

I Love Christmas

Kasha, Al
Candle On The Water

Ma (He's Makin' Eyes At Me)

Rudolph The Red-Nosed Reindeer

Telephone Hour, The

Wake Me Up Before You Go-Go

We Go Together

LOKTEV
Heiberg
Miller, The Boy And The Donkey, The

LOMAN; CRAIG
Kaye
Christmas Alphabet

LONDON, EDWIN
Enstabile, Bjorne
Christmas Music

LONGFELLOW; SIMEONE
Toti
Looks Like Spring Is Here

LOOSER, E.
Viele Volks- Und Kinderlieder

LOPEZ-CHAVARRI ANDUJAR, E.
Marco, E. Lopez-Chavarri
Colleccio De Cancons Folkloriques
Valencianes

LORRIMER
Yalanis
Chrismas Calypso

LORTZ
Foltz
Remember November

LOSCHER, SETPHAN
Blumerl

Hirtamandl

Kuckucks Polka, Die

Marschier

Rheinlandler

Schottischer

Summahansl, Der

Waldjager, Der

Warschauer, Der

Zweifacher

LOSCHER, STEPHAN
Bayrisch Polka, Die

Deutsche, Der

Steiregger, Der

LOTH, B.
Bel Astre Que J'adore

D'ou Viens-Tu, Bergere?

Fileuse

LOTT, W; KLINK, W.
Deutsche Chormusik Band I

LOTT, WALTER
Schubert, Franz (Peter)
Lindenbam, Der

LOTTI, ANTONIO
Shepherds And Maidens

LOVELACE, AUSTIN
Hospitality Carol

LOVMAND, FRODE
Joshua Fit The Battle Of Jericho

LOWA
Nowikow
Meine Heimat

LOWDEN, JEFF
Fox, Charles
I Got A Name

LOWDEN, R.J.
Handy Man

Kander, John
There Goes The Ball Game

LOWE
Lowe, Mundell
I'm Startin' A New Day
This Little Lite O' Mine

LOWE, HELENCLAIR
Choristers' Round Book, The

LOWE, J.
Gilmore, P.
When Johnny Comes Marching Home

Rachmaninoff, Sergey Vassilievich
Vocalise

LOWENS
French, Jacob
Dormant

LUBIN
Grieg, Edvard Hagerup
Verschwiegene Nachtigall, Die

Mendelssohn-Bartholdy, Felix
O Wert Thou In The Cauld Blast

LUBIN, E.
Fisherman, The

Hey 'Twas In The May

John Henry

LUBOFF
A-Roving

All Through The Night

Alouette

Andre, Fabian
Dream A Little Dream Of Me

Ash Grove, The

Beyond The Mountains

Black Is The Color

Brahms, Johannes
Vergebliches Standchen

Canto De Granada

Carmen Carmela

Click Go The Shears

Colorado Trail

Debussy, Claude
Beau Soir

Deer Chase, The

Doney Gal

Drifting And Dreaming

Emmett, Daniel Decatur
Dixie

Go To Sleepy

Goodbye, Fare You Well

Grieg, Edvard Hagerup
Schwan, Ein

Kemo Kimo

Kum Bachur Atzel

Lavender's Blue

Lift A Glass To Friendship

Liszt, Franz
Liebestraum

Lonely Birch Tree, The

Lowlands

My Shining Hour

LUBOFF (cont'd.)

Night Herding Song

Oh My Love

Old Chisholm Trail, The

Pavanne

Poor Lonesome Cowboy

Popp, W.
Love Is Blue

Riders In The Sky

Sakura

Salangadou

Schubert, Franz (Peter)
Du Bist Die Ruh

Sentimental Journey

Simons
Peanut Vendor

Skip To My Lou

Slumber Time

Streets Of Larado

Sweetheart Of Sigma Chi

Tenderly

Valencianita

Vance
Catch A Falling Star

Vigolin

When Your Hair Has Turned To Silver

Whittaker, Howard
New World In The Morning

Whoopee Ti Yi Yo

Will Ye Marry Me

Wolf, Hugo
To An Ancient Picture

LUBOFF, N.
Luboff, Peter
Utan Mal

LUBOFF, N.; CHARLES, M.
Luboff, Peter
Carousel

LUBOFF, NORMAN
Luboff, Peter
Utan Mal

When The Saints Go Marching In

Whoopee Ti Yi Yo

LUBRICH, FRITZ; HEIDUCZEK, ALOIS
Lieder Des Ostens

LUCAS
Brahe, May H.
I Passed By Your Window

Bright Mornin' Stars

LUCAS, CLARENCE
Aiken Drum

Bonnie Saint Johnston

Jolly Miller

LUCAS, JAN
Ik Weet Een Vrouwken Amoureus

Neem Mijn Leven, Laat Het Heer

Vrolijk, Herders

LUCE
Rossi, Salomone
Two Madrigals

LUCHTMAN, DICK
Costantakos, Chris Anastasios
Something To Sing About

LUCIANI, SEBASTIANO ARTURO
Antiquis, Giovanni D'
Villanelle Alla Napolitana

LUDES, ROCKY
Tyler, Keats
Christmas Present

MACKINLAY, K. STERLING
All Round My Hat

MACLEAN
Friml, Rudolf
Rose Marie (Choral Selections)

Herbert, Victor
Naughty Marietta

Romberg, Sigmund
Desert Song, The (Choral Selections)
Student Prince, The (Choral Selections)

Tate, Phyllis
Somewhere A Voice Is Calling

Tribute To Romberg, A

MACMAHON
Queen's March

MACMAHON, D.
Hook, James
Mary Of Allendale

MACMAHON, DESMOND
Bill Bones' Hornpipe

Farewell

John Peel

Lorraine

Lorraine

Pancakes

Sentinel Knight, The

MACMILLAN, ERNEST
America

MACMILLAN, SIR ERNEST
Blanche Comme La Neige

MACNUTT, WALTER
O Dear What Can The Matter Be

Streets Of Laredo

MACPHERSON
Wiegenlied

MADDEN
Seymour
Anthem Of Heritage

MADER, R.
Thurgau, Der

MADSEN, ERIK
Alle Mann Hadde Fota

MAERTENS
Telemann, Georg Philipp
Einsamkeit, Die
Friede, Sei Willkommen
Holder Segensreicher Friede
Holdsel'ge Stunden
Schlagt Die Trommel, Blast Trompeten
Sommerlust

MAERTENS, WILLI
Telemann, Georg Philipp
Friede, Sei Willkommen

MAESSEN, ANTOON
Six Old Dutch Folksongs

MAGNISON, THOR
Werner, Heinrich
Vildros

MAIER, MAX
Drei Altdeutsche Liebeslieder

Fisch Im Wasser Wohnen, Die

Lieblich Gesellet

Von Edler Art

MAILLARD-VERGER, P.
An Ader

Farandole Dauphinoise, La

Fille Du Laboureux, La

Nous Etions Trois Jeunes Filles

MAINERO; GUETTLER
Hassler, Hans Leo
Hor Va Canzona Mia

MAITLAND, J.A. FULLER
My Johnny Was A Shoemaker

MAITLAND, J.A. FULLER; BROADWOOD, LUCY E.

As I Sat On A Sunny Bank

Barkshire Tragedy, The

Chesire Man, The

Derby Ram, The

English County Songs

Farmer's Boy, The

Fly Is On The Turmut, The

Golden Vanity, The

Green Broom

Green Gravel

I'll Tell You Of A Fellow

King Arthur

Little Sir William

May-Day Carol

My Johnny Was A Shoemaker

Nottinghamshire Poacher, The

Oliver Cromwell

Peace Egging Songs

Robin-A-Thrush

Seeds Of Love, The

Souling Song, The

Sweet Nightingale, The

There Was A Lady In The West

There Was A Pig Went Out To Dig

Three Dukes, The

Tripping Up The Green Grass

Twankydillo

Wassail Bough, The

Water Of Tyne, The

MALATESTA, G.
Su In Montagna

MALHERBE, CHARLES; WEINGARTNER, FELIX
Berlioz, Hector (Louis)
Hector Berlioz Works

MALIN
Arcadelt, Jacob
Alma Mia Donna E Bella, L'
Ciel Che Rado Virtu Tanta Mostra, Il
Voi Ve N'Andat' Al Cielo

Bell'Haver, Vincenzo
Bella Pargoletta, La

Bizet, Georges
Carnaval

Choral Panorama

Chorale Perspective

Clement
Come Now, Ye Maidens

Crecquillon, Thomas
C'Est Un Grand Tort

Freire, Perez
Ay Ay Ay

Handel, George Frideric
And Draw A Blessing Down
Ritorni Omai Nel Nostro Core
We Will Rejoice In Thy Salvation
Welcome As The Cheerful Light
Your Voices Tune

Lassus, Roland de (Orlandus)
Beau Le Cristal
Gallans Qui Par Terre Et Par Mer
Grave De L'eta, Il

Lecuona, Ernesto
From One Love To Another

Longas
Cielo Azul

Mananitas, Las

MALIN (cont'd.)

Marenzio, Luca
Dissi A L'Amata Mia Lucida Stella
Ecco L'Aurora Con L'Aurata Fronte
Gia Torna A Rallegar
Ma Per Me Lasso
Mentre Qual Viva Pietra
Scaldava Il Sol
Se'l Pensier Che Mi Struggo

Monte, Philippe de
Comme La Tourterelle
Grand' Amour, La
Premier Jour Du Mois De Mai, Le

Mozart, Wolfgang Amadeus
Welches Vergnugen

Palomita

Purcell, Henry
Two Choruses

Rediscovered Madrigals

Regnart, Jacob
Dies Ist Die Zeit

Rio, Rio

Rossi
Dirmi Che Piu Non Ardo
Felice Chi Vi Mira

Schaerer
Herzlich Tut Mich Erfreuen

Serradell, Narcisco
Golondrina, La

Vecchi, Orazio (Horatio)
Fammi Una Canzonetta Capricciosa
Io Son Fenice

Widmann, Erasmus
Wer Lust Und Lieb' Zur Musik Hat

MALIN, DON
Anerio, Felice
Lieta Amanti, I

Arcadelt, Jacob
Da Bei Rami Scendea
Nous Voyons Que Les Hommes

Azzaiolo, Filippo, [Publisher]
Ti Parti, Cor Mio Caro

Choral Perspective

Franck, Melchior
Mich Erfreut, Schons Lieb, Dein Uneblick

Gombert, Nicolas
Votre Beaute Plaisante Et Lie

Hilton, John (The Younger)
If It Be Love To Sit And Mourn
Now Is The Summer Springing

Hollande, J. de
Rossignol Daus Son Nid Chante, Le

Monteverdi, Claudio
La Piaga C'ho Nel Core

Rediscovered Madrigals

Regnart, Jacob
Nun Bin Ich Einmal Frei

Renaissance Choral Music

Rore, Cipriano de
En Vos, Adieux, Dames

Youll, Henry
In The Merry Month Of May

MALMFORS, AKE
Londonderry Air

MALTBY
Oakland, Ben
I'll Take Romance

MALTZEFF, A.
Russian Carol

MAMMEL, ROLF
Gaudeamus Igitur

MANDYCZEWSKI, E.
Schubert, Franz (Peter)
Begegnung
Erklarung
Erwachen
Heimat
Lasterzungen
Nest, Das
Polterabend
Sehnsucht
Tanz, Der
Wahl, Die

MANDYCZEWSKI, E. (cont'd.)

    Wermut
    Zu Zweien

MANDYCZEWSKI, EUGEN
    Schubert, Franz (Peter)
      Deutsche Tanze

MANLEY
    Dinn, Freda
      High Barbary

MANN, JOHNNY
    Bates, Katherine
      America The Beautiful

MANNEY
    Sibelius, Jean
      Dear Land Of Home

MANNEY, C.
    Humperdinck, Engelbert
      Prayer

    Morley, Thomas
      Now Is The Month Of Maying

MANSFIELD
    Bizet, Georges
      Habanera

    Kennedy-Fraser, Marjory
      Eriskay Love Lilt, An

    Offenbach, Jacques
      Student's Chorus

    Purcell, Henry
      Fairest Isle

MANSFIELD, P.J.
    Beethoven, Ludwig van
      Coming Of Spring, The

    Chopin, Frederic
      Waltz In A Minor

    Day, Maude Craske
      Arise, O Sun

    Foster, Stephen Collins
      Beautiful Dreamer

    Handel, George Frideric
      Where E'er You Walk

    Lawreen, J.B.
      Who's That Calling So Sweet

    MacLeod, A.C.
      Skye Boat Song

    Millikin, R.A.
      Last Rose Of Summer

    Purcell, Henry
      Nymphs And Shepherds

    Schubert, Franz (Peter)
      With Thee Is Peace

    Weber, Carl Maria von
      Afforderung Zum Tanz

MANSFIELD, PURCELL J.
    I'm Troubled In Mind

MANSOURI, PARVIS
    Persian Folksongs

MARBOT, R.
    Hirondelle, Une

MARCHAL, DOMINIQUE
    Dansons La Carmagnolle

MARCHANT, A.
    Cowen, [Sir] Frederic Hymen
      Children's Home

MARECHAL, H.
    Offenbach, Jacques
      Barcarolle

MARESCOTTI
    Trois Chants Savoysiens

MARIX, JEANNE
    Musiciens De La Cour De Bourgogne Au
      XVe Siecle (1420-1467), Les

MARKI, E.
    Abschied

    Am Lagerfeuer

    Decker, W.
      'S Heimetdorfi

    Hess, C.
      Heimetvogel, Der

    Pfirstinger, Felix
      Blumen Der Heimat
      Heimatlied

MARKI, E. (cont'd.)

    S'Marlyseli Ischt Es Fyns

    Stille Tal, Das

MARKI, ERNST
    Alte Grenchnerlied, Das

    Of De Berge Mocht I Lebe

MARKOVITCH, I.
    Bergers, Les

    Fatise Kolo

    Mironosicam Zenam

    Quand On A Bu

    Touati, Raymond
      Chevre-Feuille

MARKS; JAMES
    Simons
      All Of Me

MARLOWE
    Chiapanecas

    Dichmont, William
      Ma Little Banjo

    Firestone, Idabelle
      If I Could Tell You

    Friml, Rudolf
      Bubble, The
      Donkey Serenade, The

    Gibson, Archar
      Drum, The

    Herbert, Victor
      On Parade
      Sweethearts
      Wooden Shoes

    Kountz, Richard
      God Bless Our Land

    Pierpont, J.
      Jingle Bells

    Romberg, Sigmund
      Auf Wiedersehn!
      Road To Paradise, The
      Will You Remember (Sweetheart)

    Thompson, John Jr.
      Coast Guard Victory Song

MARLOWE; DEIS
    Pierpont, J.
      Jingle Bells

MAROLT, FRANCE
    Hoch Im Gereute

    Liebe In Dieser Zeit

    Nur Dich Allein

MAROTI, GY.
    Huszonot Ev Korusdalai

MARRENBACH, R.
    Blumelein, Sie Schlafen, Die

    Es Fiel Ein Reif

    Es Wollt Ein Jagerlein Jagen

    Feinsliebchen, Du Sollst

    Jager Langs Dem Weiher Ging, Ein

    Kein Schoner Land

MARRI, ERNST
    Dur's Wiesetal

MARSH
    Barbey, Bob
      Life Is For The Birds
      Lucky To Be Me

MARSH, GERRY
    Payne, Warren
      Never Let You Go

MARSH, J.
    Wesley, S.
      Two Motets

MARSH, MARY VAL
    Watah Come A Me Eye

MARTENS
    Amner
      Woe Is Me

    Bravo, Jose de Torres Martinez
      Versa Est In Luctum

MARTENS, H.
    Neefe, Christian Gottlob
      Der Du Die Sonne Schufest

    Weber, Carl Maria von
      Preis Dir, O Ton

    Zelter, Carl Friedrich
      Lasst Fahren Hin Das Allzufluchtige

MARTENS, MASON
    Bicentennial Collection Of American
      Choral Music, The

MARTIN
    Charlottown

    Chum-Ba-Ra

    Chumbara

    Wagner, Richard
      Hymn To The Morning

MARTIN; ADES
    Jordan
      Let's Take The Long Way Around The
        World

MARTIN, DON
    Marks, Johnny D.
      A-Caroling We Go
      Anyone Can Move A Mountain
      Holly Jolly Christmas, A
      I Heard The Bells On Christmas Day
      Joyous Christmas
      Merry Merry Christmas To You, A
      Night Before Christmas, The
      Rudolph, The Red-Nosed Reindeer

MARTIN, GILBERT M.
    Sing Out

MARTIN, IVOR
    Let's Sing A Song

MARTIN, P.
    Gastoldi, Giovanni Giacomo
      Balleto

MARTIN-PREVEL
    Brel, Jacques
      Plat Pays, Le
      Sur La Place

MARTIN, UWE
    Lechner, Leonhard
      Newe Teutsche Lieder 1577
      Newe Teutsche Lieder Zu Drey
        Stimmen

MARTIN, V.
    Jamais Je N'Oublierai

MARTIN, WARREN
    O No John

MARTIN, WILLIAM
    Program Collection

MARTIN, WILLIAM R.
    Vecchi, Orazio (Horatio)
      Convito Musicale

MARTINDALE
    Day, P.
      As The Branch Is To The Vine

MARTING, ELIZABETH
    Canto Di Caccia

    Cornish May Song

    Dancing

    Golden Day Is Dying, The

    Good Night, Beloved

    Morley, Thomas
      April Is In My Mistress' Face

    Purcell, Henry
      In These Delightful Pleasant Groves

    Rosa, Let Us Be Dancing

    Swansea Town

    Tu Mi Vuoi Tanto Bene

MARTINI
    Aguirre, Julian
      Luna Blanca
      Serenata Campera

    Anonymous
      Abeto, El
      Marcha De Ituzaingo

    Beethoven, Ludwig van
      Despertar De Las Flores, El

    Bishop
      Home, Sweet Home

MARTINI (cont'd.)

Brahms, Johannes
Wiegenlied

Brogi
Vision Veneciana

Cabrera
Palito, El

Caccini
Amarilli

Chazarreta
Randera Tucumana, La

Chopin, Frederic
Tristeza

Cortijo, Vidal
Vidalita

De Rogatis, Pascual
Sombra, La

Delibes, Leo
Vals Lento

Dvorak, Antonin
Songs My Mother Taught Me

Espoile, Raoul H.
Yaravi

Foster, Stephen Collins
Buenos Noches, Viejo Hogar
Oh Susanna!
Old Black Joe
Viejos Moradores De Mi Pueblo, Los

Giordani
Aria

Gomez Carrillo, Manuel
Dos Palomitas

Grasso
Percion

Handel, George Frideric
Celebre Largo

Lopez Buchardo, Carlos
Cancion Del Carretero

Massa
Vidalita

Mendelssohn-Bartholdy, Felix
Cancion De Primavera
Primera Barcarola

Nevin
Rosario, El

Offenbach, Jacques
Celebre Barcarola

Palma, Athos
Cancion Quichua

Rimsky-Korsakov, Nikolai
Cancion Hindu

Schubert, Franz (Peter)
Serenata

Schumann, Robert (Alexander)
Campesino Alegre Que Regresa Del
Trabajo, El
Cancion Del Pastor

Silva
San Lorenzo

Strauss, Johann, [Jr.]
A Orillas Del Hermoso Danubio Azul
Cuentos De Bosque De Viena

Tchaikovsky, Piotr Ilyich
Cancion Triste
Solo El Que Sabe Amar
Vals De Las Flores

Troiani
Provincianita, La

MARTINOTTI
Stradella, Alessandro
Damone, Il

MARX KARL
Auf'm Wasa

Da Oben Uff'em Bergli

Schwefelholzle

Vo Luzern Uff Waggis Zue

MARZO, EDUARDO
Children's Carols For All Occasions

Fifty Christmas Carols Of All Nations

MARZO, EDUARDO (cont'd.)

Sixty Carols Of All Nations

MARZUKI, MARILYN S.
Davis
Music In My Life

Dorff
I Just Fall In Love Again

Gamble
I Love Music

Hamlisch, Marvin F.
Ice Castles: Theme
Nothing

Home

Love Medley

Mithrandir

Out Of The East

Smalls, Charles
Ease On Down The Road

This Is Love

Too Shy To Say

When A Child Is Born

When You're Loved

MASON
Robin Adair

MASON; BAYFORD
Reed
Last Waltz, The

MASON; CRAIG
Mozart, Wolfgang Amadeus
Scenda Amor
Three Nocturnes

Purcell, Henry
Two Choruses

MASSA
Schubert, Franz (Peter)
Momento Musical

MASSOTTI LITTEL
Brahms, Johannes
Wiegenlied

Iradier
Paloma, La

Sanchez de Fuentes, Eduardo
Tu

MASTERS
Smith
I Sing Of A Maiden

MATERASSI, M.
Primo Libro Delle Giustiniane, Il

MATERNUS, PETER
Ahoi!

MATHENY, GARY
Wayfarin' Stranger

MATTESON
Ole Chisholm Trail

MATTESON, M.
Ole Chisholm Trail

MATTESON, MAURICE
Schirmer's American Folksong Series,
Set 25

MATTFELD, VICTOR H.
Janequin, Clement
Ce Moys De May

Vecchi, Orazio (Horatio)
Fa Una Canzone

MATTHEWS, H.
Sibelius, Jean
On Great Lone Hills

MATTHIES
Chadusi, Jeff
Lied Der Bulgarischen Jugend

Hilliger
Sei Uns Gegrusst, Du Arbeitermorgen

Wenn Jemand Eine Reise Tut

MATTSON
Foster, Stephen Collins
Jeannie With The Light Brown Hair

Jobim, Antonio Carlos
Desafinado (Slightly Out Of Tune)

MATTSON, PHIL
Carmichael, Hoagy
Skylark

Gloucestershire Wassail

How Long Has This Been Going On?

S'Wonderful

MATVEJEV, M.
Galambhoz, A

MATYAS, J.
El Az Emlek

MATYAS, JANOS; RAICS, ISTVAN
Erkel, Franz (Ferenc)
Gyaszkar

MATZUKI
Bell
Love Is

MAUX, RICHARD
Zweiunddreissig Volkslieder Aus
Osterreich

MAXWELL, JAMES C.
Roberton, Hugh Stevenson
Lilt O' The Song

MAYER
Wagner, Richard
Enter With The Blest

MAYSHIP, ARTHUR
Mendelssohn-Bartholdy, Felix
Sleep My Princess

Mozart, Wolfgang Amadeus
Schlafe, Mein Prinzchen, Schlaf'
Ein

Rubenstein
Summer Is Here

Schubert, Franz (Peter)
Hey For The Road

MC AFEE
One Bad Apple

MC DONALD, J.; MC DONALD, BRIDIE
Jackie And Bridies Song Book, Book 1

Jackie And Bridies Song Book, Book 2

MC LIN
Thou Art Groovy

MCCARTHY
Farmer
Lady, My Flame Still Burning

Jones
Sing, Merry Birds

Mundy
Of All The Birds
Turn About And See Me

Phillips
Nightingale, The

Tomkins, Thomas
Woe Is Me

Vautor, Thomas
Ah Sweet, Whose Beauty
Mother, I Will Have A Husband

Whythorne
It Doth Belong More Of Good Right
Who That Will Weigh Of Ages All

Willbye
Happy, Oh Happy He

MCCARTHY, JOHN
Schubert, Franz (Peter)
Standchen

MCCAULEY, WILLIAM
C'est L'Aviron

Je Sais Bien Quelque Chose

MCCHESNEY
Golden Slumbers

Ortiz, Diego
My Heart Loves You More Each Day

Scarlatti
Lament

MCCORKLE
Hagen
Morning Star

MCCRAY
Dowland, John
Say Love If Ever Thou Didst Find

MCCRAY (cont'd.)

  Martini
    Two Motets

  Volkmann, Robert
    Evening, The

MCCULLOUGH
  Brahms, Johannes
    I Have A Wish, Dear Mother
    Pleasures In May, The

  Lassus, Roland de (Orlandus)
    My Heart Is Yours
    My Heart Leaps Up

  Schubert, Franz (Peter)
    To Spring

MCELFRESH
  Hall
    Jenny Rebecca

MCELFRESH, CLAIR
  McGlohon, Loonis
    Songbird (Thank You For Your Lovely
    Song)

MCEWEN
  Brahms, Johannes
    My Beloved

  Handel, George Frideric
    O Love Divine

MCFARLAND
  Brown, Oscar Jr.
    Brown Baby

MCFATTER, LARRY
  Paxton, Gary S.
    If You Can't Believe In Love

  You Can Build A Bridge

MCGLOHON
  Heckler
    As Long As There Is Music

MCKELVEY, J.
  Gute Nacht

MCKELVY
  Deck The Halls

  We Wish You A Merry Christmas

MCKELVY, JAMES
  Angels We Have Heard On High

  Arrival And Departure Carols

  Brahms, Johannes
    Lovesongs In Waltz Time

  Deck The Halls (In Seven-Eight Meter)

  Flaming Pudding Carol, The

  Here We Come A-Caroling

  I Saw Three Ships

  Jingle Bells Chopsticks

  Jingle Bells Scherzo

  Masters In This Hall

  Niles, John Jacob
    Lost Love

  Purcell, Henry
    Five Reasons

  Star Spangled Banner, The

MCKINNEY, HOWARD D.
  Grieg, Edvard Hagerup
    Brothers, Sing On!

MCKINNEY, RICH
  Clark, Michael
    Come On In

  Crewe, Bob
    Let's Hang On

  Only Time Will Tell

MCLEOD
  Bill Bailey Won't You Please Come
    Home

  Cannon
    Bill Bailey, Won't You Come Home?

MCLEOD, RED
  At The Jamboree Ball

MCLIN
  Herzog
    God Bless The Child

MCMURTRY, WILLIAM M.
  Selected Chansons From British
    Library, MS Add. 335087

MCNAUGHT
  Bizet, Georges
    Carmen:Selection

MCNAUGHT; KRONE
  Purcell, Henry
    Nymphs And Shepherds

MCNAUGHT, WILLIAM
  In Derry Vale (Londonderry Air)

  Oft In The Stilly Night

MCOWAT, J.
  Three German Folk Songs For Infants

MCREYNOLDS, S.A.
  Beethoven, Ludwig van
    To Victory

MCVICAR, GEORGE C.
  Brisk And Lively Lass, A

  Two Traditional Scottish Songs

MEAD
  Weber, Carl Maria von
    Chor Der Jager

  When Johnny Comes Marching Home

MEAD, G.
  When Johnny Comes Marching Home

MECHEM, KIRKE
  Aunt Rhody

  Blue-Tail Fly

  Wayfaring Stranger

MEDINGER
  Four Songs From "The Beggar's Opera"

MEHLER, F.
  Valentin, M.
    Stadens Lojtnant
    Varen Sjunger

MEHLER, FRIEDRICH
  Tva Gotlandska Brollopslatar

MEIER
  Funf Madrigale

  Willaert, Adrian
    Madrigale Um Adrian Willaert

MEIER, BERNHARD
  Rore, Cipriano de
    Opera Omnia Vol.III: Madrigals
    Opera Omnia Vol.IV: Madrigals
    Opera Omnia Vol.V: Madrigals

MEIER, W.
  Marenzio, Luca
    Mochte Die Leiden Nennen
    Schenk, Maid, Mir Deine Liebe

MEIER, WALTER
  Abschied

MEIJNS, W.
  Verdi, Giuseppe
    Va, Pensiero, Sull'Ali Dorate

MEINBERG
  Brahms, Johannes
    Zigeunerlied, No. 1
    Zigeunerlied, No. 2
    Zigeunerlied, No. 3

  Kucken, Friedrich Wilhelm
    Ach, Wie Ist's Moglich Dann

  Mucke, Franz
    Gott Grusse Dich

  Silcher, Friedrich
    Lorelei

  Taubert, [Karl Gottfried] Wilhelm
    Vom Bauern Und Den Tauben

MEISSL, E.
  In Die Berg Bin I Gern

MELANDER, ALEX
  Friml, Rudolf
    Sympathy

MELANDER, AXEL
  Ellington, Edward Kennedy (Duke)
    Solitude

  Friml, Rudolf
    Sympathy

  Kalman, Emmerich
    O Kom, O Kom Zigan

MELANDER, AXEL (cont'd.)

  Lindemann, William
    Trink, Trink, Bruderlein Trink

  Londonderry Air

  Porter, Cole
    Begin The Beguine

  Sieczynski, Rudolf
    Wien, Du Stadt Meiner Traume

  Straus, Oscar
    Sista Valsen, Den

  Strauss, Johann, [Jr.]
    Leve Var Stad

  Sundblad, Bo
    I Lissabon, Dar Dansa De
    I Lissabon Dar Dansa De

  Sylvain, Jules
    Rumba Zorina

  Sylvan, Jules
    Rumba Zorina

  Young, Victor
    Sweet Sue-Just You

MELCHERS, WALTER
  Cucaracha, La

MELFI
  Chopin, Frederic
    So Deep Is The Night

MELFI; HEWITT, T.J.
  Chopin, Frederic
    So Deep Is The Night

MELICHAR, ALOIS; ZIMMER, FRIEDRICH
  Chopin, Frederic
    In Mir Klingt Ein Lied

MELLALIEU, W. NORMAN
  Jock O' Hazeldean

MENDOZA, ANNE; RIMMER, JOAN
  Thirty Unison Folk Settings

MENDOZA; RIMMER
  Two Folk Carols

MENICHETTI, F.
  Giacobini, F.-X.
    Ajaccienne, L'

MENNES, WIM
  Morley, Thomas
    It Was A Lover And His Lass

MERCER, W. ELMO
  America The Beautiful

  God Bless America Medley

MERMAN
  Baker
    Let's Go Singin'

  Horman, John D.
    Snow

  Obenshain, Kathryn G.
    Fun, Food And Festivals

  O'Leary
    All Day Long Songs
    Saturday's Child

  Plank
    Bubble Gum Blues

  Weintraub
    Eight Bright Candles

MERMAN, JOYCE
  Barlow, Betty
    Once Around The Sun

  Herbert, Victor
    Toyland Tintype, A

MERRIFIELD
  Mothuhless Chile

  Now Look Away

MERRILL
  Brudieu, Joan
    Canas, Las

  Des Prez, Josquin
    Grillo, El

  Di Pera, Mara
    Cruel, Thy Beauty

  Encina, Juan del
    Cu-Cu, Cu-Cu

  Muchos Van De Amor

MERRILL (cont'd.)

   Rodrigo Martinez

   Steffens
      Cuckoo
      Kuckuck Auf Dem Zaune

   Vasquez, Juan
      En La Fuente Del Rosel

MERRILL, MARLIN
   Anchieta, Juan de
      Con Amores La Mi Madre
      Con Amores, La Mi Madre

   Anonymous
      Muchos Van De Amor
      Rodrigo Martinez

   Ponce, Juan
      Todo Mi Bien E Perdido

MERRITT, A. TILLMAN
   Gabrieli, Andrea
      Complete Madrigals

MESSNER, K.
   Landliche Leben, Das

MESTRES, EUG.
   Beethoven, Ludwig van
      Final De La Neuvieme Symphonie

METHFESSEL
   Wittkopp, C.
      Deutscher Sangergruss

METIS
   Alstone
      December
      Wise Man

   Barry
      Teen Age Sonata

   Brel
      Seasons In The Sun

   Brown
      What Is A Friend

   Campbell, Glen
      Less Of Me

   Carrillo
      La Mentira

   City Of New Orleans

   Cohan, George Michael
      All Our Friends
      Harrigan
      Rose

   Cole
      Lazy Moon

   Coleman, Cy
      On The Twentieth Century
      You're Never Fully Dressed Without
        A Smile

   Danoff
      Take Me Home Country Roads

   Denver
      Rocky Mountain High

   Deutschendorf, Henry John (John
      Denver)
      Annie's Song
      Back Home Again

   Donkey Of Bethlehem, The

   Even The Nights Are Better

   Gatlin, Larry
      All The Gold In California

   Heartbreaker

   Holler, Dick
      Abraham, Martin And John

   If I Could Write A Song

   I'm Coming Home Again

   Kern, Jerome
      Smoke Gets In Your Eyes

   Kirkman
      Cherish

   Kirkman, Terry
      Cherish

   Lawrence, Karen
      Eyes Of Laura Mars, Love Theme From

   Lecuona, Ernesto
      Malaguena

METIS (cont'd.)

   Lehrer, Thomas Andrew
      Pollution

   Lennon, John
      Let It Be
      Long And Winding Road, The

   Levine
      Tie A Yellow Ribbon Round The Ole
        Oak Tree

   Like A Sunday In Salem

   Loggins, David A.
      Pieces Of April

   MacDermott, Galt
      Manchester England

   Manilow, Barry
      All The Time
      Beautiful Music
      Copacabana
      One Voice

   Manning
      Morningside Of The Mountain, The

   Mr. Balloon Man

   Mr. Wonderful

   Nash, Graham
      Sounds Of Neil Young And Graham
      Nash

   New York, New York: Theme

   Oliviero
      All
      I'll Set My Love To Music

   O'Sullivan
      Clair

   Play Me A Memory

   Ross
      Lollipop

   Seals
      Hummingbird

   Sherman
      You're Sixteen

   Shorter
      Hard Road Back, The
      People Had No Faces, The

   Shoulder To Shoulder (Arm And Arm)

   Smoke Gets In Your Eyes

   Smoke Get's In Your Eyes

   Smoke Gets In Your Eyes

   Solomon
      Israeli Lullaby

   Stills, Stephen
      For What It's Worth

   Tempchin
      Peaceful Easy Feeling

   Turn To Stone

   Umiliani
      Mah Na, Mah Na

   Williams, John
      Superman

   You Take My Breath Away

   You're My World

METIS, FRANK
   Addrisi, Dick
      I Believe You

   Bacharach, Burt F.
      Close To You
      One Less Bell To Answer
      Raindrops Keep Fallin' On My Head
      What The World Needs Now Is Love

   Bone Dry

   Bread And Gravy

   Carpenter, Richard Lynn
      Top Of The World

   Carste, Hans
      Those Lazy-Hazy-Crazy Days Of
      Summer

   Cockrell, Bud
      Place In The Sun, A

METIS, FRANK (cont'd.)

   Courage, Alexander
      Star Trek

   Danoff, William Thomas
      Take Me Home Country Roads

   De Young, Dennis
      Come Sail Away

   Deutschendorf, Henry John (John
      Denver)
      Annie's Song
      Back Home Again
      Rocky Mountain High

   Dimucci, Dion Francis
      Runaround Sue

   Dominique

   Farrar, John
      Have You Never Been Mellow

   Frampton, Peter Kenneth
      I'm In You

   Friedman, Ruthann
      Windy

   Gibb, Barry
      How Can You Mend A Broken Heart?
      Love So Right

   Give Me Your Hand

   Giving And Taking

   Hi Ro Jerum

   Hiawatha's Mittens

   Holler, Dick
      Abraham, Martin And John

   I Left My Heart In San Francisco

   I'm My Own Grandpaw

   It Was A Lover And His Lass

   Jackson Scott, The Astronaut

   Lamb, The

   Leigh, Mitch
      Impossible Dream, The

   Lennon, John
      Can't Buy Me Love
      Norwegian Wood

   Little White Duck, The

   Matilda

   Must I Go Bound

   My Good Girl

   Newman, Randy
      Short People

   O Mistress Mine

   On And On

   Poetry

   Powers, Chet
      Get Together

   Preston, Billy
      You Are So Beautiful

   Richie, Lionel
      Truly

   Sayer, Leo
      Thunder In My Heart

   Simon, Paul
      America
      Fifty-Ninth Street Bridge Song, The
        (Feelin' Groovy)
      Song For The Asking
      Sound Of Silence, The

   Stevens, Ray
      Everything Is Beautiful

   Take, O Take Those Lips Away

   Temperton, Rod
      Always And Forever
      Boogie Nights

   Tennille, Toni
      Circles
      We Never Really Say Goodbye

   Under The Greenwood Tree

   Vincent, Vincent, M'sieu Vincent

MOCKL, FRANZ
Annchen, Wo Warst Du

Chore Fur Besondere Anlasse

Franck, Melchior
Lasst Uns Ein Stundlein Lustig Sein

Frankisches Liederbuch

Hochzeits-Schottisch

Hor Ich Ein Sichlein Rauschen

Ich Fand Den Liebsten Mein

In Einer Kleinen Hutte

Kad Si Bila Mala Mare

Kleiner Knabe, Grosser Gott

Kleines Gluck

Lasst Uns Das Kindlein Wiegen

Lustig, Ihr Bruder

Mit Der Liebschaft Ist's Aus

Schwarzbraunes Madchen

Was Woll'n Wir Auf Den Abend Tun?

Zwei Abendlieder

MOERAN, E.J.
Nutting Time

MOESCHINGER, ALBERT
Es Isch Kei Solige Stamme

MOFFAT
Praetorius, Michael
O Lovely Night

MOFFAT, ALFRED
Down Near The Garden Gate

Hill And Vale

In Maytime

June

Lonely House, The

Nine Years Old

Purcell, Henry
Sound The Trumpet

Silent Butterfly, The

Twilight Shadows

MOHLER, PH.
Winter Ist Vergangen, Der

MOHLER, PHILLIP
Mozart, Wolfgang Amadeus
Sei Uns Mit Jubelschalle

MOHR
Radecke, Robert
Aus Der Jugendzeit

MOINEAU
J'Ai Cueilli La Belle Rose

MOMPELLIO, FEDERICO
Striggio, Alessandro
Caccia, La

MONKEMEYER, HELMUT
Ach Herzigs Herz

Mai Tritt Ein Mit Freuden, Der

Mein Mund Der Singt

MONSON, CRAIG
Weelkes, Thomas
Thus Sings My Dearest Jewel

MONSOUR, SALLY; LAND, LOIS
Birthday Party

My Home So Far Away

MONSOUR, SALLY; LAND, LOIS RHEA
Songs Of The Middle East

MONTAN, PAUL
Green Grow The Lilacs

MONTGOMERY
Brahms, Johannes
O Wusst' Ich Doch Den Weg Zuruck

Foster, Stephen Collins
Glendy Burk, The

He's Gone Away

Sometimes I Feel Like A Motherless

MONTGOMERY (cont'd.)

Child

MOON, EARL
Godfrey, Bob
Barbershop Strut, The

MOORE
Banchieri, Adriano
Intermedio Di Solfanari

Croce
Canzonetta Da Bambini

Hughes
When Susanna Jones Wears Red

MOORE, D.
Birds' Courting Song

MOORE, RAY
Banchieri, Adriano
Madrigaletto
Se Nel Mar Del Mio Pianto

MOORHEAD, MICHAEL
Humperdinck, Engelbert
Sieben Geislein, Die: Two Choruses

MORA, FERENC
Szeghy, Endre
Altatodal

MOREN, JOHN
Berggreen, Andreas Peter
Underbar En Stjarna Blid

MORGENROTH
Fischer, Karl Ludwig
Heimat

Heim, Ignatz
Vineta

MORGENROTH, G.
Abt, Franz
Abendglocken Rufen, Die

Ebel, Eduard
Leise Rieselt Der Schnee

Es Flog Ein Kleins Waldvogelein

Es Ist Ein Schnee Gefallen

Mozart, Wolfgang Amadeus
O Isis Und Osiris

Silcher, Friedrich
So Nimm Denn Meine Hande

MORGENROTH, GUNTER
Nageli, Johann (Hans) Georg
Mensch Lebt Und Bestehet, Der

MORGENROTH, GUNTHER
Abt, Franz
Abendglocken Rufen, Die

MORGENSTERN, J.
Ich Liebe Dich, Leben

MORICZ
Kosa, Gyorgy
Iciri-Piciri

MORIERE, GUY
Aubanel, Georges
Viens Ma Bergere

MORLEY, THOMAS
It Was A Lover And His Lass

MORRIS, R. O.
Blow Away The Morning Dew

MORROW, ARTHUR
Neufeld, Rick
Moody Manitoba Morning

MORTENSEN, OTTO
Barbara Allen

Bed Is Too Small

Caleno Custure Me

Four Motets

Seven Gypsies On The Hill

'Twas Na Her Bonnie Blue

MOSER, E.
Nageli, Johann (Hans) Georg
Vaterland, Das

MOSER, HANS JOACHIM
Schutz, Heinrich
Ach Du Bitterste Sussigkeit
Brand, Der Entfessel
Dann Muss Ich Also Sterben
Du Hauch, Der Sich Dem Busen
Du Zeit Des Lenzes
Eisiger Fels Der Alpen

MOSER, HANS JOACHIM (cont'd.)

Fliehe, Fliehe, Du Mein Herze
Gluckliche Haine
Ich Sterbe, Siehe, Nun Sterb
Italienische Madrigale
Kehrt Wieder, Teure Kusse
Lachelt Die Fruhlingssonne
Lebet Wohl Denn, Teure Haine
Mich Begrusset Die Holde
Seel' In Noten
Sieh In Mir Jene Dame
So Bohrt Euch Ein, O Ihr Schlangen
Trug Ist's Nur, Lydia
Von Marmor Seid Ihr, Fraue
Weites Meer, Dem Im Busen

MOSER, HANS JOACHIM; FEDTKE, TRAUGOTT
Monteverdi, Claudio
Lamento d'Arianna

MOSER; LUBIG
Marsch Des 26. Juli

MOTTL, F.
Schubert, Franz (Peter)
Miriam's Siegesgesang
Standchen

MOTTL, FELIX
Bach, Johann Sebastian
Streit Zwischen Phoebus Und Pan,
Der

MOULIJN, J.
Klerk, Jos. de
Schip Van Staat, Het

MOY, EDGAR
Here's Health Unto His Majesty

When Johnny Comes Marching Home

MOZART, WOLFGANG AMADEUS
Handel, George Frideric
Alexander's Feast (Neue Mozart-
Ausgabe)

MUCHLER
Lissmann, Kurt
Wein Erfreut Des Menschen Herz, Der

MUCHLER; ZELTER
Lissmann, Kurt
Wein Erfreut Des Menschen Herz, Der

MUELLER
Beethoven, Ludwig van
Heavens Are Declaring, The

Foster, Stephen Collins
Come Where My Love Lies Dreaming

Franz, Robert
Dedication

Mendelssohn-Bartholdy, Felix
Liebe Und Wein
Trinklied

Schirmer's Favorite Secular Choruses

Schirmer's Favorite Selections

Winkworth
Wake, Awake, For Night Is Flying

MUELLER, FRANK
Mendelssohn-Bartholdy, Felix
Jagdlied, Op.120 No. 1
Perite Autem

Schumann, Robert (Alexander)
Tamburinschlagerin

MULLER
Achtzehn Weltliche Lieder

Christmas

Englert, Eugene E.
Wann Wir Schreiten Seit' An Seit'

Give Me Love

Greiter
Samtliche Weltliche Lieder

Humpert, Fred
Ganz Im Geheimen

I Say A Little Prayer

I'm Free

It's A Small World

Love Of The Common People

Midnight Cowboy

Night They Drove Old Dixie Down, The

Proud Mary

Raindrops Keep Fallin' On My Head

NELSON
Fiddler, The

Girl With The Buckles On Her Shoes, The

Never On Sunday

Red Rosey Bush

Schubert, Franz (Peter)
Moonlit Evening
Schmetterling, Der

Wonderland By Night

NELSON, H.
Oh! I Am Come To The Low Countrie

NELSON, HAVELOCK
Dancing The Baby

Enchanted Valley, The

Girl With The Buckles On Her Shoes, The

Has Sorrow Thy Young Days Shaded?

Has Sorrow Thy Young Days Shaded

I Wonder When I Shall Be Married

Kitty Of Coleraine

Lark In The Clean Air, The

Last Rose Of Summer, The

Lovlie Jimmie

Maid Of Bunclody, The

My Little White Home

Oh! I Am Come To The Low Countrie

Piper Thru' The Meadow Straying, The

Schubert, Franz (Peter)
Gentle Thorns, The
Schmetterling, Der

Sho—Heen, Sho—Ho

Tis My Grief And Sorrow

Ulster Lilt, An

NERSVEEN, ODD
Nielsen, A.K.
Fjell—Sangen

Olrog, Ulf Peder
Spring, Step

NETZER, EFFI
Folk Songs No. 2

NEUBAUER
Absage

Burschen Aus Mystrina

Dunayevszky, Isaak O.
Lied Vom Vaterland, Das

Ich Ging Emol Spaziere

Sedoy
Abend Auf Der Reede

NEUENDORFF
Gerhard, Fritz Christian
Drei Gesturzte Baume

NEUFELD
Herrick's Carol

NEUMAN
Mahler, Gustav
Finale From Symphony No. 2

NEUMANN, WERNER
Bach, Johann Sebastian
Schleicht, Spielende Wellen

NEUMEYER, F.
Lothringer Sing— Und Spielbuchlein

NEVIN
Pike, Harry Hale
Spring Song, A

When Love Is Kind

NEVIN; EHRET
Rogers
Rosary, The

NEVIN, GEORGE B.
When Love Is Kind

NEWBURY, KENT
Black Is The Color Of My True Love's Hair

Every Night When The Sun Goes In

I've Been Working On The Railroad

'Tis The Gift To Be Simple

NEWBURY, KENT A.
Shenandoah

NEWMAN
Bells Of Christmas, The

Shake Me I Rattle

Snow Bells

NEWMAN, JOEL
Bouquet Of Bawdy Catches

NEWMAN , RICHARD
Hackady, Hal
Shake Me I Rattle

NEWMARCH
Smetana, Bedrich
Opening Chorus From The "Bartered Bride"

NEWTON, E.
Canadian Boat Song, A

Miller Of Dee, The

Minstrel Boy, The

Old King Cole

NEWTON, ERNEST
Frog, The

NEYRAT; ERNST; BARRAUD, J.; DAVID, M.
Ane De Marion, L'

Berceuse

Celui Que Mon Coeur Aime Tant

Corbleu! Marion

Dans La Riviere D'Iturna

De Bon Matin

Fille Aux Oranges, La

La—Haut Sur La Montagne

Pauvre Laboureur, Le

Premier, C'Est Un Voyageur!, Le

Quatorze Vieilles Chansons Francaises

Rossignolet Du Bois Joli

V'la La Saint—Martin

Voici Le Joli Mois De Mai

NICHOLS
Greenback Dollar

NIEDERMANN, GUSTAV
Aenneli, Wo Bisch Gester Gsi

NIEHAUS, LENNIE
Hernandez, Frank
Rest Of My Life, The
Sunshine And Rain

Krueger, Ron
In Due Time

NIELSEN, EDWIN
Knudsen, Gunder
Hver Dag Er En Sjaelden Gave

NIELSEN, JORGEN
Gade, Niels Wilhelm
Morgonsang

NIELSEN, R.
Agostini, Lodovico
Cantava In Riva Al Fiume
Picciola Verga E Bella
Tra Giove In Cielo

Dodici Madrigali Di Scuola Ferrarese

Luzzaschi, Luzzasco
Aminta Poi Ch'a Filli
Dolce Mia Fiamma
Geloso Amante
Itene A Volo

Nicoletti, F.
Ardo Si Ma Non T'amo

Virchi, P.
Dovea La Fredda Neve
Non Fonte O Fiume
Qual Cervo Errando

NIGG
O Caille, Pauvre Caille

NIGGELING
Ich Ging Durch Einen Grasgrunen Wald

NIGGLI
Des Lebens Tage

NIGGLI, F.
Es Taget Vor Dem Walde

Hab Oft Im Kreise Der Lieben

Juheia, De Winter

Schweizer Volkslieder

Unser Leben Gleicht Der Reise

Weiss Mir Ein Blumlein Blaue

NIGGLI, FRIEDRICH
Des Lebens Tage

Im Aargau Sind Zwoi Liebi

O Schonster Schatz, Mein Augentrost

Wie Mache's De Die Zimmerlut

NIKOLSKY, A.
Fenn A Domb Hatan Kakas Szolal

Novgorod Osi Harangya

NILES
Black Is The Color Of My True Love's Hair

Frog In The Spring, The

If I Had A Ribbon Bow

Lass From The Low Countree, The

Milk Maid, The

Warrenton

Wood, Marian Louise
Lovin' Tree, The

NILES; BRANT
Down In Yon Forest

NILES; GROFF
John Henry

NILES; HELM
Lass From The Low Countree, The

NILES, JOHN JACOB
Curtains Of Night

NILES; SHEPPARD
Devil's Questions, The

Dreary Dream, The

I Gave My Love A Cherry

King William's Son

Lass From The Low Countree, The

Oh Judy, My Judy

Old Lord By The Northern Sea, The

Tiranti, My Love

Warrenton

Water—Cresses, The

Wondrous Love

NILIUS, R.
Strauss, Johann, [Jr.]
Bei Uns Z' Haus

NIN—CULMELL, JOAQUIN
Encina, Juan del
Qu'es De Ti, Desconsolado?
Triste Espana, Sin Ventura!

Ribera, Antonio de
Por Unos Puertos Arriba

Vasquez, Juan
Con Que La Lavare?
De Los Alamos Vengo
En La Fuente Del Rosel
Vos Me Matastes

NIN, J.
And The Angel Woke The Shepherds

Girl Who Cares No Longer, The

'Neath An Oak Tree

O My Love

NINIHANE, ANN
Rose
That Old Gang Of Mine

NINNIN, F.
Palanquette, La

NITSCHE, P.
Aus Der Sierra Morena

Bunt Sind Schon Die Walder

Dort Auf Den Rummelshoh'n

Geh Aus, Mein Herz, Und Suche Freud

Hab Mir Mein Weizen Am Berg Gesat

Laub Fallt Von Den Baumen, Das

Zum Fluss Ging Ich

NITSCHE, PAUL
Greensleeves

NOBLE
Antonino

Bamba, La

Butaquito, El

Canten, Senores Cantores, Tomo I

Canten, Senores Cantores, Tomo II

Carretero, El

Cielito Lindo

Coyote, El

Hughes, Herbert
I Know Where I'm Going

Ilorona, La

Noble
Keep The Song Going

Quiereme, Mariquita

Sandunga, La

Torito, El

Villancico Mexicano

Vreneli

Zihualteco, El

NOBLE, FELIXW
Down In The Valley

NOBLE, HAROLD
Old King Cole

When Johnny Comes Marching Home

NOBLE, RAMON
Bamba, La

NOBLE, RAYMOND
Antonino

NOELTE
Stock
To A Firefly

NOELTNER
Cohan, George Michael
Mary's A Grand Old Name
So Long, Mary

Rodgers, Richard
Maria

Silver
Fair Is Fair

NOETEL, K.F.
Ach Blumlein Blau

Ich Armes Maidlein Klag Mich Sehr

NONO, LUIGI
Machada, Antonio
Ha Venido, Canciones Para Silvia

NORBERT, GERHOLD
Neumann, Emil
Wenn Du Noch Eine Mutter Hast

NORDEN; FRANK
Strauss, Johann, [Jr.]
Viennese Memories

NORDMAN
Greensleeves

NORDMANN
Mozart, Wolfgang Amadeus
Bundeslied

NORDSTROM, CARL-ELOW
Duvans Sang Pa Liljekvist

Gladjens Blomster

Inga, Liten Kvarnpiga

Jag Gar I Tusen Tankar

Jag Gick Mig Ut En Aftonsund

Jag Sag Ett Ljus I Osterland

Jag Vet En Dejlig Rosa

Liten Aftonmusik, En

Om Dagen Vid Mitt Arbete

Seks Svenska Folkvisor

Till Osterland Vill Jag Fara

Vallvisa

NORGAARD, HELMER
Heav'n

NORGAARD, JOHS.
Danmark

Finland

Hartmann, Johan Peder Emilius
Sommerdag, En

Norden

NORGARD, H.
Heaven

NORMAN
Down In The Valley

Fibich, Zdenek (Zdenko)
Poeme

Little Wheel A-Turnin'

Lonesome Valley

Offenbach, Jacques
Barcarolle

NORMAN, ROBERT
Honor, Honor

In That Great Gettin' Up Mornin'

Michael, Row The Boat Ashore

Rock-A-My Soul

NORRED, LARRY
Larry Gatlin ... On Stage

NORRMAN
Violin

NORRMAN, JOHN
Anglarna Och Herdarna

Annu En Drom

Flemming, Frederich
Integer Vitae

Hedwall, Anders
Stjarnorna

Jord Och Himmel, Frojden Er

Kjerulf, Halfdan
Sang Pa Vattnet

Korling, Felix
Vandringssang

Lindblad, Adolf Fredrik
Annu En Drom
Larkan I Skyn
Med En Barnbon Pa Sin Mun
Och Drommar Nu Ga
Stilla Pa Himlen Molnen De Segla
Till Dalens Hyddor Smyga, De
Till Den Gamles Badd De Ga

Peterson-Berger, (Olof) Wilhelm
Varen Kom En Valborgsnatt

Soderman, [Johan] August
Langtan "Ser Jag Stjarnorna Sprida
Sitt Flammande Sken"

Till Varens Barn

NORRMAN, RUDOLF
Ack, Om Dagen Svunne Han

Arirang

Barn Ar Fott, Ett

Bellman, Carl Michael
Ulla, Min Ulla, Saj Far Jag Dej
Bjuda

NORRMAN, RUDOLF (cont'd.)
Jag Gick Mig Ned Till Brunnen

Jagarn Och Flickan

Late Drangen, Den

Lovavisan

Serenad

Susani

Three Ravens, The

Ulla, Min Ulla, Saj Far Jag Dej Bjuda

Varfor Ar Du Val Sa Sorgsen?

Vi Sjunger Och Spelar Hafte 1

Vi Sjunger Och Spelar Hafte 5

Viljen I Veta Och Viljen I Forsta

NORTH
Rodby
Sol-Fa Calypso
Song For You, A

NORTON
Dry Bones

NOSKE, PROF. FR.
Padbrue, Cornelis Thymans
Dat Ick Betrovert Ben

NOSSE
And Am I Born To Die?

NOTHER, WILLI
Ade, Zur Guten Nacht

Schonste Land, Das

Schulz
Mond Ist Aufgegangen, Der

NOVAK, JAN
Florilegium Cantionum Latinarum,
Fascicule II

Schola Cantans

NOWACZYK, ERWIN
Moniuszko, Stanislaw
Drobne Utwory Choralne
Trzy Piesni Choralne (Three Choral
Songs)

NOWAK
Camp
Live For Today
Somebody Who Really Cares

Christian
On This Christmas Night

He Don't Love You

Hudson
Shine On

Ley
Together We Can All Be Free

Mason
Love Takes Time

Medema, Kenneth Peter
Together

Mitchell
Teach Me To Swim

Operator

NOWAK, JERRY
Allen, Peter
I Honestly Love You

Ascher, Kenneth Lee
You And Me Against The World

Baby Come Back To Me

Bell, Thomas
You Make Me Feel Brand New

Better Than Ever

Burton, Ray
I Am Woman

Carpenter, Richard Lynn
Only Yesterday

Gamble, Kenny
Love Train

Gibb, Barry
Love You Inside Out
Night Fever

In 25 Words Or Less

NOWAK, JERRY (cont'd.)

Joel, William Martin (Billy)
Piano Man

Lambert, Dennis
Put A Little Love Away

Mcbroom, Amanda
Rose, The

Nichols, Roger Stewart
I Won't Last A Day Without You

Nilsson, Harry
Remember

Sea Of Love

Simon, Paul
Kodachrome
Loves Me Like A Rock
Sounds Of Simon And Garfunkel

Still

Turn Around

Woldin, Judd
Measure The Valleys

NOYON
Compere Guillery

Gentil Coqu'licot

Hazart, Jean
Bergere Annette, La

NOYON, JOSEPH
Rouget de l'Isle, Claude Joseph
Marseillaise, La

NYE; BARTHOLOMEW
Black-Eye Susie

Grandma Grunts

NYHOLM, HANS
Bjerre, Jens
Danmark
Solsikke

Hamburger, Povl
Advent
Indbydelse Til Sorgenfri
Skoven
Skovvandring

Ti Danske Sange

Weis, Flemming
Barcarole
Sommersang

Zacharius, Walter
Pigen Der Vandrer
Takkesprog

NYHUS, ROLF
Kvam, Oddvar S.
Blomstertid, Den Nu Kommer

NYVALL
Bishop
Home, Sweet Home

NYVALL, JACOB
Sancta Lucia

OBENSHAIN
Holiday Songbag

O'BRIEN, VINCENT
Green Isle Of Glory

OCHS, KLAUS
Zwei Jagdlieder

OCHSENFAHRT
Wedig, Hans Josef
Wo Rauchende Schlote

OCKER, V.D.
Blume, Karl
Grun Ist Die Heide

O'DONNELL
Men Of The Deeps

OETIKER, A.
Barn, Du Edle Schwizerstarn

'S Vreneli Ab Em Guggisberg

OETIKER, A.; VOGLER, C.
Alte Grenchenerlied, Das

Appenzeller Spynibueb, Der

Du Fruehlig Lirisch Neime Lang

Dur's Wiesetal Gang I Durab

Es Buurebuebli Mag I Nit

OETIKER, A.; VOGLER, C. (cont'd.)

Es Hed Es Schneeli Gschnijed

Es Isch Kei Solige Stamme

Es Taget Vor Dem Walde

Es Wott Es Magedli Frue Ufstah

Frisch Auf, Soldatenblut

Ha Am En Ort Es Bluemeli Gseh

Heimliche Liebe

Juckjuck Auf Dem Zaune, Der

Konigskinder, Die

Langweiser Lied, Das

Maien Isch Kommen, Der

Mein Hauschen Steht Im Grunen

O Du Liebs Aengeli

O Strassburg, O Strassburg

Rot Schwizer, Der

'S Heidelidomm

Sterben Ist Ein' Harte Buss

Stets In Trure Muess I Lebe

Vermahnlied An Die Eidgenossenschaft

Was Heimelig Sig

Was Stot Dene Junge Meitli Wohl A?

OETIKER, AUGUST
Ach Wie Churzen Usi Tage

OFFER, CHARLES K.
Oaken Crib, The

O'HARA
Debussy, Claude
Clair De Lune

Graff
Put Back The Star Of Bethlehem Into
Our Nation's Flag

Sully
I Want To Go Tomorrow

O'HARA; WILSON
Bratton
One World

Rowan
Sons And Daughters Of A Land Reborn

O'HARE
Kern, Jerome
Ol' Man River

OHL
Cerbus
Eternal Spring

Handel, George Frideric
Schallt Laut, Ihr Chore!

OHRWALL
Nu Skall Vi Skorda Linet

OHRWALL, ANDERS
Purcell, Henry
O All Ye People, Clap Your Hands

OKUN
Old King Cole

Stookey, Noel Paul
Christmas Dinner
Very Last Day

OLDEN, G. RONALD C.
I Love My Love In The Morning

OLIVER
Gibson
Soon It Will Be Christmas Day

Lubetkin
Calypso Serenade

Praties They Grow Small, The

Speak Softly Love

Voice Of America, The

Without You

OLIVER; DEXTER
Proud Mary

See Me, Feel Me

OLIVER; DEXTER (cont'd.)

Something

OLIVER; VISCA
Tumba

OLSEN, SPARRE
Nu Solen Gaar Ned

Sjung Hjerte, Sjung En Aftensang

Tolv Norske Folketoner

OLSON
Dance With Me, Tuka

OLSON, DANIEL
Alls Ingen Flicka Lastar Ja

Pa Brollop "E Litta Vise Vill Jag
Framstecke"

OLSON, DANIEL; OLDERMARK, BIRGER
Sopran Och Altroster Del 1. Profana
Sanger

Sopran Och Altroster Del 3. Profana
Sanger

OLSSON, DANIEL
Fyra Folkvisor

OLSSON, OTTO
Dalvisa

Domaredansen

Jan Hinnerk

OLTRA
Campana Del Pueblo, La

OMER, BENJAMIN
Twelve Folksongs

OPHAVEN, HERMANN
Horch, Was Kommt Von Draussen Rein

OPHOVEN
Ahle, Johann Rudolph
Guldene Sonne Bringt Leben Und
Wonne, Die

Albert
Waldfahrt

Rathgeber
Ist Etwas So Machtig

Schulz, Johann Abraham Peter
Mond Ist Aufgegangen, Der

OPHOVEN, H.
Friderici, Daniel
Wir Lieben Sehr Im Herzen

Silcher, Friedrich
Drunten Im Unterland

OPHOVEN, HERMANN
Beethoven, Ludwig van
An Die Freude

Bella Bionda

Charpentier, Marc-Antoine
Fur Den Frieden In Der Welt
Fur Den Frieden In Der Welt

Des Sommers Letzte Rose

Du Schones Madchen Aus Den Bergen

Engel Ohne Flugel

Glory, Glory, Halleluja

Greensleeves

Handel, George Frideric
Ombra Mai Fu

Heut Kommt Der Hans

In Der Schweiz Und In Tirol

Kalinka

Kuckuck Ruft Im Grunen Wald

Last Rose Of Summer, The

Madchen Aus Muntenia

Martini, Jean Paul Egide
(Schwarzendorf)
Plaisir d'Amour

Mein Varmeland

O Wie So Schon Und Gut

Offenbach, Jacques
Barcarolle
Galopp Infernale

OPHOVEN, HERMANN (cont'd.)

Prolog

Rubinstein, Anton
Leise Erklingt Eine Melodie

Schwarze Augen, Roter Wein

Tanz Mit Der Dordl

Tarantella, Neapolitana

Tarantella-Neapolitana

Tchaikovsky, Piotr Ilyich
Capriccio

Verdi, Giuseppe
Trinklied
Va Pensiero Sull'ali Dorate
Zigeunerchor

OPPEL, HANS
Jeep, Johann
Musika, Die Ganz Liebliche Kunst

ORCHS, S.
Handel, George Frideric
Break Fairest Dawn

O'REILLY
Kern, Jerome
Jerome Kern Medley

O'REILLY, JOHN
Palmer, Hap
Scamper
Witches Brew

Scelsa, Greg
Everybody Has Music Inside
Friends
Goodbye
It's A Beautiful Day
Sing A Happy Song
World Is A Rainbow, The

ORFF, CARL
Monteverdi, Claudio
Orfeo: Zwei Chore

ORFF, CARL; WILLERT, GERTRUD
Orff, Carl
Lieder Fur Die Schule Heft VI

ORFF; MURRAY
Eight English Nursery Songs

ORLAND, JAN
Pasierb
Four Mountaineer's Carols

ORLOV, V.
Russian Folk Songs

ORREY, L.
Purcell, Henry
Fairest Isle

ORREY, LESLIE
Lass With The Delicate Air, The

OSBORNE, CHESTER G.
Dumb, Dumb, Dumb

OSBURG, R.
Ach Lang Ist's Her

Ade, Mein Kind

Auf, Ihr Freunde In Froher Runde

Dort Drunt Im Schonen Ungarland

Du Und Ich

Eveillez-Vous

Hei, Was Braust Uber Feld Und Hugel

Ich Ging Mit Lust Und Freud

Ich Weiss Ein Rose Bluhn

Mein Weib Und Ich

Nun Eilt Euch, Bringt Die Flaschen
Her

O Juana

Schonster Abendstern

Sonne Sank, Mond Steigt Empor

Wenn Die Nachtigall Singt

Winde Wehn, Schiffe Gehn

OSBURG, RALF
Bei Uns Daheim

Liebe Freunde, Kommt Herbei

Rio Grande

OSER, H.
Isaac, Heinrich
Innsbruck, Ich Muss Dich Lassen

OSER, H. REAS
Rosenmuller, Johann
Welt Ade, Ich Bin Dein Mude

O'SHEA
Bantock, [Sir] Granville
Silent Strings

OSMOND, MARCELLA
Who Is At My Window Weeping?

OSSER
Bell
Glorious Is The Land

OSTERBERG, SVEN
Baklandets Vackra Maja

Hagbom, Hanna
Baklandets Vackra Maja

Loch Lomond

OSTERLING
I Am An American

OSTHOFF, HELMUTH
Regnart, Jacob
Einmals In Einem Tiefen Tal

OTHEGRAVEN
Gestern Bei Mondenschein

Hab Meinen Weizen Am Berg Gesat

Heller Und Ein Batzen, Ein

Is Denn Mei Vater A Leiersmann

Kimmt A Vogerl Geflogen

Rosel Wenn Du Mein Warst

Schonstes Kind, Zu Deinen Fussen

Tragische Geschichte

Wenn Zu Mein Schatzle Kommst

OTHEGRAVEN, A.VON
Wer Geht Mit

OTHMAYR
Hut Du Dich

OTHMAYR, M. CASPAR; REIN, WALTER
Mir Ist Ein Feins Brauns Maidelein

OTTEN
Greene Grow'th The Holly

Jones, Robert [2]
Dreames And Imaginations
In Sherwood Lived Stout Robin Hood

Leontovich, Mykola
Swallow's Christmas Song, The

Make We Joy Now In This Feast

Now May We Mirthe Make

OTTEN, JUDITH
Carnavalsleed

Des Prez, Josquin
Basiez Moy

Dufay, Guillaume
Ce Jour De L'an

Raregek

Weelkes, Thomas
To Shorten Winter's Sadness

OUCHTERLONY
Bonnie Wee Lassie

Darby Kelly

Night-Herding Song

Peter On De Sea Sea Sea Sea

OULD, S. G.
Savile, Jeremiah
Here's A Health Unto His Majesty

OWEN, H.
All The Pretty Little Horses

Every Night When The Sun Goes In

So Far Away

OWEN, IDLOES
Down Among The Dead Men

Handel, George Frideric
Disdainful Of Danger

OWEN, IDLOES (cont'd.)

Sospan Fach

OWENS, H; YODER, P.
Sweet Leilani

PADROS I MONTORIOL, DAVID
Sis Cancons Populars Catalanes

PAGE, N.
Cadman, Charles Wakefield
At Dawning

Wagner, Richard
Pilgerchor

PAGE, ROBERT
Bernstein, Leonard
Best Of All Possible Worlds, The
It Must Be So
Life Is Happiness Indeed
Make Our Garden Grow
This World

PAGOT, J.
Allons En Vendanges

Cloches De Vendome, Les

Delanoe
Tout Va Changer

Mere Antoine, La

Temps De Vivre, Le

Vidalin, M.
Printemps, Le

PAGOT, JEAN
Brassens, Georges
Cane De Jeanne, La
Vent, Le

Brel, Jacques
Amsterdam
Vieux, Les

C'Etait Un Cordonnier

Fugain, Michel
Bravo Monsieur Le Monde

Ma Vaque

Margoton Va-T-A l'Eau

Petite Suite Lorraine

PAHLEN
Anonymous
Pueblos Del Mundo Cantan Asi, Los

Todos A Cantar, Tomo I

PAHLEN, K.
Volkslieder Aus Aller Welt Blatt1

Volkslieder Aus Aller Welt Blatt2

Volkslieder Aus Aller Welt Blatt3

Volkslieder Aus Aller Welt Blatt4

Volkslieder Aus Aller Welt Blatt5

Volkslieder Aus Aller Welt Blatt6

Volkslieder Aus Aller Welt Blatt7

Volkslieder Aus Aller Welt Blatt8

Volkslieder Aus Aller Welt Blatt9

Volkslieder Aus Aller Welt Blatt10:
Tanzlied Von Den Hebriden

Volkslieder Aus Aller Welt Blatt11

Volkslieder Aus Aller Welt Blatt12

Volkslieder Aus Aller Welt Blatt13

Volkslieder Aus Aller Welt Blatt14

PAHLEN, KURT
Grun Sind Die Felder

'S Krahen Die Hahne

So Singen Die Volker Der Erde

Wo Gehst Du Hin?

PAKOLITZ, ISTVAN
Bardos, Lajos
Enekeljetek

PALA, J.
Speenhof, K.
Schutterij, De

PALMER
  Aura Lee

  Eddystone Light, The

  Merrill
    Take Me Along

  Scarborough Fair

PALMER, ANTHONY
  Streets Of Laredo

PALMGREN, SELIM
  Pa Dig Har Jag Tankt

PAPP, AKOS
  Sinikellot VI

PAPPERT, WALTER
  Erde Braucht Regen, Die

PARES, G.
  Saint-Saens, Camille
    Gloire, La

PARKE, DOROTHY
  Blue Hills Of Antrim, The

  By Winding Roads

PARKER
  Avenging And Bright

  Ballynure Ballad, A

  Battle Hymn Of The Republic

  Brahms, Johannes
    Nachtens

  Buffalo Gals

  By'm Bye

  Croppy Boy, The

  Girl I Left Behind Me, The

  Goin' To Boston

  Has Sorrow Thy Young Days Shaded

  I Know Where I'm Goin!

  Johnny, I Hardly Know Ye

  Mason, Lowell
    Work, For The Night Is Coming

  Minstrel Boy, The

  My Gentle Harp

  Parting Glass, The

  Silent, O Moyle, Be The Roar

  Sing, Sing

  Soldier, Soldier, Won't You Marry Me?

  'Tis Pretty To Be In Balinderry

  To Ladies' Eyes

  We May Roam Through This World

  Wearin' Of The Green

  You Fair And Pretty Ladies

PARKINSON
  Lassus, Roland de (Orlandus)
    Ich Weiss Mir Ein Meidlein

  Sermisy, Claude de (Claudin)
    Four Chansons Nos. 1 & 2
    Four Chansons Nos. 3 & 4

PARKINSON, J. A.
  Arcadelt, Jacob
    Bianco E Dolce Cigno, Il
    Gentle, Silver Swan, The
    Margot, Labourez Les Vignes

  Lassus, Roland de (Orlandus)
    Fuyons Tous D'Amour Le Jeu
    Let Us Be Gay
    Out Of Range Of Cupid's Bow
    Quand Mon Mari
    Soyons Joyeux
    When My Old Man Comes Home Too Soon

PARKINSON, JOHN A.
  Three Early Choral Songs

PARKS
  Brown
    Lullaby Moon

PARRY
  I Live Not Where I Love

PARRY, HUBERT; BENSON, LIONEL; SQUIRE,
  W. BARCLAY
  Adam de la Hale
    Love Song

  Albert, Heinrich
    Hasten Hither

  Anonymous
    Cockow, The Sweet Spring
    Cushat Dove, The
    Filles De Lyons
    My Tender Flock
    O Love Regard My Plight

  Arcadelt, Jacob
    Love's Burning Passion

  Bateson, Thomas
    O Fly Not Love
    Phillis Farewell
    Those Sweet Delightful Lillies

  Bennet, John
    Let Go, Why Do You Stay Me?

  Bertani, Lelio
    In Thy Sweet Name

  Calvisius, Seth(us)
    Wiegenlied

  Cavendish, Michael
    Come Gentle Swaines

  Certon, Pierre
    Fa La La, I Cannot Conceal It

  Clemens, Jacobus (Clemens non Papa)
    La, La, Master Peter

  Costeley, Guillaume
    Come Out My Love
    He Who Feels The Winds Of Spring
    I Behold The Streamlet Run

  Des Prez, Josquin
    Sweet Cupid's Darts

  Franck, Melchior
    Who So Doth Love

  Frederici, Daniel
    As Cupid Once

  Garnier
    Wake Me From Sleep

  Gibbons, Ellis
    Long Live Fair Oriana

  Gibbons, Orlando
    Trust Not Too Much Fair Youth

  Giovanelli, Ruggero
    As I Walked In Green Forest

  Goudimel, Claude
    When I Behold Thy Fair Locks

  Hesdin, Nicolle Des Celliers D'
    Ply, Chimney-Sweep Thine Office

  Janequin, Clement
    Ce Moys De May
    In This Lovely Month
    To Yonder Lovely Grove

  Lassus, Roland de (Orlandus)
    I Could With Anger Rage
    Ich Weiss Mir Ein Meidlein
    O Lady Fair Thy Smile
    O Let Me Look On Thee
    Once A Fuller I Espied
    S'io Ti Vedess' Una Sol
    Thou Knowest Fairest Maiden

  Le Jeune, Claude
    Thy Lips Like Roses

  Lefevre, Jacques
    Love Me Truly

  Lichfield, Henry
    All Yee That Sleepe In Pleasure

  Marenzio, Luca
    Thou Queen Of All The World

  Palestrina, Giovanni Pierluigi da
    By The Banks Of The Tiber
    My Heart It Seemed Was Dying
    Time As He Flies
    Vedrassi Prima

  Pilkington, Francis
    Rest, Sweet Nymphs

  Quintiani, Lucretio
    At Sound Of Her Sweet Voice

  Regnard, Francois
    Nymph Of The Magic Attraction

PARRY, HUBERT; BENSON, LIONEL; SQUIRE,
  W. BARCLAY (cont'd.)
  Rore, Cipriano de
    In Your Farewells

  Sandrin
    Harm Of Love, The

  Scarlatti, Alessandro
    Poor Mortal Why Must Thou Languish

  Schein, Johann Hermann
    O'er Ocean Wild

  Sermisy, Claude de (Claudin)
    Despised Be All Worldly Wealth

  Spervogel
    Maiden Beauty

  Stabile, Annibale
    Io Non So Come Vivo

  Sweelinck, Jan Pieterszoon
    O Shout With Gladness
    Thou Hast Alone John

  Tessier, Charles
    As I Saw Clora Walk
    Let Every Heart Be Merry
    O Fair Lady So Bright
    To Lovely Groves

  Verdelot, Phillippe
    I Vostr' Acuti Dardi

  Weelkes, Thomas
    Countrie Paire, A
    David's Lamentation
    Lady Your Eie
    Loe! Country Sports

  Wilbye, John
    Adieu, Sweet Amarillis
    Love Not Me For Comely Grace
    Sweet Love
    When Shall My Wretched Life
    Yee That Do Live

  Witzlav, Prince
    Many A Fool

PASCH
  Weber, Ben Brian
    Es Wollt Ein Mann Zum Weine Gehn
    Rechte Plaudertasche, Eine

PASCH, SILVIO
  Auction Block

  Muskoka

PASFIELD, W.R.
  Sullivan, [Sir] Arthur Seymour
    Climbing Over Rocky Mountains
    Prithee, Pretty Maiden
    There Lived A King
    When Britain Really Rul'd The Waves

PASIERB-ORLAND, JAN
  Gory, Nase Gory

PASS, WALTER
  Vier Deutsche Lieder Aus
    "Selectissimae Necnon
    Familiarissimae Cantiones.
    Besonder Ausserlesener
    Kunstlicher Gesang Mancherlay
    Sprachen"

PASSANI, E.
  Ducasse De Douai, La

  Trois Chansons Populaires Basques

  Trois Chansons Populaires De L'Ile De
  France

PASSANI, EMILE
  Beignets Du Mardi Gras, Les

  Catherinette

  Ce Que Je Veux

  Nid De La Caille, Le

  Ronde Des Filles Du Chat

  Trinite Des Rois, La

PASSAQUET, R.
  Dans La Troupe

  Petit Cheval, Le

  Tu Sens Bon La Terre

PASSAQUET, RAPHAEL
  Noel Noir

PERRY, DAVE
Deck The Halls

PERRY, JEAN
Perry, Dave
There Is A Melody

PERRY, JEAN; BACAK, JOYCE EILERS
Rhythm

Smiles

Special Gift, The

PERRY, L.
Betzner, Jack
Back In Dad And Mother's Day

PERRY, LOU
Godfrey, Bob
That Old Quartet Of Mine

Willson, Meredith
You And I

PERTISSAS, M.
Voici Deja Longtemps

PESSARD
Rouget de l'Isle, Claude Joseph
Marseillaise, La

PETER
Binchois, Gilles (de Binche)
Filles A Marier

PETER, DARRELL
Deck The Halls

PETER, H.A.
Bohmisk Polka

Dansvisa Fran Schlesien

Gang I Min Ungdom, En

Giftaslystna Dottern, Den

Glafs

Kohlbauernbuam Riegelts Enk!

O, Du Skona Mirzo

Osterrikisk Bondvisa

Sa Djup Som Moldau Ar

Tanzlied Aus Schlesien

Und I Wunsch Enk A Guate Gsundheit

Vantande, Den

Var Finns Ett Land

Visa Vill Jag Sjunga, En

PETER, J.
Szaz-Hatvanot Kanon

PETERSEN
Dedrick, C.
Kites Are Fun
One By One

PETERSEN, H; POULSEN, T.
Join In

PETERSEN, RALF
Spirituals For All Heft I

Spirtuals For All Heft II

PETERSON
Willson, Meredith
Seventy Six Trombones

PETERSON-BERGER, W.
Anne Knudsdatter

Compagnons De La Marjolaine, Les

PETERSON-BERGER, WILHELM
Arne Knudsdatter

Compagnons De La Marjolaine, Les

PETKER
Pachelbel, Johann
Sing Songs Of Jubilation

PETOFI, SANDOR
Juhasz, Frigyes
Ha Majd A Boseg Kosarabol

Szokolay, Sandor
Ven Epulet Mar A Vilag

PETRUCCI, OTTAVIANO; HEWITT, HELEN
Canti B: Numero Cinquanta

PETTI
Eighth Chester Book Of Motets: The
French School For Four Voices,
The

Ninth Chester Book Of Motets: The
English School For Five Voices,
The

Tenth Chester Book Of Motets: The
Italian And Spanish Schools For
Five Voices, The

PETTI, A.G.
Chester Madrigal, Bk. 5

Chester Madrigal, Bk. 6

PETTI, ANTHONY
A La Claire Fontaine

PETTI, ANTHONY G.
Chester Books Of Madrigals, The, Book
1: The Animal Kingdom

Chester Books Of Madrigals, The, Book
2: Love And Marriage

PFARR, WILHELM
Auf, Auf Zum Frohlichen Jagen

PFAUTSCH
Beautiful Yet Truthful

Schumann, Robert (Alexander)
Red, Red Rose, A

PFIRSTINGER, F.
Tobler, H.
Ode An Gott

Was Kann Schoner Sein

PFIRSTINGER, FELIX
Liederbuch Fur Gemischten Chor, band I

Liederbuch Fur Gemischten Chor, band
III

Liederbuch Fur Gemischten Chor, band
IV

Liederbuch Fur Gemischten Chor, Band
I

PFLUGER, HANS GEORG
Alleweil Ein Wenig Lustig

Altes Hiddenseer Trinklied

Blumenband, Das, Heft I

Blumenband, Das, Heft II: Ich Hab Die
Nacht Getraumet

Rheinisches Trinklied

Rundgesang Beim Trinken

Vier Trinklieder

PFUST, JOHANN
Carol Of The Bells

PHILLIPS
On Ilkla Moor Baht 'At

PHILLIPS, JOHN C.
O Waly, Waly

Three Scandanavian Songs

PHILLIPS, N.
Li'l Liza Jane

PIATELLI
Banchieri, Adriano
Barca Di Venetia Per Padova

PIATELLI, E.
Banchieri, Adriano
Vivezze Di Flora E Primavera

PICARD, MADELEINE
Roger-Ducasse, Jean-Jules Aimable
Berceuse

PICARD, P.
Bon Vigneron

PICKER, MARTIN
Fors Seulement

PIERCE
Andre, Fabian
Dream A Little Dream Of Me

Burns
Early Autumn

Coots, John Frederick
For All We Know

Liles
Let There Be Music! Let There Be
Love!

PIERCE, BRENT
McHugh, Jimmy
It's A Most Unusual Day

PIERCE, HERBERT
All Through The Night

Shadows Of Night

Twankydillo

PIERNE
Ganne
Marche Lorraine

PIERNE, G.
Gluck, Christoph Willibald, Ritter
von
Choeur Du Deuxieme Acte
Choeur Du Troisieme Acte
Fragments Du Premier Acte

PIERNE, PAUL
Chabrier, [Alexis-] Emmanuel
Espana

PILHAOUER
Quignard, Rene
Chiffonnier, Le

PILLER, BOAZ
Gretry, Andre Ernest Modeste
Garde Passe, La

PILLNEY, K.H.
Ach, Ich Werde Mich Bald Mussen
Bequemen

Drei Altdeutsche Liebeslieder

Reger, Max
Gesang Der Verklarten

PINKHAM, DANIEL
Pepusch, John Christopher
Fill Every Glass

PINNEY
Ward, Samuel Augustus
America The Beautiful

PINSUTI, CIRO
There Is Music By The River

PISANO
Angelico

Handel, George Frideric
Sadly I Languish

Hava Nagila

Iasillo
Holly In Your Heart

Lully, Jean-Baptiste (Lulli)
Gloomy Wood

Palestrina, Giovanni Pierluigi da
Scala Musicale, La

Vivaldi, Antonio
Crying, Weeping

Weelkes, Thomas
Nightingale, Organ Of Delight, The
Three English Madrigals

Zum Gali, Gali

PISK
Costeley, Guillaume
Groan (For A Dejected Suitor)
New Flames For Old
Two-Faced Love

Monkey's Wedding, The

PITCHER
Loesser
Years Before Us, The

Riders In The Sky

Robinson
Water Boy

When The Frost Punkin'

PITCHER, GLADYS
Best, Roberta L.
Teenagers Harmonize

PITFIELD
Kalinka

PITFIELD, T.B.
Carrion Crow, The

PITFIELD, THOMAS B.
Carrion Crow, The

I Live Not Where I Love

Why, Neighbours Are You So Uneasy?

PITFIELD, THOMAS P.
  Chesire Souling Song

PITSCH, ELSE
  Auf, Auf, Zum Frohlichen Jagen

  Dunkle Wolk!

  Horch, Kind, Horch

  Ich Ging Durch Einen Grasgrunen Wald

  Islandfischer

  Tod Reit't Auf Einem Kohlschwarzen
      Rappen, Der

  Wie Herrlich Ist's Im Wald

  Zwei Erntelieder

PIXLEY; WILSON; BRADLEY
  Luders, Rudiger
      Prince Of Pilsen, The

PLANEL, JEAN
  Alsace Est Un Tres Beau Pays, L'

  Aviron, L'

  Belle Francoise, La

  Cantate D'Elisabeau

  C'Est Le Vent Frivolant

  Dix Chansons Populaires De France,
      Vol. 1

  Dix Chansons Populaires De France,
      Vol. 2

  D'Ou Vient Qu'En Cette

  Faucheurs, Les

  Fille Du Labouroux, La

  Graces Soient Rendues

  Grain D'Cafe, Le

  Mon Pere Avait Cinq Cents Moutons

  Sur Le Pont D'Avignon

  Voici La Saint Jean

PLANEL, ROBERT
  Ecoutons Ces Airs De Fete

PLANK
  Clarkson
      A-Flat Cricket And A B-Flat Frog,
      An

PLANK, D.
  Nestico, G.
      Light Up The World

PLANK, DAVID
  Gentry
      Ode To Billy Joe

  McGlohon, Loonis
      Willow Creek

  Mancini, Henry
      How Soon
      Soldier In The Rain
      Tomorrow Is My Friend
      Two For The Road

  Zynczak, S.
      When Love Is Young

PLANK, DAVID L.
  Joshua

PLATH
  Sehlbach, Oswald Erich
      Gluck Auf, Gluck Auf
      Wir Sind Die Kraft Der Walzen

PLATT
  Lewis
      Our Common Heritage

PLATT, JACK
  Handel, George Frideric
      Verdi Prati

PLATT; LEWIS
  Grieg, Edvard Hagerup
      Boat Song

  Herbert, Victor
      Babes In Toyland

PLE, S.
  Aubade

  Chants D'Hier Et D'Aujourd'hui

  Etoile, L'

PLE, S. (cont'd.)
  Impression Fausse

  La-Bas

  Neige Tombe, La

  Pays Natal, Le

  Petit Bateau Du Pecheur, Le

  Pluie D'Ete

  Simone, Allons Au Verger

  Sommeil Du Chat, Le

PLIESSNIG
  Geah Nar Her Ubers Wiesale

PLOTT
  Gehring, Philip
      Shenandoah

  Schubert, Franz (Peter)
      Grave And The Moon, The
      Night, The

  Weber, Carl Maria von
      Song Of Slumber

PLOTZ
  'S Bluemli

PNO
  Stanford, Charles Villiers
      Devon, O Devon, In Wind And Rain
      Drake's Drum

POCKRISS; ADES
  Vance
      Catch A Falling Star

POCWIERZ, ANTONI
  Piesni Cieszynskie I Zywieckie

POHL, R.
  Schumann, Robert (Alexander)
      Des Sangers Fluch

POLETTI, C.
  Source, La

POMMER, HELMUT
  Grunet, Felder, Grunet, Wiessen!

  Schlaf, Mein Kindlein

  Still, Still!

  Volkslieder Und Jodler Aus Vorarlberg

  Wofferl, Hast Schon Aussiguckt

POMMER, J.
  Bas'chen, Das

  Bundesfeier

  Fuhrmannslied, Das

  Gamsenjager, Der

  Goldvogelein Gibt Bescheid, Das

  G'sundheit Und A Langs Leben

  Im Fruahjahr

  In Klangfurt Und St. Veit

  Leben In Steiermark, Das

  Nachdem San's Gar Worn

  Osterlied

  'S Peterbrundl

  Schnadahupfl

  Schnadahupfln Vom Grundlsee

  Schwere Trennung

  Seiser Almlied, Das

  Senndrin, Die

  Steirische Brauch, Der

  Vierzeiliege

  Wir Kommen Vom Gebirg

POMMER, JOSEF
  Dreiunddreizig Deutsche Volkslieder

  Ein Und Zwanzig Deutsche Volkslieder

  Funfundzwanzig Deutsche Volkslieder

  Sechzehn Volkslieder Aus Dem
      Deutschen Alpen

POMMER, JOSEF (cont'd.)
  Sechszig Frankische Volkslieder

  Siebenundzwanzig Deutsche Volkslieder

  Vierundvierzig Deutsche Volkslieder

  Vierundzwanzig Deutsche Volkslieder

PONT, KENNETH
  Seconds And Thirds

PONTEN, JAN
  Barn Ar Fott Pa Denna Dag, Ett

POOLER
  Fisher
      Simple Holiday Joys

  Knight
      Oh To Have Been

  Schmidt
      Try To Remember

  Schmidt, Harvey
      Try To Remember

  Simple Gifts

  Tum Balalaika

  Wailie, Wailie

POOLER, FRANK
  Rosaenz, E.E.
      Carnavalito Quebrandeno

POOLER, BRENT
  Pierce
      Winter Idyll, A

POOLER, FRANK
  Duda, Theodor
      Mi Y'Malel

  Kirk, Theron Wilford
      Music, I Like It A Lot!

  Neufeld
      Songs From "Twelfth Night"

  Nystedt, Knut
      Veni

  Trubitt, Allen Roy
      Madrigal

POOLER, M.
  Schumann, Robert (Alexander)
      Swallows, The

POOLER, MARIE
  Concert Sounds For Treble Voices

  Concert Time For Treble Voices

  Descants On Sixteen Traditional Songs

POOS, H.
  My Bonnie Lies Over The Ocean

  She'll Be Coming

POOS, HEINRICH
  Es Ragt Ein Berg

  Wagner, Richard
      Brautchor
      Chor Der Spinnerinnen
      Mit Gewitter Und Sturm
        (Matrosenchor)
      Steuermann, Lass Die Wacht!

POPOV, SZ.
  Olvad A Ho

PORRET, J.
  Shostakovich, Dmitri
      Au Devant De La Vie

PORTER
  Aiken, Walter H.
      All Through The Night

  Bobrowitz, David
      And I Remember

  Smith
      America

  Ward, Samuel Augustus
      America The Beautiful

PORTER, W.
  Spink
      Sleep All My Joys
      Tell Me Where The Beauty Lies
      Thus Sung Orpheus To His Strings

POSCHL, A.
  Am Samstag Auf' D'nacht

  Es Ging Ein Magdlein Grasen

POSCHL, A. (cont'd.)

    Es Ist Einer Allhier

    Jagersmann Und Sennerin

    Johannis Reigen

    Schwarze Kuahlan

    Unter Linden

    Verlassene, Die

    Vierzeiler

    Wenn Alles Wieder Aper Werd

    Wir Wollen Frohlich Heben An

POSER, HANS
    Turili-Turila

POSTON
    Penguin Book Of Christmas Carols, The

    Penguin Book Of Christmas Carols,
       The, Book 2

POSTON, ELIZABETH
    Black Chimney-Sweeper, The

    Cuckoo Dear

    Dance To Your Daddie

    Female Highwayman, The

    Spinning-Wheel Song

    Water Of Tyne, The

POTTER, A.J.
    Lovlie Jemmie

POTTLE, SAM
    Foster, Stephen Collins
       Banjo Medley
       Beautiful Dreamer
       My Old Kentucky Home

POUINARD, A.
    A Paris Y'a Eut' Un Bal

    Allons Au Bois, Ma Mignonnette

    Au Pont Du Nane

    Ave Maria Stella

    Bacchus Assis Sur Son Tonneau

    Berceuse Creole

    Bonhomm', Bonhomm'

    Bonjour La Compagnie

    Brunetta, Allons Gaiement

    Ce Sont Les Dames De Rouen

    Ce Sont Les Enfants De Babylone

    C'Est Dans L'Etat Ou Je Suis

    Chanson De L'Aveine

    Chanson De L'Ivrogne

    Chanson De Mai

    Clairon Du Roi, Le

    Diable Est Venu Dans La Ville, Le

    D'ou Reviens-Tu, Mon P'tit Louis

    Ecoliers De Pontoise, Les

    Etoile Du Nord, L'

    Fagoteur, Le

    Fille Du Soldat, La

    Gueule Au Vent, La

    J'Ai Encore A Vendre

    J'Ai Trois Vaisseaux

    Je Voudrais Bien Me Marier

    Joli Rosier

    Laissez-Moi Planter Mes Pois

    Mon Pere M'A Mariee

    Navigateurs, Les

    Nous Sommes Partis De Toulon

    Pap Me Defend D'Aller Au Bois

POUINARD, A. (cont'd.)

    Papier D'Epingle

    Papillon D'Amour

    Petit Cordonnier, Le

    Poulette Grise, La

    Pourquoi Me Mariait-On?

    Quand J'Etais Chez Mon Pere

    Quand Papa Lapin Mourra

    Ronde Du Lievre

    Sainte Catherine, La

PREIME, EBERHARD
    Neues Sing- Und Spielbuch

PRENTICE, FRED
    America The Beautiful

PREUSS, THEO.
    Christmas In Song

PRICE, MILBURN
    Turtledove, The

PRICE, NANCY
    Besig, Don
       Christmas Is...Love
       Come Follow Me
       Fly Away
       Living Free

PRIN
    Williams
       Don't Wait 'Til Tomorrow
       End Or The Beginning, The
       Merry Christmas Past

PRITCHARD, ARTHUR J.
    Polly Oliver

PRIZER, WILLIAM F.
    Libro Primo De La Croce

PROST, G.
    Bring Back

PROTHEROE
    Rider-Meyer, L.
       Dey Can't Cotch Me To Bury Me

    Songs Of Praise

PROTHEROE, DANIEL
    Faning, Eaton
       Song Of The Vikings

PROVENCHER, F.
    Chant Des Saisons, Le

PRUEFER, ARTHUR
    Schein, Johann Hermann
       Collected Works

PRUSSING, STEPHEN
    Hayo, Haya

PUDELKO, WALTHER
    Augsburger Tafelkonfekt

    Dowland, John
       Komm Zuruck
       Scheiden Muss Ich Jetzt Von Dir

    Rosentor, Das

PUERLING, GENE
    Nightingale Sang In Berkeley Square,
       A

PUERLING, GENE; MATTSON, PHIL
    Put On A Happy Face

PURRINGTON, B.R.
    Hassler, Hans Leo
       Chiara E Lucente Stella

PURRINGTON, BRUCE R.
    Hassler, Hans Leo
       Hor Va Canzona Mia

PUTZ, EDUARD
    Drei Amerikanische Volkslieder

QUAEGBER
    Ei Wie So Toricht Ist

QUEROL I GAVALDA, MIGUEL
    Cancionero Musical De Gongora

    Cancionero Musical De La Colombina

    Canconer Catala Dels s.XVI-XVIII

    Madrigales Espanoles Del s.XVI;
       Cancionero De La Casanatense

    Polifonia Profana

QUEROL I GAVALDA, MIGUEL (cont'd.)

    Teatro Musical De Calderon

    Villancicos Polifonicos Del s.XVII

QUIGNARD, JEAN-RENE
    Menuet d'Exaudet

QUILICI, F.
    A Tribbiera

    Bartalumea

    Giandarmeria Di Serra, La 3men, Acap

    O Piscador Di L'Onda

    O Ziu Andria

    U Mere Pastore

    U Trenu

    Una Sera, Per Furtuna

QUILTER
    Mellish
       Drink To Me Only

    My Lady Greensleeves

QUINN
    De Pass
       I Am One With My Black Brother

    Sometimes I Feel Like A Motherless
       Child

RAB, ZSUZSA
    Kovacs, Matyas
       Ket Kis Korus

RACEK, F.
    Schubert, Franz (Peter)
       Vaterland, Vaterland, Nimm Uns Auf

RACHLEW, A.
    Beethoven, Ludwig van
       O Welche Lust!

    Haydn, [Franz] Joseph
       Liebes Ma2dchen

RACHLEW, ANDERS
    Anonymous
       Serenade

    Beethoven, Ludwig van
       Fangekor

    Bellman, Carl Michael
       Till De Fornama

    Fem Sange

    Kuhlau, Friedrich
       Hymne

    Nielsen, Carl
       Sa Saetter Vi Piben I Ovnens Krog

    Schubert, Franz (Peter)
       Sanctus

RADEL, FRITZ
    Da Drunten Im Tale

RADERMACHER, FR.
    All Mein Gedanken

    Auf Einem Baum Ein Kuckuck

    Rathgeber
       Fratres Exultate, Was Hilft Uns
       Traurig Sein

RADERSCHEIDT
    Klefisch, Walter
       Et Log Ner Geiss

RADNOTI, MIKLOS
    Bardos, Lajos
       Himmusz A Bekerol

    Ribari, Antal
       Himnusz A Bekerol

RAFFAT DE BAILHAC
    Egunttobatez Nindaque Larik

    Mendian Zoinen Eder

    Nik Badut Maitenobat

RAHLFS
    Bein, Wilhelm
       Auf Der Luneburger Heide

RAHLWES
    Handel, George Frideric
       Triumph Von Zeit Und Wahrheit

    Heiden, Bernhard
       Triumph Von Zeit Und Wahrheit

RAICS, ISTVAN
  Ranki, Gyorgy
    Fenyben Furdik A Fold

RAINER, R.
  Lehar, Franz
    Pikanterien

RAJCS, I.
  Palestrina, Giovanni Pierluigi da
    Koszonto Enek

  Schumann, Robert (Alexander)
    Im Utnak Indul

RALEIGH
  Morley, Thomas
    April Is In My Mistress' Face

  Pilkington
    O Softly Singing Lute

RALF
  Star-Spangled Banner, The

RALF, EINAR
  Ekot

  Jatten

  Tis The Last Rose Of Summer

RALF, EINAR; BLENNOW, RAGNAR; NORRMAN,
    JOHN

  Stora Korboken

RAMBERG, PAUL
  Hosten Ar Kommen

  Min Lilla Vra Bland Bergen

  Sandstrom, Israel
    Min Lilla Vra Bland Bergen

RAMRATH
  Hirtenlied Aus Hallingtal

  Verwehrter Einlass

RAMSEY
  Handel, George Frideric
    Dove Sei

  Morley, Thomas
    Those Dainty Daffodillies

  Tchaikovsky, Piotr Ilyich
    Fair Was The Garden

  Vaughan Williams, Ralph
    Fain Would I Change That Note

RAMSEY, BASIL
  Berlioz, Hector (Louis)
    Thou Must Leave Thy Lowly Dwelling

  Haydn, [Franz] Joseph
    False Philosophy
    List, Love, To Me

  Mozart, Wolfgang Amadeus
    Happy, O Happy He
    Thou Soul Of The Universe

  Sullivan, [Sir] Arthur Seymour
    Brightly Dawns Our Wedding Day
    Sing Derry Down Derry

RAMSEY, WILLIAM
  Mendelssohn-Bartholdy, Felix
    Auf Dem See

RANDALL, PETER
  Certon, Pierre
    La, La, La, Je Ne L'ose Dire

RANDOLPH
  Bennet, John
    Weep, O Mine Eyes

  Cocchi, Gioacchino
    Colla Botiglia In Mano

  Dowland, John
    Disdain Me Still
    Fine Knacks For Ladies

  Ford, Thomas
    Since First I Saw Your Face

  Jackson, William
    Time Has Not Thinned My Flowing
      Hair

  Lassus, Roland de (Orlandus)
    Mon Coeur Se Recommande A Vous

RANDOLPH, DAVID
  Lassus, Roland de (Orlandus)
    Mon Coeur Se Recommande A Vous

  Monteverdi, Claudio
    Lagrime D'Amante Al Sepolcro
      Dell'Amata

RANSE, MARC DE
  Rouget de l'Isle, Claude Joseph
    Marseillaise, La

RAPHAELSON
  Musikanten, Die

RAPPAPORT, JONATHAN
  Hush-A-Bye, Don't You Cry

RASMUSSEN, H. BRO
  Fem Danske Sange

  Holm, Peder
    Den Forste Forarsdag
    Fugl Flyver Hvid, En
    Fuglene Tav Naesten Brat

  Jersild, Jorgen
    Lyse Naetter, De
    Natteregn

RASTALL, RICHARD
  Six Songs From The York Mystery Play
    "The Assumption Of The Virgin"

RATCLIFFE
  Five Hundred Miles

  Greenback Dollar

  Lemon Tree

  Pearsall, Robert Lucas de
    Sing We And Chaunt It

  Sing Out

RATCLIFFE, D.
  Eight For Christmas

RATCLIFFE, DESMOND
  Crimson Rose, A

  Handel, George Frideric
    Dove Sei
    Hear Thou My Weeping
    Where E'er You Walk

  Sullivan, [Sir] Arthur Seymour
    Captain Of The Pinafore
    With Catlike Tread

  This Joyful Eastertide

RATHGEBER
  Klink, Waldemar
    Freu Dich, Mein Herz

  Radermacher, Friedrich
    Es War Schon Immer So

  Spitta, Heinrich
    Ist Etwas So Machtig

RAUGEL, FELIX
  Janequin, Clement
    Ciel, Air Et Vents

  Maillard, Rene
    Amour Perdit Les Traictz Qu'Il Me
      Tira

  Sermisy, Claude de (Claudin)
    Praeparate Corda Vestra

RAUGEL, FRANZ
  Le Blanc, Didier
    O Doux Baisers, Colombin
    On Peut Feindre Par Le Cizeau
    Pour Voir Ma Fin Toute Asseuree
    Quand J'Esprouve En Aimant La
      Rigueur D'Une Dame
    Si Tost Que Vostre Oeil M'Eut
      Blesse

RAVIZE
  Wagner, Richard
    Choeur Des Fiancailles

RAVIZE, A.
  Alouette Et Le Pinson, L'

  Ane De Marion, L'

  Bateaux De La Rochelle, Les

  Berceuse Corse

  Berceuse De Visan

  Bergere Et Le Monsieur, La

  Bourree

  Carillon Chartrain

  C'etait Un P'tit Berger

  C'Etait Une Fregate

  Chanson Du Meunier, La

  Chanson Perigourdine

  Chanson Vellave

RAVIZE, A. (cont'd.)

  Chez Nous, Ietions Trois Soeurs

  Coqs, Les

  Danse Des Auvergnats

  Entrez, La Belle, En Vigne

  Guillanneuf, La

  Ile Glas

  Laute Yourn

  Lou Moulinie-Languedoc

  Mariez-Me Donc

  Mere, Mere, Mere

  Petit Jean

  Petit Mari, Le

  Peureux, Le

  Pinson, Le

  Prends Garde Au Loup

  Quand Les Conscrits Partiront

  Qu'on Apporte Ma Flute

  Sabotier, Le

  Seize Chansons Populaires

  Si Je Savais Voler

  Testament De L'ane, Le

  Tisserands, Les

  Trois Navires Sont A Toulon

  Valet D'etretat, Le

  Wagner, Richard
    Choeur Des Fiancailles
    Choeur Des Jeunes Pelerins

RAVIZE, B.; FOREST, B.; CLOUZOT, M.-R.
  Guirlande, La,deuxieme Recueil

RAY, JERRY
  Omartian, Michael
    One Song Is Not Enough

  Parnes, Paul
    Happy Is

  Scelsa, Greg
    Believe In Yourself

  Scott, Dennis
    Songs

RAYMOND
  Church
    Snow

  Curry
    Music, When Soft Voices Die
    Reuben, Reuben, I've Been Thinking

  Lincke
    Glow-Worm

  Martin
    Shepherds Nowell, The

  Rasley, John M.
    I Never Saw A Moor

  Sayers
    Who Calls?

  Scogin, Aurelia
    Look Well To This Day

  Sherman
    Autumn
    Joy
    Knowledge
    Love

  Smith
    Cape Cod Chantey

  Williams
    Dreams I Dreamed, The
    My Lord's Always Near

  Woodside
    Michael, Row The Boat Ashore

RAZEY
  Este
    How Merrily We Live

READ
  Harvest Song

  O'er Yonder In The Wood

REBAY, FERDINAND
  Du, Du Liegst Mir Im Herzen

  Hans Und Liesel

  Vetter Michel

RED, BURYL
  Getting It Together

  Pottle, Sam
    America The Beautiful

  Promised Land, The

  Radioland

REDDICK
  Humperdinck, Engelbert
    Children's Prayer

  Offenbach, Jacques
    Barcarolle

REDLICH
  Monteverdi, Claudio
    A Un Giro Sol De' Bell' Occhi
    Baci Soavi E Cari

REDMAN
  Barbara Allen

REDMAN, REGINALD
  Barbara Allen

  O Waly, Waly

REE, J.V.D.
  Swing Low Sweet Chariot

REED
  Autumn Leaves

  Brahms, Johannes
    Treue Liebe

  Dresser
    My Gal Sal

  Faure, Gabriel-Urbain
    At The Water's Edge

  Jennings
    Michigan Morn

  Pledge Of Allegiance, The

  Purcell, Henry
    Trumpet Song

  Wonderland By Night

  Work, Henry Clay
    Grandfather's Clock

REED, W.; MILCHBERG, J.; ROBLES, D.
  El Condor Pasa

REES
  Brahms, Johannes
    Wiegenlied

REES; MENDOZA
  Carols With Chimes

REESE, JAN; BACAK, JOYCE EILERS
  It's Up To You

REGEL, W.
  Drum Freunde, Trinkt Aus Vollen Fass

  Es Geht Ein Dunkle Wolk Herein

  Es Geht Wohl Zu Der Sommerzeit

  Grimmig Tod, Der

  Gutzgauch Auf Dem Zaune Sass, Der

  Von Edler Art

REGER
  Gruss

  Hermann, Nikolaus
    Ye That Have Spent The Silent Night

  Wurzburger Glockli, Die

REGER, M.
  Altfranzosisches Tanzlied

  Donati, Baldassare (Donato)
    Villanella Alla Napolitana

  Hassler, Hans Leo
    Fein'slieb Du Hast Mich G'fangen

  Meyland, J.
    Herzlich Tut Mich Erfreuen

REGER, M. (cont'd.)
  Morley, Thomas
    Fruhling Umstrahlt Ihr Antlitz Zart
    Tanzlied

REGER, MAX
  Anonymous
    Weh! Dass Ich Musste Schauen

  Gastoldi, Giovanni Giacomo
    An Hellen Tagen

  Lully, Jean-Baptiste (Lulli)
    Haltet Uns, Wonnige Banden
    Liebe Droht Auf Allen Wegen

  Morley, Thomas
    Nun Strahlt Der Mai
    Sing We And Chant It

REHM, WOLFGANG
  Binchois, Gilles (de Binche)
    Chansons

REIBEL, G.
  Nantes

REIBOLD
  Sibelius, Jean
    Finlandia

REICHARDT, J. FR.
  Rein, Walter
    Wach Auf Mein Herzens Schone

REICHENBACH, H.
  Classic Canons

  Easy Canons

  Modern Canons

REIMANN; BROWN
  Spinning Song

REIN
  Mozart, Wolfgang Amadeus
    Dir, Seele Des Weltalls

  Zuccalmaglio, Anton Wilhelm Florentin
    von
    Es Fiel Ein Reif

REIN, W.
  A, B, C, Die Katze Lief Im Schnee

  Albert, Heinrich
    Junges Volk, Man Rufet Euch

  Anke Von Tharau

  Auf Dieser Welt

  Butzemann, Der

  Drei Laub Auf Einer Linden

  Es Hat Sich Ein Bauer Ein Tochterlein

  Es War Einmal

  Frau Musica Singt, "Die Beste Zeit Im
    Jahr Ist Mein"

  Guldne Sonne, Die

  Hasleins Klage

  Ich Hatte Mein Feinsliebchen

  Im Marzen Der Bauer

  In Meiner Eltern Garten

  Jetzt Reisen Wir Zum Tor Hinaus

  Lustigen Musikanten, Die

  O Du Schoner Rosengarten

  Schatzchen, Du Liegst Mir Im Sinn

  Schifflein Sah Ich Fahren, Ein

  Vo Luzern Uff Waggis Zue

  Wer Bekummert Sich Denn, Wenn Ich
    Wandre

  Zwischen Berg Und Tiefem Tal

REIN, WALTER
  Aenneli, Wo Bist Gester Gsi

  Ahle, Johann Rudolph
    Lob Der Musik

  Eccard, Johannes
    Nun Schurz Dich Gretelein

  Es Hat Sich Ein Bauer Ein Tochterlein

  Frederici, Daniel
    Drei Schone Dinge Fein

REIN, WALTER (cont'd.)
  Gastoldi, Giovanni Giacomo
    Fahren Wir Froh Im Nachen

  Hassler, Hans Leo
    Nun Fanget An
    Tanzen Und Springen

  Im Aargau Sind Zweu Liebi

  Jetzt Reisen Wir Zum Tor Hinaus

  Praetorius, Michael
    Morgenstern Ist Aufgegangen, Der

  Scandello, Antonio (Scandellus,
    Scandelli)
    Hennlein Weiss, Ein

  Senfl, Ludwig
    Brunnlein, Die Da Fliessen, Die

  Wenn Ich Des Nachts Vor Dem Feuerlein
    Steh

REINECKE
  Beethoven, Ludwig van
    Meeresstille Und Gluckliche Fahrt

REINECKE, C.
  Beethoven, Ludwig van
    An Die Freude

  Schumann, Robert (Alexander)
    Zigeunerleben,

REINECKE, CARL
  Schumann, Robert (Alexander)
    Drei Chore

REINER
  Wenn Du Schon Warst

REINICKE, CARL
  Schumann, Robert (Alexander)
    Beim Abschied Zu Singen

REINISCH, H.
  Die Bergleut Sind Eine Edle Zier

REITER, A.
  Gute Nacht

  Jager Langs Dem Weiher Ging, Ein

  Wachtelschlag, Der

REITER, ALBERT
  Alleweil Kann Ma Net Lustig Sein

  Da Drob'n Auf'n Berg

  Drei Berg Und Drei Tal

  Es Ging Ein Bauerlein

  Fruahjahr, Das

  Hutschi Heili

  I Woass Net

REITNER, J.
  Innviertler G'sangl

REPPA
  Sendt, Willy
    Tauch An Und Pfluge

REUCHSEL, A.
  Homme Petit, Un

  Petit Mari, Le

  Roussignolet, Le

REUCHSEL, E.; MARTIN, RENE
  Bal Des Souris, Le

  Dix Vielles Chansons Populaires De
    L'Ouest

  En Revenant De Noces

  Ma Mer' M'Envoie-t-Au Marche

  Mariage Du Papillon, Le

  Mort Du Mari, La

  Noel

  Petit Ageasson, Le

  Petit Nigaud, Le

  Retour Du Marin, Le

  Turlututu

REUSCHLE
  Kammerer, Imanuel Johannes
    Tone Flug Und Silber, Der

REUSCHLE (cont'd.)
Sturmer, Bruno
Gottes Gewaltigster Flug

REUTER
Es Freit Ein Wilder Wassermann

Sibelius, Jean
Traumereien

REUTER, FRITZ
Maria Ging Ubers Weite Land

Wenn Die Soldaten

REUTTER
Muss I Denn, Muss I Denn?

REVESZ, L.
Ay Cubano

Dalok Leninrol

REYNOLDS, GORDON
Chidren's Songs From Bohemia

Children's Songs From Bohemia

REZNICEK, E.N.
Sieben Deutsche Volkslieder

RHEA
Billy Boy

Early One Morning

Handel, George Frideric
Wher'er You Walk

Haul On The Bowlin'

Home On The Range

Hubert
Gulf Clouds

I Got A Home In-A That Rock

Montrose, Jack
Clementine

Robin Adair

She Walks In Beauty

Skip To My Lou

Vocal Pizzicato

White
Billy Boy

Yeo, Heave Ho'

RHEA, LOIS; RHEA, RAYMOND
It's Time For Singing

Junior-Senior Hi In Song

RHEA, RAYMOND
Great Day

My Lord, What A Morning

RHEA, RAYMOND; RHEA, LOIS
Singing Together

RHEIN, ROBERT
Ae Fond Kiss

Kelvingrove

RICE
Purcell, Henry
More Love Or More Disdain I Crave

RICE, M.R.
Men Of Harlech

RICH
Rubinstein, Anton
Welcome Sweet Spring-Time

Wilson, Henry Lane
Carmena

RICHAR, E.
Wallfahrerlied

RICHAR, ELSA
D'vogalan, D'vogalan

Enta Da Doana

Es Kam Ein Junker

Es War Einmal Ein Abend Spat

Geh' I Zum Brunndelein

Gestern Bei Mondenschein

Heidl Popeidl

Heute Rupf' Ich Gansekraut

RICHAR, ELSA (cont'd.)
Ich Wollt' Wenn's Kohlen Schneit

Kuckuck Auf Dem Zaune Sass, Der

Lercherlein!, Das

Schone Lilofe, Die

Trost Beim Abschied

Wann Kommt Die Frohe Stunde

Zwei Blonde Konigskinder

Zwei Und Dreisig Deutsche Volkslieder

RICHARD, CHARLES
Brahms, Johannes
Es Geht Ein Wehen

RICHARDSON
Deaf Woman's Courtship, The

Down By The Riverside

Ware, John Marley
This Day Is Mine

RICHARDSON, A.
Voices In Song

RICHARDSON, JOHN A.
Down By The Riverside

RICHARDSON, MICHAEL
Blow The Candles Out

Hush-A-Bye, Don't You Cry

Poor Wayfarin' Stranger

RICHTER
Haydn, [Franz] Joseph
Augenblick, Der

Marenzio, Luca
Corran di puro latte

Morley, Thomas
Lo, She Flies

Schubert, Franz (Peter)
Lebenslust

RICHTER, C.G.
Ives, Charles
For You And Me!

RICHTER, CLIFFORD G.
Distler, Hugo
Abendlied Eines Reisenden
Es Geht Ein Dunkle Wolk Herein
Feuerreiter, Der
I Know A Lovely Rose
Lebewohl
Lied Vom Winde
Lob Auf Die Musik
Nimmersatte Liebe
Sonne Sinkt Von Hinnen, Die
Stundlein Wohl Vor Tag, Ein
Vorspruch
Wacht Auf, Es Tut Euch Not!

Ives, Charles
For You And Me!

Janacek, Leos
Kacena Divoka
Nase Pisen
Pisen V Jeseni

Lassus, Roland de (Orlandus)
Ciprine

Mendelssohn-Bartholdy, Felix
Drei Volkslieder

RICHTER-KENDELBACHER, HILDE
Singende Kreis, Der

RICKETTS, JOHN A.
I Wished To Be Single Again

RIDER
Eccard, Johannes
Nun Schurzdich Gretein

Hassler, Hans Leo
Once More We Sing

Lassus, Roland de (Orlandus)
Peasant Wants To Dance, The

Schubert, Franz (Peter)
Echo, The
Secret, The
Who Ne'er His Bread With Tears Did
Eat

RIDOUT
O Canada

RIDOUT, GODFREY
Blooming Bright Star Of Belle Isle

J'Entends Le Moulin

Sainte Marguerite

RIEDEL, PETER
Hoch Auf Dem Gelben Wagen

Horch, Was Kommt Von Draussen Rein

RIEDL, O.M.
Braune Wange, Roter Mund

Tiritomba

Wie Schon Bluht Uns Der Maien

RIEGGER
Bassett, Karolyn Wells
Take Joy Home

Brahms, Johannes
In Silent Hight

Campbell-Tipton, Louis
Spirit Flower, A

Firestone, Idabelle
In My Garden

Friml, Rudolf
Allah's Holidays
Giannina Mia

Gretchaninov, Alexander Tikhonovich
Over The Steppe

Guion, David Wendall Fentress
All Day On The Prairie

Herbert, Victor
Sweethearts

Kountz, Richard
A La Russe

Mana-Zucca, Mme. (Augusta Zuckermann)
Big Brown Bear, The

Rasbuch, Oscar
Trees

Romberg, Sigmund
Will You Remember (Sweetheart)

RIES
Schubert, Franz (Peter)
Thou Art Repose

RIETZ, JOHANNES
Gluck, Christoph Willibald, Ritter
von
Fullet Mit Schalle

Heuschreck, Der

RIETZ, JULIUS
Mendelssohn-Bartholdy, Felix
Collected Edition

RIGGS, EDWARD
Junior Hi Chorister, The

RIKKO-NEWMAN
Rossi, Luigi
Ah, Dolente Partita

RILEY
Feliciano, Jose
Feliz Navidad

Keep Your Hand On The Plow

RILEY, DAVE
Pat-A-Pan

RILEY, DAVE; SCHWARTZ, LARRY
Leigh, Mitch
Impossible Dream, The

RILEY, DAVE; WILSON, DANA
Connor, Jim
Grandma's Feather Bed

Give Me The Simple Life

Lennon, John
Eight Days A Week

Mallett, David
Garden Song

Miller
For Once In My Life

Nice 'N' Easy

Paxton, Tom
My Dog's Bigger Than Your Dog

Sir Duke

Time After Time

RILEY, DAVE; WILSON, DANA (cont'd.)

   Van Heusen, James
     Darn That Dream

RILEY, DAVID
   All Beauty Within You

RILEY, GORDON
   Lorenz, Gordon
     Grandma, We Love You

RILEY; WILSON
   Jobim, Antonio Carlos
     Jazz 'N' Samba

RIMBAULT, E.F.
   Boar's Head Carol, The

RIMMER, ROY E.
   Flies In The Buttermilk

RIMSKY-KORSAKOFF, N.
   Spinning-Top

RIMSKY-KORSAKOFF, N.; SCHINDLER, K.
   Spinning Top

RING, OLUF
   Aagaard, Thomas
     David Og Goliat
     Det Mulmer Mod Den Morke Nat
     Hjalmar Og Ingeborg
     Horer Du Rosten
     Hvem Er Det, Der Bryder Natte
      Morkets Dvalering
     Otte Salmer Og Sange
     Staerkodders Sang Om Bravallaslaget
     Vallarelat
     Ved Babylons Floder

   Stalt Vesselil

RINGWALD
   Alexander
     Christmas Is Being With Friends

   Allen
     Home For The Holidays

   Barry
     Born Free

   Bates
     America The Beautiful

   Berlin, Irving
     Easter Parade
     Give Me Your Tired, Your Poor
     It's A Lovely Day Tommorow
     Say It With Music
     White Christmas

   Geibel, Adam
     Sleep, Sleep, Sleep

   Greenwell
     Christmas Day In The Morning

   Jacobs
     This Is My Country

   Kern, Jerome
     Can't Help Singing
     I'm Old Fashioned
     Ol' Man River
     Poor Pierrot

   Kramer
     No Man Is An Island

   Lane, Burton
     On A Clear Day

   Law
     Patriot Hymn: 1775

   Leigh
     Impossible Dream, The

   Marks
     I Heard The Bells On Christmas Day

   Moline, Robert Lloyd
     You Are Now

   Muhlenberg
     Carol, Brothers, Carol

   Palitz
     While We're Young

   Porter, Cole
     In The Still Of The Night

   Redner, Lewis [Henry]
     Ev'rywhere, Ev'rywhere Christmas
      Tonight

   Rodgers, Richard
     In Concert: Carousel
     Lover
     My Romance

RINGWALD (cont'd.)

   Rox
     It's A Big, Wide, Wonderful World

   Sibelius, Jean
     Five Christmas Songs

   Smalls, Charles
     If You Believe

   Somervell, Arthur
     Walk On, Walk On!

   Sometimes I Feel Like A Motherless
     Child

   Steffe, William
     Battle Hymn Of The Republic

   Three Spirituals

   Torme
     Christmas Song, The

   Ward, Samuel Augustus
     America, The Beautiful

   Whitney, Maurice Cary
     No Man Is An Island

   Wizel
     I May Never Pass This Way Again

   Youmans
     Great Day

   Youmans, Vincent Millie
     Great Day

RINGWALD, RON
   Carribean Carol

RINGWALD, ROY
   Berlin, Irving
     Cheek To Cheek

   Gold, Ernest
     Exodus Song, The

   Harline, Leigh
     When You Wish Upon A Star

   Kern, Jerome
     Long Ago And Far Away

   Steffe, William
     Battle Hymn Of The Republic

RIPPEN, PIET
   Boer Had Maar Ene Schoen, De

RIS, F.
   Da Droben Auf Jenem Berge

   Des Abends Kann Ich Nicht Schlafen
     Gehn

   E Bissele Lieb

   Gestern Abend In Der Stillen Ruh

   Madle Ruck, Ruck, Ruck

   So Geht Es In Schmutzelputz' Hausel

RISCHE, QU.
   Ewig Werden Die Sonn' Und Sterne

   Seht Doch Unsre Madchen

RISCHE, QUIRIN
   Als Wir Jungst In Regensburg Waren

   Auf Dem Hugel Da Steht Eine Birke

   Auf Dem Hugel, Da Steht Eine Birke

   Auld Lang Syne

   Bella Italia

   Berg Fuji, Der

   Blumenstrauss, Der

   Bortniansky, Dimitri Stepanovich
     Ich Bete An Die Macht Der Liebe

   Canzonetta

   Dalmatinische Lieder

   Danza Mexikana

   Denza, Luigi
     Funiculi-Funicula

   Doring, Bruno
     Klange Aus Wien

   Einmal Noch Die Heimat Sehn

   Es Ist So Still Geworden

RISCHE, QUIRIN (cont'd.)

   Fischer, Martin
     Schwarzwaldgrusse

   Fischerlied

   Flotow, Friedrich von
     Mag Der Himmel Euch Vergeben

   Greensleeves

   Herrliche Berge

   Hore, Mein Madchen

   Ich Ging In Den Rosengarten

   Ich Kann Dich Doch Nicht Vergessen

   In Der Rosenzeit

   Jetzt Ist Die Liebschaft Aus

   Junges Madchen Sass Am Meere

   Keiner Weiss, Warum

   Komm In Meine Arme

   Leineweber, Die

   Letzter Tanz

   Liebste, Ich Wunsche Dir Gute Nacht

   Lied Der Viehtreiber

   Link
     In Der Sperlingsgasse
     Macht Die Berliner Luft, Das
     Schenk Mir Doch Ein Kleines
      Bisschen Liebe

   Lorencita

   Madchen Mit Den Blauen Augen

   Madchen Und Der Schiffer, Das

   Magdlein Wollt Wohl Fruh Aufstehn,
     Ein

   Mir Ist Ein Rot Goldringelein

   Morgen Will Mein Schatz Verreisen

   O Du Liebes Magdelein

   O Du Schoner Apfelbaum

   Otchi Tchorniya

   Pusstaliebe

   Reiter, Der

   Reiter Wollte Jagen, Ein

   Schultze, Norbert
     Fahre VII

   Silberhelle Wasser Fliessen

   Silbern Schon Fallt Der Morgentau

   Steh Auf Hohem Berge

   Strauss, Josef
     Mein Lebenslauf Ist Lieb Und Lust

   Verdi, Giuseppe
     Evviva, Beviam
     Lodern Zum Himmel
     Va, Pensiero, Sull'Ali Dorate

   Vier Baltische Volkslieder

   Von Luzern Auf Waggis Zu

   Wieder Bluhet Die Linde

   Wir Tanzen Im Maien

   Wo E Kleins Huttle

   Wohlan Die Zeit Ist Kommen

   Zogen Einst Funf Wilde Schwane

   Zwei Gitarren

   Zwei Ukrainische Volksweisen

RISHCE, QUIRIN
   Mozart, Wolfgang Amadeus
     Abendruhe

RISTENPART, KARL
   Zuccalmaglio, Anton Wilhelm Florentin
     von
     Feinsliebchen, Du Sollst Mir Nicht
      Barfuss Gehn

RITTENHOUSE; DE ARAUJO
Bac To De Dus'

RITTER
Wagner, Richard
Faithful And True. Bridal Chorus

RITTMAN
Rodgers, Richard
Preludium

RIX
Bohm, Carl
Calm As The Night

Mascagni, Pietro
Light Divine

Schubert, Franz (Peter)
Standchen

Smetana, Bedrich
Spring Chorus

RIZZO
Addrisi
Never My Love

Blues Back To Back

Carr
South Of The Border Down Mexico Way

Charnin, Martin
I Do Not Know A Day That I Did Not
Love You
Two By Two

Denver
Leaving, On A Jet Plane

Dixon
River, Stay' Way From My Door

Dubin
Lulu's Back In Town

Gershwin, George
But Not For Me
Man I Love, The
Somebody Loves Me

Green
Body And Soul

Mercer
Blues In The Night

Noble
Cherokee

Porter, Cole
Anything Goes
Just One Of Those Things

Rodgers, Richard
Choral Selections From "Two By Two"
My Heart Stood Still

RIZZO, F.
Cacavas, John
Twelve Daze Of Christmas, The

RIZZO, J.
Thanksgiving Suite

RIZZO, JACQUES
Ashford
Ain't Nothing Like The Real Thing

Goodrum, Randy
You Needed Me

Holland
How Sweet It Is (To Be Loved By
You)

Mills, Frank
Little Music Box Dancer

Nelson, Steve
Songbird

Oshrat, K.
Halleluja

Shire, David
Starting Here, Starting Now

Sing

Turk, Roy
Are You Lonesome Tonight

Weill, Kurt
Lost In The Stars

Yancy, Marvin
Our Love

RIZZO, JACQUES C.
Deutschendorf, Henry John (John
Denver)
Leaving On A Jet Plane

RIZZO, JACQUES C.; FRY, GARY D.
Deutschendorf, Henry John (John
Denver)
Leaving On A Jet Plane

ROACH; NAYLOR
Mysels
One Little Candle

ROBERTON
A-Roving

Ae Fond Kiss

Air Falalalo

Ay Waukin O

Ay, Waukin' O!

Bell, Sydney
Oran-A-Chree

Bells Of Shandon, The

Blow Away The Morning Dew

Blue Bonnets Over The Border

Bonnie George Campbell

Caleno Custureme

Carol Of The Drum

Celtic Keening Song

Celtic Lullaby, A

Charlie Is My Darling

Dance To Your Daddy

Dashing White Sergeant, The

De Battle Ob Jericho

De Battle Ob Jerico

Deep River

Devil's Awa, The

Fairest Gwen

Fairy Lullaby

Faithful Johnny

Festa, Costanzo
Down In A Flowery Vale

Fraser, K.
Eriskay Love Lilt

Glenlyon Lament

Go Down, Moses

Gradh Geal Mo Chridh

Gretna Green

Hush-A-Ba Birdie

I Got A Robe

I'll Bid My Heart Be Still

Iona Boat Song

Island Shieling Song

Joy Of My Heart

King Arthur

Kirkconnel Lea

Lassie, Wad Ye Lo'e Me

Lewis Bridal Song

Little David, Play On Your Harp

Loch Lomond

MacGregor's Gathering

Marie's Wedding

Mendelssohn-Bartholdy, Felix
In The Woods

Mingulay Boat Song

Morag's Cradle Song

My Luve Is Like A Red, Red Rose

Nobody Knows De Trouble

Nobody Knows De Trouble I See

O Waly, Waly Up The Bank

ROBERTON (cont'd.)
Oh, By An' By

Oh, Peter, Go Ring Dem Bells

One Morning In May

Peat Fire Smooring Prayer

Pipe The Music

Pratty Flowers

Prince Charlie's Farewell

Queen's Marys, The

Rising Of The Lark, The

Scots Wha Hae

Steal Away To Jesus

Sweet Nightingale

Swing Low, Sweet Chariot

Uist Tramping Song

Westering Home

When De Stars Began To Fall

When De Stars Begin To Fall

ROBERTON, H.S.
Oft In The Stilly Night

Rovin' Boy, The

Welsh Cradle Song

When Your Lamp Burns Down

ROBERTON, HUGH S.
Colledge, Patti
Chip's Carol

Dalmatian Cradle Song

Deep River

Eriskay Love Lilt, An

Fife Fisher Song, A

Flowers O' The Forest, The

Mendelssohn-Bartholdy, Felix
In The Woods

Mice And Men

Morag's Cradle Song

Over Here

Sound The Pibroch

Three Fishers Went Sailing

Wee Cooper O' Fife, The

Wee Willie Winkie

ROBERTS
Lampert
Every Little Boy Can Be President

See Me, Little Brown Boy

Tumba Cana

Tumbando Cana

ROBERTS, CARADOG
Counting The Goats

Mae Tri Pheth

Olwen A'r Gath

Two Fond Hearts

ROBERTS, D.L.
Joplin, Scott
Entertainer, The

ROBERTS, G.
Ives, Charles
Circus Band

ROBERTS, TREVOR
Five Welsh Folk Songs

ROBERTSON
A-Roving

Kennedy-Fraser, Marjory
Eriskay Love Lilt, An

Mice And Men

ROBERTSON (cont'd.)

  Poulton
    Aura Lee

ROBERTSON, K.O.
  Lindstrom, Olaf
    Akallan

ROBIN, M.-T.; DANIEL, E.
  Robin, Marie-Therese
    Trois Cailloux Ronds

ROBINSON
  Brahms, Johannes
    Im Herbst
    In Stiller Nacht
    Wie Melodien Zieht Es Mir

  Janequin, Clement
    Chant Des Oiseaux, Le

  Lampell
    Lonesome Train, The

  Mendelssohn-Bartholdy, Felix
    Nachtigall, Die

  Schubert, Franz (Peter)
    Lebenslust
    Tanz, Der

  Schumann, Robert (Alexander)
    Marienwurmchen

  Sermisy, Claude de (Claudin)
    J'Ay Fait Pour Vous Cent Mille Pas

  Vaughan Williams, Ralph
    Vagabond, The

ROBINSON, S.
  British Grenadiers

  Greene, Edwin
    Sing Me To Sleep

ROBINSON, STANFORD
  Plantation Songs, First Selection

  Polly Wolly Doodle

ROBINSON, T.E.
  Handel, George Frideric
    Wretched Lovers!

ROCHEROLLE
  Messina
    Lahaina

  Morrison
    I Shall Sing

RODBY
  Ager, Milton
    Ain't She Sweet

  Donaldson, Walter
    Yes Sir, That's My Baby

  Mango Walk

  Myrow
    Dig-A Dig-A Dum-Dum
    Doo Bee Doo Bee Dee
    Nobody's Business
    Sing Little Bird

  North
    Scat Cat!

  Rachmaninoff, Sergey Vassilievich
    Cradle Song

  Reeves, J. Flaxington
    Demon Rum

  Sherwin, William F.
    Sign Tonight

  Wish Me A Rainbow

RODBY; ROFF
  Caldara, Antonio
    Sebben Crudele

  Durante, Francesco
    Danza Danza, Fanciulla Gentile

  Lotti, Antonio
    Pur Dicesti, O Bocca Bella

  Scarlatti, Alessandro
    Gia' Il Sole Dal Gange

RODBY, W.
  Movin'

RODBY, WALTER
  Christmas Is Here

  Mulholland, James
    Banks O' Doon, The
    Green Grow The Rashes, O
    Highland Mary
    Red, Red Rose, A

RODBY, WALTER (cont'd.)

  No One's Perfect

RODBY, WALTER; ROFF, JOSEPH
  Companions All

RODER, HELMFRIED
  Donna Donna

  Du Meine

  Dunaj Iwanowitsch

  Einem Iz Doch Zeyer Gut

  Es Geht Ein Dunkle Wolk Herein

  Finnisches Tanzlied

  Hava Netse B'machol

  House Of The Rising Sun, The

  Kunz Von Kaufungen

  Limbo

  Nah Am Fluss

  Nobody's Business

  Oshima

  Pajara Pinta, La

  Papa Didn't Know

  Pastures Of Plenty

  Rosmarin

  Tanz Den Vito

  Temporal

  Troika

  Uskudar

  Walk Right In

  Wet Weather Blues

  Wo Soll Ich Mich Hinwenden

RODGERS
  Vecchi, Orazio (Horatio)
    Chi Vi Mira
    Leggiadretto Clorino

RODGERS, THOMAS
  Skye Boat Song

RODMAN
  Myers
    Feelin' Good
    Little Bit Of Love, A

RODRIGUES
  Merry, Merry Christmas Everywhere!

ROESELING, K.
  Und In Dem Schneegebirge

  Wachet Auf, Ruft Uns Die Stimme

ROESELING, KASPAR
  Gluck Auf Ihr Bergleut Jung Und Alt

ROEST, P.
  Kom, Kom, Kom, Kleine Vis

ROFF
  Bobrov
    Springtime In My Heart

  Debussy, Claude
    Clair De Lune

  Sapienza
    America, Behold Your Destiny

ROFF; CRAIG
  Magee
    High Flight

ROFF, JOSEPH
  Four Children's Songs From Uganda

  Four Folk Songs From China

  Kookaburra

  Sipping Cider Through A Straw

  Sweetly Sings The Donkey

  Three Anatolian Turkish Folk Songs

  Three Folk Songs From Sri Lanka

  Three Songs From Australia

ROGBERG, CARL
  Fabodtrall

  Ganglat Fran Svardsjo

  Glade Spelmannen, Den

  Kotilainen, Otto
    Kullerullvisan

  Kullerullvisan

  Sa Odsligt Molnen Pa Himlen Ga

  Svardsjopolska

  Svensson, Bernhard
    Glade Spelmannen, Den

  Vaggvisa Fran Dalarna

ROGER-DUCASSE
  Chansons Populaires De France

ROGERS
  Allan
    Au Clair De La Lune
    Chopsticks
    Clementine

  Bizet, Georges
    Adagietto

  Foster, Stephen Collins
    Oh Susanna

  Phillips, John
    California Dreamin'

  Puccini, Giacomo
    Musetta's Song

  Snowbird

  Somethin' Stupid

ROGERS, EARL
  All Through The Night

  Allan
    Chopsticks

  Balaloo Lammy

  Londonderry Air

  Passing By

  Row, Row, Row Your Boat

ROGERS, STEVEN
  Handel, George Frideric
    May No Rash Intruder
    Music, Spread Thy Voice Around

ROGET, H.
  Anonymous
    Gai Rossignol Sauvage

ROGNONI, L.; LEYDI, R.
  Sinigaglia, Leone
    Diciotto Vecchie Canzoni Popolari
     Del Piemonte

ROHDE
  Tanze, Du Mein Madchen

  Wie Schon Bluht Uns Der Maien

ROHDE, WALTER
  Dat Du Min Leevsten Bust

ROHWER
  Komm Mit Ins Klingende Neuland

ROHWER, J.
  Auf, Du Junger Wandersmann

ROIDER
  New River Trail

ROLAND-MANUEL
  Trois Chansons Populaires Francaises

ROOS
  Widele, Waddele

ROOSLI; WILLISEGGER; ZIHLMANN
  ...Und Die Spatzen Pfeifen Lassen

ROOT
  Gounod, Charles Francois
    Ring Out, Wild Bells

ROPARTZ, J.-GUY
  Bergers Les Bergeres, Les

  J'm'en Vas Chantant, Riant

  Nous Etions Trois Filles

  P'tite Charmette, La

  Rossignolet Du Bois

  Viens Avec Moi, Charmante Brune

ROS, J.A.
  Tre Svenska Folkvisor

ROSAS, JOHN
  Getabocken Och Vargen

  Morgonvisa

  Skalvisa

  Till En Yngling

  Tva Skalvisor

  Ungkarlsvisa

  Ungmorsskal Fran Kokar

ROSENBAUM, H.
  Dowland, John
    Flow My Tears
    In Darkness Let Me Dwell

ROSENBECKER
  Foster, Stephen Collins
    My Old Kentucky Home

ROSENBERG
  Ahlstrom, Johan Alfred
    Serenade

ROSENSTENGEL, A.
  Texaslied

  Ungarisches Fest

ROSENSTENGEL, ALBRECHT
  Abgeblitzt

  Abschied Von Texas

  All Mein Gedanken

  Bamba, La

  Bauernlied

  Cucaracha, La

  D-Zug Kommt, Der

  Drei Alte Volkslieder—Neu Dargeboten

  Eine Seltene Schonheit

  Fiedelhans

  Gelbe Rose Von Texas, Die

  Good Bye, Lisa Jane

  Gut Nacht, Ladies

  Hannele Und Steffele

  Hava Nagila

  Hochzeit In Bukarest

  Ich Komm Von Alabama

  Katjuschka

  Lach Mein Schatz

  O Hein!

  Oben Auf Dem Berge

  Old Zip Coon

  Polenmadchen

  Schlaflied Fur Juliska

  Serbischer Tanz

  Singen, Lasst Uns Singen

  Sur Le Pont D'Avignon

  Swing, Mr. Schumann

  Tanzlied Aus Israel

  Tarantella

  Tic E Tic E Toc

  Trinkt Aus, Schenkt Ein!

  Uber Lander Und Meere

  Vier Alte Volkslieder—Im Neuen Gewand

  What Shall We Do?

  Wollt Ihr Wissen?

ROSS
  Niles, John Jacob
    Go'way From My Window

ROSS, HUGH
  Tchaikovsky, Piotr Ilyich
    Golden Cloud, The

ROSSA, E.
  Lassus, Roland de (Orlandus)
    Oly Szep Ma Minden

  Tchaikovsky, Piotr Ilyich
    Altatodal

ROSSA, ERNO
  Karai, Jozsef
    Szabadsag, Szallj Kozenk

ROSSEL, W.
  Lindenlaub

ROSSI
  Berlioz, Hector (Louis)
    Wondrous Night

  Haydn, [Franz] Joseph
    Oxford Canon, The

  Musical Masterpieces For Male Voices

  Musical Masterpieces For Women's
    Voices

  Musical Masterpieces For Young Voices

  Schubert, Franz (Peter)
    Lusty Horn, The

ROSSI, NICK
  Castelnuovo-Tedesco, Mario
    Thanksgiving

  Mozart, Wolfgang Amadeus
    Barcarole

  Strauss, Richard
    Morgen

ROSSIN
  Goin' Home

ROSSMAYER, R
  Strauss, Richard
    Tageszeiten, Die

ROTH; HEIBERG
  Brahms, Johannes
    Evening Serenade

ROTHEROE
  March, Myrna Fox
    Shadow, The

ROTMAN
  Rameau, Jean-Philippe
    O, Nuit!

ROTMAN, JOH.
  He's Got The Whole World

ROULLIER
  O'Sullivan
    Alone Again (Naturally)

ROUSSEAU
  Strauss, Johann, [Jr.]
    An Der Schonen Blauen Donau

ROW
  Sibelius, Jean
    Vale Of Tuoni

ROWLAND, EDITH
  Ayres From Playford

ROWLAND, EDITH; SHAW, MARTIN
  Ives, Simon
    Now We Are Met

  Lanier, Nicholas
    Though I Am Young

  Lawes, Henry
    I Saw Fair Chloris

ROWLEY
  Bobby Shafto

  Coates
    Tell Me Where Is Fancy Bred?
    Who Is Sylvia?

  Coates, Eric
    Who Is Sylvia

  Fire Down Below

  Fraser, K.
    Road To The Isles

  Genee, Richard
    Italienischer Salat

  Hughes
    I Have A Bonnet Trimmed With Blue

  Hughes, Herbert
    I Know My Love

ROWLEY (cont'd.)

  Keel, Frederick
    Port Of Many Ships

  Kennedy-Fraser, Patuffa
    Road To The Isles, The

  Lark In The Clear Air

  Molloy, James Lyman
    Kerry Dance
    Kerry Dance, The

  Oh Dear! What Can The Matter Be?

  Rio Grande

  Road To The Isles

  Roving

  Shenandoah

  Somervell, Arthur
    Young Love Lies Sleeping

  Suo-Gan

  Vaughan Williams, Ralph
    Linden Lea

  Williams
    Linden Lea

ROWLEY, A.
  Casson
    Cuckoo, The

ROWLEY, ALEC
  All Round My Hat

  Arne, Michael
    Under The Greenwood Tree

  Bishop, [Sir] Henry (Rowley)
    Dashing White Sergeant, The

  Bobby Shafto

  Farmyard, The

  Gentle Maiden, The

  Hook, James
    Lass Of Richmond Hill, The

  Jensen, Adolf
    Mill, The

  Lark In The Clear Air, The

  Oh Dear! What Can The Matter Be?

  Rising Of The Lark, The

  Sacramento

  Strawberry Fair

  Suo-Gan

  There Was A Maid, And She Went To The
    Mill

  Youthful Year, The

ROY, FRED
  Lavalee, Calixa
    O Canada

  O Canada!

ROY, KLAUS G.
  Among The Maidens

  Pride Goeth Before A Fall

ROYER
  Echo Carol

RUAULT
  Schubert, Franz (Peter)
    Hymne A La Musique

RUBBEN, HERMANNJOSEF
  Ich Weiss Nicht, Wie Mir Ist

  Kleiner Fisch

  Kommt Und Singt

  Nehm' Ich Die Bandura

  Willst Du Feine Fische Fangen

  Wo Man Singt

  Zwei Volkslieder

RUBBEN, HERMANNJOSEPH
  Apfel Fallt Vom Baume

  Danza Cantata

  Gut'n Abend Euch Allen

RUBBEN, HERMANNJOSEPH (cont'd.)

Herbst Kommt Nun

Komm Mein Madchen

Lasst Uns Froh Beim Czardas Singen

Nach Island

Quer Durch Europa

Schlaf Mein Liebchen

Wahre Freundschaft

Weisse Perlen

Wer Geht Mit Juchhe

RUBBRA, EDMUND
Afton Water

Dance To Your Daddie

Dear Liza

My Tocher's The Jewel

RUBIN
Oyf'n Prip'chok

Stevens, Richard John Samuel
With Conscious Pride

RUBISCH, E.
Rundadinella

RUDNYTSKY
From Behind A Mountain

Tell Me Where You're Going

RUE, PIERRE DE LA
Blume, Karl
Ja, Grun Ist Die Heide

Foster, Stephen Collins
Beautiful Dreamer

Schubert, Franz (Peter)
Heidenroslein
Leise Flehen

RUIZ
Marenzio, Luca
Innocentes

RUMERY, LEONARD
Strauss, Richard
Waldesgesang

RUNEBERG
Sibelius, Jean
Gleichheit
Nicht Mit Klagen

RUNG, HENRIK; LAUB, THOMAS
Aage Og Else

Herr Lovmand

Jeg Ser Sa Mangt Et Orlogsskib

Jeg Stod Mig Ved En Baek Af To

Liden Kirsten

Oluva-Kvadet

Ramund

Ravnen

Ribolt Var En Greveson

Saerhefte I

Var Bohmerlands Dronningen, Det

Var Bolden Herr Rimmer, Det

Var Jomfru Gundelin, Det

Var Vel Syv Og Syvsindstyve, Det

RUNKEL, K.
Brahms, Johannes
How Lovely Are Thy Dwellings Fair

RUNNER
Dallier, H.
Pastorale Pour Noel

RUPPEL, PAUL E.
French Folksongs

Icelandic Folksongs

Negro Songs

RUSSEL-SMITH
Hall, George
Elizabeth I And II

RUSSELL
Clinton
Dipsy Doodle, The

Michael, Row The Boat Ahore

Smetana, Bedrich
Fountain, The

RUSSELL-SMITH
Gibbs, Cecil Armstrong
Five Eyes

Hughes, Herbert
I Know Where I'm Goin'

Kodaly, Zoltan
Arms Of Hungary, The
Evening Song
Good Housewife, The
Grow, Tresses
'Mid The Oak Trees
Wine, Sweet Wine

RUSSELL-SMITH, GEOFFRY
O Let Us Sing A Sweet Lullay

RUSSELL, WELFORD
Sleep Wayward Thoughts

RUST, WILLIAM; RIETZ, J.; HAUPTMANN, M;
BECKER, C.F.; KROLL, F.;
DOERFFEL, A.; NAUMANN, E; VON
WALDERSEE; KRETZCHMAR, H.

Bach, Johann Sebastian
Complete Works. Bach-Gesellschaft
Edition

RUTHENBERG, O.
Au Clair De La Lune

Chanson Des Scieurs

Es Hatt' Ein Bauer Ein Schones Weib

Jetzt Gang I Ans Brunnele

Leute, Hort, Ich Will Euch Singen

Schlaf, Mein Kindchen

Wo Man Singt, Bin Ich Zu Hause

Zwei Schwane Kamen Gezogen

RUTHENBERG, OTTO
Es Wollt Ein Schneider Wandern

Ist Nichts Mit Den Alten Weibern, 'S

Kommt Herbei, Feiert Mit

Reim Dich, Oder Ich Fress Dich

Zwei Schlesische Schnurren

RUTHERFORD
Bricusse, Leslie
What Kind Of Fool Am I

Ellington, Edward Kennedy (Duke)
It Don't Mean A Thing
Mood Indigo

RUTHERFORD, P.
Gibb, Barry
Saturday Night Fever

RUTHERFORD, PARIS
Gibb, Barry
I Just Want To Be Your Everything

RUTTER
Dancing Day

Eight Christmas Carols, Set 2

RUTTER, JOHN
Five Traditional Songs

O Waly, Waly

Two American Folk-Songs

SAABY, S.
Alfven, Hugo
Swedish Rhapsody

SAABY, SV.
Reesen, Emil
To, Som Elsker Hinanden

SAABY, SVEND
Annie Laurie

Auld Lang Syne

Benatzky
Vardshuset Vita Hasten

Gamla Goda Dar

Loch Lomond

SAABY, SVEND (cont'd.)

Rapee, Erno
Charmaine

Rode Sarafan, Den

Rosen Fran Provence

Vita Akasiorna, De

SAAR
Keys Of Heaven, The

Schubert, Franz (Peter)
An Die Musik
Standchen

Strauss, Johann, [Jr.]
Dreams Of Spring

Tambourin

SAAR, LOUIS V.
Cox, Persis
Song Of The Hunt

Kaferhochzeit

Mein Madel Hat Einen Rosenmund

Menuet De Martini

Twelve Days Of Christmas, The

SABEL, H.
Auf, Auf Zum Frohlichen Jagen

Jager Langs Dem Weiher Ging, Der

SACCO
Charles, Ernest
House On A Hill, The

Coombs, Charles Whitney
Four-Leaf Clover

Guion, David Wendall Fentress
Carry Me Home To The Lone Prairie

Mana-Zucca, Mme. (Augusta Zuckermann)
Big Brown Bear, The

Schubert, Franz (Peter)
Allmacht, Die

SACCO, JOHN
Strauss, Johann, [Jr.]
Selections From "Die Fledermaus"

SAINT-SAENS, C.
Charpentier, Marc-Antoine
Malade Imaginaire, Le

Rameau, Jean-Philippe
Oeuvres Completes Tome III

SAINT-SAENS, CAMILLE; MALHERBE, CH.;
EMMANUEL, M.; TENEO, M.

Rameau, Jean-Philippe
Complete Works

SALISBURY
Morley, Thomas
My Bonny Lass She Smileth

SALLMANN, HANS GERD
De Gospel Ship

SALMONS, CYRIL L.
Dvorak, Antonin
Gipsy Songs

SALONEN, S.
Cruger, Johann
Var Ar Den Van

SALONEN, SULO
Min Sjal, Du Maste Nu Glomma

Seventeen Finnish Folksongs

Sixteen Finnish Folksongs

Upp, Du Min Sjal, Och Sjung

SALTER
Brahe, May H.
I Passed By Your Window
Speedwell

Foster, Stephen Collins
Come Where My Love Lies Dreaming

Keel, Frederick
Trade Winds

Martin, (Frederick John) Easthope
Come To The Fair

Newton
Madrigal In May

SALTER (cont'd.)

Ronald, [Sir] Landon
O Lovely Night

Weatherly, Fred E.
Danny Boy

SALTER; MAXWELL
Heron
Keep On Hopin'

SALTZMAN, H.
Schumann, Robert (Alexander)
Beim Abschied Zu Singen

SAMM, J.
Rameau, Jean-Philippe
Rondeau Des Songes

Saint-Saens, Camille
Choeur Des Philistines

SAMPLE, ARTHUR
Annie Laurie

Banks Of Allan Water, The

Sally In Our Alley

SAMSON, J.
Bergere Nanon

Deux Bransles

Nanette

Trois Bransles De La Vallee De La
Valouse

Violette Doublera, La

SAMSON, JOSEPH
Philippot Le Savoyard
Ode Bacchique

SAMUELSON
Hazelhurst
O Leave Your Sheep

Head, Michael (Dewar)
When I Think Upon The Maidens

Kennedy-Fraser, Patuffa
Road To The Isles, The

Ronald, [Sir] Landon
Prelude

Weatherly, Fred E.
Danny Boy

When Love Is Kind

SANCHEZ, B.
Recueils De Chants Faciles

Vingt Chants De France Et D'ailleurs

SANDBERG
Foster, Stephen Collins
Stephen Foster Chrestomathy, A

SANDBERG, RHONDA
Bridge Over Troubled Water

SANDERS, VERNON
Foster, Stephen Collins
Oh, Susanna Stomp

SANDERSON, WILFRED
Pellissier, H.G.
Awake

SANDOR, ARANY
Buzavirag

SANFORD
Fryson
Give Yourself To Jesus

Jagger, Mick
Angie

McCartney, [John] Paul
Give Ireland Back To The Irish

Ruby
Cecilia

Seals
Summer Breeze

Stewart
Everyday People

Withers
Lean On Me

Woyaya

Young
Heart Of Gold
I Am A Child

SANTO
Anonymous
Cantos Italianos De La Montana

SARBEK, BORIS
Drake, Ervin
I Believe

SARGENT
Cowboy Carol

Earth's Joy

Hawaiian Lullaby

Three Far Eastern Carols

Zither Carol

SARGENT, MALCOLM
All God's Chillun

Lis'en To De Lams

Little David Play On Yo' Harp

SARKOZI, I.
Forradalmi Dalok

SATEREN
Grieg, Edvard Hagerup
When Summits Pierce The Blue

SATEREN, LELAND
A Kjore Vatten

Kjerringa Med Staven

Prairie Song

SATEREN, LELAND B.
Rachmaninoff, Sergey Vassilievich
Soft Hills And Soothing Wind

SAUL, FELIX
Sang I Skogen

Staffan Var En Stalledrang

SAUNDERS, NEIL
Sermisy, Claude de (Claudin)
Fair Is The Grove

Two Chansons

SAXTON
Come By Here

SCARMOLIN
Montanye
Sunset In The Alps

SCHAEFERS, ANTON
Schwartz, Gerhard von
Komm, Trost Der Nacht, O Nachtigall

SCHAFER
Bein, Wilhelm
Post Im Walde, Die

SCHAFER, EWALD
Kein Schoner Land

SCHAFER, L.
Hoffmann, G.K.
I Mocht So Gern

SCHAGER
Mozart, Wolfgang Amadeus
Bundeslied

SCHAGER, KARL
Brahms, Johannes
Wiegenlied

Drei Rippm, Drei Rappm

Ei Wiar I Va Wean Auffageh

Mozart, Wolfgang Amadeus
Osterreichische Bundeshymne
Wiegenlied

Urbanek, Hans
Du Lieber Augustin

Verstehst

War Immer So, 'S

SCHALLER, ARTHUR
Eberwein, Max
Ergo Bibamus

SCHALLER, PAUL
Haydn, [Johann] Michael
Abschied

SCHARWENKA
Beethoven, Ludwig van
Chorfantasie

SCHECK, H.
Auf Der Brucke Von Nantes

Kuhl War Und Neblig Der Morgen

Umbluhet Ist Meine Hutte

SCHECK, HELMUT
Meine Kuhlein, Ihr Lieben

SCHEFFER, P.I.
Gospel Rhapsody

SCHEFFLER, J.J.
Glockchen, Das

Stenka Rasin

SCHEHL, J.A.; BRUNSMAN, W.J.
Midnight Ride Of Paul Revere, The

SCHEIBLAUER, MIMI; PFISTERER, TRUDI
Lueg Und Sing

SCHEID, OTTO
Suss, Rudolf
Jagabuam, D'

SCHEIDER, WERNER
Down By The Riverside

Ev'ry Time I Feel The Spirit

My Bonnie Is Over The Ocean

When The Saints Go Marchin' In

SCHEIDL, OTTO
Suss, Rudolf
Lied Der Waldviertler
Wachaulied

SCHEIERLING, KONRAD
Ich Bin Das Ganze Jahr Vergnugt

SCHELLE, HENRIETTE
Reger, Max
Mein Schatzelein

SCHEMITSCH
Strauss, Johann, [Jr.]
An Die Schonen Blauen Donau
Wein, Weib Und Gesang

Strauss, Josef
Dorfschwalben Aus Osterreich

SCHEMITSCH, H.
Elsner, Toni
Wenn Man Verliebt Ist

Hammerschmiedg'solln, Die

SCHEMITSCH, HANS
A Bauernbuble Mag I Net

Abt, Franz
Wo Die Alpenrosen Bluh'n

Andulka

Auf, Auf Zum Frohlichen Jagen

Auf Du Junger Wandersmann

Aus Grauer Stadte Mauern

Dirndal, Merk Dir Den Bam

Dirnderl, Geh Her Zum Zaun

Dirndl, Willst An Edelknaben

Erzherzog-Johann-Lied

Es War Amal Am Abend Spat

Geh I Zum Brunndelein

Gluck Auf, Gluck Auf!

Gruss Gott, Du Schoner Maien

Handwerksgesell, Der

Hofmann, O.
Stadt Der Lieder, Die

I Bin A Steirerbua

Im Marzen Der Bauer

Inverno E Passato, L'

Kreutzer, Konradin
Hobellied

O Tannenbaum

Raimund, Ferdinand
Bruderlein Fein

Salzburger Glockenjodler

Schon Ist Die Jugend

SCHEMITSCH, HANS (cont'd.)

Schonste Auf Der Welt Ist Mein
    Tirolerland, Das

Schrammel, Hans
    Was Ost'reich Is

Seydler, W.C.
    Hoch Vom Dachstein An

Suppe, Franz von
    Ist Mein Osterreich, Das

Wachtelschlag, Der

Wann Der Guggu Schreit

Wanns Nur Lei Regna Tuat

Werner, H.
    Heidenroslein

Wia Lustig Ist's Im Winter

Wohl Ist Die Welt

Wohlan Die Zeit Ist Kommen

Zillertal, Du Bist Mei Freud

SCHERCHEN
    Beethoven, Ludwig van
        Glorreiche Augenblick, Der

    Blomdahl, Karl-Birger
        In The Hall Of Mirrors

SCHERCHEN, HERMANN
    Abschied: Muss I Den

    Drunten Im Unterland

SCHERZBERG
    Wie Ist Die Moldau Tief

SCHESSL
    Werdenfelser Liederheft

SCHIBLER, A.
    Somebody's Knocking

SCHIETZ, HENRIK
    Norge

SCHILLING
    Purcell, Henry
        Nymphs And Shepherds

SCHILLING, K.H.
    Beim Kronewirt

SCHILLIO
    Nine Hundred Miles From Home

    There Was A Little Maiden

SCHILLIO, E.
    Boll Weevil Song, The

    Dulcie

    Grandma Grunts

    Krugman, Lillian D.
        Down In Trinidad

SCHILLIO, EMILE
    Nine Hundred Miles

SCHIMMERLING, H.A.
    Beyond The Village

    Love's Lament

    Yuri Benka

SCHINDLER
    Lefebre, Jacques
        Aime-Moi, Bergere

    Shalitt
        Eli, Eli

SCHINDLER, K.
    Tchaikovsky, Piotr Ilyich
        Nightingale, The

SCHINELLI
    Canzoniere Dei Fanciulli Vol.III:
        Canti D'argomento Diverso

    Canzoniere Dei Fanciulli Vol.v: Brani
        D'opere Teatrali

    Selezione Di Cinquando Canti Corali

SCHINELLI, A.
    Anonymous
        Violetta, La

    Banchieri, Adriano
        Tre Graziani

    Collana Di Composizioni Polifoniche
        Vocali Sacre E Profane Vol. II

SCHINELLI, A. (cont'd.)

    Sessantaquatro Composizioni
        Profane

    Collana Di Composizioni Polifoniche
        Vocali Sacre E Profane Vol. III
        Composizioni Profane

    Vecchi, Orazio (Horatio)
        Imitazione Del Veneziano
        So Ben Mi Ch'a Bon Tempo

SCHINELLI, A.; SOMMA, B.
    Nanini, Giovanni Maria (Nanino)
        Primo Libro Delle Canzonette, Il

SCHINELLI, ACHILLE
    Croce, Giovanni
        Triaca Musicale

    Trentacinque Canti Populari Italiani

SCHIOTS, H.
    Go Where Glory Waits Thee

    Golden Slumbers

    Now, Robin, Lend To Me Thy Bow

    Sigh No More, Ladies

SCHIOTZ, H.
    Bellman, Carl Michael
        Gubben Ar Gammal

SCHIPA
    Liszt, Franz
        Liebestraum

SCHIRMUNSKI, VICTOR
    Volkslieder Aus Dem Bayrischen
        Kolonie Jamburg Am Dnjepr

SCHLAGETER, WALTER
    Alte Meister

    Donati, Baldassare (Donato)
        Wenn Wir Hinausziehen

    Lassus, Roland de (Orlandus)
        Landsknechtsstandchen

SCHLEGL, H.
    Frisch Auf Zum Streit

SCHLEICHER, L.
    Polyfonia Starych Majstrov Na
        Latinske Texty

SCHLIPPENBACH
    Silcher, Friedrich
        Nun Leb' Wohl, Du Kleine Gasse

SCHLOSSER
    Mozart, Wolfgang Amadeus
        Berceuse

SCHLOSSER, P.
    Rameau, Jean-Philippe
        Chantons Bacchus
        Chantons Platee
        Chantons Sur La Musette
        Choeur Des Nymphes

SCHLOTEL
    Bridges
        First Spring Morning
        Gay Robin Is Seen No More

SCHMALZ, OSKAR FR.
    Barggruess

    Bluemli, Ds

    Bluemli Rosmari, Ds

    Das Isch Ja Gang Eso Gsy!

    Das Isch U Blybt Eso!

    Es Wunschli

    Ha Gmeint

    Hochzytsmorge

    Langi Zyti

    Lerchli, Ds

    Maientag

    Mailied

    Mys Guggisberg

    Ryfeli, Ds

    Schoni Stunde

    Sunnsyte, D'

    Sunntig, Der

    Zwoi Sunnegi Ouge

SCHMALZ, P.
    Drei Roselein, Die

    Freud Und Leid

SCHMALZRIEDT
    Heinrich Schutz Und Andere
        Zeitgenossische Musiker In Der
        Lehre Giovanni Gabrielis

SCHMID, A.
    Abgeblitzt

    Kaperfahrtslied

    Mazurka Lockt, Die

    Petruschka

    Rote Sarafan, Der

    Timokwein

SCHMID, ALFONS
    Am Unteren Hafen

    Fern Nach Sud Kosaken

    Kaljinka

    Mazurka Lockt, Die

    Petruschka

    Timokwein

    Winde Weh'n Schiffe Geh'n

SCHMID, ALFRED
    Kaperfahrtslied

SCHMID, ERNST
    Sandmannchen

SCHMID, ERNST FRITZ
    Lechner, Leonhard
        Neue Lustige Teutsche Lieder

    Schramm, Melchior
        Edler Jager Wohlgemut, Ein

SCHMID, R.
    Strauss, Johann, [Jr.]
        Kaiser-Walzer

SCHMID, REINHOLD
    Bauer, Bauer, Bauer

    Gern, Oh Gern

    Gingen Einst Drei Magdelein

    Komm Doch Her

    Marjanne

    Meines Gartners Schonste Nelke

    Moge Euch, Ihr Junggesell'n, Der
        Teufel Baden

    Nekutej

    Retzer Pfarrer, Der

    Such Nicht Lange

    Was Hat Die Nachtigall

    Weisse Taube, Eine

    Wenn Du Mir, Bauer

    Wie Scheinst Du, Liebste Mir

SCHMID, W.
    Lanner, Josef
        Im Fruhling

    Mendelssohn-Bartholdy, Felix
        Fruhlingslied

    Zur Guten Nacht

SCHMID, WALTER
    Lanner, Josef
        Im Fruhling

SCHMIDT
    Gastoldi, Giovanni Giacomo
        Introduttioni A I Balletti
        Quindici Balletti A Cinque Voci
            Vol. I
        Quindici Balletti A Cinque Voci
            Vol. II
        Quindici Balletti A Cinque Voci
            Vol. III
        Quindici Balletti A Cinque Voci
            Vol. IV

    Lassus, Roland de (Orlandus)
        Zanni

    Marenzio, Luca
        Due Rose Fresche

SCHMIDT (cont'd.)

Wagner, Richard
Spinnerlied

SCHMIDT-BARRIEN, HEINRICH
Keen Groter Freud

SCHMIDT-DOLF
Nentwich, Josef
Heinzelmannchen

Schumann, Robert (Alexander)
Zigeunerleben

SCHMIDT, H.C.
Gastoldi, Giovanni Giacomo
Fifteen Balletti, Vol. I
Fifteen Balletti, Vol. II
Fifteen Balletti, Vol. III
Fifteen Balletti, Vol. IV
O Compagni Allegrezza

SCHMIDT, H.W.
Wenn Die Nachtigallen Schlagen

SCHMIDT, HAROLD
Marenzio, Luca
Gia Torna A Rallegrar

SCHMIDT, HUGO WOLFRAM
Coenen, Hans
Konzert Der Bremer Stadtmusikanten

Cosacchi, Stephan
Hymne
Jahresschlussfeier

Haass, Walter
Festliche Kantate

Hammerschlag, Walter
Gute Fahrt

Hofer, Karlheinz
Shanties From The Seven Seas

Loebner, Roland
Integer Vitae
Titanic

Putz, Eduard
Kalendermann, Der

Roeseling, Kaspar
Gericht Uber Reinecke Fuchs

Rosenstengel, Albrecht
Max Und Moritz
Vater Und Sohn

Rubben, Hermannjosef
Musikalisches Ratselraten
Wird Wieder Sein

Schafer, Karl
Herz, Werde Wach
Kantate Zur Schulentlassung

Schmidt, Hugo Wolfram
Zwei Festgesange

Werner, Fritz
Fruhlingskantate
Jagdkantate
Wanderkantate

Woll, Erna
Siehe Die Sonne

Zipp, Friedrich
Machet Die Tore Weit

SCHMIDT, HUGO WOLFRAM; PUTZ;
ROSENSTENGEL

Negro Spirituals

SCHMIDT, HUGO WOLFRAM; WEBER, ALOYS
Chorbuch

Liederbuch

SCHMIDT, LEOPOLD
Deutsche Volkslieder Aus Niederdonau

SCHMITT, WILHELM K.
Dat Du Mien Leevsten Bust

SCHMUCKLE
Krietsch, Georg
Ist Der Himmel Dir Gewogen

SCHNEBEL, DIETER
Bach, Johann Sebastian
Contrapunctus I
Contrapunctus VI
Contrapunctus XI

SCHNEIDE-HEISE, A.
Abschied

SCHNEIDER
Rote Sarafan, Der

Waldteufel, Emil
Dolores
Ganz Allerliebst
Patineurs, Les
Sirenenzauber

SCHNEIDER, B.
Schone Mallone, Die

SCHNEIDER; HEISE
Susser Die Glocken Nie Klingen

Wie Lustig Ist's Im Winter

SCHNEIDER-HEISE, A.
Dort Jenes Brunnlein Hat Kaltes
Wasser

SCHNEIDER-HEISE, ALFRED
Stehn Zwei Stern

SCHNEIDER; REGULA
Lortzing, (Gustav) Albert
Holzschuhtanz

SCHNEIDER, W.
Zwei Heitere Tanzlieder

SCHNEIDER, WALTHER
Andulka

Bei Sonn Und Himmel

Bruder Lustig

Es War Einmal Ein Gartner

Ich Liebte Einst Ein Madchen

Lustig, Ihr Bruder

Musik Erfullt Die Welt

SCHNELLI, A.
Banchieri, Adriano
Balletto Di Villanelle

SCHNITLER
Bauer, Der Hatte Ein Tochterlein, Ein

SCHNITZER, K.
Walter
Wald Am Hollabrunnen, Der

SCHNITZLER
Drei Raben

Jagerlied

Lustige Hochzeit

Mai Ist Da, Der Mai, Der

Wollt Ihr Meine Senn'rin Kennen?

SCHNURL, KARL
Gute Nacht

Jagrische Leben, Das

SCHOENDLINGER
Es Steht Ein Lind

Es Steht Ein Lind In Jenem Tal

SCHOENFELD
Caesar
Pledge Of Allegiance To The Flag

SCHOLLUM, R.
Aber Rossknecht, Steh Auf

Da Summa Is Aussi

Diandl Wullst An Edelknabn

Jag'rische Leb'n, Das

Und Im Feld Singt Die Lerch'n

Wann Der Guggu Schreit

Wiar I Bin Auf D'alma Ganga

SCHOLLUM, ROBERT
Abschied Von Der Jugend

Auf, Auf

Ballade

Dirndal, Merk Dir Den Bam

Europaische Volkslieder

Fastnachtslied

Flachgauer Schnadahupfl

Flieg, Mein Falke

Fliegt Mein Herz Davon

SCHOLLUM, ROBERT (cont'd.)

Fuhrmannslied

Gamla Goda Dar

Geh I Hinaus

Griass Di God!

Hirte, Der

Hugelhin Mein Bachlein

I Tua, Was I Will

Junge Krabbenkocherin

Klage Des Leibeigenen

Klappernd Zog Ich Durch Das Landchen

Lied Der Hirten

Lied Des Hirten

Lied Vom Schafer

Lord Lovell

Madchen, Horch

Madchen Im Wald

Oan Widl Garn

Roselil

Schaferliedchen

Spottlied

Tanzlied "La Capucine"

Taube, Die

Traumte Mir

Und Bin I Net A Fescher

Vier Weberlein

Werbung

Zizalbeer

SCHOLTES, WALTER
Oft In The Stilly Night

SCHOLTYS
Lanner, Josef
Schonbrunner, Die

Strauss, Johann, [Jr.]
Kaiser-Walzer

SCHOLTYS, H.H.
Schubert, Franz (Peter)
Endlich Ist's Mai Geworden
Entra L'Uomo Allo Che Nasce
Hoch Uber Mir, Unendlich Klein
Quell' Innocente Figlio
Seit Ich Dich Zuletzt Gesehen

Ziehrer, Carl Michael
Herrreinspaziert
Singen, Lachen, Tanzen
Singen, Lachen Tanzen

SCHOLUCH, A.
Eintonig Klingt Das Glockchen

SCHONAICH; CHAROLATH
Rische, Quirin
Starke Fruhling, Der

SCHONAUER, HEINRICH
Reichardt
Fichtelgebirgslied

SCHONBERG
Nageli, Johann (Hans) Georg
Spinn, Magdlein, Spinn

Rathgeber, Valentin
Mein Stimme Klinge

SCHONEBAUM, I.
Ich Ging Einmal Spaziere

SCHONENBERGER, W.
Hej, Wer Geht Denn Dort

Kehr Ich Abends Heim Mit Singen

Wenn Mir In Stunden Kummerschwer

SCHONENBERGER, WALTER
Wenn Mir In Stunden Kummerschwer

SCHONHERR, M.
Komzak, Karl
Volksliedchen

SCHONHERR, M. (cont'd.)

  Strauss, Johann, [Sr.]
    Radetzky Marsch
    Radetzky-Marsch

  Strauss, Johann, [Jr.]
    Bei Uns Z' Haus
    Champagner Her!
    Stiergefecht In Der Sierra De
      Suazzo
    Vergessenes Lied
    Wienerblut Muss Was Eigenes Sein

  Strauss, Josef
    Wiener Kinder Singen Gern

  Suppe, Franz von
    Vorwarts Mit Frischem Mut

SCHONHERR, MAX
  Komzak, Karl
    Marchen

SCHONNING, JOHNNY
  Nu Star Jag Pa Min Resa

SCHOULTZ
  Bergman, Erik
    Springtime
    Vogel, Die

SCHOUSBOE, TORBEN; LINDHOLM, STEEN
  Hartmann, Johan Peder Emilius
    Braender Lonligt I Mit Sind, Der
    Da Skulle Du Vaere Kommen
    Engel Har Rort Ved Din Pande, En
    I Varen Knoppes En Lind
    Jeg Sadled Min Hest En Morgenstund
    Jeg Ved, Jeg Vorder Dig Aldrig Kaer
    Seks Sange

SCHRADE, LEO; BOORMAN, STANLEY
  Machaut, Guillaume de
    Motets

SCHRADE, LEO; BOORMAN, STANLEY H.
  Machaut, Guillaume de
    Complete Works Of Guillaume De
      Machaut, Vol. III

SCHRAMMEL
  Spielman
    Mankind Should Be My Business

SCHREUDER, G.
  Daal, O Nacht, Stille Nacht

  Wilt Heden Nu Treden

SCHREY
  Dowland, John
    Susses Lieb, O Kom Zuruck

  Haydn, [Franz] Joseph
    Drei Heitere Kanons

  Morley, Thomas
    Launisch Ist Sie

  Rivander, Paulus
    Vinum, Der Edle Rebensaft

  Widmann, Erasmus
    Ich Hab Ein Boses Weib

  Zangius, Nikolaus
    Mein Lieber Wirt

SCHREY, W.
  Ade, Jetzt Muss Ich Scheiden

  Alle, Die Mit Uns Auf Kaperen Fahren

  Alte Weiber-Junge Madel

  Bergleut Sind Die Schonsten Leut

  Breite Fluss, Der

  Da Sass Ein Weib, Das Spann

  Dort Unten In Der Gasse

  Ei Wohl Ein' Schone Zeit

  Es Leuchten Zwei Sterne

  Es Ritt Ein Jager Wohlgemut

  Es Wollt Ein Jager Jagen

  Es Wollt Ein Magdlein Tanzen Gehn

  Flogen Einst Drei Wilde Tauben

  Frisch Auf, Ihr Bergleut, Auf

  Frisch Auf, Ins Weite Feld

  Grunet Die Hoffnung

  Gruss Gott, Du Schoner Maien

  Hore, O Weibchen

SCHREY, W. (cont'd.)

  Ich Ging Mit Lust Wohl Durch Den Wald

  Ich Hab Mir Einen Garten Gepflanzet

  Ich Habe Bei Meiner Hutte

  Im Sommer, Die Liebe Lange Zeit

  Ist Etwas So Machtig

  Ja, Der Berg'sche Fuhrmann

  Jetzt Kommt Das Schon Fruhjahr

  Kappen, Der Sturmann, Der

  Lass Doch Der Jugend Ihren Lauf

  Laub Fallt Von Dem Baumen, Das

  Lustig, Ihr Bruder

  Mai, Der Mai, Der Lustige Mai, Der

  Mai Tritt Ein Mit Freuden, Der

  Mein Schatzelein

  Mein Stimme Klinge

  Schon Ist Die Welt

  Schone Mai Ist Kommen, Der

  Stimmt Mit Uns Ein

  Viel Freuden Mit Sich Bringet

  Vor Meines Herzliebchens Fenster

  Wenn Ich Ein Kleins Waldvoglein War

  Wer Will Mit Nach Frankfurt Fahren

  Wer Will Schone Rosen Pflucken

  Wilddieb Wollte Jagen Gehn, Ein

  Winde Wehn, Schiffe Gehn

  Zwei Mailieder Aus Dem Tessin

SCHRIFT, HL.
  Gerhard, Fritz Christian
    Wache Auf, Der Du Schlafst

SCHROCK
  Schubert, Franz (Peter)
    Geburtstaghymne

SCHROEDER
  Eccard, Johannes
    Nichts Bessers Ist Auf Erden

  I've Got Peace Like A River

SCHROEDER, H.
  Ach Blumlein Blau

  Ach Elslein, Liebes Elselein

  Ade Zur Guten Nacht

  All Mein Gedanken

  Drei Laub Auf Einer Linden

  Es Fiel Ein Reif

  Es Sass Ein Klein Wild Vogelein

  Es Sass Ein Schneeweiss Vogelein

  Es Steht Ein Lind

  Es Steht Ein Lind In Jenem Tal

  Es Zogen Drei Sanger

  Frisch Auf, Gut G'sell

  Gott G'segn Dich, Laub

  Gruss Gott, Du Schoner Maien

  Ich Hab Die Nacht Getraumet

  Ich Kann Des Abends Nicht Schlafen
    Gehn

  Ich Wollt, Dass Ich Doheime War

  Jetzt Gang I Ans Brunnele

  Kleines Trinkgelage

  Maienzeit Bannet Leid

  Mayen, Der Mayen, Der

  Mein Madel Hat Einen Rosenmund

SCHROEDER, H. (cont'd.)

  Praetorius, Michael
    Nach Gruner Farb Mein Herz Verlangt

  Schwesterlein

  Sollt Heut Der Mond Nicht Heller
    Scheinen

  Stehn Zwei Stern Am Hohen Himmel

  Verstohlen Geht Der Mond Auf

  Viel Freuden Mit Sich Bringet

  Wach Auf, Meins Herzens Schone

  Wenn Alle Brunnlein Fliessen

  Wie Schon Bluht Uns Der Maien

  Zum Tanze, Da Geht Ein Madel

  Zwei Frohliche Lieder

SCHROEDER, HERMANN
  Frisch Auf In Gottes Namen

  Matrosenlied

  Vorm Himmel Hangt Ein Graues Tuch

SCHROTH
  Every Year At Christmas

SCHRUEDER, C.
  Geluckig Is Het Land

SCHUBERT, H.
  Auf, Auf, Ihr Wandersleut

  Hopsa, Hopsa, Rieber, Nieber

  Nach Suden Nun Sich Lenken

SCHULER
  Lissmann, Kurt
    Empor Aus Nacht

SCHULER; DU VINAGE
  Erdlen, Hermann
    Nun Jubiliert Der Morgen

SCHULER, G.
  Niedermann, Gustav
    Friede, Friede Sei Auf Erden

SCHULLER, GUNTHER
  Medieval Christmas, A

SCHULTZ
  Ade Nun Zur Guten Nacht

  Wenn Alle Brunnlein Fliessen

SCHULTZ, H.
  Feld Ist Weiss, Das

  Hopsa, Schwabenliesel

  Lass Dich Schneiden

  Zwei Rheinische Volkslieder

SCHULTZ, SV. S.
  Verdi, Giuseppe
    Triumfmarch

SCHULZE, W
  Brahms, Johannes
    Sieben Deutsche Volkslieder

SCHUMANN
  Hampel, V.
    Bei Der Bergschmiede
    Ewige Bergheimat
    Habmichlieb Und Enzian
    Sommer In Den Vorbergen

  Kotzschke
    Stehauflied, Das

SCHUMANN, CLARA; BRAHMS, JOHANNES
  Schumann, Robert (Alexander)
    Collected Works, Vol. 1
    Collected Works, Vol. 2
    Collected Works, Vol. 3
    Collected Works, Vol. 5
    Collected Works, Vol. 6
    Collected Works, Vol. 7
    Complete Works

SCHUMANN, G.
  Handel, George Frideric
    Abschied

SCHUMANN, WALTER
  Fum, Fum, Fum

  He's Gone Away

  When The Saints Go Marching In

SCHUMANN, WALTER; ALLMAN
  Patapan

SCHUMANN, WALTER; ERICKSON
  Drunken Sailor

  Wells
    All You Need Is A Song

SCHUSTER
  Knab, Armin
    Vaterland, Das Ist Ein Baum, Das

SCHWADRON
  Artsah Alinu

SCHWAEN
  Den Schonsten Fruhling Sehn Wir
    Wieder

  Frisch Auf, Mein Volk

  Immer Frohlich, Immer Munter

  So Treiben Wir Den Winter Aus

  Zelter
    Epiphanias

SCHWARTZ
  Beethoven, Ludwig van
    Himmel Ruhmen, Die

SCHWARTZ, BORIS
  Glinka, Mikhail Ivanovich
    Complete Works

SCHWARTZ, DAN
  Morgan, Russ
    You're Nobody 'Til Somebody Loves
      You

SCHWARZ
  Schmidt
    Ich Trage Eine Fahne

SCHWARZ, GERHARD
  Trader, Willi
    Wieder Einmal Ausgeflogen

SCHWEIGER, MAX
  Reger, Max
    Maria Wiegenlied: Maria Sitzt Am
      Rosenhag

SCHWIND, GUNTER
  Schwerer Abschied

SCHYBERGSON
  Sibelius, Jean
    Brausend Rauscht Eine Woge
    Draussen Braust Der Sturm

SCOGIN; RAYMOND
  Christmas Bells

  Here We Go A-Caroling

SCOTSON
  Wenrich, Percy
    Put On Your Old Grey Bonnet

SCOTT
  All The Pretty Little Horses

  Chopin, Frederic
    Prelude

  Drummer And The Cookie

  Erie Canal, The

  Gloucestershire Wassail

  Jacobs
    This Is My Counry
    This Is My Country

  Jenny Jenkins

  One Flag Of Brotherhood

  Shenandoah

  Wondrous Love

SCOTT, D.
  Invitation To Madrigals-Book 7

SCOTT, JAMES A.
  Foster, Stephen Collins
    American Troubadour, The

SCOTT, T.
  Soldier, Soldier, Will You Marry Me?

SCOTT; TRUSLER
  A'Soalin

SEARS
  Golden Earrings

SEAV
  Dvorak, Antonin
    Wedding Song

SEAY
  Certon, Pierre
    Zehn Franzosische Chansons

  Consilium
    If Now Again

  De Villiers, Pierre
    Ne Te Plains Tant

  Gold And Blue

  Has He Left Me?

  Hesdin, Nicolle Des Celliers D'
    Grief, Double Grief

  Hurt I Have

  Janequin, Clement
    Zehn Chansons

  Le Peletier
    Si Mon Malheur

SEAY, ALBERT
  Attaignant, Pierre, [publisher]
    Vingt Deuxiesme Livre

  Genet, Elzear (Carpentras)
    Collected Works Vol. V: Residium

  Heurteur, Guillaume le
    Souvent Amour

  Moderne, Jacques, [publisher]
    Quart Livre
    Cinquiesme Livre

  Sandrin, Pierre
    Opera Omnia

  Sermisy, Claude de (Claudin)
    Jour Robin, Une

  Thirty Chansons For Three And Four
    Voices From Attaingnant's
    Collections

SEAY; LE JEUNE
  Chadieu
    ModeI: TIME, GOD AND THE WORLD
    ModeII: All Things Are Inconstant
      Save God
    ModeIII: All Pleasure Is But For A
      Moment
    ModeIV: Earthly Love Is Passing
    ModeV: ALL THINGS VANISH LIKE SMOKE
    ModeVI: The Black Night Of
      Disbelief
    ModeVII: On The World As A Monster
    ModeVIII: Of The Ambitious And The
      Miserly
    ModeIX: On The Nature And The World
      Reflections On The Vanity And
      Inconstancy Of The World

SEBESTYEN, ANDRAS; NADAS, KATALIN
  Kabalevsky, Dmitri Borisovich
    Dal A Voros Csillagrol

SECHLER
  Zawinul
    Mercy, Mercy, Mercy

SECHLER, CLYDE
  Simon, Paul
    Bridge Over Troubled Water

SECKINGER, KONRAD
  Volkslieder Aus Fremden Landern,
    HeftIV

  Volkslieder Aus Fremden Landern, Heft
    I

  Volkslieder Aus Fremden Landern, Heft
    II: MUSIKANTEN, WARUM SCHWEIGT
    IHR

  Volkslieder Aus Fremden Landern, Heft
    III

SEEGER
  Leineweber, Die

SEEGER, P.
  Bei Meiner Blondine

  Blume Am Hut, Eine

  Gloria Im Himmel

  Happy Farmer, The

  Happy Farmer, The

  Maienlied

  Molly Malone

  Monsieur Rousselle

SEEGER, P. (cont'd.)
  Ringlein, Das

  Schoner Summer

  Seht, Konig Dagobert

  Verliebte, Der

  Vier Tschechische Lieder

  Zog Einst Durch Paris

SEEGER, PETER
  Bleib Doch Stehn

  Es Zogen Drei Sanger

  Grabe Tag Um Tag

  Liebeshandel

  Nimm Von Uns, Herre

  O Kam' Das Morgenrot

  Schaferin Und Konigssohn

SEEGER; RINGWALD
  Carawan
    We Shall Overcome

SEEKERS
  Seekers, The

SEGERSTAM, SELIM
  Jungfrun Och Bergakungen

SEHLBACH, ERICH
  Albert, Heinrich
    Jetzund Heben Wald Und Feld

  Schulz, Johann Abraham Peter
    Mond Ist Aufgegangen, Der

SEIB, V.
  Heimkehr

  Tanzlied

SEIB, VALENTIN
  Fruhling Ist Kommen

  Jascha Liebt Katjuschka

  Kalinka

  Kleine Senorita

  Zwei Gitarren--Rasposchol

SEIBER
  Handsome Butcher, The

  Three Hungarian Folk Songs

  Three Hungarian Folk Songs

SEIFFERT, MAX
  Sweelinck, Jan Pieterszoon
    Chansons, Rimes Francoises Et
      Italiennes

SEIGMEISTER; EHRET
  He's Gone Away

  Let There Be Song

SEITZ, RUDIGER
  Zwei Kanonische Volkslieder

SEKTBERG
  Rossini, Gioacchino
    Danza, La

SENA, SURYA
  Doyi, Doyi

SENART, J.-F.
  Ah! Si Mon Moine

  Vigneault, Gilles
    Doux Chagrin, Le

SENDELBACH; GOTZ
  Weber, Ben Brian
    Diese Erde Ist Ein Stern

SENDT
  Knab, Armin
    Zwei Sich Herzlich Lieben, Das

SENDT, W.
  Es Ist Ein Schnitter

  Frau Nachtigall Im Wald

  Jeder, Der Im Kopfe Hell

  Jetzt Kommen Die Lustigen Tage

  Mond Ist Aufgegangen, Der

  Reife Frucht Ruft Euch

SENDT, W. (cont'd.)
  Schone, Die Du Mein Leben
  Verstohlen Geht Der Mond Auf
  Will Ein Lustig Liedchen Bringen
  Zwei Altdeutsche Liebeslieder
  Zwei Altdeutsche Liebeslieder
SENFT, JOCHE
  Gospels, Shanties, And Folklore
SENNELS, R.
  Alouette, L'
SEPHULA, M.
  Sing, Africa!
  Sing Again, Africa!
SERKOW, PETER
  House Of Rising Sun, The
  Kleiner Czardas
SEROCKY, K.
  Berceuse
SERPOSS
  Giordano, Umberto
    O Pastorelle, Addio
SERPOSS, EMILE
  Verdi, Giuseppe
    Va, Pensiero, Sull'Ali Dorate
SEUFFERT
  Bruckner, Anton
    Trosterin Musik
SEXTON; CLARK
  Fun, Folk And Frolic Songs
SHACKLEY
  Rachmaninoff, Sergey Vassilievich
    In The Silence Of Night
SHACKLEY, GEORGE
  Tchaikovsky, Piotr Ilyich
    Nur, Wer Die Sehnsucht Kennt
SHAND, DAVIS
  Gluck, Christoph Willibald, Ritter
    von
    From The Realm Of Souls Departed
SHARP
  Carrion Crow, The
  Frog And The Mouse, The
  Frog He Would A-Wooing Go, A
  Lord Rendal
  Sweet Nightingale
  Tailor And The Mouse, The
  Three English Folk Songs
  Three Nonsense Folk Songs
  Wraggle Taggle Gipsies O!, The
SHARP, CECIL
  As I Walked Through The Meadows
  Bingo
  Briery Bush, The
  Brisk Young Widow, The
  Coasts Of High Barbary, The
  Crystal Spring, The
  Cuckoo, The
  Geordie
  I'm Seventeen Come Sunday
  Keeper, The
  Keys Of Canterbury, The
  Lark In The Morn, The
  Lover's Tasks, The
  My Boy Willie
  My Man John
  Nightingale, The
  O No, John
  O Waly, Waly
  Riddle Song, The

SHARP, CECIL (cont'd.)
  Sailor From Sea, The
  Searching For Lambs
  Sheep Shearing, The
  Spanish Ladies
  Three Little Tailors Driving Up To
    London
  William Taylor
SHARP; KARPELES
  Vaughan Williams, Ralph
    Rich Old Lady, The
SHARPE, EVELYN
  All Through The Night
  As I Sat On A Sunny Bank
  Ash Grove, The
  At The Mid-Hour Of Night
  Banks Of Allan Water, The
  Barkshire Tragedy, The
  Bonnie Banks O' Loch Lomond, The
  Castle Of Dromore, The
  Charlie Is My Darling
  Cockles And Mussels
  Crocodile, The
  Derby Ram, The
  Early One Morning
  Gathering Daffodils
  Gentle Maiden, The
  Green Bushes
  Herding Song
  Last Rose Of Summer, The
  May Day Carol
  My Johnny Was A Shoemaker
  My Mother Bids Me Bind My Hair
  North Country Maid
  Now Robin, Lend Me Thy Bow
  O Can Ye Sew Cushions
  O, The Oak And The Ash
  Oft In The Stilly Night
  Oh! Dear, What Can The Matter Be?
  Robin A Thrush
  Seeds Of Love, The
  Skye Boat Song
  Snowy Breasted Pearl, The
  Summer Is A Coming In
  Sweet Music Is King
  Sweet Nightingale, The
  There Was A Pig Went Out To Dig
  Twankydillo
  Water Of Tyne, The
  When Daisies Pied
  Where Be Going?
  Where The Bee Sucks
  Where'er You Walk
SHAW
  Haydn, [Franz] Joseph
    Jahreszeiten, Die
  Hook, James
    Lass Of Richmond Hill, The
  Set Down Servant
SHAW, G.
  Arne, Thomas Augustine
    Mists Before The Sunrise Fly

SHAW, G. (cont'd.)
  Handel, George Frideric
    Silent Worship
SHAW, G.T.
  There's Nae Luck About The House
  Wi' A Hundred Pipers
SHAW, GEOFFREY
  Barbara Allan
  Clychau Aberdyfi
  David Of The White Rock
  Early One Morning
  Flight Of The Earls, The
  I Live Not Where I Love
  In Derry Vale — Londonderry Air
  John Peel
  Mermaid, The
  Minstrel Boy, The
  Oh Dear! What Can The Matter Be?
  Spring Bursts Today
  There's Nae Luck
SHAW, GEOFFREY T.
  Drink To Me Only With Thine Eyes
  Golden Vanity, The
  John Peel
SHAW; HUNTER
  Bishop, [Sir] Henry (Rowley)
    Home, Sweet Home
  Buckley, R. Bishop
    Wait For The Wagon
  Little Liza Jane
  Thomas, John Rogers
    Bonnie Eloise
  Work, Henry Clay
    Grandfather's Clock
SHAW, J.K.
  Morley, Thomas
    Six Drinking Songs
SHAW, KIRBY
  All I Want For Christmas Is My Two
    Front Teeth
  Ballin' The Jack
  Cannon, Hughie
    Bill Bailey, Won't You Please Come
    Home
  Carole King Collage
  Chestnuts Roasting On An Open Fire
  Come Again, Sweet Love
  Every Day I've Got To Sing Some
  Festival Fanfare
  Fire In The Furnace
  Garner, Erroll
    Misty
  Gershwin, George
    Summertime
  Honeysuckle Rose
  Jazz Hot, Le
  Kander, John
    Show Stopper
  Let's Do It
  Lullabye Of Birdland
  Next To Lovin'
  On Broadway [2]
  Rodgers, Richard
    My Romance
  Say Hello!
  Since I Fell For You
  Sing For You America
  Star Spangled Banner, The

SHAW, KIRBY (cont'd.)

Sweet Georgia Brown

Twenties Medley

Varsity Drag

We're So Glad

SHAW, MARTIN
Clarke, Jeremiah
Saint George's Day

Elves, The

Hark! The Echoing Air

My Bonnie Cuckoo

Nature Song-Bookvol. II

Nature Song-Bookvol. III

Nature Song-Bookvol. IV

Purcell, Henry
Come Unto These Yellow Sands
Fairest Isle
Fly, Bird Of Song
If Music Be The Food Of Love
In Spring Every Creature
Let Us Awake
Nymphs And Shepherds
O The Sweet Delights Of Spring
Store Away Your Happy Hours
Two Daughters Of This Aged Spring

Sing Three

SHAW; PARKER
Amour De Moy, L'

Annie Laurie

Aupres De Ma Blonde

Billings, William
Chester

Black, Black, Black

Blow The Man Down

Brahms, Johannes
Down Low In The Valley
Still Of The Night

Cherry Tree Carol, The

Da Unten Im Thale

Darling Nelly Gray

Death Of Nathan Hale, The

Deep River

Drummer And The Cook, The

Du, Du Liegst Mir Im Herzen

Fletcher, J.
Seeing Nellie Home

Flow Gently, Sweet Afton

Foster, Stephen Collins
Beautiful Dreamer
Come Where My Love Lies Dreaming
De Camptown Races
Dolcy Jones
Gentle Lena Clare
Jeanie With The Light Brown Hair
Laura Lee
My Old Kentucky Home
Oh! Susanna
Oh Susanna!
Old Black Joe
Old Folks At Home
Ring De Banjo
Some Folks Do
'Way Down In Cairo

Gamla Goda Dar

Haul Away, Joe

He's Gone Away

Johnny Has Gone For A Soldier

Juanita

Kuchen, F.
Treue Liebe

Lowlands

Marianina

Purcell, Edward C.
Passing By

SHAW; PARKER (cont'd.)

Schubert, Franz (Peter)
Pastorella, La

Shenandoah

Soldier Boy, The

Spanish Ladies

Spilman, James E.
Flow Gently, Sweet Afton

Stodole Pumpa

Swansea Town

Vecchi, Orazio (Horatio)
Fa Una Canzone

Vive L'amour

Wassail Song

What Shall We Do With The Drunken
Sailor

Yellow Rose Of Texas, The

SHAW, PAT
Simi Jadech

SHAW, ROBERT
Brahms, Johannes
Liebeslieder Walzer

SHAW, RUBY
Can't Stay Away

Three Blind Mice

SHAW, WATKINS
Blow, John
Awake, Awake My Lyre
Awake, Awake, My Lyre

SHAW, WATKINS; BERGMANN
Blow, John
Marriage Ode

SHAY
Lightfoot, Gordon
Sundown

Loggins, David A.
Love Song, A

Raposo, Joseph G.
You Will Be My Music

Seals
Diamond Girl

Simon
Haven't Got Time For The Pain

Young
After The Gold Rush

SHELBY
Gillespie
Content

SHEPPARD
Adam Lay Ybounden

De Word

Dunstable, John
Agincourt Song

Hickory Stick, The

Lonesome Whistle

Rebel Soldier, The

Sweet Betsy From Pike

World's So Wide, The

SHEPPARD-JONES
Hole In The Bucket

Whistle, Daughter, Whistle

SHERIDAN
Foster, Stephen Collins
Old Folks Medley

SHERMAN
Gordon
So What?

SHERMAN; SIMEONE
Sherman
Chim Chim Cher-Ee
Supercalifragilisticexpialidocious

SHIELD, WILLIAM
O Happy Fair

O Happy Fair (The Loadstars)

SHIPP
Bennet, John
Drive Him Back To London

Costeley, Guillaume
Allons Au Vert Boccage

East, Michael
Corydon Would Kiss Her Then
In The Merry Month Of May

Ward, Samuel Augustus
Fly Not So Fast

Weelkes
Come, Let's Begin
Ha Ha! The World Doth Pass

Youll, Henry
Come, Merry Lads, Let Us Away
Only Joy, Now Here You Are

SHIPP, C.M.
Weelkes, Thomas
Ha Ha! This World Doth Pass

SHIPP, CLIFFORD M.; SHIPP, MARY JANE
Bennet, John
Drive Him Back To London

SHOOK, JEAN
Simons
You Can Have Ev'ry Light On
Broadway

SHORT, HENRY
Schumann, Robert (Alexander)
Liebesgarten

SHUR
Tee Lee Bee Lee Boo

SICARDI
Schubert, Franz (Peter)
Como Pesca Ulfrido

SICKLES
O'Hara, Geoffrey
She Could Only Sing A "C"

SIEFFERT, MAX; GEHRMANN, HERMANN
Sweelinck, Jan Pieterszoon
Collected Works

SIEGL, O.
Alma Wasserl

Alte Fiakerlied, Das

Des Abends Ist Es Gut

Weiss Ich Ein Schones Roselein

Winter Ist Vergangen, Der

SIEGL, OTTO
Regiment Sein Strassen Zieht

Wachauer Schifferlied

SIEGLER, CHR.
Donna, Donna, Komm Nach Haus

Mozart, Wolfgang Amadeus
Bald Prangt, Den Morgen Zu
Verkunden
Bald Prangt Den Morgen Zu Verkunden

Strauss, Johann, [Jr.]
Auf Der Jagd

Strom Trag Mich

SIEGLER, WINFRIED
Kein Feuer, Keine Kohle

SIEGMEISTER
Birds' Courting Song

Deaf Woman's Courtship

SIEGMEISTER, E.
Shenandoah

SIEGMEISTER; EHRET
Massenet, Jules
Open Thy Blue Eyes

SIEGMEISTER, ELIE
Bird's Courting Song

SIEGMUND-SCHULTZE
Handel, George Frideric
Friedensode: Ode Fur Den Geburtstag
Der Konigen Anna
Wahl Des Herakles, Der

SIEGMUND-SCHULTZE, WALTHER
Handel, George Frideric
Ode Fur Den Geburtstag Der Konigin
Anna
Wahl Des Herakles, Die

SIGURDSSON, BIRGIR
  Sveinsson, Gunnar Reynir
    Eg Vakti I Nott

SILCHER
  Gluck, Christoph Willibald, Ritter
    von
    Untreue

SILCHER, F.
  Blaublumlein

  Es Ist Vollbracht

  Es Loscht Das Meer Die Sonne Aus

  Schubert, Franz (Peter)
    Lindenbaum, Der

  Schwimm Hin, Ringelein

SILCHER, FRIEDRICH
  Jordan, Hellmut
    So Nimm Denn Meine Hande

  Schubert, Franz (Peter)
    Lindenbaum, Der

SILTMAN
  Danoff
    Take Me Home, Country Roads

  Deutschendorf, Henry John (John
    Denver)
    Annie's Song

  Mezzetti
    Morning Train

SILTMAN, BOBBY
  Very Last Day

SILTMAN, BOBBY L.
  Danoff, William Thomas
    Take Me Home Country Roads

SILVER
  Block
    Lamb, The

  North, Alex
    Such Lovely Things

SILVERMAN
  Wilder
    Evening Song

SIMEON
  Millet
    Deep Are The Roots

  Secunda, Sholom
    Dona Dona

SIMEONE
  Allen
    Which Way America?
    Which Way America

  Bacharach, Burt F.
    Walk On By

  Berlin, Irving
    Alexander's Ragtime Band
    This Is A Great Country

  Bigard, Albany Leon (Barney)
    Mood Indigo

  Boland
    Holiday

  Bono, Salvatore Phillip (Sonny)
    Beat Goes On, The

  Bricusse
    Feeling Good

  Burch
    Dream On, Little Dreamer

  Burke
    Country Style

  Burnette
    Magnificent Sanctuary Band

  Carlos
    Easy Days - Easy Nights

  Colwell, Paul
    Up With People!

  Comin' Through The Rye

  Cowell, Henry Dixon
    Walk Hand In Hand

  Darby, Kenneth Lorin
    T'was The Night Before Christmas

  Diamond
    Song Sung Blue

SIMEONE (cont'd.)
  Ellington, Edward Kennedy (Duke)
    Mood Indigo

  Emmett, Daniel Decatur
    Dixie

  Faith
    Christmas Is...

  Feller
    Snow, Snow, Beautiful Snow
    Snow, Snow Beautiful Snow

  Hamblen
    Open Up Your Heart
    This Ole House

  Have Songs—Will Sing!

  Hello Tomorrow

  Hirsch
    Anytime Of The Year

  Hubbard, Jerry
    Thing Called Love, A

  Jacobs, Jim
    Grease Medley

  Jameson
    Summertime Summertime

  Jingle Bells

  Karlin, Frederick James
    For All We Know

  Kells
    Dear Santa, Have You Had The
    Measles

  Lee
    Manana

  Let's Sing The Old Songs

  Little Brown Jug

  Loesser
    New Ashmolean Marching Society And
    Students Conservatory Band, The

  Mancini, Henry
    Charade

  Marks
    Anyone Can Move A Mountain
    Holly Jolly Christmas
    Holly Jolly Christmas, A
    Joyous Christmas
    Rockin' Around The Christmas Tree
    Rudolph, The Red-Nosed Reindeer

  Mills
    Red Wing
    Sweet Sounds Of Music

  My Bonnie Lies Over The Ocean

  Nichols, Roger Stewart
    Rainy Days And Mondays
    We've Only Just Begun

  Rise And Shine

  Sahner
    Sing Of A Merry Christmas

  Schwartz
    Rock-A-Bye Your Baby With A Dixie
    Melody

  Sherman
    Chim Chim Cher-Ee
    Spoonful Of Sugar, A
    Supercalifragilisticexpialidocious
    You Gotta Be A Football Hero

  Songfest

  Sousa, John Philip
    Stars And Stripes Forever, The

  South, Joe
    Games People Play

  Stallman
    Everybody's Got The Right To Love
    Round And Round

  Stevens, Cat
    Morning Has Broken

  Styne, Jule (Jules Stein)
    Diamonds Are A Girl's Best Friend

  Tchaikovsky, Piotr Ilyich
    Dance Of The Sugar Plums
    Dance Of The Toy Flutes
    Nutcracker Suite, The
    Overture
    Trepak
    Waltz Of The Flowers

SIMEONE (cont'd.)
  This World

  Thomas
    Spinning Wheel

  Van Heusen
    Country Style
    Like Someone In Love

  Weston
    Gandy Dancers Ball

  Whiting
    Louise

  Woods
    When The Red, Red Robin Comes Bob,
    Bob, Bobbin' Along

  Wrubel, Allie
    Zip-A-Dee-Doo-Dah

  Youth Sings At Christmas

  Youth Sings

SIMKINS
  Purcell, Henry
    My Heart Is Inditing

SIMOENE
  Toti
    Looks Like Spring Is Here

SIMON
  All Things Are Possible

  Alleluia

  Arizona...Has Anybody Ever Seen It
    All?

  Barry, John
    Moonraker

  Bernstein, Elmer
    Good Friend
    Moondust

  Coleman, Cy
    Our Private World

  Dancin' Slow

  Here's To Good Friends

  I'll Come Running

  It All Comes Out Of The Piano

  Loewe, Frederick
    Almost Like Being In Love

  MacDermott, Galt
    Easy To Be Hard

  Manilow, Barry
    Slow Dance, A

  O, Beautiful America

  One Star

  Rogers, Kenneth Ray (Kenny)
    You Decorated My Life

  Rowen, Ruth Halle
    Whoa, Mule, Whoa!

  Skip To My Lou

  Steps

  Strouse, Charles Louis
    It's The Hard-Knock Life
    Tomorrow

  Taylor
    I Will Be In Love With You

  Time Has Come, The

SIMON, H.
  Kume, Kum Geselle Min

  Silcher, Friedrich
    Ich Hatt' Einen Kameraden

SIMON, HERMANN
  Silcher, Friedrich
    Ich Hatt' Einen Kameraden

SIMONE
  Irvine
    To Be Young, Gifted And Black

SIMONITI, R.
  Plovi, Plovi

SIMONTON, D.
  Godard, Benjamin Louis Paul
    Lullaby

SIMPSON
  Lewis
    Sing Happy Child
    Song Of The Refuge Children

SIMPSON, KENNETH
  MacDougall's Farm

  Vive L'Amour

SINCLAIR, J.
  Ives, Charles
    They Are There! (A War Song March)

SINGERLING, J.W.
  Koennemann, M.
    Fremersberg, De

SJOBERG, P.A.
  Stiby, Tue
    Jar Alskar Dig

SJOBERG, PER-ANDERS
  Foster, Stephen Collins
    Oh Susanna

  Most Beautiful Song, The

  Vackraste Visan Om Karleken, Den

SKEAT
  Aiken, Walter H.
    All Through The Night

  Foster, Stephen Collins
    Old Folks At Home

  Minstrel Boy, The

SKEI, ALLEN B.
  Handl, Jacob (Jacobus Gallus)
    The Moralia Of 1596: Part I
    The Moralia Of 1596: Part II

  Rossetti, Stefano
    Madrigals For Three To Eight Voices
    Primo Libro De Madregali A Quattro
      Voci, Il

SKIPP
  Regnard, Francois
    Ma Mie Et Moy

  Weelkes, Thomas
    Messalina's Monkey

  Youll, Henry
    Pity Me, Mine Own Sweet Jewel

SKOLD, SVEN
  Sa Alskade Gud Varlden All

SLATER
  Bunnell
    Ventura Highway

  Elgar, [Sir] Edward (William)
    Land Of Hope And Glory

  Fulterman
    Beside You

  Gershwin, George
    Gershwin Revisted

  John
    Salvation
    Your Song

  Kamen
    Fields Of Joy

  Legrand, Michel
    Summer Knows, The
    Summer Me, Winter Me

  Lennon, John
    Fool On The Hill, The

  Lodge
    Eyes Of A Child

  O'Day, Alan Earle
    Train Of Thought

  Raleigh
    Laughing On The Outside (Crying On
      The Inside)

  Rice, Tim
    Everything's Alright
    Heaven On Their Minds
    Hosanna
    I Don't Know How To Love Him
    I Only Want To Say Gethsamene
    Superstar

  Robertson, J. Robbie
    Night They Drove Old Dixie Down,
      The

  Russell
    Song For You, A
    Superstar

SLATER (cont'd.)
  Simon
    Sparrow
    That's The Way I've Always Heard It
      Should Be

  Thomas
    Eternity Road
    Floating

  Webb
    Everybody Gets To Go To The Moon

  Williams
    Baby, Please Don't Go

SLATER, NEIL
  Deutschendorf, Henry John (John
    Denver)
    Like A Sad Song
    Sunshine On My Shoulders

  Williams, Linda
    Costa, La

SLATER, NEIL; FRY, GARY D.
  Deutschendorf, Henry John (John
    Denver)
    Sunshine On My Shoulders

SLEPT; RIZZO
  Green
    I'll Always Be In Love With You

SLIM, H. COLIN
  Gift Of Madrigals And Motets, A, Vol
    II

  A Gift Of Madrigals And Motets Vol.
    II

  A Gift Of Madrigals And Motets Vols.
    I & II

SMATEK, M.
  Bendl, Karel
    Smrt Prokopa Velikeho

SMEETS, LEO
  Giordani, Tommaso
    Caro Mio Ben

SMITH
  All Through The Night

  Ash Grove, The

  Blow The Candles Out

  Blue-Tail Fly, The

  Cuckoo, The

  Drunken Sailor, The

  Foster, Stephen Collins
    Come Where My Love Lies Dreaming
    Some Folks

  Hays
    Put The Right Man At The Wheel

  Heav'n Bells Ringin' In Mah Heart

  Heirlooms

  High Barbary

  Hutchinsons
    Horticultural Wife, The

  Kittridge
    Tenting On The Old Camp Ground

  Lieben Bringt Gross Freud, Das

  Minstrel Boy, The

  Riddle, The

  Riqui, Riqui, Riquirran

  Rodgers, Richard
    Climb Ev'ry Mountain
    Lonely Goatherd, The

  Shenandoah

  Sorrento Folk Song

  Stehn Zwei Stern'

  Stehn Zwei Stern

  S'vivon

  Tell Me Where The Dove Has Flown

  Winner, Septimus ("Alice Hawthorne")
    Listen To The Mocking Bird

SMITH, GREGG
  Ives, Charles
    Old Home Day
    Son Of A Gambolier, A
    Waltz

  Paper Of Pins

  Railroad Corral, The

SMITH, JAMES G.
  Bradbury, William Batchelder
    Sleep Well

  Ives, Charles
    Lincoln, The Great Commoner

  Jenks, Stephen
    Death Of General Washington

  Minstrel's Catch And Eight Canons

  New Liberty Bell, The

  Work, Henry Clay
    Crossing The Grand Sierras

SMITH, R.E.
  We Wish You A Merry Christmas

SMITH, TIM
  Sing With Life

SMITH; WILSON; BRADLEY
  Herbert, Victor
    Fortune Teller, The

SMITHERS
  Monteverdi, Claudio
    Tu Dormi

SMITS, W.A.M.
  Nu Zijt Wellekome

  O Kerstnacht Schoner Dan De Dagen

SMOLDEN
  Visitatio Sepulchri

SMOLDON
  Peregrinus

SNEL, D.J.
  Gezang 136

  Kortjakje
    Altijd Is Kortjakje Ziek

SNESRUD, ARLIN
  Ivey, Anne
    Hello, Old Friend

  Kendrick, Warren
    Laurel

SNOW
  Willson
    I See The Moon

SNR, L. KEAN
  All Through The Night

  Men Of Harlech

SOBAJE, MARTHA
  I'm So Glad

  Longfellow
    Arrow And The Song, The

SODERHOLM, V.
  Kihlberg, Rob
    Jag Sjunga Vill Min Julesang

SODERLUNDH, L.B.
  Talgper

SODERO
  Liszt, Franz
    Liebestraum

SODERSTEN, AXEL
  Tempelklockan

SODERSTROM
  Foster, Stephen Collins
    I Dream Of Jeanie

SODERSTROM, EMIL
  Bortniansky
    Russian Vesper Hymn

  Clychau Aberdyfi

  Foster, Stephen Collins
    I Dream Of Jeanie

  Go, Tell It On The Mountains

  Marzials, Theo
    Twickenham Ferry

  Rise Up, Shepherd, An' Foller

SODERSTROM, EMIL (cont'd.)

Van Grove, Isaac
Road To Vaux

Wilson
Turn Ye To Me

Ye Banks And Braes

SOLDAN
Brahms, Johannes
Quartette
Thirty-Five Secular Choruses
Zigeunerlieder Op.103, Op.112

SOMERS, HARRY
We Wish You A Merry Christmas

SOMERVELL
Handel, George Frideric
Umbra Mai Fu

Lully, Jean-Baptiste (Lulli)
Sun, The

Shield, William
O Happy Fair

Stevens, Richard John Samuel
Blow, Blow Thou Winter Wind
Sigh No More Ladies

Vaughan Williams, Ralph
Linden Lea

SOMERVELL, ARTHUR
Melody Of May

Touch Not The Nettle

SOMERVILLE
Love Is Come Again

SOMMA, B.
Banchieri, Adriano
Festino Nella Sera Del Giovedi
Grasso Avanti Cena
Pazzia Senile, La

Monteverdi, Claudio
Su, Su, Su, Pastorelli Vezzosi

Palestrina, Giovanni Pierluigi da
Cruda Mia Nemica, La

Vecchi, Orazio (Horatio)
Amfiparnaso

SOMMA, BONAVENTURA
Striggio, Alessandro
Cicalamento Delle Donne Al Bucato,
Il

Vecchi, Orazio (Horatio)
Veglie Di Siena, Le

SOMMA, BONAVENTURA; BIANCHI, LINO
Torelli, Guasparri
Fidi Amanti, I

SOMMERVILLE, TOM
Johnnie Cope

SOPRAPORTE
Beckerath, Alfred von
Seele, Die Das Haus Des Lebens
Baut, Die

SORAAS, LARS
Bruk Makd

Mitt Hjerte Alltid Vanker

Sangermars-Etter Hamma

Songar Av Rasofiel Rise

SORENSEN, H.
Soraas, Lars
Sangermarsj

Wennerberg, Gunnar
Gluntarne

SORENSEN, HANS
Heise, Peter Arnold
Hver En Smafugl Blunder

Henriques, Fini Valdemar
Moder, Jeg Er Traet, Nu Vil Jeg
Sove

Mortensen, Otto
Du Danske Sommer Jeg Elsker Dig

Mozart, Wolfgang Amadeus
Hvor Sodt, Nar Aftenklokker Kime

Og Sneen Den Fog

Varfor Sitta Vi Sa Still Och Tysta

Weyse, Christoph Ernst Friedrich
Danser Majen Skon I Mode

SORENSEN, HEIDE
Soraas, Lars
Sangermarsj

SORENSON, TORST
Yndig Og Frydefuld Sommertid, En

SORENSON, TORSTEN
Alskades Lov, Den

Gota Kampavisa

Jag Blaste I Min Pipa

Olafur Reid

Ramund Den Unge

Sigurdskvadet

Sorjande, Den

Yndig Og Frydefuld Sommertid, En

SORLI, ARNE
Kvam, Oddvar S.
Samisoga Lavlla

SOSSI, SERGIO
Italian Folksongs

SOTOLAR, K.
Abschiedslied

Es Steht Ein Baum Im Tiefen Tal

Himmelslucka, Die

I Hor Nix Mehr Wischpln

Mutter Und Tochter

Treue Liebe

SOUTHALL, MITCHELL
Nobody Knows The Trouble I've Seen

Steal Away

SOYER, A.
Chansons Canadiennes

SPAETH
Lehar
My Little Nest Of Heavenly Blue

SPAETH, S.
Barber Shop Harmony

SPAETH, SIGMUND
More Barbershop Harmony

SPANDL, J.
Mullers Abschied

SPAUN, ANTON R. VON
Osterreichesche Volkslied, Das

SPEVACEK, LINDA
Do You Know?

Mozart, Wolfgang Amadeus
Alleluja

Shenandoah

Shout Glory

Simple Gifts

Soon I Will Be Done

Take Time For Love

What A Day It Will Be!

Yankee Spectacular

SPICKER
Brahms, Johannes
Little Dustman, The

Grieg, Edvard Hagerup
Landerkennung

Mozart, Wolfgang Amadeus
Wiegenlied

Offenbach, Jacques
O Lovely Night

Schubert, Franz (Peter)
Allmacht, Die

Strauss, Johann, [Jr.]
By The Beautiful Blue Danube

SPINNER, LEOPOLD
Six Canons On Irish Folksongs

SPITTA, H.
Gruss Gott, Du Schoner Maien

SPITTA, PHILIPP; SCHERING, ARNOLD;
SPITTA, HEINRICH

Schutz, Heinrich
Collected Works

SPRINGFIELD
Fum, Fum, Fum

SPRONGL, N.
Wiegenlied

SPROSS, C.
Handel, George Frideric
Where E'er You Walk

SQUIRE, W.B.
Conversi, Girolamo
Sola Soletta

Croce, Giovanni
Cynthia, Dein Holdes Singen

Gibbons, Orlando
Ich Schwor Nicht Freundschaft

Wilbye, John
Wozu Als Mann In Sklavenketten
Bluten

SREBOTNJAK
Two Macedonian Folk Songs

SREBOTNJAK, A.
Aj Nu, Hor Mir Zu

Ajde, Die Sonne Sinkt Nun

Ja, Da Kommen Sie

Komm Nur Fido

Mile Aus Tschaikovo

Rumgezankt Und Zugeschlagen

STADLMAIR, H.
Ach Elslein

Acht Volkslieder

Du Mein Einzig Licht

Es Sass Ein Klein Wild Vogelein

Es Taget Vor Dem Walde

Gar Lieblich Hat Sich Gesellet

Gesegn Dich Laub

Ich Armes Maidlein

Ich Woll' Gern Singen

STADLMAIR, HANS
Kommt, Ihr G'speilen

STAEPS, H.U.
Haus, K.
Vier Villanellen

STALMEIER, P.
Grieg, Edvard Hagerup
Landkjenning

Verdi, Giuseppe
Choeur Des Tziganes
Coro d'Introduzione

STAMMLER
Foltz, Karl
Segen Uber Dich, Brot

STANBRIDGE, C.
Brahms, Johannes
Wiegenlied

STANFORD
Rowley, Alec
My Love's An Arbutus

STANFORD, C.V.
Quick! We Have But A Second

STANFORD, CHARLES VILLIERS
My Love's An Arbutus

STANFORD, CHARLES VILLIERS; ROWLEY,
ALEC

My Love's An Arbutus

STANGE, MAX
Bach, Johann Sebastian
I Natten

STANNEK
Am Flusse

STANTON
Gently, Gently

STICKLES (cont'd.)

I Feel Pretty
Maria
One Hand, One Heart
Somewere
Tonight

Bluebird Of Happiness

Bohm, Carl
Calm As The Night

Brahms, Johannes
Wiegenlied

Charles, Ernest
Let My Song Fill Your Heart

Connor, Tommie
I Saw Mommy Kissing Santa Claus

Dickinson
I'm Nobody

Dietz
Haunted Heart

Fields
Close As Pages In A Book
Fireman's Bride, The

Flag Without A Stain

Friml, Rudolf
Giannina Mia

Greensleeves

Herbert, Victor
Angelus

Kahal, Irving
I'll Be Seeing You

Kaihan, M.
Now Is The Hour

Kennedy
South Of The Border

Kentucky Babe

Kern
All Through The Day

Kern, Jerome
Can't Help Lovin' Dat Man
I've Told Every Little Star
Long Ago (And Far Away)
Look For The Silver Lining
Ol' Man River
Smoke Gets In Your Eyes
Song Is You, The
They Didn't Believe Me
Way You Look Tonight, The

Let There Be Peace On Earth

Leveen, Raymond
Christmas Candles

Little White Duck, The

Loesser
I've Never Been In Love Before
Rodger Young

Loesser, Frank
Anywhere I Wander
Big D
Don't Cry
Inch Worm, The
Sit Down You're Rockin' The Boat
Standing On The Corner
Thumbelina
Ugly Duckling, The
Wonderful Copenhagen

Lovely To Look At

Luther
Down In The Valley

Lyon
One Rose, The

MacDowell, Edward Alexander
To A Wild Rose

Make Believe

Malotte
Brotherhood

Marais, Josef
Marching To Pretoria

Marais, Marin
A-Round The Corner

Mendelssohn-Bartholdy, Felix
Auf Flugeln Des Gesanges

Orchids In The Moolight

STICKLES (cont'd.)

Poor Pierrot

Rodgers, Richard
All At Once You Love Her
All Through The Day
Bali Ha'i
Cock-Eyed Optimist, A
Dites-Moi
Everybody's Got A Home But Me
Fellow Needs A Girl, A
Getting To Know You
Happy Christmas, Little Friend
Happy Christmas Little Friend
Happy Christmas, Little Friend
Happy Talk
Hello, Young Lovers
I Whistle A Happy Tune
If I Loved You
I'm Gonna Wash That Man Right Outa
My Hair
I'm Your Girl
In My Own Little Corner
It Might As Well Be Spring
It's A Grand Night For Singing
Kansas City
Keep It Gay
Lovely Night, A
Many A New Day
Merry Christmas, Little Friend
My Romance
No Other Love
Oh, What A Beautiful Mornin'
Oklahoma
Oklahoma [Selection]
Out Of My Dreams
People Will Say We're In Love
Pore Jud
Rodgers And Hammerstein Showtime
So Far
Some Enchanted Evening
Stan' Up An' Fight
Surrey With The Fringe On Top, The
Ten Minutes Ago
That's For Me
There Is Nothin' Like A Dame
This Nearly Was Mine
We Kiss In A Shadow
Wonderful Guy, A
You'll Never Walk Alone
Younger Than Springtime

Rogers, J.H.
Wind And Lyre

Ruggiero, Gabrielle
Farewell, Dear Alma Mater

Scott, Clement
Now Is The Hour

Shenandoah

Showtime: Choral Collection, Vol. 2

Sibelius, Jean
Broken Melody, The

Tenderly

Vercamp
Protect America

Ware, John Marley
This Day Is Mine

Whatever Will Be, Will Be

Who

Why Do I Love You?

Willson
Goodnight, My Someone
May The Good Lord Bless And Keep
You
May The Good Lord Bless You And
Keep You
May The Lord Bless And Keep You

Willson, Meredith
It's You
Seventy Six Trombones
Till There Was You

Winter Wonderland

With This Ring

Wright, Robert Craig
And This Is My Beloved
Baubles, Bangles And Beads
Stranger In Paradise

You'll Never Walk Alone

Youmans, Vincent Millie
Carioca

STICKLES, WILLIAM
Bizet, Georges
Selections From "Carmen"

STILZ
Zelter, Carl Friedrich
Konig In Thule, Der

STOCKMEIER, WOLFGANG
Wagner, Richard
Parzival Vor Der Gralsburg

STOCKTON, ROBERT
Gastoldi, Giovanni Giacomo
When May's Bright Days Are Shining

Lechner, Leonhard
To Win My Dear A Hundred Boys Are
Trying

Morley, Thomas
'Tis The Time Of Yuletide Glee

STOLTE
Budjonny Lied

Im Januar Um Mitternacht

Trotz Alledem

STOLZENAU
Meyer
Deutsche Volkslied, Das

STONE
Ash Grove

Come, Let's Be Merry

Drunken Sailor, The

Franck, Melchior
Du Bist Aller Dinge Schon
Ich Sucht Des Nachts
Meine Schwester, Liebe Braut

Handel, George Frideric
Choice Of Hercules, The

Rimsky-Korsakov, Nikolai
Glory

Wilson
Take, Oh Take Those Lips Away

STONE, DAVID
Dance To Your Daddy

STONE, KURT
Dvorak, Antonin
Cradle Song
Deep Within The Forest
Forsaken Lover, The
I Cannot Answer

Feld, Jindrich
Pidy Bidy Bim Pim
Tam Tam Ta Dam

Janequin, Clement
Chant Des Oiseaux, Le

Jeppesen, Knud
Four Shakespeare Songs
Four Shakespeare Songs

Rossini, Gioacchino
Chant Funebre
La Foi

Shostakovich, Dmitri
Face To Face
Have Courage, Friends
Invincible Victors

STONE, L.
Black Is The Color Of My True Love's
Hair

STONE, LEONARD
Wayfaring Stranger

STONE, NORMAN
Come Let's Be Merry

Dutch Spring Carol

Flower Carol

How Should I Your True Love Know?

Maiden Of Morven

Purcell, Henry
In These Delightful Pleasant Groves

Willow Song

STONE, PAMELA
Gibbons, Orlando
Silver Swan, The

STORACE
No Song No Supper

STOTHART; MARLOWE
Herbert, Victor
Wooden Shoes (Clip, Clop, Clop)

SUCHOFF (cont'd.)

   Brown
     Song Of Peace

   Debussy, Claude
     Beau Soir

   Delius, Frederick
     Appalachia
     Once Paumanok

   Dvorak, Antonin
     Prsten

   Fields
     Miami Beach Rumba

   Glee Reigns In Galilee

   Goldfarb
     I Have A Little Dreydl

   Grieg, Edvard Hagerup
     Old Song, The

   Massenet, Jules
     Elegy

   Naumann, Johann Gottlieb
     O You Kinsmen Of The People

   Paradies, Pietro Domenico (Paradisi)
     'Tis Love That Rogue So Wily

   Pergolesi, Giovanni Battista
     Nina

   Purcell, Henry
     Sound The Trumpet

   Schubert, Franz (Peter)
     Death And The Maiden

   Schumann
     Two Thoughts For Children's Chorus

   Tchaikovsky, Piotr Ilyich
     None But The Lonely Heart

   Tum Balalaika

   Two Thoughts For Children's Chorus

SUCHOFF, BENJAMIN
   Dvorak, Antonin
     Prsten

SUDETAN
   Rein, Walter
     Es Ritten Drei Reiter

SUERTE
   Green Grow The Rushes, Oh

SULLIVAN, ARTHUR
   Long Day Closes, The

   O Hush Thee, My Baby

SUND, ROBERT
   Alouette

   Bellman, Carl Michael
     Trad Fram, Du Nattens Gud

SUNDBERG, HOLLIS
   Courage, Alexander
     Star Trek

SUNDBLAD, HENRIK
   Ga Du Listige Gosse

   Gossen Uppa Berget

SUNDERMAN
   Walker
     I'll Take You Home Again Kathleen
     Rose Of Tralee, The

SUNDQVIST, RUDOLF
   Gammalt Brollopskvade Fran Malung

   Kullerullvisan

SURDO
   Three Blind Mice

SURREY, CHARLES
   Schubert, Franz (Peter)
     Wandering Miller

SUSCINIO, J.
   Chansons De La Mer Et De La Voile

SUTCLIFFE
   Love Will Find Out The Way

SUTER
   Emmentaler Hochzeitstanz

SUTER, H.
   Es Kam Ein Herr Zum Schlossli

   Im Aargau Sind Zwei Liebi

SUTER, H. (cont'd.)

   Mein Schatz Der Ist Auf Die
     Wanderschaft Hin

   Schaferin Und Der Kuckuck, Die

SUTER, HERMANN
   Schonster Abestarn

   Un Uf Der Walt Si Kener Lut

SVADER, ROMY
   Keen, Marta Lynn
     Christmas On The Beach At Waikiki

SVEDBOM, VILHELM
   Hej Dunkom

   Hej, Dunkom Sa Lange Vi Levom

SVEDLUND, K.E.
   Cruger, Johann
     Var Ar Den Van, Som Overallt Jag
     Soker

SVEDLUND, KARL-ERIC
   Nordqvist, Gustaf
     Men Jag Horde En Sang

SVEDLUND, KARL-ERIK
   Men Jag Horde En Sang

SVEINBJORN, BEINTEINSSON
   Sveinsson, Gunnar Reynir
     Saungvar Dalabarnsins

SVEINSSON, GUNNAR REYNIR
   Icelandic Folksongs

   Songs

SWAFFIELD, R.
   Schumann, Robert (Alexander)
     Traumerei

SWANWICK, KEITH
   Five Songs From America

SWEENEY, JAMES JOHNSON
   Hemberg, Eskil
     Eighteen Movements

SWEETING, E.T.
   Aye Waukin' O!

   Broadwood, Lucy E.
     Derby Ram, The
     My Johnny Was A Shoemaker

   Cooper Of Fife, The

   King Arthur

   Leezie Lindsay

   MacLeod, A.C.
     Skye Boat Song

   Twankydillo

   Willow Tree, The

SWEETMAN, PAUL W.
   False Face Legend

SWICKARD
   Rachmaninoff, Sergey Vassilievich
     To The Children

SWIFT
   Copland, Aaron
     Younger Generation

   Ding Dong Merrily On High

   Evans
     Lady Of Spain

   Kreutzer, Conrad
     Herman The Violinist

   Nolan
     Tumbling Tumbleweeds

SWIFT, R.
   Black Sheep

SWING, R.
   Four Welsh Folk Songs

SWINGLE
   Bach, Johann Sebastian
     Badinerie
     Fruehling, Der
     Gigue
     Largo
     Menuetto
     Solfeggietto

   Handel, George Frideric
     Air

   Mozart, Wolfgang Amadeus
     Allegretto
     Fugue

SWINGLE (cont'd.)

   Rondo

SWINYARD
   Schubert, Franz (Peter)
     Serenade (Softly Stealing Through
     The Stillness)

SZABOLCSI
   Ranki, Gyorgy
     Kodaly Emlekezete

SZABOLCSI, BENCE
   Bartok, Bela
     Ungarische Volkslieder Aus
     Siebenburgen

SZADOVSZKIJ; NADAS, KATALIN
   Kompanyejec
   Harcjatek

SZEGO, I.
   Eneklo Nep 1945-1965

SZEKELY, E.
   Estharang, Az

SZEKERES
   Schutz, Heinrich
     Ket Olasz Madrigal

SZEKERES, F.
   Gastoldi, Giovanni Giacomo
     Regi Mesterek Vegyeskarai XIII

   Gumpeltzhaimer, Adam
     Regi Mesterek Egynemukarai V

   Janequin, Clement
     Regi Mesterek Vegyeskarai IV
     Regi Mesterek Vegyeskarai VII
     Regi Mesterek Vegyeskarai XV
     Szel, Te Vig, Lenge Szel

   Ket Madrigal

   Monteverdi, Claudio
     Regi Mesterek Vegyeskarai VI

   Regi Mesterek Egynemukarai I

   Regi Mesterek Egynemukarai II

   Regi Mesterek Egynemukarai III

   Regi Mesterek Egynemukarai VI

   Regi Mesterek Vegyeskarai I

   Regi Mesterek Vegyeskarai II

   Regi Mesterek Vegyeskarai III

   Regi Mesterek Vegyeskarai V

   Regi Mesterek Vegyeskarai VIII

   Regi Mesterek Vegyeskarai X

   Regi Mesterek Vegyeskarai XI

   Regi Mesterek Vegyeskarai XII

   Regnart, Jacob
     Regi Mesterek Egynemukarai IV

   Weckerlin, Jean-Baptiste-Theodore
     Regi Francia Szerelmi Dalok A XVII.
     Sz.

SZEKERES, FERENC
   Arma, Paul (Pal) (Imre Weisshaus)
     Francia Bordalok

   Gibbons, Orlando
     Cries Of London, The

SZWEYKOWSKI, Z.
   Bazylik, Cyprian
     Songs

SZWEYKOWSKI, Z.M.
   Waclaw of Szamotuly
     Songs

SZWEYKOWSKI, Z.M.; OCHLEWSKI, T.
   Caccini, Francesca
     Prologue

TAILLANDIER, SAINT-RENE
   Saboly, Nicholas
     C'est Le Bon Lever

TALDIR
   Vingt Chansons Populaires

TALMADGE, ARTHUR S.
   Bach, Johann Sebastian
     Nun Ruhen Alle Walder

TAPP
   Vaughan Williams, Ralph
     Orpheus With His Lute

TAPP, FRANK
Eton Boating Song

TAPP, FRANK; HAYWOOD, E.
Eggs To Market

Schubert, Franz (Peter)
Cloud-Boats

TAPP; HAYWOOD
Good Soil, The

Grape Gathering, The

TAPPAN
MacDowell, Edward Alexander
Two MacDowell Songs

Schubert, Franz (Peter)
Two Schubert Songs

Scottish Medley, A

TAPPAN, HOWARD
Ash Grove, The

Blow The Wind Southerly

TAPSCOTT, CARL
Au Clair De La Lune

Canadian Boat Song

Harris, Neil
Golden Land, A

Il Etait Une Bergere

I'se The B'y That Builds The Boat

Something To Sing About

Two Canadian Folk Songs

Watson, Gordon P.
Manitoba

TARP, SVEND ERIK
Negro Spirituals Og Amerikanske
Folkesanger

TARP, SVEND ERIK; SAABY, SV.; THOMSEN,
KNUD

Aloha Oe

Black Joe

Carry Me Back

Darling Nelly Gray

De Camptown Races

Heav'n Heav'n

My Old Kentucky Home

Oh Susanna

Old

Old Folks At Home

Polly Wolly Doodle

TARTARIN, A.
Belle Rose Du Printemps

Chaloupe A L'Eau, La

Isabeau Se Promene

Petit Bouquet De Fleurs

Selection D'airs Populaires
Americains

Sur La Plus Haute Cime

Sur La Rive De La Mer

Vieux Pelerin

Vive La Rose Et Le Lilas

TATE
Cielito Lindo

Dry Bones

In Paris Lived A Lady

Noel Alsacien

Old Macdonald Had A Farm

Terre Est Froide, La

Venez, Venez Vite

TATE, PHYLLIS
Johnston, Lyell
Ould John Braddleum

TATGENHORST
Foltz
Walk With Me In The Sun

TATTON
I Will Give My Love An Apple

TAUPIN
John, Elton
Goodbye Yellow Brick Road

TAURMAN
Dougherty, Celius H.
Love In The Dictionary

Schuman, William Howard
Orpheus With His Lute

TAUSKY
Offer, Charles K.
Up And Down The River Danube

TAYLOR
Lowlands

TAYLOR, DEEMS
Mayday Carol

TAYLOR, J.
Songbook One

Songbook Two

TAYLOR, JOHN W.R.
Up The Raw

TAYLOR, M.C.; WINDHAM, M.; SIMPSOM,
CLAUDE

Catch That Catch Can

TELEMANN
Schrey, Wilhelm
Auf, Fordre Von Dem Besten Wein

TELLEP
Tcherepnin, Alexander
Tranquil Light

TELLEP, L.
Deck The Halls

TERRAL, FRANCOIS
Aznavour, Charles
Comediens, Les

Barbeau, M.
Berceuse Indienne

TERRI
Chi-Chi Pap-Pa

Child Of God, A

Come All Ye Fair And Tender Ladies

Foster, Stephen Collins
De Camptown Races

Frere Jacques

I've Been Workin' On Duh Railroad

Oh, No, John!

San Sereni

Shenandoah

Streets Of Laredo, The

Tone Duh Bell Easy

When Love Is Kind

TERRI, SALLI
Cindy

Come All Ye Fair And Tender Ladies

Drunken Sailor

Dyin' Californian, The

Foster, Stephen Collins
Oh, Susanna

Unconstant Lover, The

TERRI, SALLY
All Around The Year

Rounds For Everyone From Everywhere

TERRY
Bound For The Rio Grande

When Love Is Kind

TERRY, RICHARD RUNCIMAN
Sailor Shanties, Second Selection

TEUSCHER, H.
Es Sass Ein Schneeweis Vogelein

THALER, S.
Kremser, Eduard
Wir Treten Zum Beten

THEHOS, A.
Conradi, J.G.
Herzliebchen Mein

Trara, Die Post Ist Da

THEHOS, ADAM
Es Tont Des Abendglockleins Schlag

Isaac, Heinrich
Innsbruck, Ich Muss Dich Lassen

THERSTAPPEN
Lassus, Roland de (Orlandus)
Busstranen Des Heiligen Petrus-Teil
1
Busstranen Des Heiligen Petrus-Teil
2
Busstranen Des Heiligen Petrus-Teil
3
Prophetiae Sibyllarum

THEURING, G.
Mozart, Wolfgang Amadeus
A-B-C, Das

THIBODEAU, Y.
Boite A Chanson, La

THIEBAUT, THIERRY
Calango

THIEL, E.
Jag Vet En Dajlig Rosa

THIEME, K.
Wahre Freundschaft

THIJSSE, W.H.
Mendelssohn-Bartholdy, Felix
Musikantenprugelei

THIMAN
All Thro' The Night

Austin, Frederick
Twelve Days Of Christmas, The

Flag Of Canada

Henman, Geoffrey
Ploughman's Song, The

Monro, George
My Lovely Celia

Oft In The Stilly Night

Oh Breathe Not His Name

THIMAN, E. H.
Austin, Frederick
Twelve Days Of Christmas, The

THIMAN, ERIC H.
Drink To Me Only

Flowers In The Valley, The

Gentle Maiden, The

Greensleeves

Jolly Waggoner, The

Keel Row, The

Kitty Of Coleraine

O! No, John

O Waly, Waly

Oft In The Stilly Night

Oh No, John

Silent, O Moyle

Young May Moon, The

THIRY, A.
Borodin, Alexander Porfirievich
Danses Polovtsiennes

Trois Chansons Bretonnes

THOMAS
Leslie
Lullaby Of Life

Two Welsh Love Songs

THOMAS, C. EDWARD
It's Me (Standin' In The Need Of
Prayer)

THOMAS, CHRISTOPHER
This Train

THOMAS, ELIZABETH
Frog He Would A-Wooing Go, A

THOMAS, GERARD
Lafarge, Guy
Boites A Musique, Les

THOMAS, MANSEL
Cariad Coll

If She Were Mine

Lost Love

Pe Cawn I Hon

THOMAS, W.; AMELN, K.
Kleine Quempas-Heft, Das

Quempas-Heft, Das

THOMAS; WHEAR
Elliot
Bonnie Eloise

THOMAS, WYNDHAM
Robin And Marion Motets, Vol 1

THOMPSON
Addrisi
Time For Livin'

Dukelsky, Vladimir ("Vernon Duke")
Autumn In New York

Fain
Secret Love

Gershwin, George
'S Wonderful

Harburg
April In Paris

Livingston
Twelfth Of Never, The

Ortolani
You Know

Rodgers, Richard
Mountain Greenery

Silver
Aim For Heaven

Tijuana Jail, The

Warren
September In The Rain

When The Saints Go Marching In

Williams
Bet You Never Guessed
Friends, Relatives, Parents
That's A Very Good Sign
This Is An Opening
We Never Sing Opening Numbers
We're Through

Willson
American Legion, The

Wright, Robert Craig
Little Hands

THOMPSON, ANNE H.
Julian's Garden

THOMPSON, DICK
Danoff, William Thomas
I Guess I'd Rather Be In Colorado

Marks, Johnny D.
Rockin' Around The Christmas Tree

THOMPSON, RANDALL
Lark In The Morn, The

THOMPSON, RICHARD
Mama-Chu

THOMSON, VIRGIL
Chabrier, [Alexis-] Emmanuel
Fete Polonaise

Thomson, Virgil Garnett
There Is A Garden In Her Face

THORNE
Woodforde-Finden, Amy
Pale Hands I Loved

THORPE, RAYMOND
Seven Contrasted SATB Songs

THYGERSON, ROBERT
Sometimes I Feel Like A Motherless
Child

THYGERSON, ROBERT W.
Barbershop Choir, The

Cindy

TIARKO-RICHEPIN
Choeurs De France

TIEDEMANN, H.-J.
Klang, Klang, Glockenschlag

Musikanten, Spielt Auf!

Sehnsucht

TIEMERSMA, S.
Wagner, Richard
Pilgerchor

Weber, Carl Maria von
Chor Der Jager

TIESSEN
Kucken
Wenn Ich Ein Voglein War

TIESSEN, H.
Ach Elslein, Liebes Elslein

Englert, Eugene E.
Wann Wir Schreiten Seit An Seit

Erfreue Dich, Himmel

Es, Es, Es Und Es

Es Geht Ein Dunkle Wolk Herein

Es Taget Vor Dem Walde

Franck, Melchior
Kommt, Ihr G'spielen

Fuchs, Du Hast Die Gans Gestohlen

Gassle, Das I Gange Bin,Das

Herrlicher Baikal

Ihren Schafer Zu Erwarten

Krieger, Adam
Ihr Schonen Augen

Kucken, Friedrich Wilhelm
Ach, Wie Ist's Moglich Dann

Lippe Detmold Eine Wunderschone Stadt

Muss I Denn

Nageli, Johann (Hans) Georg
Freut Euch Des Lebens
Von Uns Gehst Du Still Und Stumm

Nun Will Der Lenz Uns Grussen

O Strassburg, Du Wunderschone Stadt

Silcher, Friedrich
Annchen Von Tharau

Telemann, Georg Philipp
Rechte Stimmung, Die

Wenn Ich Ein Voglein War

Wir Tanzen Im Maien

TIESSEN, HEINZ
Alle Meine Kleider

Alle Vogel Sind Schon Da

Ehlers, Wilhelm
Da Droben Auf Jenem Berge

Fuchs, Du Hast Die Gans Gestohlen

Hoffner, Paul Marx
Schafer Putzte Sich Zum Tanz, Der

In Der Fremde

Josephson, Jacob Axel
Dem Schlafenden Kinde

Klage Der Maria

Maienfahrt

Mozart, Wolfgang Amadeus
Komm, Lieber Mai!

O Strassburg, Du Wunderschone Stadt

O Strassburg, O Strassburg, Du
Wunderschone Stadt

Schlaf, Mein Kindelein

Schwarz, Erika
Es Ist Ein Schnee Gefallen

TIESSEN, HEINZ (cont'd.)

Varlamov, Alexander
Rote Sarafan, Der

Wiegenlied

TIFFAULT
Dickinson
I'm Nobody! Who Are You?

Milliman
Man In The Bright Red Suit, The

TIFFAULT, LEIGHTON
Milidantri, Mary Ann
Music Belongs

TILLINGHAST
Bach, Johann Sebastian
August, Lebe, Lebe Konig

Brahms, Johannes
Liebe Schwalbe

Handel, George Frideric
Endless Pleasure, Endless Love

Mozart, Wolfgang Amadeus
O Winds, Blow Ye Softly

Schumann, Robert (Alexander)
Ins Freie

TIMMS, COLIN
Steffani, Agostino
Gettano I Re Dal Soglio

TIPPETT; BERGMAN
Purcell, Henry
Come Ye Sons Of Art
Ode For St. Cecelia's Day (1692):
Hail Bright Cecilia

TIPPETT; BERGMANN
Purcell, Henry
Come Ye Sons Of Art

TISCHLER, HANS
Medieval Motet Book, A

Montpellier Codex, The

TISHMAN, MARIE
Dayenu

TITTEL, ERNST
Es Liegt Ein Schloss In Osterreich

Osterreichischer Heimatchor

TODD
Handel, George Frideric
Hymen, Hastel
In Gentle Murmurs

Leighton, Z.E.
My Heart's Prayer

TODT, B.
Bach, Johann Sebastian
Auf, Schmetternde Tone
Lasst Uns Sorgen, Lasst Uns Wachen
Mer Hahn En Neue Oberkeet

TOLBY; DAVIS
Poling
Get Thee Behind Me, Satan

TOLMAGE
Ding, Dong, Merrily On High

Lassus, Roland de (Orlandus)
Patience

TOLMAGE, GERALD
Fum, Fum, Fum

Michael, Row The Boat Ashore

TOMASI, H.
Barcarolle

Cantu Di Malinconia

Chanson De La Pipe

Chanson De Pecheur

Chanson Politique

Cheta, Cheta, Chet'O Sagra

Ciuciarella

Lamento

Lamentu Di Spanettu

Lamentu Serenata Di Spanettu

Nelli Monti Di Cuscioni

Ninina

O Cinciarella

TREHARNE (cont'd.)

Shanty Man's Life, The

Star Lullaby

Sullivan, [Sir] Arthur Seymour
Lost Chord, The

Tchaikovsky, Piotr Ilyich
Waltz Of The Flowers

Tell Bruddah 'Lijah

There Was An Old Soldier

Thompson, H.S.
Cousin Jedediah

Three Farmers, The

Two Little Kittens

Two Sisters, The

Tyson, Mildred Lund
Sea Moods

Van Hagen, Peter Albrecht
Morn Of May, The

Waving Blanket, The

Work, Henry Clay
Kingdom Comin'

TREHARNE, B.
Birds, The

Coventry Carol, The

TREHARNE, BRYCESON
Brahms, Johannes
Fahr' Wohl

TREHARNE; MUELLER
Humperdinck, Engelbert
Prayer

TREML, ROBERT
Kanons Zum Singen Und Spielen

TRINDER, WALTER
Afton Water

TRINKAUS
Day In, Day Out

When Love Is Kind

Winter Wonderland

TROJAN, JAN
Janacek, Leos
Drei Gemischte Chore

TROMMENSCHLAGER, M.
Sans Verser De Larmes

TROST, HANS-JAKOB
Drei Laub Auf Einer Linden

Wohl Heute Noch Und Morgen

TRUED
A Janta A Ja

Buck, Dudley
Blow The Trumpets

TRUITT, R.
Matesky, T.
Four American Songs

TRUNK
Beethoven, Ludwig van
Elegischer Gesang

TRUNK, R.
Schubert, Franz (Peter)
Fullest Wieder Busch Und Tal
Ich Wollt, Ich War Ein Fisch
Mich Ergreift, Ich Weiss Nicht Wie
Schaff' Das Tagwerk Meiner Hande
Tiefe Stille
Uber Allen Gipfeln

TRUSLER
Chumbara

Come All Ye Shepherds

Kumbayah

Schubert, Franz (Peter)
Radiant Morn, The

Sing We All Noel

TSAREHRADSKY
Quiet Water, The

TUCAPSKY, ANTONIN
Janacek, Leos
True Love

Wood, Charles
Ethiopia Saluting The Colours
Ethiopia Saluting The Colours

TUMBLESON, RAY
Hurry! Hurry!

TUNLEY, D.
Lefevre, Jacques
Chambriere, Chambriere
Tu Ne L'Entends Pas

TURELLIER, J.
Adieu Paniers

TURNBULL, FEDORA
Water Of Tyne, The

TURNER
Carpenter, John Alden
When I Bring To You Coloured Toys

TURNER, E.
Bye An' Bye

TUTTLE, S.D.
Hasten, Shepherds, Hasten

TUTTLE, STEPHEN
Costeley, Guillaume
Silvery Flowing Brooks

Mauduit, Jacques
By You So Gently

TVEIT
Day By Day

TVEIT, SIGVALD
Bred Dina Vida Vingar

Fremad Norske Menn

UHLMANN, OTTO
Ich Weiss Nicht, Bin Ich Reich Oder
Arm

Schwyzer Heiweh

ULVAEUS
Andersson
Thank You For The Music

UNRUH, GARY L.
Des Prez, Josquin
Scaramella Va Alla Guerra

URBANEK
Sieczynski, Rudolf
Wien, Du Stadt Meiner Traume

URBANEK, H.
Mozart, Wolfgang Amadeus
Hai Di Diana Il Core

Strauss, Johann, [Jr.]
Tritsch-Tratsch Polka

URBANEK, HANS
Des Abends

Frau Nachtigall Als Botin

URQUHART, PETER W.
Chickens They Are Crowin', The

Come, All You Fair And Tender Ladies

VAAL, O.DE
Faignient, Noel
Overloedigen Rijckdom

Kerstzang
Herders Hebt Gij Al Vernommen

Op, Op Die 'T Rijkbewonen

Turnhout, Gerard de
Komt Al' Uit Zuiden

Villard, Jean (Gilles)
Trois Cloches, Les

VACCARO, JUDITH
March Of The Toy Soldiers

VACCHI, G.
Composizioni Corali D'Ispirazione
Popolare

VACI, MIHALY
Lendvay, Kamillo
Ejszaka II

Lorand, Istvan
Tenger, A

VALANIS
Jones
Christmas Calypso

VAN
Dowland, John
Come Again, Sweet Love

VAN BEEKUM, JAN
Bonnie's Medley

VAN CAMP
Foster, Stephen Collins
If You've Only Got A Moustache

Janequin, Clement
Ouvrez Moi L'huis

Mendelssohn-Bartholdy, Felix
Choral Responses

Peuerl, Paul
O Musica' Thou Noble Art

VAN CAMP, L.
America

VAN CAMP, LEONARD
Belcher, Supply
Welcome To Spring

Billings, William
Jargon
Meet America's William Billings
Modern Music
Rose Of Sharon

Casey, Thomas
Drill, Ye Tarriers, Drill

Foster, Stephen Collins
Beautiful Dreamer
Come Where My Love Lies Dreaming
If You've Only Got A Moustache
Jeanie With The Light Brown Hair

Hail To Thee, O Music

Kimball, Jacob, Jr.
Music Of Jacob Kimball, Jr.

Kittredge, Walter
Tenting On The Old Campground

Mason, Lowell
Dozen Rounds, A

Mendelssohn-Bartholdy, Felix
Auf Dem See
Fruhzeitiger Fruhling
Lerchengesang
Liebe Und Wein
Open Air, The

Poor Old Man, The

Star-Spangled Banner Through History,
The (1814-1942)

Women Are Wanting The Vote

VAN DEN DYCK
Molloy, James Lyman
Love's Old Sweet Song

VAN, GUILLAUME DE
Anonymous
Or Sus Vous Dormes Trop

Jacopo da Bologna
Non Al Suo Amante

VAN HEUSEN; JAMES
Burke
Imagination

VAN IDERSTINE, A.P.
Sourwood Mountain

VAN, JEFFERY
Christmas Lullaby

VAN WYATT
Raise A Ruckus

VANCE
America The Beautiful

He's Gone Away

I Am A Woman

Kjelson
Secular Music For Treble Voices

VANCE, MARGARET
Cowboy's Lament, The

Turtledove, The

What Love Can Do

VANCE, MARGARET SHELLEY
Ash Grove

Holly And The Ivy, The

Pretty Saro

VOGG, H.
Lortzing, (Gustav) Albert
Heil Sei Dem Tag

Millocker, Karl
Bei Solchem Feste
Pole Trinkt Galant, Der

Strauss, Johann, [Jr.]
Jetzt Ist Zeit Zur Lustbarkeit
Zur Serenade!

Verdi, Giuseppe
Libiamo Ne' Lieti Calici

VOGHT, RICHARD
Brubeck, David (Dave) Warren
They All Sang Yankee Doodle

VOGL
Sehlbach, Oswald Erich
Ich Bin Ein Grosser Hasser

VOGLER, C.; OETIKER, A.
Singstubete

VOGRICH
Drink To Me Only With Thine Eyes

Schubert, Franz (Peter)
Standchen

Wagner, Richard
Faithful And True. Bridal Chorus

VOLGYFY, HANS
Bruckner, Anton
Trosterin Musik

VOLKSMUND
Knab, Armin
Sonne Und Regen

Taubert, Karl Heinz
Wachter Tutet In Sein Horn, Der

VOLLINGER, WILLIAM
Caldara, Antonio
Though You've No Pity

Cornyshe, William (Cornish)
Ah, Robin

VONESCH, R.
Krenger, R.
Daheim

Wunderlin, T.
Gruss An Die Heimat

VONESCH, RICO
Amapolita

Andulka

Little David

So Singen Die Volker Der Erde, Blatt
1

So Singen Die Volker Der Erde, Blatt
2

So Singen Die Volker Der Erde, Blatt
3

So Singen Die Volker Der Erde, Blatt
4

So Singen Die Volker Der Erde, Blatt
5

So Singen Die Volker Der Erde, Blatt
6

So Singen Die Volker Der Erde, Blatt
7

So Singen Die Volker Der Erde, Blatt
8

When The Stars Begin To Fall

VOROSMARTY, MIHALY
Balazs, Arpad
Szavak A Konyvhoz

VRANKEN, J.
Archangelsky
Wnoeschi Bozje

VREE
Janequin, Clement
Plus Belle De La Ville, La

Lassus, Roland de (Orlandus)
Quand Mon Mari

Monteverdi, Claudio
Ch'ami La Vita Mia
Lasciatemi Morire

VREE, M.
Fum, Fum, Fum

O Love, Forlorn

Shenandoah

VREE, MARION
Janequin, Clement
Frolicsome Nymph
Oh, The Prettiest Of The City
Petite Nymphe Folatre

Lassus, Roland de (Orlandus)
When Home From Work My Husband
Comes

Sermisy, Claude de (Claudin)
Ring, Ring High The Pipes

Shenandoah

Ye Banks And Braes

VUILLERMOZ, J.
Chanson De Route

Marseillaise, La

Noel

Nostalgie

WADELY, F. W.
Oranges And Lemons

WADSWORTH
Eddystone Light

Mermaid, The

WADSWORTH, ROBERT
I Had Four Brothers Over The Sea

Napoleon

When Pa

When Pa...

WADSWORTH, ROBERT W.
Teens In Tune

WADWSORTH, ROBERT; BOCK, FRED
Old Man Noah Knew A Thing Or Two

WAESCHE
Meyer
On The Way To Home Sweet Home

WAGNER
A-Roving

All Through The Night

Amour De Moy

Ayer Te He Visto

Foster, Stephen Collins
Glendy Burk, The
I Dream Of Jeanie
My Old Kentucky Home
Nelly Bly
Oh! Lemuel

Gluck, Christoph Willibald, Ritter
von
Come Thou Now

Gruner Hanf

Handel, George Frideric
Galatea Dry Thy Tears
Mourn, All Ye Muses
Must I My Acis Still Bemoan

Haydn, [Franz] Joseph
Beredsamkeit, Die

J'ai Du Bon Tabac

Kommt, Wir Gehn Am Engen Stege

Lowlands

Mendelssohn-Bartholdy, Felix
Auf Flugeln Des Gesanges

Mozart, Wolfgang Amadeus
O Vote Tremendo
Placido E Il Mar

Oh, Bury Me Not

Palestrina, Giovanni Pierluigi da
Could I But Capture
These Are My Heartfelt Tears

Skip To My Lou

Sometimes I Feel Like A Motherless
Child

Swing Low, Sweet Chariot

WAGNER; AHROLD
Baile De Gaita

WAGNER, DOUGLAS E.
Handel, George Frideric
Where'er You Walk

WAGNER, FR.
Wagner, Richard
Deutsches Weihelied

WAGNER, HANS
Schneiderlied Aus Kals

WAGNER, HERMANN
Als Ich Einmal Reiste

An Die Freunde

Aus Herzensgrund

...Da Draussen Auf Der Landstrass'

Draussen Auf Gruner Waldheid

Entlaubet Ist Der Walde

Es Geht Ein' Dunkle Wolk Herein

Europa

Freunde, Das Ist Unsre Zeit

Frisch Auf, Ihr Musici

Guten Abend Euch Allen

Hejo! Spann Den Wagen An

Immer Strebe Zum Ganzen

Jetzt Fangt Das Neue Fruhjahr An

Kommt, Ihr G'spielen

Lob Der Musik

Moseler-Chorhefte

Moseler Chorhefte

Schamet Euch Der Tranen Nicht

Sei Unser Weg

Singet Dem Tag Ein Lied

Singet Den Sommer An

Trara, So Blasen Die Jager

Unverlierbare Heimat

Wann Wir Schreiten

...Wetten, Dass Dann Winter Ist

Wir Zogen In Das Feld

Wogen Und Wind

WAGNER, LAVERN J.
Turnhout, Gerard de
Sacred And Secular Songs For Three
Voices
Sacred And Secular Songs For Three
Voices, Vol. I
Sacred And Secular Songs For Three
Voices, Vol. II

WAGNER, ROGER
Brahms, Johannes
Neue Liebeslieder

Roger Wagner Program Of S.A.T.B.
Choral Music, A

WAGNER; SCHONKIRCH, H.
Das Almfahren

Wia Lusti Is's In Winter

WAHLGREN, H.
Sjostrom, F.
Ulla Katarinas Brudmarsch

WAILES
Peerson, Martin
At Her Faire Hands
Hey The Horne
Locke Up, Fair Lids
Open The Dore
Resolve To Love
See, O See Who Is Here
Selfe Pitties Teares
Sing, Love Is Blind
Upon My Lap

WALES, EVELYN
Brahms, Johannes
Hungarian Dance No. 5

Weber, Carl Maria von
Hunting Song

WARNICK (cont'd.)

Simone
Cotton-Eyed Joe
Flo Me La
In The Evening By The Moonlight
Little Liza Jane

Simons
Marta
Peanut Vendor

Skylar, Sunny (Selig Sidney Shaftel)
Nola

Smith
Ballin' The Jack

Spielman
Christmas Spirit, The

Stookey, Noel Paul
Early In The Morning

Stormy Weather

Swift
Fine And Dandy

Telephone Hour

This Could Be The Start Of Something

Von Tilzer, Harry
I Want A Girl

Wagner
Under Freedom's Flag

Warren
I Only Have Eyes For You

Washington
Give A Little Whistle

Watch What Happens

What A Country

What The World Needs Now Is Love

Wildcat Medley

Willson
Big Clown Balloons, The
Gary, Indiana
Here's Love
I Ain't Down Yet
Lida Rose
Pick-A-Little, Talk-A-Little
Pine Cones And Holly Berries
That Man Over There
Wells Fargo Wagon, The

Winter Wonderland

With This Ring

Yarrow, Peter
It's Raining

Yesterdays

You'll Never Walk Alone

WARNICK, CLAY
Bernard, Felix
Winter Wonderland

WARRELL
Keys Of My Heart, The

We Wish You A Merry Christmas

WARRELL, ARTHUR
Sweet Nightingale

WARREN
Romay
From This Summer Garden

WARREN, BETTY
Handel, George Frideric
Ask If Yon Damask Rose

WARREN, DAVID
Mozart, Wolfgang Amadeus
Kleine Freimaurer-Kantate, Eine

WARREN, EDWIN B.
Fayrfax, Robert
Collected Works Vol. III: Secular
Works

WARREN-SMITH, A.G.
Broad, D.F.
Born To Be King

WARRINGTON
Wolfson
I Love A Sousa March

WASNER
Brahms, Johannes
Waldesnacht, Du Wunderkuhle

Hume, Alexander
Flow Gently, Sweet Afton

Likiokalani, Queen of Hawaii
Aloha Oe

Mozart, Wolfgang Amadeus
Song Of Loyal Brotherhood

Schulz, Johann Abraham Peter
Ihr Kinderlein, Kommet

WASNER, FRANZ
Gluck
Sangen Om Kvarnen

WASSERMAN, A.
Nicht Der Wind Rauscht

Wie Ein Regenschauer

WASSERMANN, A.
Aus Dem Schonen Fernen Lande

WATKINS, J.J.F.
Carrion Crow, The

WATKINS SHAW; BERGMAN
Blow, John
Marriage Ode

WATKINSON, P.G.
Scottish Folksongs

Swedish Folksongs

WATKINSON, PERCY G.
Scottish Folksongs

Swedish Folksongs

WATSON
Bergh, Leif
Honor And Glory

Hanson
Be As A Lion
Children's Dance

WATSON, J.P.
Landlord, Fill The Flowing Bowl

WATSON, MICHAEL
Married To A Mermaid

WATSON, RUSSELL
Dry Bones

Steffe, William
Battle Hymn Of The Republic

WATSON, RUTH
Mary Ann

Raftsmen, Les

WAXMAN
Carter
Lord Of The Dance

WAXMAN, DONALD
Boar's Head, The

Coventry Carol

English Noel, An

God Send You A Happy New Year

Green Grow'th The Holly

Wassail Song

WEATHERLY; EHRET
Danny Boy

WEATHERLY; HAUSMAN
Danny Boy

WEAVER
Song Of The Volga Boatmen

WEBB
Lovering
Pablo, The Reindeer

WEBB; RAYMOND
On Top Of Old Smoky

WEBB, TREVOR R.
Come Out And Dance

WEBER
Ach Blumlein Blau

Nicolai, Otto
Mondchor

WEBER, B.
Ach, Bin Ich Nicht Ein Armer Mann

Als Ich Ein Junggeselle War

Bleich Sind Heut Meines Madchens
Wangen

Catina Bellina, Wie Bist Du So Schon

Dort Drunten Im Tale

Dort Jenes Seechen Hat Kaltes Wasser

Drei Woche Vor Ostern

Es Tanzt Ein Bi-Ba-Butzemann

Es War Einmal Ein Kleines Schifflein

Es Wollt Ein Schneider Wandern

Gestern Abend War Vetter Michel Hier

Gestern Bei Mondenschein

Hab Ein Madchen Heute Mir Erwahlt

Ich Ging In Einer Nacht

In Den Karpaten

Isaac, Heinrich
O Welt, Ich Muss Dich Lassen

Knablein Ging Spazieren, Ein

Kommt, Freunde, In Die Runde

Lasst Mich Singen

Madchen, Liebes, Sollst Nicht Weinen

Mein Lieb Ist Wie Der Morgenstern

Nun Ruhen Alle Walder

Schwarzbraunes Augelein

Sommer Will Uns Kommen, Der

Sonne Gluht, Die Rose Bluht, Die

Und Unser Liebe Frauen

Was Hab Ich Denn Meinem Feinsliebchen
Getan?

Widele, Wedele

WEBER, BERNHARD
Am Schonsten Sommerabend

An Einem Maienmorgen

Auld Lang Syne

Heut Noch Sind Wir Hier Zu Haus

In Der Barke

In Der Karpathen

John Peel

Jungfer Cathleen

Komm, Herzens Freud

Matrosenleben

Old MacDonald Had A Farm

Old McDonald

Schonster Abendstern

Se Amor Mai Da Vu Se Vede

Seht Ihr Im Tale

Seht Nur Mein Madchen

Stehn Zwei Stern

Sur Le Pont D'Avignon

Wiegenlied

Zecherweisheit

Zwiegesprach

WEBER, ERNHARD
Sur Le Pont D'Avignon

WEBER, LUDWIG KARL
Tanz, Nur Tanz

WEBER, W.
Arcadelt, Jacob
Weisse Schwan, Der

Dowland, John
Come Again! Sweet Love Doth Now
Invite

WETTSTEIN, ALBERT
  Fry Schwyzerland

  Lied Des Soldners Im Walschland
WETZLER
  Brahms, Johannes
    Mainacht, Die

  Little Red Drum, The
WETZLER, ROBERT
  Keeper, The

  Little Red Drum, The

  Variations On A Camp Song
WHAPLES, MIRIAM K.
  Anonymous
    Carmina Burana
WHAW, MARTIN
  Nature Song-Bookvol. I
WHEELER
  Chopin, Frederic
    Rolling High, Rolling Low

  Lizette

  Siegmeister
    Lift Every Voice
WHEELER, A.
  Road To The Isles
WHEELER; WADSWORTH
  Jr. Hi
WHITCOMB
  Millay
    Wide World, The
WHITE
  Dis Train

  Golden Slumbers

  Wilding
    My Nannie, O
WHITE; BENNETT
  Star-Spangled Banner, The
WHITECOTTON
  Three Scottish Songs
WHITEHEAD, A.
  King Arthur
WHITEHEAD, ALFRED
  At The Mid-Hour Of Night

  Farewell To Sliev Morna

  God Save The Queen

  King Arthur

  Leezie Lindsay
WHITFIELD, J.B.R.
  Highland Lad, A

  Three Burns Songs
WHITFIELD, JOHN B.R.
  O John, Come Kiss Me Noo

  Treble And Bass Song Book, Book 1

  Treble And Bass Song Book, Book 2
WHITFORD, HOMER J.
  Bortniansky, Dimitri Stepanovich
    Bird, Let Loose In Easter Skies,
      The
WHITING
  Hundred Pipers, The
WHITNEY
  Ward, Samuel Augustus
    From Sea To Shining Sea
WHITTAKER
  Blow The Wind Southerly

  Water Of Tyne, The
WHITTAKER, W.G.
  Purcell, Henry
    Moon Reappears, The
WIBERGH, JULIUS
  Gaskvisor
WICKENHAUSER, K.
  Abschiedslied
WICKENS, DENNIS
  Old Woman And The Pedlar, The

WIDDECOMBE
  Macpherson
    Shepherd's Cradle Song
WIDDICOMBE
  Crystal Fountain, The

  Gospel Trail

  Gospel Train, The

  I Got A Robe

  Little David, Play On Your Harp

  Macpherson
    Shepherds Cradle Song

  Macpherson, Charles
    Shepherds' Cradle Song, The

  O Sleep, Thou Heav'n Born Treasure

  Offer, Charles K.
    Crystal Fountain, The
    Knocking Carol, The

  Seiber, Matyas Gyorgy
    Three Hungarian Folk Songs

  Swing Low, Sweet Chariot

  Sykes, Harold H.
    As We Sailed Out Of London River

  Wiegenlied
WIDDICOMBE; JACOBSON
  Seiber, Matyas Gyorgy
    Three Hungarian Folk-Songs
WIDEEN, IVAR
  Ack, Varmeland, Du Skona

  Brollopsvisa

  Geijer, Erik Gustaf
    Kvall Och Frid

  Lindblad, Otto
    Dalkarlasang
    Langtan Till Landet

  Uti Var Hage Dar Vaxa Bla Bar
WIDMAIER, W.
  Ach Elslein, Liebstes Elselein

  Es Fuhr Ein Bauer Ins Holz
WIDMANN
  Lassus, Roland de (Orlandus)
    Audite Nova
    Farmer, What's That In Your Bag?
    Ola! O Che Bon Eccho!
    Villanella
WIDNER, I.
  Olin, Stig
    Gang Jag Seglar I Hamn, En

  Turesson, Gunnar
    Flicka Fran Backafall
WIDNER, IVAR
  Liljefors, Ruben
    Nar Det Lider Mot Jul

  Nar Det Lider Mot Jul
WIENINGER, H.
  Zum Beschluss
WIESEHAHN, W.
  Vijf Volksliederen
WIESENTHAL, JOHN
  Au Claire De La Lune
WIKANDER, DAVID
  Adam de la Hale
    Kom, Du Ljuva Hjartevan

  Peterson-Berger, (Olof) Wilhelm
    Danslek

  Sang I December

  Till Osterland Vill Jag Fara

  Varvindar Friska

  Wennerberg, Gunnar
    Min Sjal Langtar Och Trangtar
WILDGANS, A.
  Etti, Karl
    Wer Im Werk Den Lohn Gefunden
WILDING-WHITE
  Copland, Aaron
    Little Horses

WILEY
  Handel, George Frideric
    Brotherhood Of Man, The
WILHOUSKY
  Lambert
    When Johnny Comes Marching Home

  Niles
    Black Is The Color Of My True
      Love's Hair

  Perrin
    Sleeping Lake
WILIMEK, E.
  Alle Bama Bluahn Weiss

  Hansel Und Gretel

  Ihr Herren, Schweigt Ein Wenig Still

  Vier Jahreszeiten, Die
WILKINS
  Kinkel, Johanna
    Farewell

  Molloy, James Lyman
    Kerry Dance, The
WILKINS, F.E.; KINKEL, J.
  Farewell
WILKINS, NIGEL E.
  Adam de la Hale
    Lyric Works
WILKINSON, PETER
  Swing Low, Sweet Chariot
WILKINSON, PHILIP
  I Got A Robe

  Joshua Fight De Battle Ob Jericho
WILKINSON, PHILIP G.
  My Man John

  Nobody Knows De Trouble I See

  Peter, Go Ring Dem Bells

  She's Like The Swallow

  Sweet Nightingale

  Swing Low, Sweet Chariot
WILKINSON, S.
  Brahms, Johannes
    Christmas Cradle Song
WILKINSON, STEPHEN
  Nightingale, The
WILLAN
  Agincourt Song, The

  What Is This Lovely Fragrance?
WILLAN, HEALEY
  Navire De Bayonne, Le

  O Canada

  Sainte Marguerite
WILLCOCKS
  Five Christmas Carols

  Five Folk Songs

  Sussex Carol
WILLCOCKS, DAVID
  Barbara Allen

  We Wish You A Merry Christmas
WILLERT, GERTRUD
  Orff, Carl
    Lieder Fur Die Schule Heft II
    Lieder Fur Die Schule Heft IV
WILLIAMS
  Bach, Johann Sebastian
    Bach, By Jove!
    Bourree For Bach
    Breezy Bach
    Fugue In Du
    Gavotte For Bach
    Preludio
    Sleepytime Bach

  Bornn
    Blossom

  Farmer's Daughters, The

  Leather-Winged Bat

  Nolan
    Tumbling Tumbleweeds

  Pearly Adriatic

WITTKOPP
  Hutter
    Nun Noch Einmal

  Wagner, Richard
    Hochzeitsmarsch

WITTMER, E.L.
  Frisch Frohlich Woll'n Wir Singen

  Geh Aus, Mein Herz, Und Suche Freud

WITTMER, EBERHARD L.
  Winzerin, Die

WOHLEGEMUTH, G.; RUBISCH, E.
  Wir Singen, Band 1: Chor- Und
    Volksliedsatze Alter Meister

WOHLGEMUTH
  Reinitz
    Bundeslied

WOHLGEMUTH, G.; RUBISCH, E.
  All Mein Gedanken

  Wir Singen, Band 2: Alte Volkslieder
    In Neuen Satzen

  Wir Singen, Band 4: Jungere
    Volkslieder In Neuen Satzen

  Wir Singen, Band 5: Lieder Der
    Gegenwart

WOHRLE
  Biebl, Franz
    Den Gefallenen "Habt Ruh Und
      Frieden"

WOIKE
  Lissmann, Kurt
    Deutsche Erde
    Jubelsturmend Soll Es Klingen
    Rausche, Machtiger Psalm

  Sturmer, Bruno
    In Die Welt Mit Bunten Fahnen

WOLD, A.
  Wahlin, C.P.
    Lilla Stina

WOLDIKE, MOGENS; ARNHOLTZ, ARTHUR
  Laub, Thomas
    Age Og Else
    Danske Folkviser
    Dronning Dagmars Dod
    Dronning Dagmars Dod
    Ebbe Skammelson
    Himmelbruden
    Jomfruen I Hindeham
    Jomfruen I Ormeham
    Kong Didrik Og Hans Kaemper
    Kongemordet I Finderup
    Kvindemorderen
    Lave Og Jon
    Liden Kirstens Dans
    Marsk Stigs Dotre
    Moens Morgendrom
    Ramund
    Stolt Elselil
    Svend Vonved
    Valravnen

WOLF
  Livingstone
    Call Of The May
    Old Fashioned Girl
    Wind Of The West

  Viva La Musica!, Tomo I

  Viva La Musica!, Tomo II

WOLFRAM, H.F.
  Fahnengelobnis

WOLFRAM, HEINZ
  Fahnengelobnis

WOLFRUM
  Abgeblizt

WOLFURT, K.V.
  Es Ritt Ein Jager Wohl Jagen

WOLL, E.
  Es Sungen Drei Engel

  Zu Kronstadt Vor Dem Burgentor

  Zu Maien, Zu Maien Die Vogelein
    Singen

WOLTERS
  Bachofen, Johann Caspar
    Viele Verachten Die Edele Musik

  Lassus, Roland de (Orlandus)
    Musica, Dei Donum Optimi

  Monteverdi, Claudio
    Lamento D'Arianna
    Sestina

WOLTERS (cont'd.)

  O Musica

WOLTERS, G.
  Bin Ich Nicht Ein Lustiger Fuhrmann

  Dort Nied'n In Jenem Holze

  Heller Und Ein Batzen, Ein

  O Du Stille Zeit

  Trara, Die Post Ist Da

WOLTERS, GOTTFRIED
  Ars Musica-Band 2

  Ars Musica-Band 3

  Ars Musica-Band 4

  Ars Musica-Band 5

  Baumann, Hans
    In Allerliebster Nacht

  Trubel, Gerhard
    Nach Dem Winter, Da Kommt Der
      Sommer
    Wohlauf, Gut Gsell, Von Hinnen

WOLTERS, KARL-HEINZ
  Frisch Auf, Ihr Bergleut

WOOD
  Cowan, Marie
    Waltzing Matilda

  Gone Away

  Hilke
    Ever Again

  King
    Song Of The Islands

  Lazicki
    Song Of The Storm

  Pretty Saro

  White
    Morning Trumpet

WOOD; GLASER
  Ding-Dong! Merrily On High

WOODGATE
  Quilter, Roger
    Fair House Of Joy
    To Daisies, Not To Shut So Soon

  Somervell, Arthur
    World's Good Morrow

  Wraggle Taggle Gipsies

  Wraggle Taggle Gipsies, O!, The

WOODGATE, L.
  Elgar, [Sir] Edward (William)
    Like To The Damask Rose
    Rondel
    Shepherds Song, The

  Hughes, Herbert
    Little Bo-Peep
    Sing A Song Of Sixpence

WOODGATE, LESLIE
  Barri, Occardo
    Old Brigade

  Bonnie Strathyre

  Hieland Laddie

  Pretty Polly Oliver

  Richard Of Taunton Dene

  Songs Of Erin, Fantasia On Irish
    Folk-Songs No. 1

  Songs Of Erin, Fantasia On Irish
    Folk-Songs No. 2

  Wraggle, Taggle Gipsies, The

WOODSIDE
  Lawes, William
    Power Of Musick

  Palestrina, Giovanni Pierluigi da
    Ah! Thou Would'st Rather See

WOODWORTH
  Dvorak, Antonin
    Gram
    Magdlein Im Walde

  Handel, George Frideric
    Draw The Tear From Hopeless Love

WOODWORTH (cont'd.)

  Hutchinson, Francis
    How Sleep The Brave

  Offenbach, Jacques
    Choruses

  Purcell, Henry
    Three Catches

  Schein, Johann Hermann
    Studentenschmauss

  Webbe, Samuel, Sr.
    Glorious Apollo

WOODWORTH, G.W.
  Gounod, Charles Francois
    Chorus Of Bacchantes

  Gute Nacht

  Morley, Thomas
    Now Is The Month Of Maying

  Weelkes, Thomas
    Cease Sorrow Now
    Come, Sirrah Jack Ho
    Four Arms, Two Necks, One Wreathing
    On The Plains Fair Trains
    On The Plains, Fairy Trains
    Strike It Up, Tabor

  Wilbye, John
    Weep, O Mine Eyes

WOODWORTH, G.W.; DAVISON, A. T.
  Gute Nacht

WORK
  All I Want

WORK, J.W.
  This Ol' Hammer

WORMSBACHER, HELLMUT
  Dat Du Min Leevsten Bust

  Jan Hinnerk

  Kiekbusch

  Min Jehann

  Zemanovsky, Alfred
    Wunderwagen, Der

WORMSBACHER, HELMUT
  Dat Du Mien Leevsten Bust

WORTLEY; RAYMOND
  Happy Days With Jingle Bells

WRIGHT
  Farmer
    Little Pretty Bonny Lass, A

  Grigg, W.E.
    When You Walk Away

WRIGHT, DON
  Farewell To Nova Scotia

  This Land Is Your Land

WRIGHT; FORREST; FRANK
  Grieg, Edvard Hagerup
    Hand In Hand
    Life Of A Wife Of A Sailor, The
    Little Hands
    Rhyme And A Reason, A
    Ribbons And Wrappings
    When We Wed

WULZ, HELMUT
  Es Hat Ja Schon Drei G'schlagn

  In Da Molltalleiten

  Neujahrslied

WYATT
  Ching-A Ring Chaw

  Crawdad

WYNN, HUBERT
  Schubert, Franz (Peter)
    Heidenroslein

YALANIS
  Jones
    Christmas Calypso

YARON, A.
  Doniach, Shula
    Rhymes, Vol. 1
    Rhymes, Vol. 2

YEATS, W.B.
  Johnson, Reginald
    Down By The Salley Gardens

ZOLLNER, KARL
  Wandern Ist Des Mullers Lust, Das

ZOTTO, G.
  Cantar Veneto

ZSCHIEGNER, FRITZ
  An Das Rosenherze

  Blumenblute, Madchentreu

  Brucke Von Avignon, Die

  Feder Im Wind, Die

  Frau Nachtigall

  Junggeselle, Der

  Konig Dagobert

  Timokwein

  Weiber Von Arlon, Die